Immigrant America

A CENTENNIAL BOOK

One hundred books
published between 1990 and 1995
bear this special imprint of
the University of California Press.
We have chosen each Centennial Book
as an example of the Press's finest
publishing and bookmaking traditions
as we celebrate the beginning of
our second century.

UNIVERSITY OF CALIFORNIA PRESS

Founded in 1893

Immigrant America

A Portrait

Second Edition

Alejandro Portes and Rubén G. Rumbaut

UNIVERSITY OF CALIFORNIA PRESS
BERKELEY   LOS ANGELES   LONDON

University of California Press
Berkeley and Los Angeles, California

University of California Press, Ltd.
London, England

© 1996 by the Regents of the University of California

Library of Congress Cataloging-in-Publication Data

Portes, Alejandro, 1944–.
   Immigrant America : a portrait / Alejandro Portes and
Rubén G. Rumbaut. — 2nd ed.
     p.   cm.
"A centennial book."
  Includes bibliographical references and index.
  ISBN 0-520-20786-6 (cloth : alk. paper). —
ISBN 0-520-20765-3 (pbk . : alk. paper)
    1. Immigrants—United States—History.   2. United
States—Emigration and immigration—History.
3. Americanization—History.   I. Rumbaut, Rubén G.
II. Title.
JV6450.P67   1996
304.8′73—dc20   96-16209
                                                CIP

Printed in the United States of America
9 8 7 6 5 4 3 2

The paper used in this publication meets the minimum
requirements of American National Standard for
Information Sciences—Permanence of Paper for Printed
Library Materials, ANSI Z39.48-1984.

To Eulalia and Carmen,
immigrant mothers

Contents

List of Illustrations   xiii

List of Tables   xv

Preface to the Second Edition   xix

Preface to the First Edition   xxiii

Acknowledgments for the Second Edition   xxvii

Acknowledgments for the First Edition   xxxi

1. Introduction: Who They Are and Why They Come   1

   The Origins of Immigration   8

   Immigrants and Their Types   14

   Overview   25

2. Moving: Patterns of Immigrant Settlement and Spatial Mobility   28

   The Pioneers   29

   Following in the Footsteps   32

   Contemporary Settlement Patterns: A Map of Immigrant America   34

   Preferred Places   43

   Persistent Ethnicity   49

   Conclusion: The Pros and Cons of Spatial Concentration   53

3. Making It in America: Occupational and
      Economic Adaptation   57
   Immigrants in the American Economy   58
   Explaining the Differences: Modes of
      Incorporation   82
   Contexts of Reception   84

4. From Immigrants to Ethnics: Identity,
      Citizenship, and Political Participation   93
   Immigrant Politics at the Turn of the Century   96
   Immigrant Politics Today   107
   The Future of Immigrant Politics   124
   Conclusion   138

5. A Foreign World: Immigration, Mental Health, and
      Acculturation   155
   Marginality and Freedom   158
   Early Psychopathology: The Eugenics Approach to
      Mental Illness   159
   From Nationality to Class and Context: The
      Changed Etiology of Mental Illness   164
   Immigrants and Refugees: Contemporary Trends   168
   Contexts of Incorporation: Mental Health and
      Help Seeking   176
   Acculturation and Its Consequences   180
   Conclusion: The Major Determinants of
      Immigrant Psychology   187

6. Learning the Ropes: Language and Education   192
   Patterns of English Language Acquisition in the
      United States   195
   Language Diversity and Resilience in the United
      States Today   207
   Assimilation and Linguistic Pluralism in America   219
   Conclusion   229

7. Growing Up American: The New Second
      Generation   232
   The New Second Generation at a Glance   233
   Leaving the Parental Fold   239
   Dissonant and Selective Acculturation: Four
      Examples   243
   Acculturation, Assimilation, and Contexts of
      Adaptation   247
   Segmented Assimilation: Five Examples   253
   Achievement and Identity: Survey Evidence   256
   Conclusion   267

8. Conclusion: Immigration and Public Policy   269
   Theories of Immigration   271
   Immigration Controls   278
   Determinants of Unauthorized Immigration:
      A Summary   282
   Immigration Types and the Law   284
   Conclusion   298

   Notes   301

   References   323

   Index   357

Illustrations

Figures

1. Composition of legally admitted immigrant flows to seven major metropolitan destinations, 1993 36
2. Principal destinations of the eight largest immigrant groups, 1987 38
3. Contexts of reception of recent immigrant groups in the United States, 1990 89
4. Immigrants admitted, 1970–1979, and proportions naturalized, 1970–1993, by selected countries of birth 120
5. Mental health over time for different immigration categories 175
6. Determinants of immigrant psychological orientations and types 189
7. Language retention and acquisition among immigrant groups: a typology 220
8. Type of immigration, social context of settlement, and hypothetical community and linguistic outcomes 228
9. Types of acculturation across generations 242
10. Types of acculturation, social context, and predicted second-generation outcomes 252
11. Types of immigration and modes of entry 286

Photographs   following page 140.

Tables

1. Destinations of the Eight Largest Immigrant Groups, 1987   39
2. Metropolitan Areas of Destination of the Five Major Refugee Groups Admitted in 1987 and 1993   42
3. Destinations of Major Immigrant Groups in Selected Years   46
4. Educational Attainment of Principal Immigrant Groups, 1990   59
5. Educational Attainment of Immigrants Age 25 and Over, 1990   61
6. Foreign-Born Groups with Highest Proportion of College-Educated Persons, 1990, and Characteristics of Countries of Origin   65
7. Labor Force Participation and Professional Specialty Occupations of Selected Immigrant Groups, 1990   68
8. Immigrant Nationalities with Highest Number of Persons Classified as Professionals and Managers and as Operators and Laborers, 1993   70
9. Self-Employment Among Selected Foreign-Born Groups, 1990   72

10. Minority Firm Ownership and Indicators of
    Firm Performance, 1987   74
11. Median Household Incomes and Poverty Rates
    of Principal Immigrant Nationalities and
    Regions of Origin, 1989   78
12. Naturalizations for Selected Countries and
    Regions, 1976–1993   116
13. The 1970 Immigrant Cohort and Its
    Naturalization History over the Following
    Decade for Selected Countries and Regions   118
14. Median Years of U.S. Residence, by Year of
    Naturalization and Region of Birth,
    1975–1993   121
15. Professional Immigrants and Eastern
    Hemisphere Immigrants Admitted Under
    Third Preference, by Region, 1975   122
16. The Spanish-Origin Vote in the Southwest   128
17. Political Orientations of Contemporary
    Immigrants   131
18. Contexts of Exit: Stressful Life Events in the
    Post-1975 Migration of Indochinese Refugees
    Resettled in San Diego County   172
19. Prevalence of Demoralization Among
    Indochinese Refugees in San Diego County, by
    Ethnic Group, Gender, and Level of Education   173
20. Sociodemographic and Mental Health
    Characteristics of Cuban and Haitian Entrants
    in Miami, 1987   177
21. Help Seeking for Emotional Problems and
    Facilitational Factors, Cuban and Haitian
    Entrants, 1987   179
22. Perceptions of Discrimination Among Cuban
    and Mexican Immigrants, 1973–1979   183

23. Perceptions of American Society and Its
    Correlates, Cuban and Mexican Immigrants   184
24. Satisfaction and Plans, Cuban and Mexican
    Immigrants, 1976 and 1979   187
25. Percentage Classified as LEP, FEP, and
    English-Only Among Two Cohorts of San
    Diego High School Students, 1986–1987 and
    1989–1990, by Selected Ethnic Groups and
    English Language Status   202
26. Academic Grade Point Averages of Two
    Cohorts of San Diego High School Students,
    1986–1987 and 1989–1990, by Selected
    Ethnic Groups and English Language Status   204
27. Annual Dropout Rates for the 1989–1990
    Cohort of San Diego High School Students, in
    Rank Order, by Selected Ethnic Groups and
    English Language Status   206
28. Language Spoken at Home and Related
    Characteristics for Selected Immigrant
    Groups and the Native-Born, 1990, Ranked by
    Proportion of Foreign-Born Who Speak
    English Only   208
29. Language Spoken at Home, Ability to Speak
    English "Very Well," and "Linguistically
    Isolated" Households Among Immigrants, by
    Year of Immigration and Age Group   210
30. Ability to Speak English "Very Well" and
    "Linguistically Isolated" Households Among
    Selected Immigrant Groups, by Year of
    Immigration   212
31. Generation, Nativity, and Language Use
    Among Selected Foreign-Origin Groups, 1976   215
32. Monolingualism and Bilingualism Among
    Hispanic Adults in the United States, by
    Nativity, 1976

217

33. Characteristics of Second Generation
    Children, 18 Years or Less, Living in
    Immigrant-Headed Households, 1990   236

34. Situation and Experiences of Second
    Generation Students in South Florida and
    Southern California Schools, 1992   238

35. Profile of Five Second Generation
    Nationalities, 1992   258

36. Net Effects of Immigrant Community on
    Academic Achievement   266

37. Effects of the Presence of Immigrant Workers
    on Native Workers' Wages, 1980   288

38. Economic and Social Indicators of Source
    Countries of U.S.-Bound Professional
    Emigration   295

39. Refugee Arrivals in the United States by
    Selected Nationalities and Presumed Reasons
    for Departure   296

Preface to the Second Edition

Six years have passed since we completed, in January 1989, the manuscript for the first edition of *Immigrant America*. In that brief span, the world changed—and so did immigrant America.

The Cold War ended, yet refugee admissions increased significantly; a massive amnesty program for three million formerly unauthorized immigrants was implemented; the Immigration Act of 1990 increased regular immigrant visas by 40 percent over the levels reached in the 1980s; and despite a variety of official efforts to stem the flow, undocumented immigration has not only grown but diversified since 1989. From the collapse of the former Soviet Union at the beginning of the 1990s to the collapse of the Mexican economy at mid-decade; from the passage of the Immigration Act of 1990 and the 1993 North Atlantic Free Trade Agreement to the normalization of relations with the governments of Vietnam and Cambodia; from the ill-fated voyage of the *Golden Venture*, the smuggling ship carrying Chinese immigrants that ran aground off the coast of New York, to the interdiction of 30,000 Cuban *balseros* in the Florida Straits and the reversal of a favorable thirty-year U.S. policy toward Cuban émigrés; from Tiananmen Square to the Persian Gulf War to the U.S. interventions in Somalia and Haiti; all of these are but bits and pieces of a larger set of forces which—alongside the sustained demand for immigrant labor by U.S. employers, the vagaries of U.S. foreign policies and public opinion, the enabling presence of social networks of family

and friends—have had substantial if often unintended reper-
cussions for immigration flows and policies.

The vertiginous pace of recent historical change requires
that we bring our analysis up to date, a task that has become all
the more compelling in view of the sharply politicized and increasingly acrimonious public debate on immigration issues in
the 1990s. Indeed, the past several years have not only witnessed an *acceleration* of immigration flows into the U.S.—the
twenty million foreign-born persons counted by the 1990 U.S.
Census formed the largest immigrant population in the world,
and admissions during the 1990s appear certain to eclipse the
record set in the first decade of this century—but also an *inten-
sification* of public alarm and nativist resistance to it, exacer-
bated by the prolonged recession of the early 1990s and capped
by the passage in 1994 of Proposition 187 in California, home
to fully a third of the nation's immigrants. As a result, immigration has risen to the top of the policy agenda and become a salient campaign issue in the 1996 presidential elections.

Accordingly, we have revised the text to reflect the latest
available evidence, making extensive use of the wealth of new
data from the 1990 census, the Immigration and Naturalization
Service, and other sources from a rapidly accumulating research literature through the mid-1990s. The result is a thor-
ough updating of the book; most of the several dozen tables
and figures in the first six chapters are new or have been
wholly revised, as is their accompanying text. Moreover, two
new chapters have been especially written for this second edition. Chapter 7 examines the new second generation of children
of immigrants now coming of age in American cities, a vastly
understudied topic that nonetheless is key to a serious understanding of the long-term consequences of contemporary immigration for American society. Chapter 8 concludes with an
effort not only to assess critically the sometimes paradoxical
effects of present policies, but also to confront and to specify
the policy implications of our own analysis, placing our findings in historical perspective and seeking to tease out the complex dynamics of U.S.-bound immigration.

Throughout, we maintain our original analytical approach, focusing on immigration as a process, not an event, and on the diversity of today's immigrants—their social origins and contexts of exit and their adaptation experiences and contexts of incorporation. We noted in the preface to the first edition that we sought to grasp at once the diversity and the underlying structures of the new immigration, and to make it accessible to a broader audience whose understanding of today's immigrants can be clouded by common media clichés and widespread stereotypes. That was and remains the aim of this book.

Preface to the First Edition

America, that "permanently unfinished" society, has become anew a nation of immigrants. Not since the peak years of immigration before World War I have so many newcomers sought to make their way in the United States. Each year during the 1980s an average of six hundred thousand immigrants and refugees have been legally admitted into the country, and a sizable if uncertain number of others enter and remain without legal status, clandestinely crossing the border or overstaying their visas. The attraction of America, it seems, remains as strong as ever—as does the accompanying ambivalence and even alarm many native-born Americans express toward the newest arrivals. Unlike the older flows, however, today's immigrants are drawn not from Europe but overwhelmingly from the developing nations of the Third World, especially from Asia and Latin America. The heterogeneous composition of the earlier European waves pales in comparison to the current diversity. Today's immigrants come in luxurious jetliners and in the trunks of cars, by boat and on foot. Manual laborers and polished professionals, entrepreneurs and refugees, preliterate peasants and some of the most talented cosmopolitans on the planet—all are helping reshape the fabric of American society.

Immigrant America today differs from that at the turn of the century. The human drama of the story remains as riveting, but the cast of characters and their circumstances have changed in complex ways. The newcomers are different, reflecting in their motives and origins the forces that have forged a new world order in the second half of this century. And the America that receives them is not the same society that processed the "huddled masses" through Ellis Island, a stone's throw away from the nation's preeminent national monument to liberty and new beginnings. As a result, theories that sought to explain the assimilation of yesterday's immigrants are hard put to illuminate the nature of contemporary immigration.

Certainly much has been said and written about the newest inflows, both in the popular and academic media, and nonspecialists are beginning to get glimpses of the extraordinary stories of ordinary immigrants in the contemporary American context. Missing still is an effort to pull together the many strands of our available knowledge about these matters, to grasp at once the diversity and the underlying structures of the new immigration, and to make it accessible to a general public. Such is the aim of this book.

A subject as complex and controversial as recent immigration to the United States cannot, of course, be exhaustively considered within the scope of this or any other single volume. Nor is it our purpose to present the results of original research, to assess systematically the myriad impacts of post–World War II immigration on American institutions, or to cover in any significant depth the trajectories of each of the scores of national groups that are in the process of becoming, with or without hyphens, the newest members of American society. Instead, we have sought to comb through a vast literature and to offer a synthesis of its major aspects in a way that is both comprehensive and comprehensible. Throughout, our focus on today's immigrants is on the diversity of their origins and contexts of exit and on the diversity of their adaptation experiences and contexts of incorporation. Although the emphasis is on contemporary trends, the discussion seeks to understand present realities in historical perspective and in the context of competing theories of immigrant adaptation.

The book consists of seven chapters. "Who They Are and Why They Come" is the basic issue addressed in chapter 1, and a typology of contemporary immigrants that serves to organize the subsequent analysis of their processes of economic, political, social, cultural, and psychological adaptation is proposed. Chapter 2, "Moving," examines their points of destination and patterns of settlement, and the formation and function of new ethnic communities in urban America. Chapter 3, "Making It in America," looks at the incorporation of immigrants in the American economy and seeks to explain their differences in education, occupation, entrepreneurship, and income within specific contexts of reception. That is, the economic adaptation of immigrants needs to be understood not merely in terms of their resources and skills, but as it is shaped by specific government policies, labor market conditions, and the characteristics of ethnic communities. Chapter 4, "From Immigrants to Ethnics," analyzes immigrant politics, including the underlying questions of identity, loyalty, and determinants of current patterns of naturalization among newcomers who are "in the society but not of it."

Chapter 5, "A Foreign World," switches lenses to focus on the psychology of immigrant adaptation, looking at the emotional consequences of varying modes of migration and acculturation, the major determinants of immigrants' psychological responses to their changed circumstances, and immigrant patterns of mental health and help seeking in different social settings. Chapter 6, "Learning the Ropes," proceeds to a detailed discussion of English acquisition, the loss or maintenance of bilingualism across generations, and new data on the educational attainment of diverse groups of young immigrants in American public schools. The concluding chapter seeks to clarify the origins of that most controversial segment of today's immigration—the illegals—and to assess how this inflow and its recorded counterpart are likely to affect the nation in years to come.

This then is a portrait of immigrant America in the waning years of the twentieth century. Like any portrait, selective in its hues and brushstrokes, it is an interpretation of a subject too rich and elusive to be rendered in a single picture. Our goal has been not to reach exclusively colleagues and specialists, but rather a broader audience whose understanding of today's immigrants can be clouded by common media clichés and widespread stereotypes. If the reader finds in this book a challenge to these prevailing views and a stimulus to gain additional knowledge about the newest members of this society, its purpose will have been fulfilled.

Acknowledgments for the
Second Edition

This new edition has relied extensively on original research carried out during the 1990s by the authors. In particular, since 1989 we have collaborated on a continuing study of children of immigrants in southern California and south Florida—the largest such survey to date—results from which form the core of chapter 7. We gratefully acknowledge the financial support of the Andrew W. Mellon Foundation, the Russell Sage Foundation (889.503), the Spencer Foundation, and the National Science Foundation (SBR 9022555), which jointly made this study possible. We are very much indebted to the administrators, principals, and teachers and staff of scores of secondary schools in the San Diego Unified School District, and the Dade County and Broward County school districts for their unstinting cooperation throughout the various phases of data collection. We are grateful as well for the generous assistance extended to us by the sociology departments of San Diego State University, Florida International University, Michigan State University, and the Johns Hopkins University, through which the study has been conducted.

In San Diego, we have benefited from the extraordinary commitment and competence of our research staff, especially James Ainsworth, Linda Borgen, Norm Borgen, Kevin Keogan, and Laura Lagunas. We appreciate as well the work of a team of over two dozen interviewers fluent in Spanish, Tagalog, Vietnamese, Cambodian, Lao, Hmong, and other Asian languages representative of the immigrant families that have settled in the San Diego area. While the mix of languages is less diverse in south Florida, the effort and capabilities of our research staff there are no less noteworthy. Our colleague, Lisandro Pérez, who directed fieldwork in that area from the start, deserves much credit for the success of this challenging research program. So does his Florida International University team of Liza Carbajo, Ana María Pérez, Victoria Ryan, and the trilingual team of interviewers who took the final stage of the survey to successful completion.

At Johns Hopkins, Richard Schauffler, Dag MacLeod, and Tomás Rodríguez were responsible for data entry and editing and the management of data files. Their dedicated and professional work made possible the timely analysis of survey data for inclusion in this new edition. We also appreciate the comments on the new chapter 7 by Guillermina Jasso, Aristide Zolberg, Charles Tilly, Douglas Massey, and Patricia Fernández-Kelly.

In addition, chapters 5 and 6 have been revised to reflect more recent research supported by grants awarded to Professor Rumbaut, respectively, by the U.S. Department of Health and Human Services, Bureau of Health Care Delivery, Division of Maternal and Child Health, for a study of infant health risks and outcomes among low-income immigrants, carried out in collaboration with Professor John R. Weeks of San Diego State University; and by the U.S. Department of Education, Office of Educational Research and Improvement, for a study of school contexts and educational achievement among language-minority immigrant students in San Diego city schools. Their support is gratefully acknowledged.

Additional original photography was contributed specifically for this new edition by Steven J. Gold, to whom we are once again greatly indebted. The images captured by his camera in communities throughout the country illustrate the diversity of immigrant America today. Finally, we owe a special debt of gratitude to our editors at the University of California Press, Naomi Schneider and William Murphy, who gave us unfailing support during the preparation of this new edition, and to Angie Decker at Johns Hopkins, who is really the key person without whose dedication and effort in assembling disparate text corrections, references, maps, and tables, the final manuscript could not have been produced. We can only hope that the contents of this new edition are up to the quality of her work.

Acknowledgments for the
First Edition

In the years since we first conceived the idea of this book, many unexpected events have affected its progress. As often happens, its execution proved far more time-consuming and difficult than originally planned. However, we have had the support of many people and institutions along the way. In California, Chanthan S. Chea, Duong Phuc, Vu Thanh Thuy, and Prany Sananikone gave a first powerful impulse to the project by organizing field visits to the Vietnamese and Cambodian business communities of San Diego and Santa Ana. These experiences persuaded us that there was here an unwritten human story, different from that depicted in official statistics and media reports, that needed to be told. Tong Vang supplemented these visits with interviews and translations of views of Hmong refugees, some of which are included in chapter 5.

Much of the writing took place while Portes conducted field surveys of recently arrived Mariel Cubans and Haitian refugees in south Florida. Data from these projects and qualitative observations garnered while conducting them have been extensively used in the book. For financial support to implement these surveys, we acknowledge the Sociology Program of the National Science Foundation (grant #SES-8215567), of the National Institute of Mental Health (MH-41502), and the Sloan Foundation (87-4-15). In Miami, the president of Florida International University, Modesto Maidique; the dean of the Arts and Sciences School, James Mau; and the chair of the Sociology and Anthropology Department, Lisandro Pérez, deserve our thanks for making available the facilities of the institution and for their unwavering support during the months of fieldwork.

The close ties of this project with FIU also involved many members of its faculty, in particular Douglas Kincaid, Anthony Maingot, Mark Rosenberg, and Alex Stepick. Together with the previously cited officials, they helped us unravel the intricacies of ethnic relations in Miami and the distinct characteristics of its different foreign communities. Stepick and his wife, Carol Dutton Stepick, directed three successive surveys of post-1980 Haitian refugees. Their close ties with leaders of the Haitian community and their dedication and patience made possible the successful completion of each stage under unusually adverse conditions. The parallel Cuban surveys were led by Juan Clark of Miami-Dade Community College. The expertise of Clark and his team of interviewers made it possible to gain access and obtain reliable data from a large sample of Mariel refugees, a group afflicted at that time by numerous difficulties of adaptation.

We have also made extensive use of results from two large surveys of recently arrived Southeast Asian refugees conducted by Rumbaut in Southern California. For financial support, we acknowledge the National Institute of Child Health and Human Development (#HD-15699), the U.S. Office of Refugee Resettlement (#100-86-0214), and the San Diego State University (SDSU) Foundation. Kenji Ima of SDSU was the co-investigator in one of these studies. Both owe much to the commitment and ability of a staff of Indochinese interviewers and translators recruited from the refugee communities of San Diego.

Many colleagues have helped us by reading and commenting on various chapters. At Hopkins, we thank Andrew Cherlin, William Eaton, Patricia Fernández-Kelly, and Melvin Kohn for their valuable input. At SDSU, we acknowledge the advice of Richard L. Hough, John R. Weeks, and James L. Wood. Elsewhere, Charles Hirschman, Leif Jensen, Ivan Light, Silvia Pedraza-Bailey, Peter I. Rose, Rubén D. Rumbaut, Marta Tienda, and William A. Vega also read and commented on several parts of the manuscript. All have our deep appreciation but are exempted from any responsibility for the contents.

Original photography was contributed specifically for this book by several individuals, adding a visual dimension to our portrait of immigrant America in ways that mere words cannot. We wish to thank Estela R. García and Luis E. Rumbaut for scenes of immigrant communities in Miami and Washington, D.C., Steven J. Gold for his photos of diverse immigrant groups in California and along the Mexican border, Erica Hagen for her portraits of Southeast Asians awaiting resettlement to the United States in various refugee camps in Thailand, and the *San Diego Union* and Michael Franklin for his photos of Mexican migrant farmworkers in southern California.

At the University of California Press, Naomi Schneider adopted the idea of the book as her own and has given it indispensable encouragement. We are thankful to her, as well as to the press's reviewers, who provided numerous useful suggestions. Anna Stoll not only typed multiple versions of each chapter but coordinated the many tasks required by the supporting field projects and the various stages of the manuscript. Thanks to her diligence and competence, the idea of this book has become reality.

1

Introduction

Who They Are and
Why They Come

In Guadalajara, Juan Manuel Fernández worked as a mechanic in his uncle's repair shop making the equivalent of $150 per month. At thirty-two and after ten years on the job, he decided it was time to go into business on his own. The family, his uncle included, was willing to help, but capital for the new venture was scarce. Luisa, Juan's wife, owned a small corner grocery shop; when money ran out at the end of the month, she often fed the family off the store's shelves. The store was enough to sustain her and her children but not to capitalize her husband's project. For a while, it looked as if Juan would remain a worker for life.

Today Juan owns his own auto repair shop, where he employs three other mechanics, two Mexicans and a Salvadoran. The shop is not in Guadalajara, however, but in Gary, Indiana. The entire family—Luisa, the two children, and a brother—have resettled there. Luisa does not work any longer because she does not speak English and because income from her husband's business is enough to support the family. The children attend school and already speak better English than their parents. They resist the idea of going back to Mexico.

Juan crossed the border on his own near El Paso in 1979. No one stopped him, and he was able to head north toward a few distant cousins and the prospect of a factory job. To his surprise, he found one easily and at the end of four months was getting double the minimum wage in steady employment. Almost every worker in the plant was Mexican, his foreman was Puerto Rican, and the language of work was uniformly Spanish. Three trips from Gary to Guadalajara during the next two years persuaded him that it made much better sense to move his business project north of the border. Guadalajara was teeming with repair shops of all sorts, and competition was fierce. "In Gary," he said, "many Mexicans would not get their cars fixed because they did not know how to bargain with an American mechanic." Sensing the opportunity, he cut remittances to Mexico and opened a local savings account instead.

During his last trip, the "migra" (border patrol) stopped him shortly after crossing; that required a costly second attempt two days later with a hired "coyote" (smuggler). The incident put a stop to the commuting. Juan started fixing cars out of a shed in front of his barrio home. Word got around that there was a reliable Spanish-speaking mechanic in the neighborhood. In a few months, he was able to rent an abandoned garage, buy some equipment, and eventually hire others. To stay in business, Juan has had to obtain a municipal permit and pay a fee. He pays his workers in cash, however, and neither deducts taxes from their wages nor contributes to Social Security for them. All transactions are informal and, for the most part, in cash.

Juan and Luisa feel a great deal of nostalgia for Mexico, and both firmly intend to return. "In this country, we've been able to move ahead economically, but it is not our own," she says. "The gringos will always consider us inferior." Their savings are not in the bank, as before the shop was rented, but in land in Guadalajara, a small house for his parents, and the goodwill of many relatives who receive periodic remittances. They figure that in ten years they will be able to return, although they worry about their children, who may be thoroughly Americanized by then. A more pressing problem is their lack of "papers" and the constant threat of deportation. Juan has devised ingenious ways to run the business, despite his illegal status, but it is a constant problem. A good part of his recent earnings is in the hands of an immigration lawyer downtown, who has promised to obtain papers for a resident's visa, so far without results.

At age twenty-six, Nguyen Van Tran was a young lieutenant in the army of the Republic of South Vietnam when a strategic retreat order from the ARVN high command quickly turned into the final rout. Nguyen spent three years in communist re-education camps, all the while attempting to conceal his past as a skilled electronics technician. He finally got aboard a boat bound for Malaysia and after two more years in a refugee camp arrived in Los Angeles in 1980. He had neither family nor friends in the city, but the government provided some resettlement aid and the opportunity to improve his English. At the end of a year, he had secured a job in a local electronics assembly plant, which brought in enough to support himself and his wife and child.

Seeing this plant double in a single year, Nguyen realized the opportunities opening up in electronics. He enrolled in the local community college at night and graduated with an associate degree in computer science. He pooled his savings with another Vietnamese technician and a Chinese engineer and in 1983 launched his own firm. Two years later Integrated Circuits, Inc., employed approximately three hundred workers; most were not Asians, but undocumented Mexican women. By 1985, the company sold about $20 million worth of semiconductors and other equipment to the local IBM plant and other large firms. ICI has even started its own line of IBM-compatible personal computer, the Trantex, which has sold well so far in the local market.

Nguyen, who is chairman of the company, sports a mustache, a sleek Mercedes, and a brand new name, George Best. Perhaps for fear of the "protection gangs" re-created by former Vietnamese policemen in Los Angeles, he has kept a low profile within the Vietnamese community. The name change is part of this approach. "Mr. Best" is not particularly nationalistic, nor

does he dream of returning to Vietnam. He attributes his remarkable five-year ascent to hard work and a willingness to
take risks. To underline the point, he has hung a large portrait
of himself in his community college graduation gown behind
his oversize desk. He and his wife are already U.S. citizens.
They vote Republican, and he has recently joined the local
chamber of commerce.

———————

Lilia González-Fleites left Cuba at fifteen, sent alone by her
formerly wealthy parents, who remained behind. The Catholic
Welfare Agency received her in Miami, and she went to live with
other refugee children in an orphanage in Kendall, Florida,
until released to an aunt. She finished high school promptly
and married, without her parents' consent, her boyfriend from
Cuba, Tomás. There was little work in Miami, and the young
couple accepted an offer from the Cuban Refugee Center to resettle them, along with the rest of Tomás's family, in North
Carolina. Everyone found work in the tobacco and clothing factories except Lilia, whom Tomás kept at home. At eighteen, the
formerly pampered girl found herself a cook and maid for Tomás's entire family.

By sheer luck, the same order of nuns who ran her private
school in Havana had a college nearby. Lilia used her school
connections to gain admittance with a small scholarship and
found herself a part-time job. Those were hard years, working
in one city and attending school in another. Tomás and Lilia
rarely saw each other because he also decided to return to
school while still working.

At age thirty-nine, Lilia is today a successful Miami architect.
Divorced from Tomás, she has not remarried, instead pursu-
ing her professional career with single-minded determination.
When Cuban refugees finally abandoned their dreams of return, Lilia entered local politics, affiliating with the Republican
party. She ran for state office in 1986 but was defeated. Un-
daunted, she remained active in the party and became increas-

ingly prominent in south Florida political circles. More than an immigrant success story, she sees herself at the beginning of a public career that will bridge the gap between the Anglo and Cuban communities in south Florida. Her unaccented English, fierce loyalty to her adopted country, and ability to shift easily between languages and cultures bodes well for her political future.

––––––––––

After finishing medical school, Amitar Ray confronted the prospect of working *ad honorem* in one of the few well-equipped hospitals in Bombay or moving to a job in the countryside and to quick obsolescence in his career. He opted instead for preparing and taking the Educational Council for Foreign Medical Graduates (ECFMG) examination, administered at the local branch of the Indo-American Cultural Institute. He passed it on his second attempt. In 1972, there was a shortage of doctors in the United States, and U.S. consulates were directed to facilitate the emigration of qualified physicians from abroad.

Amitar and his wife, also a doctor, had little difficulty obtaining permanent residents' visas under the third preference of the U.S. immigration law, reserved for professionals of exceptional ability. He went on to specialize in anesthesiology and completed his residence at a public hospital in Brooklyn. After four years, nostalgia and the hope that things had improved at home moved the Rays to go back to India with their young daughter, Rita. The trip strengthened their professional and family ties, but it also dispelled any doubts as to where their future was. Medical vacancies were rare and paid a fraction of what he earned as a resident in Brooklyn. More important, there were few opportunities to grow professionally because he would have had to combine several part-time jobs to earn a livelihood, leaving little time for study.

At fifty-one, Amitar is now associate professor of anesthesiology at a midwestern medical school; his wife has a local practice as an internist. Their combined income is in the six figures, affording them a very comfortable life-style. Their daughter is a senior at Bryn Mawr, and she plans to pursue a graduate degree in international relations. There are few Indian immigrants in the mid-sized city where the Rays live; thus, they have had to learn local ways in order to gain entry into American social circles. Their color is sometimes a barrier to close contact with white middle-class families, but they have cultivated many friendships among the local faculty and medical community.

Ties to India persist and are strengthened through periodic trips and through the professional help the Rays are able to provide to colleagues back home. They have already sponsored the immigration of two bright young physicians from their native city. More important, they make sure that information on new medical developments is relayed to a few selected specialists back home. However, there is little chance that they will return, even after retirement. Work and new local ties play a role in this, but the decisive factor is a thoroughly Americanized daughter whose present life and future have very little to do with India. Rita does not plan to marry soon; she is interested in Latin American politics, and her current goal is a career in the foreign service.

After a lapse of half a century, the United States has again become a country of immigration. In 1990, the foreign-born population reached 19.8 million or 7.9 percent of the total. Although a far cry from the situation eighty years earlier, when immigrants accounted for 14.7 percent of the American population, the impact of contemporary immigration is both significant and growing. Numerous books and articles have called attention to this revival and sought its causes—first in a booming American economy and second in the liberalized provisions of the 1965 immigration act. A common exercise is to compare this "new" immigration with the "old" inflow at the turn of the century. Similarities include the predominantly urban destination of most newcomers, their concentration in a few port cities, and their willingness to accept the lowest paid jobs. Differences are more frequently stressed, however, for the "old" immigration was overwhelmingly European and white; but the present inflow is, to a large extent, nonwhite and comes from countries of the Third World.

The public image of contemporary immigration has been colored to a large extent by the Third World origins of most recent arrivals. Because the sending countries are generally poor, many Americans believe that the immigrants themselves are uniformly poor and uneducated. Their move is commonly portrayed as a one-way escape from hunger, want, and persecution and their arrival on U.S. shores as not too different from that of the tired, "huddled masses" that Emma Lazarus immortalized at the base of the Statue of Liberty. The "quality" of the newcomers and their chances for assimilation are sometimes portrayed as worse because of their non-European past and the precarious legal status of many.

The reality is very different. The four previous cases, each a composite of real life experiences, are certainly not representative of all recent immigrants. Clearly, not all newcomers are doctors or skilled mechanics, and fewer still become politicians or millionaires. Still, these are not isolated instances. Underneath its apparent uniformity, contemporary immigration features a bewildering variety of origins, return patterns, and modes of adaptation to American society. Never before has the United States received immigrants from so many countries, from such different social and economic backgrounds, and for so many reasons. Although pre–World War I European immigration was by no means homogeneous, the differences between successive waves of Irish, Italians, Jews, Greeks, and Poles often pale by comparison with the current diversity. For the same reason, theories coined in the wake of the Europeans' arrival at the turn of the century have been made obsolete by events during the last decades.

Increasingly implausible, for example, is the view of a uniform assimilation process that different groups undergo in the course of several generations as a precondition for their social and economic advancement. There are today first-generation millionaires who speak broken English, foreign-born mayors of large cities, and top-flight immigrant engineers and scientists in the nation's research centers; there are also those, at the other extreme, who cannot even take the first step toward assimilation because of the insecurity linked to an uncertain legal status.

This book describes that diversity. Many of the countries from which today's immigrants come have one of their largest cities in the United States. Los Angeles' Mexican population is next in size to those of Mexico City, Monterrey, and Guadalajara. Havana is not much larger than Cuban Miami, and Santo Domingo holds a precarious advantage over Dominican New York. This is not the case for all groups; others, such as Asian Indians, Laotians, Argentines, and Brazilians, are more dispersed throughout the country. Reasons for both these differences and other characteristics of contemporary immigrant groups are not well known—in part because of the recency of their arrival and in part because of the common expectation that their assimilation process would conform to the well-known European pattern. But immigrant America is a different place today from the America that emerged out of Ellis Island and grew up in the tenements of New York and Boston.

The Origins of Immigration

Why do they come? A common explanation singles out the 1965 change in American immigration law as the principal factor. According to this view, today's immigrants come because they can, whereas before 1965 legal restrictions prevented them from doing so. Although the 1965 law certainly explains qualitative and quantitative changes in immigration during the last three decades, it is an insufficient explanation. Not everyone in even the major sending countries has immigrated or is planning to do so. Compared to the respective national populations, those who decide to migrate generally represent a minuscule proportion. The question can thus be reversed to ask not why many come, but why so few have decided to undertake the journey, especially with difficult economic and political conditions in many sending countries.

Moving to a foreign country is not easy, even under the most propitious circumstances. It requires elaborate preparations, much expense, giving up personal relations at home, and often learning a new language and culture. Not so long ago, the lure of higher wages in the United States was not sufficient by itself to attract foreign workers and had to be activated through deliberate recruitment. Mexican immigration, for example, was initiated by U.S. growers and railroad companies who sent recruiters into the interior of Mexico to bring needed workers. By 1916, five or six weekly trains full of Mexican workers hired by the agents were being run from Laredo to Los Angeles. According to one author, the competition in El Paso became so fierce that recruiting agencies stationed their employees at the Santa Fe bridge, where they literally pounced on immigrants as they crossed the border.[1]

The question then remains, What are the factors motivating some groups but not others to seek entry into the United States at present? The most common answer is the desperate poverty, squalor, and unemployment of many foreign lands. Two authors offer this somber assessment:

> We call the poorest countries of the world "developing countries," as though the use of a progressive adjective could make a country progressive. But the overwhelming evidence is that most of these countries are not "developing" countries but "never-to-be-developed" countries. Most of the world's poor will stay poor for our lifetimes and for several generations to come, and there is nothing the developed nations can do to alter this fact.[2]

They go on to argue that as these countries "sink into squalor, poverty, disease, and death," their poor will seek to migrate en masse to the United States and other developed countries to escape these terrible conditions.[3] Other less alarmist accounts tend to share the same basic view of migration as a consequence of foreign destitution and unemployment.[4]

These statements are made despite a mounting body of evidence that points in the exact opposite direction. Consider legal immigration. The proportion of professionals and managers among occupationally active immigrants consistently exceeds the average among U.S. workers. During the last two decades, immigrant professionals represented around 33 percent of the total, at a time when professionals and managers ranged between 17 and 27 percent of the American labor force. Although the gap may be somewhat exaggerated by the available immigration data, other sources confirm that recent immigrants are as well represented as the native-American population at the higher educational and occupational levels. For 1990, the census reported the percentage completing four or more years of college as 20.3 percent for natives and 20.4 percent for the foreign born; the number in professional specialty occupations was about the same for both groups: 12 to 14 percent. For this reason, the gap in median household incomes in favor of the native born did not exceed U.S. $2000 in that year, despite the fact that over 40 percent of the foreign born had been in the United States for ten years or less.[5]

But even if legal immigrants represent a select group from most sending countries, what about the illegals? The evidence here is more tentative because of the difficulty of investigating a surreptitious flow. However, the available studies coincide on two points: The very poor and the unemployed seldom migrate, either legally or illegally; and unauthorized immigrants tend to have above-average levels of education and occupational skills in comparison with their homeland populations. More important, they are positively self-selected in terms of ambition and willingness to work.

Mexico is the source of over 95 percent of unauthorized aliens apprehended in the United States during the last two decades. Although the socioeconomic origins of most immigrants are modest by U.S. standards, they consistently meet or surpass the average for the Mexican population. Illiteracy among Mexican unauthorized immigrants has been estimated at between 3 and 10 percent, at a time when the figure for Mexico as a whole was 22 percent. At the other end, those with at least some secondary education have been estimated by four different studies to hover around 30 percent while only 21 percent had reached similar schooling in the Mexican population.[6] Contrary to the stereotype of Mexican immigrants as overwhelmingly impoverished peasants, up to 48 percent of the unauthorized have been found to originate in cities of twenty thousand or more, in comparison with 35 percent of all Mexicans.

During the 1970s, around 45 percent of Mexican workers made their living from agriculture; a study of apprehended illegals estimated a similar proportion, 49 percent, but another of former illegals who had regularized their situation reduced it to 18 percent. White-collar and urban skilled and semiskilled occupations employed between 35 and 60 percent of unauthorized immigrants prior to their departure from Mexico; these occupations absorbed approximately 30 percent of the Mexican population in comparable years.[7] All studies coincide in that few of these immigrants were unemployed in Mexico, the figure hovering around 5 percent. As one author states, "the findings indicate that it is not the lack of jobs, but of *well-paid* jobs, which fuels migration to the U.S."[8]

Even more conclusive findings come from research in the Dominican Republic, another important source of illegal immigration. Several independent studies conclude that Dominicans who migrate internationally, including those without documents, are more likely to come from the cities, have much higher levels of literacy, be relatively more skilled, and have lower levels of unemployment than the Dominican population as a whole. Among those from rural areas, migrants come predominantly from the sector of medium to large farmers rather than from the landless peasantry.[9]

The main reason the poorest of the poor do not migrate

across international borders is that they are not able to. In Mexico, "those at the very bottom of the local income distribution are not likely to migrate to the States because they lack even the resources needed to cover the costs of transportation and fees charged by the smugglers."[10] In the Dominican Republic, "there are major legal and financial barriers that prevent the poor from migrating . . . reports suggest that it costs several thousand dollars to be provided with papers and smuggled out of the country."[11] Studies of Haitian unauthorized migration also report that it costs thousands to buy passage aboard barely seaworthy craft bound for south Florida.[12]

But if migrants do not come to escape unemployment or destitution, why do they come? Why, in particular, should middle-class professionals and skilled workers embark on a costly journey, sometimes surreptitiously, and sacrifice work, friends, and family back home? The basic reason is the gap between life aspirations and expectations and the means to fulfill them in the sending countries. Different groups feel this gap with varying intensity, but it clearly becomes a strong motive for action among the most ambitious and resourceful. Because *relative*, not absolute deprivation lies at the core of most contemporary immigration, its composition tends to be positively selected in terms of both human capital and motivation. The United States and the other industrialized countries play a double role in this process. First, they are the source of much of the modern culture of consumption and of the new expectations diffused worldwide. Second, the same process of global diffusion has taught an increasing number of people about economic opportunities in the developed world that are absent in their own countries.

It is thus not surprising that most of today's immigrants, even the undocumented, have had some education and come from cities, for these are precisely the groups most thoroughly exposed to life-styles and consumption patterns emanating from the advanced world. These are also the groups for whom the gap between aspirations and local realities is most poignant and among whom one finds the individuals most determined to overcome this situation. Educated and skilled workers and small farmers are generally better informed about employment opportunities abroad than the illiterate and the destitute. Those at the bottom of the social structure not only lack the means to migrate, but often the motivation to do so because they are less exposed to the lure of consumption styles in the developed nations and are less aware of the work opportunities in them.

The form that this gap takes varies, of course, across countries and social groups. For skilled workers and small farmers, migration is the means to stabilize family livelihoods and meet long-desired aspirations—a car, a TV set, domestic appliances of all sorts, additional land and implements. For urban professionals, it provides a means of reaching life standards commensurate with their past achievements and to progress in their careers.[13] Seen from this perspective, contemporary immigration is a direct consequence of the dominant influence attained by the culture of the advanced West in every corner of the globe. The bewildering number and variety of today's immigrants reflect this worldwide reach and the vision of modern life and individual fulfillment that goes with it.

Back in the nineteenth century, the United States was a growing industrializing country that needed labor; but because its life standards were not a global model and its economic opportunities were not well known, it had to resort to deliberate recruitment. Thus, the vaunted "pull" of U.S. wages had to be actualized by American migration agents sent to Mexico, Ireland, southern Italy, and the Austro-Hungarian empire to apprise people of the "better meals and higher wages" available for work in the eastern canal companies, the western railroads, and later on in industry.[14]

The enormous variety of today's immigrants and the fact that they come spontaneously rather than through deliberate recruitment reflect the attraction of American life-styles and their gradual conversion into a world standard. Immigrants do not come to escape perennial unemployment or destitution in their homeland. Most undertake the journey instead to attain the dream of a new life-style that has reached their countries but that is impossible to fulfill in them. Not surprisingly, the most determined individuals, those who feel the distance between actual reality and life goals most poignantly, often choose migration as the path to resolve this contradiction.

Immigrants and Their Types

Within this general picture, there are significant differences in migration goals and their relative fulfillment. Any typology implies simplification, but it is useful at this point to present a basic classification of contemporary immigrants to organize the upcoming analysis of their process of adaptation. Each basic type is represented by several nationalities; conversely, a national group may include individuals representing different types. These are distinguished by a series of common characteristics of socioeconomic origin and reasons for departure that tend to be associated with different courses of adaptation once in the United States.

Labor Migrants

Manual labor immigration corresponds most closely to popular stereotypes about contemporary immigration. The movement of foreign workers in search of menial and generally low paid jobs has represented the bulk of immigration, both legal and undocumented, in recent years. The Immigration Reform and Control Act (IRCA) of 1986 was aimed primarily at discouraging the surreptitious component of this flow while compensating employers by liberalizing access to legal temporary workers. A decade later, Proposition 187, an initiative passed by the California electorate in 1994, sought to discourage undocumented immigration by barring illegal aliens from access to public services. We discuss the intent and effectiveness of these two measures in chapter 8. For the moment, it suffices to note the principal ways manual labor immigration has materialized in recent years.

First, migrants can simply cross the border on foot or with the help of a smuggler or overstay a U.S. tourist visa. In official parlance, illegal border crossers have been labeled EWIs (entry without inspection); those who stay longer than permitted are labeled visa abusers. In 1993, the U.S. Immigration and Naturalization Service (INS) located 1.33 million deportable aliens, of which 1.29 million were EWIs. Predictably, the overwhelming majority of illegal border crossers—97 percent— were Mexicans.[15]

A second channel of entry is to come legally by using one of the family reunification preferences of the immigration law (left untouched, for the most part, by the 1986 reform and reaffirmed by the Immigration Act of 1990). This avenue is open primarily to immigrants who have first entered the United States without legal papers or for temporary periods and who have subsequently married a U.S. citizen or legal resident. Marriage automatically entitles the immigrant to a legal entry permit; spouses of U.S. citizens are given priority because they are exempt from existing quota limits. A study of 822 legal Mexican immigrants arriving during 1973–74 found that about 70 percent of respondents had lived in the United States prior to legal entry, most for periods of six months or more. Forty-eight percent of this sample came with visas granted to spouses of U.S. citizens; another 45 percent came under the quota as spouses of U.S. legal residents.[16] In 1987, the situation was not very different: Of the 72,351 legal Mexican immigrants arriving in that year, 50,793 (70.2 percent) were exempt from quota limits as spouses, children, or parents of U.S. citizens; an additional 16,632 (23.0 percent) came as spouses or close relatives of citizens or legal residents. By 1993, an identical 93 percent of the 69,784 legal Mexican immigrants who arrived in that year entered under family preferences or as immediate relatives of U.S. citizens. An additional 56,777 were also legalized in 1993 under IRCA's amnesty provisions, of whom 69 percent were immediate family members who entered as "legalization dependents" under a provision of the Immigration Act of 1990.[17]

The last avenue is to come as a contract laborer. There was a provision in the 1965 immigration act for the importation of temporary foreign laborers when a supply of "willing and able" domestic workers was not available. This provision was maintained and actually liberalized by the 1986 reform. In both cases, the secretary of labor must certify that a labor shortage exists before Immigration authorizes the entry of foreign workers. Because the procedure is cumbersome, especially in the past, few employers sought labor in this manner. An exception is the sugar industry in Florida, for which "H-2" workers, as they are labeled because of their type of visa, have become the mainstay of its cane-cutting labor force. They come after a selection process in Jamaica and other West Indian countries, live in company barracks during the harvest, and return home immediately after its end. Contract workers are also found in lesser numbers throughout the Eastern Seaboard working in the fruit orchards of Georgia and the Carolinas and in the shade tobacco crop of Connecticut.[18] During the 1970s, 1980s, and early 1990s, approximately twenty thousand H-2 workers per year have been imported, primarily from the West Indies.

The principal magnet drawing foreign manual workers to the United States is undoubtedly the level of U.S. wages relative to those left behind. At $4.25 an hour, the U.S. minimum wage is approximately six times the prevailing one in Mexico, which is, in turn, higher than most in Central America. The actual wage many U.S. employers pay their foreign workers exceeds the legal minimum and is significantly higher than that available for skilled and even white-collar work in Mexico and other sending countries. This is why relatively well-educated and skilled foreigners are willing to accept these frequently harsh jobs. To them, the trek to the United States and the economic opportunities associated with it often represent the difference between stagnation or impoverishment and attainment of their life's goals.[19]

Whatever their motivation, however, immigrants could not come if there were not a demand for their labor. That demand is strong and growing. Employers value immigrant workers' diligence, reliability, and willingness to work hard for low pay. They argue that American workers are either unavailable or unwilling to perform hard menial jobs. Garment contractors, small electronics firms, and other employers of immigrants have further argued that they would have to close their doors or move abroad if this labor supply were cut off.[20]

This demand is fueled by the favorable position in which employers find themselves. There are no recruitment or other costs in hiring immigrant laborers because they come on their own and bear all the dangers and expenses of the journey. Until recently, there were no legal costs either because the law specifically exempted employers from any liability for hiring illegal aliens. Although the 1986 immigration reform has altered this situation, a number of loopholes still facilitate access to immigrant laborers, regardless of their legal status. In addition, the new law itself has expanded channels for the legal importation of temporary workers.[21]

Under these conditions, it is not surprising that manual labor immigration has continued and grown from year to year. This flow does not represent an "alien invasion," as some authors have called it, because an invasion implies moving into someone else's territory against their will. In this instance, the movement is very much welcomed, if not by everyone, at least by an influential group—namely, the urban employers and rural growers who have come to rely on this source of labor. The match between the goals and aspirations of foreign workers and the interests of the firms that hire them is the key factor sustaining the movement from year to year.

A more appropriate conclusion than the "alien invasion" notion is that labor immigration occurs because there is a strong demand for it. Immigrants are regarded as superior workers for the performance of certain tasks, especially those Americans accept only unwillingly. The men and women who come under these circumstances find in the modest entry jobs available on this side of the border the means to fulfill expectations blocked in their own countries. Some do stay and attempt to carve a new life in America. Many return, however, because although U.S. wages are higher, the "yield" of these wages in terms of consumption, investments, and social status is often greater back home. Having accumulated enough savings, most immigrants seek to reestablish or gain a position of social respectability, a goal more easily accomplished in their home communities.[22] Manual labor immigration is thus not a one-way flow away from poverty and want, but rather a two-way process fueled by the changing needs and interests of those who come and those who profit from their labor.

Professional Immigrants

A major preference category of the U.S. visa allocation system is reserved for "members of the professions of exceptional ability and their spouses and children." This category provides the main entry channel for the second type of immigrants. Unlike the first, these come legally and are not destined to the bottom layers of the American labor market. Labeled "brain drain" in the countries of origin, this flow of immigrants represents a significant gain of highly trained personnel for the United States. In 1993, 109,760 persons classified as professionals and managers arrived as permanent residents; the main contributors included mainland China (13,954), the Philippines (11,164), India (10,210), Great Britain (5,508), and Taiwan (4,708). The overall number and the principal contributors changed little during the 1980s.[23] However, since 1992, under the new provisions of the Immigration Act of 1990, the number of these visas tripled the level that had been the annual norm for the previous twenty-five years.

Foreign professionals and technicians seldom migrate because of unemployment back home. The reason is that they not only come from the higher educational strata, but that they are probably among the best in their respective professions in order to pass difficult entry tests, such as the ECFMG examination for physicians, or to attract U.S. job offers. The gap that generally makes the difference in their decision is not the invidious income differential between prospective U.S. salaries and those at home. Instead, it is the gap between available salaries and work conditions *in their own countries* and those regarded there as acceptable for people with their education.

Professionals who earn enough at home to sustain a middle-class standard of living and who are reasonably satisfied about their chances for advancement seldom migrate. Those threatened with early obsolescence or who cannot make ends meet start looking for opportunities abroad. A fertile ground for this type of migration are countries in which university students are trained in advanced Western-style professional practices, but then find the prospects and means to implement their training blocked because of poor employment opportunities or lack of equipment.[24]

Because they do not come to escape poverty, but to improve their careers, immigrant professionals seldom accept menial jobs in the United States. However, they tend to enter at the bottom of their respective occupational ladders and to progress from there according to individual merit. This is why, for example, foreign doctors and nurses are so often found in public hospitals throughout the country. But in recent years, a number of foreign professionals—primarily of Asian origin—have had to turn to other pursuits because of new entry barriers to their respective careers in the United States. Common alternatives have been small business or even the unregulated practice of their profession while awaiting better times.[25] Despite these difficulties, these immigrants' economic success has been remarkable. For example, immigration from India during the last two decades has been heavily skewed toward university-educated professionals and technical personnel. In 1990, the median household income of Indian immigrants was $48,320—$18,000 above the median for the U.S. population and $20,000 above the figure for the foreign born, despite the fact that almost 60 percent of these immigrants had been in the United States ten years or less.[26]

An important feature of this type of immigration is its inconspicuousness. We seldom hear reference to a Filipino or an Indian immigration "problem," although there are over one million Filipinos and over five hundred thousand Indians living in this country. The reason is that professionals and technicians, heavily represented among these nationalities, seldom form tightly knit ethnic communities. As the case of Amitar Ray and his family exemplifies, professional immigrants are among the most rapidly assimilated—first because of their occupational success and second because of the absence of strong ethnic networks that reinforce the culture of origin. However, assimilation in this case does not mean severing relations with the home country. On the contrary, because successful immigrants have the means to do so, they attempt to bridge the gap between past and present through periodic visits and cultivating family and friends left behind. During the first generation at least, a typical pattern is the attempt to juggle two different social worlds. Although this is a difficult and expensive task, many foreign professionals actually succeed in it.

Entrepreneurial Immigrants

Near downtown Los Angeles there is an area approximately a mile long where all commercial signs suddenly change from English to strange pictorial characters. Koreatown, as the area is known, contains the predictable number of ethnic restaurants and grocery shops; it also contains a number of banks, import-export houses, industries, and real estate offices. Signs of "English spoken here" assure visitors that their links with the outside world have not been totally severed. In Los Angeles, the propensity for self-employment is three times greater among Koreans than among the population as a whole. Grocery stores, restaurants, gas stations, liquor stores, and real estate offices are typical Korean businesses. They also tend to remain within the community because the more successful immigrants sell their earlier businesses to new arrivals.[27]

A similar urban landscape is found near downtown Miami. Little Havana extends in a narrow strip for about five miles, eventually merging with the southwest suburbs of the city. Cuban-owned firms increased from 919 in 1967 to 8,000 in 1976 and approximately 28,000 in 1990. Most are small, averaging 8.1 employees at the latest count, but they also include factories employing hundreds of workers. Cuban firms are found in light and heavy manufacturing, construction, commerce, finance, and insurance. An estimated 60 percent of all residential construction in the metropolitan area is now done by these firms; gross annual receipts of Cuban manufacturing industries increased 1,067 percent during a recent ten-year period.[28]

These areas of concentrated immigrant entrepreneurship are known as ethnic enclaves. Their emergence has depended on three conditions: first, the presence of a number of immigrants with substantial business expertise acquired in their home countries; second, access to sources of capital; third, access to labor. The requisite labor is not too difficult to obtain because it can be initially drawn from family members and then from more recent immigrant arrivals. Sources of capital are often not a major obstacle either, because the sums required initially are small. When immigrants do not bring them from abroad, they can accumulate them through individual savings or obtain them from pooled resources in the community. In some instances, would-be entrepreneurs have access to financial institutions owned or managed by co-nationals. Thus, the first requisite is the critical one. The presence of a number of immigrants skilled in what sociologist Franklin Frazier called "the art of buying and selling" can usually overcome other obstacles to entrepreneurship.[29] Conversely, their absence tends to confine an immigrant group to wage work even when enough savings and labor are available.

Entrepreneurial minorities are the exception in both turn-of-the-century and contemporary immigrations. Their significance is that they create an avenue for economic mobility unavailable to other groups. This avenue is open not only to the original entrepreneurs, but to later arrivals as well. The reason is that relations between immigrant employers and their co-ethnic employees often go beyond a purely contractual bond. When immigrant enterprises expand, they tend to hire their own for supervisory positions. Today Koreans hire and promote Koreans in New York and Los Angeles, and Cubans do the same for other Cubans in Miami, just as sixty years ago the Jews of Manhattan's Lower East Side and the Japanese of San Francisco and Los Angeles hired and supported those from their own communities.[30]

A tightly knit ethnic enclave is not, however, the only manifestation of immigrant entrepreneurship. In other cities, where the concentration of these immigrants is less dense, they tend to take over businesses catering to low-income groups, often in the inner cities. In this role as "middleman minorities," entrepreneurial immigrants are less visible because they tend to be dispersed over the area occupied by the populations they serve. Koreatown in Los Angeles is not, for example, the only manifestation of entrepreneurship among this immigrant group. Koreans are also present in significant numbers in New York City, where they have gained increasing control of the produce market, and in cities like Washington, D.C., and Baltimore, where they have progressively replaced Italians and Jews as the principal merchants in low-income inner-city areas.[31] Similarly, roughly two-thirds of Cuban-owned firms are concentrated in Miami, but they are also numerous in other cities such as Los Angeles and Jersey City. The percentage of firms per thousand Cuban population is actually higher in these secondary concentrations than in Miami.[32]

The rise of ethnic enclaves and middleman minorities is generally fortuitous. There are no provisions so far in the U.S. immigration law to encourage foreign businessmen to come here, except as visitors. Congress is currently considering a provision that will grant U.S. residence to a limited number of foreign capitalists who invest in sizable job-creating enterprises. However, no explicit entry preference exists for small immigrant entrepreneurs with little or no capital, and none is likely to be implemented in the future. In general, entrepreneurial minorities come under preferences designated for other purposes. Koreans and Chinese, two of the most successful business-oriented groups, have availed themselves of the employment-based preference categories for professionals and skilled workers and, subsequently, of the family reunification provisions of the 1965 and 1990 immigration laws. Cubans came as political refugees and were initially resettled in dispersed localities throughout the country. It took these refugees more than a decade after initial arrival to start regrouping in certain geographic locations and begin the push toward entrepreneurship.

Refugees and Asylees

The Refugee Act of 1980, signed into law by President Carter, aimed at eliminating the former practice of granting asylum only to escapees from Communist-controlled nations. Instead, it sought to bring U.S. policy into line with international practice, which defines as a refugee anyone with a well-founded fear of persecution or physical harm, regardless of the political bent of his or her country's regime. In practice, however, the United States during the Reagan administration continued to grant refugee status to escapees from communism, primarily from Southeast Asia and Eastern Europe, while making it difficult for others fleeing non-Communist regimes such as Guatemala and El Salvador. The granting of asylum has significant advantages over other alternatives. The central difference is that while refugees have legal status, the right to work, and can avail themselves of the welfare provisions of the 1980 act, those denied asylum have none of these privileges and, if they stay, are classified as illegal aliens.[33]

Being a refugee is therefore not a matter of personal choice, but of governmental decision based on a combination of legal guidelines and political expediency. Depending on the relationship between the United States and the country of origin and the international context of the time, a particular flow of people may be classified as a political exodus or as an illegal group of economically motivated immigrants. Given past policy, it is thus not surprising that there are few escapees from rightist regimes living legally in the country. Major refugee groups have arrived, instead, after the Soviet army occupation of Eastern Europe, after the rise to power of Fidel Castro in Cuba, and after the takeover by Communist insurgents of three Southeast Asian countries. Ironically, after the end of the Cold War in 1989 and the collapse of the Soviet Union in 1991, the number of refugees admitted actually grew—once again due to foreign policy interests, and once again largely from the same source countries.

In 1993, a total of 127,343 refugees arrived and were admitted for legal residence in the United States. Of these, 37,604 or 30 percent came from Vietnam, Cambodia, and Laos; Cuba accounted for another 9 percent; the Soviet Union, Poland, and Romania combined represented 39 percent; and Afghanistan and Ethiopia added another 5 percent. Iran and Iraq— the only major non-Communist sources of refugee migration— accounted for 5 percent. Admissions from the Communist or former Communist world still represented about 90 percent of the total in this year.[34]

Major refugee groups living at present in the United States thus tend to share strong anti-Communist feelings, although they are different in many other respects. Their entry into the American labor market, for example, has been heterogeneous, paralleling and even exceeding the diversity among regular immigrants. Political refugees are found today in low-paid menial work, as is the case with many Cambodians, Laotians, Afghans, Ethiopians, and 1980 Mariel Cubans. They are also found at the higher end of the labor market, in prominent and well-paid professional careers, as is often the case with Eastern Europeans and Iranians. Others have veered toward business and self-employment after giving up hopes of returning to their countries. Cubans in south Florida and increasingly the Vietnamese, concentrated in Orange and Los Angeles counties, have followed this route. Finally, there is even the option of remaining out of work, made possible by the welfare provisions of the 1980 refugee act. Asian refugees with little education and work skills are commonly found in this situation.[35]

The official label of refugee conceals differences not only between national groups but within each of them as well. Two categories are generally found in most refugee flows. First, there is an elite of former notables who left because of ideological and political opposition to their countries' regimes. They tend to be among the earlier arrivals and usually have little difficulty validating their claim of political persecution. Second, there is a mass of individuals and families of more modest backgrounds who left at a later date because of the economic exactions and hardships imposed by the same regimes.[36] Depending on the relationship between their home country and the United States, they can be classified as bona fide refugees or as illegal aliens. This diversity in the origins of refugees and the interaction between the earlier elite arrivals and subsequent cohorts goes a long way toward explaining each group's economic and social adaptation. We examine the particulars of each case in the following chapters.

Overview

In 1995, well over a hundred foreign countries and possessions sent immigrants to the United States. Aside from basic statistical data supplied by INS and the Census Bureau, little is yet known about most of these groups. Tracing their evolution and patterns of adaptation is a task well beyond the scope of this book. Instead, we delineate the basic contours of contemporary immigration by focusing on major aspects of the adaptation experience. The emphasis throughout is on diversity in both the immigrants' origins and their modes of incorporation into American society. The typology outlined in this chapter serves as the basic organizing framework as we follow immigrants through their location in space, their strategies for economic mobility, their efforts at learning a language and a new culture, their decision to embrace the country as naturalized citizens, and their struggle to raise their children in America and, inevitably, as Americans.

Although there are significant differences within each major type of immigration, there is reason to believe that manual labor migrants, foreign professionals, entrepreneurial groups, and refugees share a number of characteristics with others in a similar position. In other words, immigrants from different nations who enter the United States as professionals and find positions in their fields tend to have more similar adaptation experiences than those typical of immigrant laborers from their respective countries. As in all typologies, empirical reality registers exceptions and combinations. Refugees and university-trained professionals may become entrepreneurs and the latter, if unsuccessful, may turn to manual wage labor. The category of refugee is particularly problematic because, as seen previously, it is not an economic mode of incorporation but a political status, validated by an explicit decision of the U.S. government. Yet despite their internal diversity, refugees possess certain common characteristics that set them apart from other immigrants. Subsequent chapters clarify the nature of these characteristics.

A description of present-day immigration and its diversity would be incomplete if not supplemented by a discussion of what all this means for the host society. Is it good or bad for the United States that so many foreigners from so many different countries are arriving at present? Should the country move decisively to prevent or restrict at least some of these flows? Alternatively, should it continue to maintain, as in the recent past, one of the most liberal immigration policies in the world? Our reply to these questions will be generally optimistic. Overall, immigration has been and will continue to be positive for the country both in terms of filling labor needs at different levels of the economy and, more important, injecting into society the energies, ambitions, and skills of positively selected groups. Qualifications exist, and we discuss them. But in our view, they do not detract from this general assessment.

The political debate about immigration in the United States has always been marked by vigorous calls for restriction. The most ardent advocates of this policy are often children and grandchildren of immigrants who wear their second-generation patriotism outwardly and aggressively. This position forgets that it was the labor and efforts of immigrants—often the parents and grandparents of today's restrictionists—that made much of the prosperity of the nation possible. Even the fiercest xenophobes have had a hard time arguing that turn-of-the-century groups such as Italian and Polish peasants or the much attacked Chinese and Japanese had a long-term negative effect on the country. Instead, these now successful and settled groups are presented as examples, but exception is taken to the newcomers. There is irony in the spectacle of Americans who bear clear marks of their immigrant origins being among the most vocal adversaries of continuing immigration. Consequences of heeding their advice would be serious, however. Although regulation and control of the inflow from abroad are always necessary, suppressing it would deprive the nation of what has been so far one of its main sources of energy, innovativeness, and growth.

2

Moving

Patterns of Immigrant Settlement and Spatial Mobility

In his 1926 study, *Migration and Business Cycles*, Harry Jerome concluded that the inflow of population was "on the whole dominated by conditions in the United States. The 'pull' is stronger than the push."[1] By that time, the gradual integration of the world economy had advanced sufficiently to make many Europeans aware of economic opportunities on the other side of the Atlantic, so deliberate recruitment became unnecessary. The question remains, however, about the destination of these flows. Labor economists frequently write as if immigrants have perfect information about labor market conditions in the receiving country and adjust their locational decisions accordingly.

The reality is very different because a number of factors other than wage differentials impinge on the actual destination of migrant flows. This chapter examines the locational distribution of immigrant groups with an emphasis both on diversity among nationalities and types of migration and on the unequal distribution of the foreign population in space. Although our main interest is on contemporary trends, we must go back in time, because the roots of the locational patterns of immigrants arriving today are often found in events that took place earlier in the century.

The Pioneers

The settlement decisions of contemporary immigrants are decisively affected by the ethnic concentrations established by their compatriots in the past. Because earlier flows consisted overwhelmingly of manual laborers, it is important to examine first how these foreign working-class communities came to settle where they did.

A first significant factor was geographical propinquity. It is not by chance that the bulk of turn-of-the-century European immigrants settled along the mid- and north-Atlantic seaboard while their Asian counterparts settled in California and other Pacific states. It is also not surprising that the bulk of early Mexican immigration concentrated in the Southwest, especially along the border. For immigrant workers, proximity to the homeland has two important economic consequences: First, for those who come on their own, it reduces the costs of the journey; second, for everyone, it reduces the costs of return, which most labor migrants plan to undertake at some point. In those cases where migration occurs along a land border, as with Mexicans, proximity to the sending area also provides a familiar physical and climatic environment.

The impact of propinquity is most vividly reflected in those immigrant communities established right by the waterside, at points of debarkation in port cities of both coasts. The "Little Italys" huddled close to the water in Boston, New York, Philadelphia, and Baltimore and the "Chinatowns" of San Francisco and other cities offer living testimony of a type of immigration that, having reached U.S. shores, would go no farther.[2]

This is not the whole story, however, because many other groups pushed inland. For foreign laborers, the decisive factor for the latter type of settlement was recruitment either in the home country or at ports of entry. The concentration of some Central and Eastern European peoples in the Midwest reflects the turn-of-the-century development of heavy industry in this area—first steel and later auto making. This concentration was coupled with the minimal skills required for most new industrial jobs, which made recruiting cheap immigrant labor attractive to employers. Consequences of this recruitment pattern last to our day: Only 5 percent of the population reporting foreign ancestry in 1980 lived in Ohio, but it is the home state of 15 percent of the nation's Croatians, 14 percent of the Hungarians, 15 percent of the Serbs, 22 percent of the Slovaks, and 45 percent of the Slovenians.[3]

Similarly, during the nineteenth century, labor recruitment by the Hudson and other canal companies moved contingents of Irish and Italian workers inland along the routes followed by canal construction. In the West, Chinese coolie workers also moved inland after mass recruitment by the railway companies.[4] The Union Pacific and the Central Pacific also recruited Mexicans, trainloads of whom were dispatched from El Paso and other border cities. About the same time, Finnish workers made their appearance in northern Wisconsin, Minnesota, and the Michigan Peninsula—hired by the copper mine and timber companies.[5]

Not every group arriving during the nineteenth century consisted exclusively of wage workers, however. Those coming before the Civil War in particular were often able to take advantage of cheap land in the West to go into business for themselves. This was especially the case of German settlers arriving since before the Revolutionary War. Germans were able to push inland toward the sparsely settled lands of Ohio, Indiana, Illinois, and beyond. In their wake, the landscape of the Midwest became dotted with rural farm enclaves in which the settlers' language and customs dominated.[6]

The influence of what were, in fact, the entrepreneurial migrations of its day have also lasted to the present. Descendants of the original settlers and those coming later on during the nineteenth century represent today the paramount ethnic concentrations throughout the Midwest. In the west north central states (Wisconsin, Minnesota, Iowa, the Dakotas, and Nebraska), over 50 percent of the population reported some German ancestry in 1990, a figure that quintuples that corresponding to the English. Germans are by far the dominant ethnic group in Cincinnati (39 percent), Indianapolis (27 percent), Milwaukee (45 percent), Minneapolis-St. Paul (39 percent), and St. Louis (36 percent).[7]

A similar pattern of independent Midwest farm settlement was followed by early Scandinavian and Czech immigrants. Scandinavian enclaves in the west north central region and especially in Minnesota attracted immigrants from the same nationalities throughout the century; their descendants represent today the fourth largest ancestry group in the region and the third largest (15 percent) in Minneapolis-St. Paul. Czech farming made its appearance in Wisconsin around the mid-1800s; from Racine and earlier farming enclaves, Czechs pushed inland toward the Nebraska frontier and then to Oklahoma and Texas. In 1990, Czech ancestry still accounted for about 25 percent of the populations of several rural counties in these states.[8]

In the Far West, Japanese immigrants attempted to follow the same path by buying land and engaging in independent farming during the early 1900s. In their case, however, land was neither plentiful nor empty. Japanese farmers faced the united opposition of domestic growers, who had welcomed their arrival as laborers but who resisted violently their shift into self-employment:

> So long as the Japanese remained willing to perform agricultural labor at low wages, they remained popular with California ranchers. But . . . many Japanese began to lease and buy agricultural land for farming on their own account. This enterprise had the two-fold result of creating Japanese competition in the produce field and decreasing the number of Japanese farmhands available.[9]

As a result, the California state legislature passed the Alien Land Law of 1913 restricting Japanese land acquisition. This legal instrument was refined in 1920 when these immigrants were forbidden to lease land or act as guardians of native-born minors in matters of property.[10] These measures drove many Japanese off the land and into urban small businesses, but the development of an urban enclave economy was also stunted by the end of Japanese immigration, following the Gentleman's Agreement of 1907. As a consequence of these restrictions, Japanese-Americans, although a highly successful group, number at present less than one million and, with the exception of Hawaii, represent a minuscule proportion of the population of the states where they concentrate.[11]

Pioneer migrants—whether settling in places of arrival, following labor recruiters inland, or charting an independent course through farming and urban trade in different locations—had a decisive influence on later arrivals. Once a group settled in a certain place, the destination of later cohorts from the same country often became a foregone conclusion. Migration is a network-driven process, and the operation of kin and friendship ties is nowhere more effective than in guiding new arrivals toward preestablished ethnic communities. This process may continue indefinitely and accounts for the high concentration of most foreign groups in certain regions of the country and their near absence from others.

Following in the Footsteps

At the time of the Mexican Revolution in the early 1900s, large contingents of Mexican refugees migrated northward to find employment in the slaughterhouses of Chicago, the breweries of Milwaukee, and the steel mills of Gary, Indiana. Communities established then continue to serve as magnets for Mexican migrants today. Despite the distance and the different climatic conditions, remote villages in the interior of Mexico continue sending their sons, year after year, for a stint of work in the urban industries of the Midwest.[12]

The same pattern is found in the East, where small Jamaican, Dominican, and Haitian colonies in New York City provided the nucleus for guiding mass labor migration during recent years. Again distance and a colder climate were no obstacle for these Caribbean migrants to follow in the wake of their predecessors. Out West, most contemporary Asian and Pacific Islander migrations such as the Japanese and the Filipinos continue to be overwhelmingly concentrated in their areas of traditional settlement.[13]

The influence of preexisting networks on locational patterns tends to be decisive among contemporary manual labor migrants because they are not guided by recruiting agents, but by spontaneous individual and family decisions, usually based on the presence in certain places of kin and friends who can provide shelter and assistance. Exceptions to this pattern are found most often among other types of immigrants. Professionals, such as physicians, engineers, and scientists, tend to rely less on the assistance of preexisting ethnic communities than on their own skills and qualifications. They often come only after securing job offers from U.S. employers and tend to be more dispersed throughout the country than manual labor migrants. Although no national contingent is formed exclusively by professionals and their families, a few—such as recent Indian immigrants—approximate this pattern and provide examples of its characteristic dispersion.[14]

Entrepreneurial minorities tend to settle in large urban areas that provide close proximity to markets and sources of labor. Like working-class migrants, foreign entrepreneurs are often found in the areas of principal ethnic concentration because of the cheap labor, secluded markets, and access to credit that they make available. This is the case, for example, of Koreans, concentrated in Los Angeles; Chinese entrepreneurs in San Francisco and New York; and Cubans in Miami. However, other business-minded immigrants choose to move away from the principal areas of ethnic concentration in quest of economic opportunity. The latter are commonly found in the role of middleman merchants and lenders for the domestic working class. Koreans and Chinese in several East Coast cities and Cubans in Puerto Rico provide examples.[15]

Finally, the early locational patterns of political refugees and seekers of political asylum are often decided for them by government authorities and private resettlement agencies. In the past, the goal of official programs has been to disperse refugee

groups away from their points of arrival to facilitate their cultural assimilation and attenuate the economic burden they are
supposed to represent for receiving areas. This official decision
accounts for the multiplicity of locations in which groups such
as the Cubans and the Vietnamese are found today. Gradually,
however, refugees trek back toward areas closer to their homeland and more compatible in terms of culture. The presence of
ethnic communities of the same nationality or a related one has
frequently played a decisive role in promoting these secondary
migrations.

The rapid growth of the Cuban population in Dade County,
Florida, and of the Vietnamese population in Orange County,
California, can be traced directly to this process. By 1979, half
of the Cuban-origin population of the United States was found
in the Miami metropolitan area (Dade), a result primarily of return migration by refugees originally resettled elsewhere. Similarly, by 1984, Orange County had more Vietnamese refugees
than any state of the Union except California. *Calle Ocho* (S.W.
8th Street) in Miami is the heart of "Little Havana"; Bolsa Avenue in Westminster (Orange County) has been called the Vietnamese capital of America.[16]

Contemporary Settlement Patterns:
A Map of Immigrant America

These various processes have led to a settlement pattern among
recent immigrants to the United States that combines two apparently contradictory outcomes: concentration, because a few
states and metropolitan areas receive a disproportionate number of the newcomers, and diffusion, because immigrants are
found in every state of the Union and because different immigrant types vary significantly in their locational decisions. In
1993, 71 percent of the 904,292 foreign persons admitted for
legal permanent residence went to just six states: California
(28.8 percent), New York (16.7 percent), Texas (7.5 percent),

Florida (6.8 percent), New Jersey (5.6 percent), and Illinois (5.2 percent). At the other extreme, no state received fewer than two hundred immigrants, the least favored being Wyoming (263) and Montana (509).[17]

Figure 1 portrays the national composition of immigrant flows to seven major receiving urban areas. Together these cities accounted for 43 percent of legal immigration during 1993. With small variations, this settlement pattern is representative of those registered throughout the 1980s. Along with numerical concentration, there is much diversity in the origins of immigrants going to these seven cities. Three of the five principal flows to New York—the premier destination of immigrants— come from the Caribbean, with those from the Dominican Republic accounting for a fifth of the total, followed by Jamaica and Guyana. The same Caribbean origins typify immigration to Miami, except that here Cubans are by far the dominant nationality.

Mexicans form the largest contingent to the second and seventh areas of destination—Los Angeles and Houston, respectively. As with Mexicans, the play of geography and prior ethnic settlement is also reflected in the remaining major flows to each city. In Los Angeles, Asian immigrants account jointly for over one-fourth of the total; in Chicago, they are also present but share pride of place with Mexicans and with a major European group—Poles who have traditionally settled in this area. The same forces underlie the composition of immigration to San Francisco, a traditional place of settlement for Asians, where Chinese, Filipinos, and Vietnamese account jointly for a large share of the inflow.

Perhaps the most peculiar case is Washington, D.C., where most immigrant communities are of recent vintage and where, unlike other East Coast destinations, Caribbean groups are not predominant. Instead, migration to Washington is dominated by entrepreneurial Asian groups along with former political refugees. Vietnamese and Salvadorans represent the latter trend. Although there is some logical affinity between the

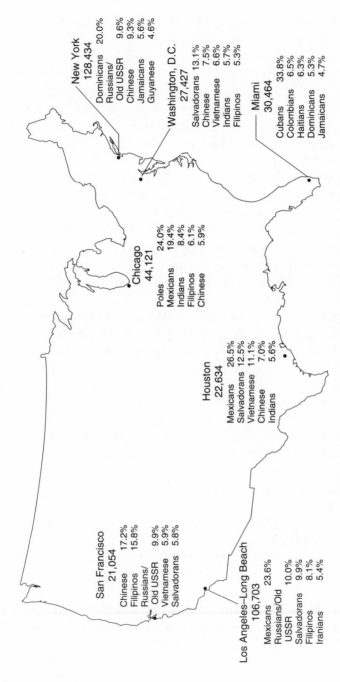

San Francisco
21,054

Chinese	17.2%
Filipinos	15.8%
Russians/	
Old USSR	9.9%
Vietnamese	5.9%
Salvadorans	5.8%

Los Angeles–Long Beach
106,703

Mexicans	23.6%
Russians/Old	
USSR	10.0%
Salvadorans	9.9%
Filipinos	8.1%
Iranians	5.4%

Houston
22,634

Mexicans	26.5%
Salvadorans	12.5%
Vietnamese	11.1%
Chinese	7.0%
Indians	5.6%

Chicago
44,121

Poles	24.0%
Mexicans	19.4%
Indians	8.4%
Filipinos	6.1%
Chinese	5.9%

New York
128,434

Dominicans	20.0%
Russians/	
Old USSR	9.6%
Chinese	9.3%
Jamaicans	5.6%
Guyanese	4.6%

Washington, D.C.
27,427

Salvadorans	13.1%
Chinese	7.5%
Vietnamese	6.6%
Indians	5.7%
Filipinos	5.3%

Miami
30,464

Cubans	33.8%
Colombians	6.5%
Haitians	6.3%
Dominicans	5.3%
Jamaicans	4.7%

Figure 1.   Composition of legally admitted immigrant flows to seven major metropolitan destinations, 1993.

SOURCE: U.S. Immigration and Naturalization Service, *1993 Statistical Yearbook* (Washington, D.C.: U.S. Government Printing Office, 1994), table 19.

NOTES: (1) "Chinese" includes migrants from mainland China only. (2) Orange County, just south of Los Angeles, was the sixth-largest metropolitan area of immigrant destination in 1993.

motives for departure of these politically motivated outflows and their settlement in the nation's capital, the actual processes leading to this outcome have not been studied in detail so far.[18]

An alternative portrait of the settlement process emerges when we examine locational decisions of the major immigrant groups themselves, rather than major areas of destination. Although there is overlap between both forms of arranging the data, the two vary because national contingents differ in their levels of concentration and their propensity to locate in metropolitan areas. Figure 2 and table 1 present the relevant information for 1987. This year is representative of basic trends during the last decade, prior to the IRCA legalization program. The three largest immigrant groups arriving in that year share a preferred place of destination: Los Angeles. Miami is the choice of the fourth and New York of the next three. The last group, the Vietnamese, split about evenly between Los Angeles and nearby Santa Ana. Only two groups did not have Los Angeles as one of their preferred destinations; four did not include New York.

Next to Los Angeles and New York come San Francisco, the second choice of Chinese and Filipinos, and San Diego, the third for Filipinos and Mexicans. Finally, several cities are the specific destinations of only one group for reasons of history or propinquity. Cubans are the single largest immigrant group in both Miami and Tampa; Dominicans predominate in San Juan and Mexicans in El Paso. Third settlement choices have alternated in the past with other locations for several nationalities. For example, Chicago has only recently ceased to be such a choice for Mexicans and Honolulu for Filipinos.

The locational decisions of all major contemporary inflows tend to reflect both historical patterns of settlement and types of contemporary immigrants. Most concentrated and least rural are Cubans, over three-fourths of whom settled in Miami. In 1987, as in prior years, recorded immigration from Cuba did not correspond to actual arrivals, but was formed instead by former political refugees who adjusted their legal status. As refugees, Cubans were far more dispersed following the deliberate resettlement policy of government agencies. The high

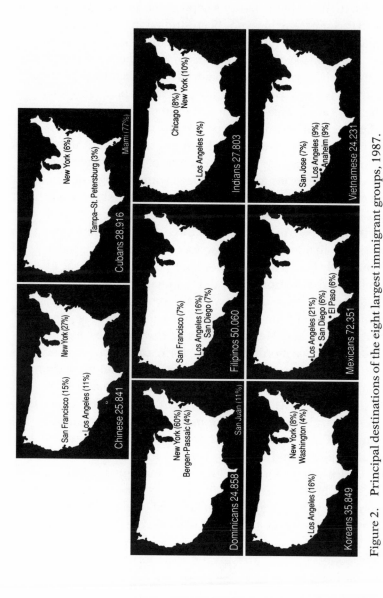

Figure 2. Principal destinations of the eight largest immigrant groups, 1987.

SOURCE: U.S. Immigration and Naturalization Service, *1987 Statistical Yearbook* (Washington, D.C.: U.S. Government Printing Office, 1988), table 18.

NOTE: "Chinese" includes migrants from mainland China only.

Table 1

Destinations of the Eight Largest Immigrant Groups, 1987

Nationality	Most Common Destination		% at Top Three Destinations	% at Other Metropolitan Destinations	% at Non-metropolitan Destinations	As % of Total Immigration
	City	%				
Mexican	Los Angeles	21	33	55	12	12
Filipino	Los Angeles	16	30	59	11	8
Korean	Los Angeles	16	29	62	9	6
Cuban	Miami	77	86	13	1	5
Indian	New York	10	22	71	7	5
Chinese[a]	New York	27	53	44	3	4
Dominican	New York	60	76	21	3	4
Vietnamese	Anaheim–Santa Ana	9	25	71	4	4

SOURCE: U.S. Immigration and Naturalization Service, *1987 Statistical Yearbook* (Washington, D.C.: U.S. Government Printing Office, 1988), table 18.

[a] Immigrants from mainland China only.

concentration of Cubans as "immigrants" thus reflects voluntary individual decisions to migrate back to south Florida. As a result, the majority of Miami's population is today of Cuban origin, and close to half of the metropolitan population of Dade County is classified as Hispanic. Undoubtedly, geographic and climatic reasons have played a role in the process, but more important seems to have been the business opportunities made available by the emergence of an ethnic enclave economy in the area.[19]

Next in concentration are Dominicans, a group whose rapid growth has taken place during the last two decades and that is composed primarily of industrial operatives and laborers. Employer recruitment and the existence of an older Dominican colony in New York City appear to have been the decisive factors channeling this labor inflow in that direction.[20]

Most dispersed spatially are Indian immigrants—the group with the highest proportion of university graduates and professionals. The greater geographic mobility of this type of immigration is also reflected in the two top destinations of Indians, who, unlike other Asians, do not settle predominantly in West Coast cities. Instead, close to one-fifth of Indian immigrants settle in New York and Chicago, and the rest are found dispersed throughout other metropolitan locations.

The mainland Chinese share with Indians a preference for New York City and with Cubans a relatively high level of concentration in their major place of destination. These similarities are not casual because, like Indians, a high proportion of recent Chinese immigrants possess university educations; and, like Cubans, they are often bound toward those areas where an ethnic economy already exists. In this case, New York's flourishing Chinatown and adjacent areas seem to provide the lure for newcomers.[21]

The three largest national contingents are relatively similar in their levels of metropolitan concentration, although this convergence is not the outcome of the same historical process. The largest group—Mexicans—is formed overwhelmingly by workers and their families. The proportion of professionals and managers among occupationally active Mexican immigrants in 1987 was the lowest among all eight major immigrant groups (6.0 percent), as it had been in prior years; the percentage of urban workers and farm laborers was, however, the highest (70.8 percent). Although originally a rural flow, Mexican immigration has become mostly urban, as reflected in the 88 percent of new arrivals going to metropolitan areas. The considerable dispersion of this group can be attributed to its size and its long-standing character as a source of wage labor throughout the Southwest and Midwest.

Filipinos represent another group with a long history of settlement in the United States. Earlier arrivals, in particular those going to Hawaii, were mostly rural workers.[22] Unlike Mexicans, however, contemporary Filipino immigrants are a diverse group, combining family reunification with a sizable contingent of new professionals. The latter represented close to half (46 percent) of occupationally active migrants in 1987. The occupationally inactive, presumably kin of earlier arrivals, comprised an absolute majority (63 percent) of the total flow in 1987.

Koreans are a professional and business-oriented group of more recent vintage. Their main destination is Los Angeles, where an ethnic enclave economy has grown rapidly during the last decade. Koreans have also become prominent in produce retailing and other small businesses in East Coast cities. New York and Washington came next to Los Angeles as their places of destination in 1987; they were also the single largest foreign group arriving in large mid-Atlantic cities such as Philadelphia and Baltimore.[23]

Like Cubans, the Vietnamese are not newly arrived immigrants, but mostly former refugees who have adjusted their legal status. The influence of government resettlement programs in the spatial distribution of refugee groups can be seen clearly in this instance. Vietnamese immigrants are the least concentrated of all major nationalities, including Indians. Only 9 percent of 1987 Vietnamese immigrants planned to settle in Orange County, their preferred location. There is evidence that the

Table 2

Metropolitan Areas of Destination of the Five Major Refugee Groups Admitted in 1987 and 1993

Nationality	N	Most Common Destination	(%)	Second Most Common Destination	(%)
1987					
Cuban	26,952	Miami, FL	78.5	New York, NY	5.9
Vietnamese	20,617	Orange County, CA	9.2	Los Angeles, CA	7.4
Cambodian	12,206	Stockton, CA	9.3	Los Angeles, CA	6.0
Laotian	6,560	Minneapolis–St. Paul, MN	12.1	Fresno, CA	6.4
Iranian	5,559	Los Angeles, CA	40.3	New York, NY	5.8
1993					
Soviet Union	45,900	New York, NY	24.5	Los Angeles, CA	8.7
Vietnamese	30,249	Orange County, CA	17.9	San Jose, CA	10.3
Cuban	11,603	Miami, FL	76.5	Jersey City, NJ	3.7
Laotian	6,547	Fresno, CA	24.6	Minneapolis–St. Paul, MN	9.4
Iranian	3,875	Los Angeles, CA	60.9	New York, NY	6.2

SOURCES: U.S. Immigration and Naturalization Service, *1987 Statistical Yearbook* (Washington, D.C.: U.S. Government Printing Office, 1988), table 40, pp. 65–66, and *1993 Statistical Yearbook* (Washington, D.C.: U.S. Government Printing Office, 1994), table 37, pp. 92–93.

Vietnamese, like the Cubans in the past, have been leaving areas of initial settlement and concentrating in other cities, primarily in California. As table 2 shows, by 1993 the proportion of Vietnamese settling in Orange County had doubled to 18 percent. Los Angeles, San Jose, and San Diego are also areas with a sizable population of this nationality.[24]

In general, however, refugee groups that are sponsored and resettled through official programs tend to exhibit higher levels of spatial dispersion than those that do so on their own. This pattern is illustrated in table 2, which presents data on preferred states of residence of the five largest refugee groups admitted in 1987 and 1993. All three Southeast Asian nationalities, generally resettled through officially sponsored programs, chose California as their preferred destination, but much smaller fractions were initially settled there. Over time, however, family sponsorships lead to increasing concentrations in preferred locales. In 1987, only 6 percent of mostly Hmong refugees from Laos were resettled in Fresno, but by 1993 the proportion going to Fresno had quadrupled to 25 percent. The proportion of Iranians settling in Los Angeles increased from two-fifths in 1987 to three-fifths in 1993. Like immigrants of the same nationality, Cuban "refugees" in 1987 were not new arrivals, but mostly individuals who had come during the Mariel boatlift and then adjusted their earlier "entrant" status. After the initial resettlement period, Mariel refugees were thus free to select their place of residence. Like other Cubans, they gravitated toward south Florida. As shown in table 2, 78 percent of all 1987 Cuban refugees settled in Miami, as did 76 percent of all Cubans admitted six years later.

Preferred Places

Immigration to the United States is today an urban phenomenon and one concentrated in the largest cities. In 1993, less than 5 percent of legal immigrants went to live in nonurban areas, and more than half settled in just ten metropolitan locations. In particular, recent years have seen the gradual end of what was a significant component of pre–World War I immigration: rural-bound groups coming to settle empty lands or work as farm laborers.

This trend is probably less marked among undocumented immigrants, many of whom continue working in agriculture. There are no reliable figures on the size and occupational distribution of the undocumented population, but a series of studies conducted among returning immigrants in their places of origin indicates both a continuing rural presence and an increasing urban concentration. Many undocumented immigrants apparently begin as rural workers but gradually drift into the cities, attracted by higher wages and better working conditions.[25] As seen in chapter 1, there is a close interaction between legal and illegal immigrants from the same countries. A large proportion of legal migration from countries like Mexico and the Dominican Republic is composed of formerly undocumented immigrants who managed to legalize their situation. Hence, the spatial distribution of the recorded component of these inflows gives us a partial glimpse of what takes place underground.[26]

The bias of contemporary immigration toward a few metropolitan places is not a phenomenon of recent years, but one that has occurred regularly during the last three decades. Year after year, with remarkable regularity, the same cities emerge as the preferred sites of destination of the total inflow and of its major national components. Table 3 illustrates this trend with data for selected years, beginning in 1967. During the following three decades, approximately one-fourth to one-third of total immigration concentrated in the three principal areas of destination. New York remained always the preferred site while the next two places alternated among Los Angeles, Chicago, and Miami. The single most significant change during the period is the consolidation of Los Angeles as the second preferred destination of immigrants and the diminishing gap between the size of this inflow and that bound for New York.

Table 3 presents trends for the four nationalities for which data are available during the entire period. Mexicans and Dominicans represent approximately the same proportion of total immigration throughout these years, increasing slightly in 1993. Filipino immigration experienced a significant absolute and relative increase between 1967 and 1975 and then stabilized at about 8 percent of the total. Cuban immigrants—mostly adjusted former refugees—declined significantly until the mid-1980s and then increased again to about 5 percent of total immigration in 1987. This quantum jump is an outgrowth of the Mariel exodus, which also accounts for an extraordinary rise in spatial concentration. Close to 90 percent of recent Cuban immigrants cluster in just three cities, with the overwhelming majority going to Miami. Next in concentration are Dominicans, although their strong preference for New York has declined slightly during the last years. Filipinos and Mexicans are far more dispersed; but, with some exceptions, their preferred areas of destination remain the same. Los Angeles consolidated its place during this period as the major area of settlement for both groups, and San Diego surged ahead to third place, replacing more traditional destinations.

Reasons for the spatial concentration of immigrant flows, the strong urban bias of recent ones, and the consistency of their destinations over time are all linked to the characteristic economics of immigration. Like native youth, newly arrived immigrants are newcomers to the labor market who tend to search for immediately available opportunities. Regardless of their qualifications and experience, recent immigrants generally enter at the bottom of their respective occupational ladders. Thus, foreign manual workers are channeled toward the lowest paying and most arduous jobs; immigrant professionals, such as physicians and nurses, also must accept less desirable entry jobs within their professions and even outside of them.[27] Lastly, entrepreneurs also start small, with shops catering to their own community or in riskier "middleman" ventures in the inner city.

Table 3

Destinations of Major Immigrant Groups in Selected Years

Nationality	Year	N	As % of Total Immigration	% in Top Three Destinations	Most Common Destinations		
					First	Second	Third
Mexican	1967	42,371	11.7	19.6	Los Angeles	Chicago	El Paso
	1975	62,205	16.1	22.7	Los Angeles	Chicago	El Paso
	1979	52,096	11.3	17.3	El Paso	Los Angeles	Houston
	1984	57,557	10.6	27.9	Los Angeles	Chicago	El Paso
	1987	72,351	12.0	33.0	Los Angeles	El Paso	San Diego
	1993	126,561	14.0	31.4	Los Angeles	Chicago	Houston
Cuban	1967	33,321	9.2	59.0	Miami	New York	San Juan
	1975	25,955	6.7	57.9	Miami	New York	San Juan
	1979	15,585	3.4	59.1	Miami	New York	San Juan
	1984	10,599	1.9	51.8	Miami	Jersey City	New York
	1987	28,916	4.8	86.0	Miami	New York	Tampa
	1993	13,666	1.5	81.5	Miami	Jersey City	Tampa
Dominican	1967	11,514	3.2	90.6	New York	San Juan	Miami
	1975	14,066	3.6	84.7	New York	San Juan	Jersey City
	1979	17,519	3.8	80.6	New York	San Juan	Bergen-Passaic
	1984	23,147	4.3	78.7	New York	San Juan	Bergen-Passaic
	1987	24,858	4.1	76.0	New York	San Juan	Bergen-Passaic
	1993	45,420	5.0	71.1	New York	San Juan	Boston

Filipino	1967	10,865	3.0	25.6	San Francisco	Honolulu	New York
	1975	31,751	8.2	20.1	San Francisco	Los Angeles	Honolulu
	1979	41,300	9.0	17.8	San Francisco	Los Angeles	Honolulu
	1984	42,768	7.9	28.1	Los Angeles	San Francisco	Honolulu
	1987	50,060	8.3	30.0	Los Angeles	San Francisco	San Diego
	1993	53,457	7.0	26.0	Los Angeles	New York	San Diego
Total	1967	361,972		26.1	New York	Miami	Chicago
	1975	386,194		28.2	New York	Los Angeles	Chicago
	1979	460,348		25.5	New York	Los Angeles	Miami
	1984	543,903		29.8	New York	Los Angeles	Chicago
	1987	601,516		33.2	New York	Los Angeles	Miami
	1993	904,292		30.9	New York	Los Angeles	Chicago

SOURCE: U.S. Immigration and Naturalization Service, *Statistical Yearbooks* (Washington, D.C.: U.S. Government Printing Office, 1968, 1976, 1980, 1985, 1988, 1994).

In the absence of deliberate recruitment or other ad hoc factors, entry jobs at the bottom of the respective ladders are more easily accessible in large urban agglomerations and in those experiencing processes of rapid economic growth. Once immigrants from a particular nationality "discover" the existence of such opportunities in an urban area, the process becomes self-perpetuating through the operation of ethnic networks. It is thus not surprising that the principal concentrations of the three largest immigrant groups at present are found in Los Angeles, a large metropolitan area that has experienced rapid economic expansion in recent years. It is not surprising either that Cubans concentrate in Miami, another fast-growing city that has become the center of U.S. trade with Latin America. Washington, D.C., is also an attractive area of destination for entrepreneurially oriented groups because of the presence of a large inner-city minority population, along with a sizable segment of highly paid government workers.

Less obvious are reasons for the continuation of New York–bound immigration given the industrial decline of the area in recent years. Between 1970 and 1980, New York lost close to half a million jobs; the most affected sector was manufacturing, where employment decreased by almost one-third. New York's industrial decline raises the question of why immigrants persist in going there instead of following manufacturing jobs to their new locations in the Carolinas, Florida, or Texas. One reason is that, despite declines in both population and employment, New York continues to be the nation's largest urban agglomeration. Another is that large established ethnic communities continue to serve as a magnet for new immigrants from their home countries. More important, however, amid industrial decline there has been significant economic growth spurred by other sectors such as services and construction. From 1977 to 1980, there was a 17 percent increase in the nine major service industries, including a 20 to 30 percent growth in producer services. Total construction activity in New York was up 7.1 percent between 1980 and 1981, compared with 1.2 percent nationwide. Demand for office space remained strong, with preleased space exceeding the actual inventory for several consecutive years during the 1980s.[28]

About half of the jobs generated in distributive and producer services in New York City are in the highest paid earning classes; this is particularly true in the so-called FIRE sector (finance, insurance, and real estate) and in transportation, communications, and utilities. However, about 45 percent of employment in producer services and 65 percent in consumer services are formed by jobs paid minimum or near minimum wages. Approximately 20 percent of employment in construction is also in this low-wage class, a figure that increases significantly among nonunion workers.[29]

Immigrants have found in these low-paid jobs a continuing and expanding entry point into New York's labor market; in turn, their presence has been a significant element fueling the city's economic expansion. In addition to producer services, consumer services, and construction, there are also indications of renewed industrial activity, but one that takes place through subcontracting, sweatshops, homework, and other informal arrangements. Several field studies point to a heavy concentration of immigrants among both owners and workers in this informal industrial economy.[30] Thus, recent economic growth in New York has been accompanied by a profound reorganization of production and distribution activities in a number of sectors. As Sassen-Koob states: "The large influx of immigrants from low-wage countries over the last fifteen years . . . cannot be understood separately from this restructuring. . . . It is the expansion in the supply of low-wage jobs generated by major growth sectors that is one of the key factors in the *continuation* of the current immigration to New York."[31]

Persistent Ethnicity

A final question is what locational trends can be expected in the future. In other words, will recent immigrants and their descendants continue to be disproportionately concentrated in a few metropolitan places, or will they gradually disperse throughout the country? Theories of immigrant assimilation have consistently assumed the latter outcome: Insofar as immigrants and their children become more like native Americans, their patterns of spatial mobility will become more similar to those of the rest of the population. In this view, the gradual disappearance of concentrated immigrant communities represents the spatial counterpart of cultural assimilation as foreign groups "melt" into the host society. In some writings, the process is described as an elementary version of queuing theory, with older immigrant groups leaving urban ethnic areas to new ones:

> There has also been an historical pattern of one group replacing another in neighborhoods, jobs, leadership, schools, and other institutions. Today's neighborhood changes have been dramatized by such expressions as "white flight" but these patterns existed long before. . . . In nineteenth century neighborhoods where Anglo-Saxons had once fled as the Irish moved in, the middle-class Irish later fled as the Jews and Italians moved in.[32]

We showed previously that new immigrants tend to be persistent in their choice of spatial location. This pattern says little, of course, about the long-term preferences of particular groups once they have settled in the country. To explore this question, we must move back in time and examine locational patterns of groups that have been in the United States for longer periods.

A recent study provides initial support for the assimilation hypothesis by reporting a negative correlation between time in the country and spatial concentration as measured by the index of dissimilarity (D) from the American population as a whole. For ten European nationalities, most of which were already well represented in the country at the time of independence, the correlation between these two variables is −.72.[33] However, the same study goes on to report that immigrant groups' initial settlement patterns have had a decisive influence on the ethnic composition of each of the country's regions. For example, with

few exceptions, the five largest ancestry groups within each regional division include groups that were among the five largest
immigrant contingents already living in the area in 1850, 1900,
or 1920. Thus, German and Irish are among the largest ancestry groups in New England, where they were also among the
principal immigrant nationalities in each of these earlier years;
Norwegians and Swedes are strongly represented in the west
north central region at present, just as their ancestors were at
the turn of the century.[34]

What is true of regions is also true of specific nationalities.
Descendants of late nineteenth- and early twentieth-century
immigrants, particularly those coming from the Mediterranean and from non-European countries, tend to remain in their
original areas of settlement. At present, the five most highly
concentrated ethnic groups are Mexicans, Portuguese, Japanese, Filipinos, and Norwegians. As seen previously, Mexicans
and Filipinos continue to arrive in large numbers and to go
to the places in which they were concentrated half a century
ago. The remaining groups are, however, descendants of immigrants who arrived in the United States mostly before World
War II. Despite long residence in the country, they cluster in the
same areas as their forebears. Three-fourths of all Portuguese-
Americans reside at present in only four states: Massachusetts
and Rhode Island in the East and California and Hawaii in the
West; a similar proportion of Japanese-Americans is found in
just the latter two states.[35]

Within major areas of settlement, there has been, of course,
outward movement and dispersal, and this pattern has often
been taken as evidence of full assimilation. However, the telling fact is that, after several generations, particular nationalities continue to be associated with specific patches of national territory, giving them their distinct idiosyncrasies and
cultural traits. Such stable locations are a far cry from the
image of a thoroughly homogenized "melted" population with
identical proportions of the same original nationalities found
everywhere.

There are few grounds for belief that the resilience of these ethnic communities is likely to give way in the future. The American population as a whole is gradually moving away from the Northeast and Midwest toward the South and Southwest. If present trends continue indefinitely, New England and the mid-Atlantic region will see their combined share of the total population reduced from 21 to just 10 percent, and the west south central and Pacific regions will increase theirs from 24 to 36 percent. However, this spatial displacement will not lead to greater dispersion of ethnic communities. If trends observed during the late 1980s continue, their overall spatial concentration will either not change or actually increase.

Reasons for this somewhat unexpected outcome are three-fold: First, ethnic groups concentrated in regions losing population are less likely to leave so that, over time, their relative proportion increases. Second, when members of an ethnic minority move, they are more likely to go to areas where their own group is already numerous, including those experiencing out-migration. Third, when an ethnic group moves en masse from its traditional area, it does not become necessarily dispersed, but often regroups in another region. The outcome of these trends, when projected into the future, is that nationalities such as the Poles will tend to remain heavily concentrated in the Northeast and Midwest, Norwegians in the west north central states, and Cubans in the Southeast; Russians (mostly Jews) will tend to abandon the mid-Atlantic region to reconstitute themselves as a major ethnic group in the Pacific.[36]

A recent instructive example involves the one hundred thirty thousand Indochinese refugees who arrived in the United States in 1975. Upon arrival, they were sent to four major reception centers, from which they were resettled in 813 separate locations spread throughout all fifty states. Data collected at the reception centers show that less than half of these refugees (47.3 percent) were sent to the state of their choice. By 1980, however, 45 percent lived in a state other than the one to which they had been sent. Nearly 40 percent had moved to areas of high ethnic concentration in California. Conversely, the proportion that lived in dispersed communities with less than five hundred refugees of the same nationality dropped from 64.7 to 40.1 percent. Secondary migration trends during the 1980s and 1990s continued reinforcing the predominance of a few areas of Indochinese concentration.[37]

Given these past experiences and the propensity of major contemporary immigrations to remain clustered, there is little reason to expect a dispersal of recent immigrants and their children. Contrary to assimilationist views, the safest prediction is that ethnic communities created by present immigration will endure and will become identified with their area of settlement, giving to the latter, as other immigrants had before them, a distinct cultural flavor and a new "layer" of phenotypical and cultural traits.

Conclusion: The Pros and Cons of Spatial Concentration

The question of why ethnic communities tend to stay put in certain parts of the country can be discussed jointly with advantages and disadvantages of this pattern because the two issues are closely intertwined. Overall, the entire process of immigrant settlement is "sticky" because new arrivals tend to move to places where earlier immigrants have become established, and later generations do not wander too far off. Following assimilation theory, it could be argued that this pattern is irrational because economic opportunities, especially for the American-born generations, are often greater elsewhere. Individualistic aspirations should lead to dispersal because upward economic mobility often requires spatial mobility.[38]

There is, however, an alternative logic that contradicts this reasoning. By moving away from places where their own group is numerically strong, individuals risk losing a range of social and moral resources that make for psychological well-being as well as for economic gain. A large minority that becomes dispersed risks lacking a significant presence or voice anywhere; on the contrary, even a small group, if sufficiently concentrated, can have economic and political weight locally. For members of the immigrant generation, spatial concentration has several positive consequences: preservation of a valued life-style, regulation of the pace of acculturation, greater social control over the young, and access to community networks for both moral and economic support.

For subsequent generations, preservation of the ethnic community, even if more widely dispersed, can also have significant advantages. Among the entrepreneurially inclined, ethnic ties translate into access to sources of working capital, protected markets, and pools of labor.[39] Others also derive advantages from an enduring community. There is strength in numbers, especially at the ballot box, and this fact allows minority groups to assert their presence and their interests in the political process. As chapter 4 shows, politics can also serve as an avenue of individual upward mobility when other paths remain blocked. The ascendance of urban Irish politicians in the late nineteenth century and that of their Italian counterparts later on provide the classic examples.[40]

The question of relative advantages and disadvantages can be turned around, however, and asked from the point of view of American society. Many writers have expressed fears of continuing immigration precisely because it leads to growing ethnic concentration, which, they believe, will alter the cultural fabric of the nation. At worst, secessionist movements have been anticipated in those areas where immigrants and their descendants become the majority.[41]

There is little doubt that the best way of minimizing the impact of immigration is either to stop it or to disperse new arrivals, but this is also a way of minimizing the potential long-term contribution that immigrant communities can make. Throughout the history of the United States, communities created by foreign groups have been a significant force in promoting the growth and economic vigor of cities like New York, Boston, San Francisco, and Los Angeles, as well as entire regions like the Midwest. Once immigrants have settled and integrated into the society, their traditions and folkways have entered local

culture. After a while, these syncretic products become institutionalized and are proudly presented by all as "typical" of the
local lore. St. Patrick's Day parades, German beer fests, Chinese
New Year celebrations, Mardi Gras carnivals, Mexican fiestas,
and the like are many manifestations of this process.

But what about separatism? During the first two decades of
the century, immigrants came to represent over one-fifth of the
American labor force, and they and their children composed
absolute majorities of the country's urban population. This
situation, in which the foreign presence relative to the native
population vastly exceeded that found today, did not give rise to
any secessionist movement. Immigrants focused their energies
instead on carving an economic niche for themselves; their
children learned English and gradually entered native social
circles and the local political process. Perhaps the most telling
case against nativist fears is that of Mexican-Americans in the
Southwest. Despite the large size of this minority, its proximity
to the home country, and the fact that these territories were
once Mexico's, secessionist movements within the Mexican-
American population have been insignificant. During World
War II and the Korean War, Mexican-American youths could
easily have avoided military service by taking a short ride into
Mexico; instead, they contributed tens of thousands of both soldiers and battle casualties to the nation's war effort.[42]

Ethnic communities have been much less the Trojan horses
portrayed by the xenophobes than effective vehicles for long-
term adaptation. As Andrew Greeley states: "It could be said
that the apparent inclination of men . . . to consort with those
who, they assume, have the same origins provides diversity
in the larger society and also creates substructures that meet
many functions the larger society would be hard put to service."[43] Greeley also notes, however, that "the demons of suspi-
cion and distrust prove very hard to exorcise from interethnic
relationships."[44] At a time when such "demons" are again on the
rise, it may be well to recall past experience, where spatial concentrations of immigrants from all over the globe did not lead
either to political separatism or to cultural alienation. Within

their respective areas of settlement, ethnic communities created by immigration have grown and diversified; later generations' efforts to maintain a distinct culture have been invariably couched within the framework of loyalty to the United States and an overarching American identity. Today's immigrants in all likelihood will follow the same path.

3

Making It in America
Occupational and
Economic Adaptation

As we noted in chapter 1, a common perception of contemporary immigration is that it is predominantly a low-skill labor flow and that its quality is declining over time. This perception is not only common among the public at large, but has been given academic credibility as well. An economist describes his version of the trend as follows:

> As one moves from one country to another . . . one begins to believe that there is something in common among jobs held by migrants in widely diverse geographic areas and very different historical periods: the jobs tend to be unskilled, generally but not always low-paying and to connote inferior social status; they often involve hard or unpleasant working conditions and considerable insecurity.[1]

In testimony before Congress, another economist puts forth a different version of this argument: "The labor market quality of immigrant cohorts has changed substantially over time and has declined in the last 20 or 30 years; the kinds of skills and the kinds of people we are getting now are different from the kinds of skills and the quality of immigration we were getting 20 or 30 years ago."[2]

Thirty years ago there was little immigration, of course, and what there was came under a quota system that effectively barred most nationalities. Statements about an overwhelmingly low-skill flow may be applicable to undocumented immigration but, like those about declining quality, neglect the sizable recorded immigration of recent years. The socioeconomic profile of the foreign born is quite different from what such statements would make us believe. In 1990, the proportion of college graduates among all immigrants was the same as in the total U.S. population. More significantly, that proportion was higher among immigrant cohorts arriving between 1987 and 1990 than among those coming earlier.[3] In 1993, 34 percent of newly arrived immigrants who listed an occupation were classified by the Immigration and Naturalization Service as professionals and managers. The figure significantly exceeds the national average.

It is unlikely that the occupational profile of these immigrants in future years will reproduce exactly the one at arrival; there is evidence, however, that highly educated immigrants remain strongly represented at the top of the U.S. occupational pyramid.[4] In this chapter, we examine this evidence along with that pertaining to the occupations, business enterprises, and income of recent immigrants. Through this analysis, we seek to establish the validity of alternative theories about the economic progress of the foreign born and, in particular, of those views that rely exclusively on individual skills and motivation.

Immigrants in the American Economy

Education

Within the general picture of an educationally advantaged population, there is great diversity. If most immigrants are not illiterate, they are not all college graduates. Variation in educational background highlights again the central theme of great heterogeneity among the foreign born. In table 4, for example, the Taiwanese appear as the most educated immigrants

Table 4
Educational Attainment of Principal Immigrant Groups, 1990

Country of Birth	Total Persons	% Completed 4 Years of College or More[a]	% High School Graduates[a]	% Immigrated 1980–1990
Total Native-Born	228,942,557	20.3	77.0	—
Total Foreign-Born	19,767,316	20.4	58.8	43.8
Above U.S. Average				
India	450,406	64.9	87.2	55.7
Taiwan	244,102	62.2	91.6	65.4
Iran	210,941	50.6	86.7	49.6
Hong Kong	147,131	46.8	83.3	44.3
Philippines	912,674	43.0	82.5	49.0
Japan	290,128	35.0	86.4	52.7
Korea	568,397	34.4	80.1	56.1
China	529,837	30.9	60.6	53.5
Near U.S. Average				
Former Soviet Union	333,725	27.1	64.0	39.4
United Kingdom	640,145	23.1	81.3	24.1
Canada	744,830	22.1	72.6	16.6
Peru	144,199	21.0	78.6	60.8
Germany	711,929	19.1	75.9	11.2
Poland	388,328	16.3	58.1	30.0
Vietnam	543,262	15.9	58.9	61.8
Cuba	736,971	15.6	54.1	25.5
Colombia	286,124	15.5	66.8	51.2
Jamaica	334,140	14.9	67.9	46.2
Greece	177,398	14.8	50.0	12.8
Ireland	169,827	14.6	63.9	19.4
Nicaragua	168,659	14.6	58.8	74.0
Below U.S. Average				
Ecuador	143,314	11.8	60.3	43.3
Haiti	225,393	11.8	57.6	58.9
Italy	580,592	8.6	39.3	6.4
Dominican Republic	347,858	7.5	41.7	53.1
Guatemala	225,739	5.8	37.5	68.3
Cambodia	118,833	5.5	35.4	85.8
Laos	171,577	5.1	37.8	76.4
El Salvador	485,433	4.6	32.7	75.2
Portugal	210,122	4.6	32.1	21.6
Mexico	4,298,014	3.5	24.3	49.9

SOURCE: U.S. Bureau of the Census, *The Foreign-Born Population in the United States*, CP-3-1 (Washington, D.C.: U.S. Department of Commerce, July 1993), tables 1, 3.

[a] Persons aged 25 years or older.

because close to 100 percent are high school graduates; if the indicator is college rather than high school graduation, then Asian Indians take first place.

The largest national contingent—Mexicans—has the lowest level of schooling, according to both indicators. The generalization that low-educated immigrants come mostly from Latin America is contradicted, however, by the presence of European nationalities in the bottom educational category. Immigrants from Italy and Portugal, in particular, resemble those from Mexico in their low average educational attainment. Nationalities that are close to the educational mean come predominantly from traditional countries of emigration in northeastern Europe and from Canada. In this category are also several Latin American countries, the most important of which numerically are Colombia and Peru.

The portrait of education among the foreign born presented in table 4 is puzzling and does not lend itself to ready interpretation. The view that the educational level of immigration has been declining over time does not find support in these data, either in terms of general averages or when disaggregated by national origins. The last column of table 4 presents the proportion of immigrants coming during 1980–90 as a rough indicator of recency of arrival. Close to 50 percent or more of the best-educated groups—such as those from India, Iran, Taiwan, Korea, and the Philippines—arrived in recent years. By contrast, high proportions of those groups with lower averages of education were already in the country before 1980.

This conclusion is also supported by results in table 5, which indicate higher proportions of college and high school graduates among immigrants who arrived during the last ten years than among the entire foreign-born population. Note, however, the marginal declines of these proportions among immigrants from Asia, Africa, and Latin America, partially compensated for by significant increases in the number of educated immigrants from Europe and Canada. These tendencies reflect the interplay of a complex array of factors, including the growing presence of dependent kin in immigrant flows, partially compensated

Table 5

Educational Attainment of Immigrants Age 25 and Over, 1990

Region	All Immigrants		Immigrated 1980–1990	
	% Completed College	% Completed High School	% Completed College	% Completed High School
All Immigrants	20.4	58.8	23.7	59.4
Africa	47.1	87.9	44.1	87.6
Asia	38.4	75.8	37.2	73.6
Europe and Canada	18.6	64.9	34.8	81.4
Latin America and Caribbean	9.1	39.0	8.4	39.7

SOURCE: U.S. Bureau of the Census, *The Foreign-Born Population in the United States*, CP-3-1 (Washington, D.C.: U.S. Department of Commerce, July 1993), table 3.

for by the youth of recent arrivals. Dependents tend to lower the average educational level of their national groups, and young immigrants tend to increase it because of the global trend toward high educational attainments. The resulting ups and downs cannot be appropriately summarized by any simplistic conclusion about "declining quality."

A full interpretation of educational differences among the foreign born requires consideration of a plurality of factors. There are actually two different levels of explanation: that of differences between nationalities and that of differences among individuals.

At the first or aggregate level, relevant factors involve the countries of both origin and destination. Concerning the latter, immigration policies and labor demand are the most important explanatory variables. Prior to 1965, U.S. immigration policy made it difficult for Asians and Africans to come. After that date, a new immigration policy opened the doors on the basis of two criteria: family reunification and occupational qualifications. Unlike European and certain Latin American nationalities, Africans and Asians had few families to reunite with in the United States; hence, the only path open to them was that of formal credentials. This situation explains the high average levels of education of most Asian and African immigrants. It also helps account for its slight decline in the last few years as family reunification gained growing significance.

Apart from regular immigration, the U.S. government has also chosen to admit certain groups at particular times for political considerations. As seen in chapter 1, most of these refugee groups came from Communist-dominated countries. The educational profile of each such nationality depends on the evolution over time of the inflow. Initial waves of refugees tend to come from the higher socioeconomic strata; but as the movement continues, they are increasingly drawn from the lower classes. The decline in schooling tends to be faster when refugees originate in poor countries where the well educated represent a small proportion of the total population. In combination, these factors explain the low average levels of education of some Southeast Asian refugee groups (such as Cambodians and Laotians), the middling average levels of Vietnamese and Cubans, and the high educational profile of recently arrived Iranians, Soviet Jews, Ethiopians, and Afghans.[5]

Finally, demand for low-wage labor in agriculture and other U.S. industries has given rise, as seen earlier, to a sustained underground flow. Not surprisingly, this demand has had its greatest impact in less-developed countries near America's borders rather than in distant or more developed nations. Although undocumented migration tends to be temporary rather than permanent, a substantial number of migrants eventually settles down in the United States and manages to legalize the situation.[6] Given the size of the undocumented inflow and the modest educational origins of most participants, it is not surprising that, even if only a minority change their status to legal residence, they will have a strong downward effect on the aggregate statistics. This pattern helps explain the low average education of legal immigrants from Mexico, the Dominican Republic, and most of Central America, countries that have been the primary sources of undocumented migration in the past.[7]

However, political and economic forces in the receiving country do not explain the diversity of educational achievement among the foreign born. The relative opening of American borders after 1965 may have been a godsend to the highly educated in certain countries, but it was a matter of indifference to others. Similarly, American growers' demand for low-wage rural workers had a significant impact on Mexico, but a very limited one on Canada. Finally, the relative decline in the numbers of European immigrants after 1965 took place despite the expanded facilities for immigration from these countries—through either family reunification or occupational preferences. Clearly, an increasingly prosperous European population did not see changes in American law as a cause for much excitement.

The greatest impact of the new preference system was elsewhere, namely on the less-developed countries of Asia and Africa. Unlike Western Hemisphere nations, for which the doors were never closed, the possibilities to migrate to the United States from Africa or Asia had been absent until this time. The 1965 act changed this situation, and the well educated in these countries took note. For illustration, table 6 lists the eighteen nations contributing the highest proportions of college graduates to the United States in 1980. These countries share three notable characteristics: First, they are all distant, being located, without exception, in Asia or Africa; second, those immigrants are of recent origin, as indicated by the proportion that emigrated after 1970; nearly all came after that date, with proportions ranging from 79 percent for Egypt to 99 percent for Uganda. Third, they are all less developed countries, including several, like Bangladesh, India, and Kenya, that are among the poorest in the world. As shown in table 6, for many of these countries substantial percentages of the respective sending populations are illiterate and the per capita product did not exceed U.S.$1000 in 1993. It is thus clear that the lure of economic and occupational opportunities in the United States, created by the new preferences system, had its greatest effect on countries where similar opportunities are most scarce and where the well educated did not have this alternative in the past.

A second approach to explaining educational differences is identifying individual background factors that affect the process. Hirschman and Falcón analyzed educational attainment among twenty-five religioethnic groups in the United States, including both recent immigrants and descendants of earlier arrivals. A sample size close to seven thousand cases and information on a number of relevant variables makes results of this study worth careful attention.[8]

Not surprisingly, parental schooling, followed by father's occupational characteristics, were the most important individual factors accounting for educational differences across groups. Parental schooling alone explained about a third of these differences. The net advantages of Jews, Asians, and British ancestry groups were thus due, in large measure, to their having been reared by parents with above-average levels of education. Conversely, the large disadvantage of Italians, Eastern Europeans,

Table 6

Foreign-Born Groups with Highest Proportion
of College-Educated Persons, 1990, and
Characteristics of Countries of Origin

Country	% College Graduates Among Foreign-Born, 1990[a]	% Immigrated to U.S. 1970–1990	GNP per Capita ($), ca. 1993	% Literate Population, ca. 1993
India	64.9	87.9	290	25
Nigeria	64.2	96.2	310	51
Taiwan	62.2	91.4	9,630	94
Zaire	59.6	84.8	235	72
Egypt	54.5	79.1	660	50
Pakistan	53.7	93.4	430	35
South Africa	53.4	87.6	2,900	76
Kenya	52.0	93.2	270	69
Bangladesh	51.9	97.9	220	36
Iran	50.6	91.0	2,230	74
Uganda	47.1	99.5	190	48
Zimbabwe	47.0	76.5	540	74
Hong Kong	46.8	77.4	17,860	77
Cameroon	46.4	94.4	770	56
Malaysia	46.3	96.3	3,160	78
Myanmar (Burma)	45.8	89.3	530	81
Sri Lanka	44.7	86.0	600	89
Philippines	43.0	82.3	830	90
United States	20.4	68.4	24,750	98

SOURCES: U.S. Bureau of the Census, *The Foreign-Born Population in the United States,* CP-3-1 (Washington, D.C.: U.S. Department of Commerce, July 1993), tables 1, 3; 5% Public Use Microdata Sample (PUMS) of the 1990 U.S. Census; Population Reference Bureau, *1995 World Population Data Sheet* (Washington, D.C.: PRB, 1995); United Nations, *Demographic Yearbook, 1993* (New York: United Nations, 1995).

[a] Persons 25 years or older.

and Mexicans was reduced by about half once parental schooling is statistically controlled. Less obvious was the finding that
mother's education is more important than father's in deter-
mining schooling.

Also significant was the finding that immigrant generation
did not affect education. There was a rise in average schooling from the first to the third generations and a decline in the
fourth and subsequent ones. The net impact of generation was
not, however, of much consequence. This result indicates that
time in the United States does not compensate for low educational endowments among earlier immigrant generations.
First-generation newcomers from higher socioeconomic backgrounds are hence better educated on the average than established ethnic groups from more modest origins.

After controlling statistically for a series of individual factors, Hirschman and Falcón found that the original differences in education were significantly reduced, but that important ones remained. For example, Asians who were statistically
"equal" to others in parental schooling and other background
factors retained a 1.6-year educational advantage over the rest;
Mexicans suffered a 1.4-year disadvantage.[9] These persistent
differences suggest the existence of broader cultural or social
factors, not captured by the analysis of individual variables that
affect the collective performance of each group. We return to
this point after discussing occupation and income below.

Occupation and Entrepreneurship

In 1990, 64 percent of the foreign-born population in the United
States was in the labor force, a figure nearly identical to the
national average. Labor force participation was higher among
immigrants from Latin America (71 percent), Africa (75 percent), and Asia (66 percent) and especially high among certain
nationalities such as Indians (75 percent). Immigrant unemployment in 1990 was 7.8 percent, a higher rate than for the
native born. There is some variation around this figure, but im-

migrant groups differ much less in their commitment to work and their ability to find employment than in other dimensions.[10]

A partial exception to this pattern are refugees from Southeast Asian countries, among whom levels of nonparticipation and unemployment remain high. In 1990, Cambodian and Laotian refugees had a labor force participation rate of only 49 percent, and unemployment among participants ranged between 10 and 20 percent. The Vietnamese had a much higher level of participation, 64.4 percent, a figure comparable to the average for the foreign born. However, compared to the refugees who arrived in the 1970s from these countries, more recent arrivals have had lower participation rates, higher joblessness, and a less rapid increase in labor market involvement, indicating the greater difficulty of the less skilled to find employment.[11]

The same diversity among nationalities in levels of education is found when we examine types of occupation in the United States. Given the close association between both variables, it is not surprising that highly educated groups are those most frequently represented in professional and managerial occupations. The wide occupational diversity among the foreign born conceals, however, a bimodal pattern in which certain groups concentrate at the top of the occupational distribution while others are found mostly at the bottom. Table 7 illustrates this pattern with data for selected groups of more than one hundred thousand persons in 1990. Immigrant nationalities that exceed by a significant margin the proportion of professionals in the American labor force come, most notably, from Asia. Particularly noteworthy is the occupational profile of Indians, where professionals represent over a third of occupationally active immigrants, and that of the Taiwan Chinese, where they represent almost a third.

At the other extreme are nationalities from Latin America and southern Europe, where the relative number of those in high-level occupations is half or less the national average. Note that the low presence of these groups at the top of the occupational distribution is not correlated with weak labor force

Table 7
Labor Force Participation and Professional Specialty
Occupations of Selected Immigrant Groups, 1990

Country of Birth	Number of Persons	% in U.S. Labor Force [a]	% in Professional Specialty Occupations [b]
United States	248,709,873	65.3	14.1
Above U.S. Average			
India	450,406	74.6	34.0
Taiwan	244,102	64.9	28.7
Iran	210,941	67.9	24.0
Hong Kong	147,131	75.1	22.5
Canada	744,830	52.1	21.1
United Kingdom	640,145	57.3	20.8
Former Soviet Union	333,725	39.7	20.1
Philippines	912,674	76.3	18.0
Japan	290,128	54.2	17.6
China	529,837	62.3	16.9
Below U.S. Average			
Colombia	286,124	73.7	8.8
Italy	580,592	46.4	8.5
Nicaragua	168,659	74.6	5.0
Dominican Republic	347,858	63.8	5.2
Portugal	210,122	71.6	3.8
Cambodia	118,833	48.4	5.5
Laos	171,577	49.7	4.4
Guatemala	225,739	75.7	3.3
El Salvador	486,433	76.3	2.4
Mexico	4,298,014	69.7	2.6

SOURCE: U.S. Bureau of the Census, *The Foreign-Born Population in the United States*, CP-3-1 (Washington, D.C.: U.S. Department of Commerce, July 1993), table 4.

[a] Persons 16 years or older.
[b] Employed persons 16 years or older.

participation. Latin American male immigrants, in particular, are among the most active in the U.S. labor market.

Immigrant arrivals during the 1990s have, by and large, continued these occupational patterns, with the difference that aging European nationalities are less heavily represented among the economically active, and Asians and Latin Americans more so. Table 8 presents an alternative portrait of occupational diversity among the foreign born by listing the ten countries that sent the largest absolute number of immigrants classified as professionals and managers in 1993 and those that sent the largest number of operators and laborers in the same year. Asian countries continue to occupy the top of the occupational distribution. The four Asian nationalities listed in table 8 accounted jointly for 60 percent of the total among the top ten of all persons classified as professionals and managers. In second place come the United Kingdom, Canada, and Ireland, which together represent another 21 percent, while recent refugees from Poland and the former Soviet Union added 15 percent. Professionals represent a high proportion of several English-speaking African nationalities as well, although their absolute numbers are much lower.

The opposite situation is that of Mexico and the Dominican Republic, which send a substantial contingent of professionals to the United States but whose number gets buried in the total statistics. Mexico is also the prime source of immigrant operators and laborers, accounting by itself for 30 percent of this category and exceeding the next four largest working-class contingents combined. About half of occupationally active Mexican immigrants in 1993 were classified in this manual labor category, a proportion exceeded only by Cambodians. Other sizable manual labor contingents come from the Caribbean and Central America (Cuba, the Dominican Republic, Guatemala, and El Salvador), Southeast Asia, and mainland China. As noted in chapter 2, "immigrants" from Cuba and Southeast Asia during the 1990s were mostly former political refugees who adjusted their status. Their origins in the exodus of *balseros* and in the tail end of the Southeast Asian flow account

Table 8
Immigrant Nationalities with Highest Number of Persons Classified as Professionals and Managers and as Operators and Laborers, 1993

Country of Birth	Economically Active Immigrants	Professionals and Managers	
		N	%
China	26,076	13,954	53.5
Philippines	21,500	11,164	51.9
India	14,013	10,210	72.9
Poland	15,605	6,074	38.9
United Kingdom	9,337	5,508	59.0
Canada	7,348	4,938	67.2
Taiwan	6,056	4,708	77.7
Former Soviet Union	11,982	3,835	32.0
Ireland	9,781	3,312	33.9
Dominican Republic	15,533	2,912	18.7

		Operators and Laborers	
		N	%
Mexico	47,201	21,478	45.5
Vietnam	18,302	6,685	36.5
Dominican Republic	15,533	5,782	37.2
Cuba	6,025	3,968	65.9
El Salvador	10,672	3,849	36.1
Former Soviet Union	11,982	3,445	28.8
Colombia	4,575	2,672	58.4
China	26,076	2,661	10.2
Poland	15,605	2,076	13.3
Guatemala	3,958	1,962	49.6

SOURCE: U.S. Immigration and Naturalization Service, *1993 Statistical Yearbook* (Washington, D.C.: U.S. Government Printing Office, 1994), table 21, pp. 68–69.

for their overrepresentation at the bottom of the occupational ladder.

The immigration and refugee policies of the United States, the demand for labor by American employers, and the differential impact of these forces in countries at various levels of development are factors explaining the broad occupational diversity among immigrant groups. To take one example, the bimodal occupational pattern of recent migration from mainland China is due to the combination of the occupational preferences system established in 1965 with the prior existence of a sizable Chinese community in the U.S. West Coast, Hawaii, and New York. This ethnic community was able to use family reunification provisions once the door to China reopened during the early 1970s.

Microlevel studies of individual occupational attainment among immigrants have consistently identified education and, secondarily, parental socioeconomic background as the major explanatory factors.[12] However, as in the case of education, these factors do not account entirely for differences in occupation among either individuals or nationalities, a result that suggests again the presence of broader cultural or social structural forces.

As important as the relative status of the jobs that newcomers occupy is their relative propensity for self-employment. It is a familiar sociological observation that immigrant minorities are more prone than the native population to work for themselves. In the 1820s, 80 percent of free white Americans were self-employed, but the proportion declined continuously, at least until 1970. In that year, the self-employed represented only 7.8 percent of the employed American labor force. The figure was, however, 8.5 percent among the foreign born, 12 percent among Chinese and Japanese immigrants, and over 15 percent among those of Greek and Russian origin.[13]

The rate of self-employment is important as an indicator of economic self-reliance and also as a potential means for upward mobility. In general, immigrants who own their own established businesses earn significantly more than those working

Table 9
Self-Employment Among Selected
Foreign-Born Groups, 1990

Nationality	Number Self-Employed	Rate of Self-Employment per Thousand Employed Population[a]
All Foreign-Born	728,335	68.29
Above U.S. Average		
Korean	56,279	180.46
Greek	14,774	147.22
Iranian	14,472	119.51
Russian	10,441	100.97
Italian	25,393	100.90
Canadian	33,913	95.24
Near U.S. Average		
Japanese	10,849	79.43
Polish	14,027	79.17
Cuban	31,421	73.37
Chinese[b]	38,335	72.77
Colombian	11,618	65.75
Indian	18,586	63.48
Vietnamese	16,088	57.77
Below U.S. Average		
Portuguese	6,772	51.47
Dominican	8,407	50.80
Salvadoran	12,880	46.61
Mexican	105,073	45.02
Ecuadoran	2,609	41.90
Jamaican	8,453	39.69
Haitian	4,850	35.29
Filipino	19,492	32.51

SOURCE: U.S. Bureau of the Census, *The Foreign-Born Population in the United States*, CP-3-1 (Washington, D.C.: Department of Commerce, July 1993), table 4.

[a] Population 16 years of age and over.
[b] Sum total of the foreign-born population from Hong Kong, the People's Republic of China, and Taiwan.

for wages.[14] As in other forms of socioeconomic achievement, there is, however, considerable diversity across nationalities. Table 9 presents results of an analysis of self-employment among foreign-born groups in the 1990 Census.

In 1990, the rate of self-employment was 69.74 per thousand population in the United States. Diversity among immigrant nationalities is highlighted by the sizable gap between the lowest and highest self-employment rates: from 32 per thousand among Filipinos and 35 per thousand among Haitians to 180 per thousand among Koreans. Greeks, Iranians, Italians, and Russians also exhibit high rates of self-employment. Other Asian nationalities, notably the Japanese and Chinese, also have rates exceeding the national average. Latin American groups generally fall below this level, with the exception of Cubans and Colombians.

The meaning of self-employment in the 1990 Census remains somewhat obscure, however, because no distinction is made, for example, between odd jobbers working for a casual wage and professionals with an established practice. Therefore, it is not possible to say a priori whether high rates of self-employment among a particular group represent a means of material survival or a vehicle for economic mobility. The survey of minority business ownership, conducted by the census every five years, refines this information by distinguishing between firms with or without paid employees and by providing information on their relative size. Unfortunately, these data have been gathered only for a few specific minorities and not for all immigrant or ancestry groups. Nevertheless, this information provides a useful point of comparison, as shown in table 10.

The main findings from these data are that minorities with the highest rates of self-employment—defined in this case by total number of firms per one hundred thousand population— are also the ones with the highest rates of ownership of firms with paid employees. There is also a rough correspondence with the 1990 figures in terms of the relative positions of the nationalities listed in both tables. This correlation suggests that

Table 10

Minority Firm Ownership and Indicators of Firm Performance, 1987

Group	All Firms			Firms with Paid Employees			
	N	Firms per 100,000 Population[a]	Gross Receipts per Firm ($1,000s)	N	Firms per 100,000 Population[a]	Employers per Firm	Gross Receipts per Firm ($1,000s)
Korean	69,304	119.49	110.85	21,657	37.33	3.2	254.05
Asian Indian	52,266	90.73	128.47	16,370	28.42	4.0	316.83
Japanese	53,372	73.61	71.89	10,186	14.05	3.8	273.36
Chinese	89,717	68.53	107.11	26,531	20.27	4.8	281.28
Vietnamese	25,671	60.68	53.02	5,840	13.81	2.3	143.32
Filipino	40,412	37.49	47.36	6,711	6.22	2.5	186.79
Cuban	61,470	69.61	89.18	10,768	12.19	4.4	392.56
Central or South American	66,356	34.34	48.25	10,793	5.59	2.5	188.25
Mexican	229,706	26.08	51.52	49,078	5.57	3.0	171.23
Black	424,165	22.79	46.59	70,815	3.80	3.1	199.54

SOURCES: U.S. Bureau of the Census, *Survey of Minority-Owned Business Enterprises: Blacks, Hispanics, and Asian Americans* (Washington, D.C.: Department of Commerce, April 1992); and U.S. Bureau of the Census, *The Foreign-Born Population in the United States*, CP-3-1 (Washington, D.C.: Department of Commerce, July 1993), table 1.

[a] Population 16 years of age and over.

self-employment rates are an acceptable, if still imperfect measure of established-business ownership. In 1987, Koreans, Indians, and Chinese owned the highest relative number of firms with paid employees among the groups studied. Among Latin American groups, Cubans had the highest rate of business ownership—with or without employees. Cuban and Asian Indian firms were also the largest in terms of both average gross receipts and number of employees.[15]

The incidence of self-employment and ownership for firms with employees was least common among Mexicans, Filipinos, and other Latin Americans in 1987. Filipino firms with employees, for instance, were only one-fourth as common as among Asian Indians and slightly more than half as common as among Cubans. However, the rate of business ownership among even the least entrepreneurial of these foreign minorities still exceeded the figure for the largest domestic minority, American blacks, as indicated in the bottom row of table 10.

Several theories have been advanced to explain the differential propensity for self-employment and entrepreneurship among various groups. The most common explanation is the distinct cultural endowment of certain nationalities that leads them to seek avenues for profitable enterprise while others remain content with wage employment. As Light has noted, all these cultural theories trace their origin, directly or indirectly, to Max Weber's thesis about the Protestant ethic and its effect on the development of capitalism.[16]

A first problem with culturalistic theories, however, is that they are always *post factum* (that is, they are invoked once a group has achieved a notable level of business success, but they seldom anticipate which ones will do so). A second problem is the diversity of national and religious backgrounds of entrepreneurially oriented groups. Among minorities with high rates of business ownership, we find Jews and Arabs, southern and northern Europeans, Asians, and Latin Americans. They practice Protestantism, Catholicism, Greek Orthodoxy, Buddhism, Confucianism, Shintoism, and Islam. If a set of unique entrepreneurial "values" must be associated with each of these distinct religiocultural backgrounds, it is difficult to see what is left out as a point of comparison. This theoretical untidiness is compounded by the presence of other groups of similar cultural or religious origins that are not significantly represented among minority business owners. Why, for example, are Chinese Buddhists prone to entrepreneurship, but not Buddhist Cambodians; why Catholic Cubans and not Catholic Dominicans? A theory that must invent a unique explanation for each positive instance or for each exception ends up explaining nothing.

For this reason, sociologists have moved away from exclusively cultural interpretations to try to find in the situational characteristics of various groups the key to their economic behavior. One such theory, advanced by Bonacich and her associates, is that groups that consider themselves and are regarded by others as temporary residents have every incentive to engage in business and accumulate profits. According to this view, such groups are set apart from the native majority, and they themselves long to go home, a situation that promotes their distinct economic behavior.[17]

This theory explains, for example, why immigrant groups in the United States are more entrepreneurially oriented than domestic minorities, such as blacks. It fails to explain, however, differences in business ownership between Jews and other European immigrant groups at the turn of the century or between Cubans and Mexicans at present. Unlike most pre–World War I immigrants who aimed at returning to their countries once they had "made it in America," Eastern European Jews came escaping czarist oppression and did not intend to return.[18] Similarly, Mexican immigrants are part of a cyclical flow, and many plan to return to or retire in Mexico.[19] Cuban refugees—at least after the failure of the 1961 Bay of Pigs invasion—left the island with few prospects for return. These and other empirical examples contradict the "sojourner" theory of immigrant entrepreneurship. Other authors have argued that sojourners, as "birds of passage," are in fact more willing to engage in low-wage labor and other forms of temporary employment than in long-term business planning.[20]

A second situational theory emphasizes the social disadvantages newcomers face in a strange society and their negative economic consequences. Minorities are frequently discriminated against in the labor market and are thus either excluded from employment or relegated to the least attractive jobs. Given this situation, it is not surprising that they find self-employment, even in marginal businesses, an attractive alternative. According to this "disadvantage theory," self-employment is not, at least initially, an avenue for economic mobility but a means for material survival. Groups that are discriminated against tend to pool their resources, forming rotating credit associations and other similar cooperative organizations in order to provide mutual support.[21]

This theory explains the high propensity for self-employment among Asian minorities, such as the Chinese and the Japanese, who were subjected to a great deal of discrimination and even direct persecution during the first decades of the century. However, it fails to explain the low rates of self-employment among Filipinos and Mexicans, also discriminated-against minorities and also subject to persecution in different periods. Nor does it provide a satisfactory account for the very low levels of entrepreneurship among American blacks, despite their being the prototypical victims of prejudice. In contrast, several nationalities with high rates of business ownership—such as the Lebanese, Greeks, Koreans, and Cubans—do not seem to have suffered much political or economic persecution in the United States.[22] Hence, just as in the cases of education and occupation, we find that existing theories account only partially for the significant variability in self-employment and business ownership among the foreign born. Factors other than those identified so far must be brought into play in order to achieve a satisfactory explanation.

Income

The best summary measure of the relative position of an immigrant group in the United States is probably its average income level. Given the variability of education, occupation, and business ownership among the foreign born, it is not too sur-

Table 11

Median Household Incomes and Poverty Rates of Principal
Immigrant Nationalities and Regions of Origin, 1989

		Income		Age
Region/Country of Birth	Persons N	Median Household Income	Poverty Rate[a] (%)	% 60 Years and Older
Total Native-Born	228,942,557	30,176	12.7	16.7
All Immigrants	19,767,316	28,314	18.2	18.0
Asia	4,979,037	35,318	16.2	10.6
Africa	363,819	30,907	15.7	6.2
Europe and Canada	5,095,233	30,066	9.3	40.0
Latin America and Caribbean	8,416,924	24,385	24.3	9.6
Above $32,000 household income				
India	450,406	48,320	8.1	6.4
Philippines	912,674	45,419	5.9	14.7
Hong Kong	147,131	42,033	12.7	3.2
Taiwan	244,102	38,966	16.7	3.6
Iran	210,941	35,836	15.7	9.1
Portugal	210,122	35,053	7.0	17.3
Japan	290,128	34,999	12.8	12.5
United Kingdom	640,145	34,339	6.6	33.9
Greece	177,398	33,500	9.1	26.6
Between $26,000 and $32,000				
Ireland	169,827	31,562	8.4	43.6
Germany	711,929	30,652	7.7	37.0
Jamaica	334,140	30,599	12.1	12.0
China	529,837	30,597	15.7	25.1
Peru	144,199	30,465	14.6	8.4
Canada	744,830	30,186	7.8	40.7
Korea	568,397	30,147	15.6	8.1
Vietnam	543,262	30,039	25.5	5.3
Italy	580,592	29,369	8.0	48.3
Colombia	286,124	29,139	15.3	8.2
Cuba	736,971	27,292	14.7	30.1
Poland	388,328	26,948	9.7	46.9

(Continued on next page)

Table 11 (*continued*)

Region/Country of Birth	Persons N	Income		Age
		Median Household Income	Poverty Rate[a] (%)	% 60 Years and Older
Below $26,000				
Haiti	225,393	25,454	21.7	7.3
Nicaragua	168,659	24,944	24.4	7.1
Guatemala	225,739	24,362	25.8	4.2
El Salvador	485,433	23,533	24.9	3.9
Mexico	4,298,014	21,926	29.7	7.0
Dominican Republic	347,858	19,996	30.0	7.9
Cambodia	118,833	19,728	38.4	5.1
Laos	171,577	19,671	40.3	4.9
Former Soviet Union	333,725	19,125	25.0	45.8

SOURCE: U.S. Bureau of the Census, *The Foreign-Born Population in the United States,* CP-3-1 (Washington, D.C.: U.S. Department of Commerce, July 1993), tables 1, 5.

[a] Percent of persons below the federal poverty line.

prising that average incomes also vary widely, although the patterns observed are not what other factors would suggest. Table 11 presents the available evidence from the 1990 Census in 1989 dollars. Median immigrant incomes lag about $3,700 for families and about $1,800 for households in comparison to the total U.S. population. When figures are aggregated by continents, European immigrants have the highest per capita income and the only one far surpassing the national average, although European household incomes fall slightly below that standard. Asian households are the only ones that notably exceed the national average, despite lower individual incomes, a fact suggesting the importance of income pooling among these families. Latin American immigrants rank at the bottom of both distributions, and also had much higher poverty rates.

This level of aggregation is somewhat deceptive because it conceals significant differences within geographic regions.

Table 11 lists foreign groups of 100,000 people or more in 1990 that occupied the top and bottom of the household income distribution, as well as those that came close to the national median ($26,000–$32,000). Although a number of factors, including household size, household composition, and length of time in the country, affect these average figures, it is noteworthy that the top category is occupied mostly by the same Asian nationalities that were well represented at the top of the educational and occupational distributions. Two of these groups (the Iranians and the Greeks) also have very high rates of self-employment.

Close to the national median income are a varied array of Latin American, Asian, and European nationalities. Several groups in this set are among the most entrepreneurially oriented, including the Chinese, Koreans, and Cubans. The Italians and Portuguese, who rank much below the national schooling average (see table 4), have household incomes at or above the national average, as well as much lower poverty rates.

At the bottom, with low household incomes and high poverty rates, are Southeast Asian refugees (Laotians and Cambodians) and immigrants from the Dominican Republic, Mexico, and Central America. The indeterminate relation between education and income is again highlighted by the low incomes of immigrants from the former Soviet Union, despite high average levels of education. Recency in the country and an aging population are the most apparent explanations for this contradiction because, as seen in table 4, roughly two-fifths of them arrived as refugees in the United States during the 1980s, and as seen in table 11, nearly half of this population consists of elderly persons on fixed incomes.

Several studies have attempted to establish the effect of individual characteristics on the earnings of the foreign born. Perhaps the best known is the study by Chiswick, who analyzed male immigrant earnings in 1970 on the basis of such characteristics as education, work experience, and time since immigration. He found that education had a positive effect on earnings among immigrants, but that the effect was not as high as among the native born. Every year of education increased earnings by about 7 percent among natives, but only by 5.5 percent among the foreign born. Similarly, the positive effect of work experience was "discounted" for immigrants whose earnings increased less per year of past work than among natives. For all immigrants, earnings increased by about 7 percent after five years in the United States, 13 percent after ten years, and 22 percent after twenty years.[23]

This study also found that, after controlling statistically for individual background characteristics, immigrants from Mexico, Cuba, Asia, and Africa had significantly lower earnings than the rest. Chiswick attributed the Cuban gap to the recency of their arrival because 80 percent of this group had arrived in the decade prior to the 1970 Census. Cubans with ten to fifteen years of U.S. residence had already reached economic parity with the native born. Although the study did not pursue a comparable analysis, the same explanation is probably applicable to most Asian nationalities, which also contained a high proportion of recent arrivals in 1970. Most significant, however, is the finding that the earnings gap for Mexicans—by far the largest non-European immigrant group—did not decline significantly with time in the United States. Chiswick attributed this large and persistent gap to a Mexican "ethnic-group effect."[24]

Subsequent studies have generally confirmed this finding. In an econometric analysis of the earnings of Spanish-origin males in 1976, Reimers found that, after she controlled for education, work experience, and other background traits, Mexican men earned about 6 percent less than non-Hispanic whites; Cubans earned about 6 percent more. There were no such differences among women, in part because average earnings of native-born and immigrant women alike were so low. Contrary to results for men, the study found no clear-cut pattern of wages increasing with time in the United States among females.[25]

A comparative study of Cuban and Mexican immigrants who arrived in the United States in 1972–73 discovered that the process of economic attainment differed significantly between both groups after six years of U.S. residence. Occupation and education had stronger effects on earnings among Cubans; length of U.S. residence prior to legal entry and knowledge of English were the major predictors among Mexicans. Individual characteristics accounted for about 40 percent of the income differences within the Cuban sample, but only 20 percent among Mexicans. Cuban men earned about $1,000 more per year in 1979 than their Mexican counterparts; equalizing statistically for individual background characteristics reduced the gap only by half.[26] This low ability of predictive models based on individual variables to explain differences within and across immigrant groups indicates, once again, the need for an alternative and more encompassing explanation. This task must necessarily focus on factors other than those employed by prior studies incorporating variables at a broader level of analysis.

Explaining the Differences: Modes of Incorporation

There are two ways to "make it" in America, at least legally. The first is the salaried professional/managerial route; the other is independent entrepreneurship. There is no doubt that what immigrants "bring with them"—motivation, knowledge, and resources—is a decisive feature affecting whether they will gain entry into one or another path of economic mobility. The typology of immigration in chapter 1 is essentially a qualitative summary of basic resource endowments. For example, manual immigration is generally characterized by low levels of education and occupational skills and an absence of prior entrepreneurial experience. This scarcity of human capital, characterizing immigrants of modest origin, makes raw physical power their principal marketable asset in the American labor market.

Professional immigration is characterized by high levels of education and skill. These resources may not translate immediately into highly paid positions because of language difficulties and lack of job-seeking experience. Over time, however,

education and professional training tend to give these immigrants a significant edge in gaining access to better-paid positions. Similarly, entrepreneurial flows are distinguished by a
substantial number of immigrants with prior business experience. These skills may remain dormant for a while, as new arrivals struggle with language and customs at the receiving end.
However, with increasing time and familiarity with the host
economy, many are able to reenact past experience by eventually moving into self-employment.

Hence, time is an important variable influencing socioeconomic achievement, but it is so for some groups more than for
others. As the previously discussed research shows, earnings
tend to increase with number of years since arrival. However,
the process is likely to be more accelerated for those who possess skills and resources than for those who must rely on their
physical energy. Among refugee groups, time has a different
meaning because it is often associated with a declining socioeconomic background. Earlier refugees tend to come from the
elite and middle classes; later cohorts increasingly resemble the
mass of the sending country's population. The fate of these late
arrivals depends, to a large extent, on the kind of community
created by their co-nationals. This contingent outcome already
calls attention to the significance of the contexts of reception
met by newcomers.

An emphasis on the different modes in which immigrants
can become incorporated into the host society is a way to overcome the limitations of exclusively individualistic models of
immigrant achievement. The basic idea is simple: Individuals
with similar background skills may be channeled toward very
different positions in the stratification system, depending on
the type of community and labor market in which they become
incorporated. This process can help explain differences in occupation, business ownership, and income among immigrants
who are statistically "equal" in a host of individual characteristics. However, it is not sufficient to point to the importance of
context, just as it is not enough to attribute persistent income

differences to an "ethnic group effect." We must move beyond this level of generalization to specify at least what some of these contextual factors are and how they operate.

Contexts of Reception

For immigrants, the most relevant contexts of reception are defined by the policies of the receiving government, the conditions of the host labor market, and the characteristics of their own ethnic communities. The combination of positive and negative features encountered at each of these levels determines the distinct mode of newcomers' incorporation. Governments are important because their policies determine whether sizable immigration flows can begin at all and, once under way, the forms they will take. Although occasional surreptitious immigrants may filter in, regular migration flows of predictable size and direction emerge only with the consent of governments. This consent need not be explicit, however. Underground labor flows may be tacitly permitted, as has been the case in the United States at least until the 1980s.[27] In every instance, governmental policy represents the first stage of the process of incorporation because it affects the probability of successful immigration and the legal framework in which it is to take place.

Although a continuum of possible governmental responses toward foreign groups exists, basic options are only three: exclusion, passive acceptance, or active encouragement. When enforced, exclusion precludes immigration or forces immigrants into a wholly underground existence. The second alternative is defined by the act of granting access, explicitly or implicitly, without any additional effort to facilitate or impede the process. Most economically motivated immigration to the United States in recent years has taken place under this alternative. The third governmental option occurs when authorities take active steps to encourage a particular inflow or to facilitate its resettlement. At various times during the nineteenth and twentieth centuries, the U.S. government was directly involved in recruiting laborers or skilled workers deemed to be in short supply domestically.[28]

During the last three decades, active governmental intervention to stimulate migration or facilitate its resettlement has been restricted to selected refugee inflows. Governmental support is important because it gives newcomers access to an array of resources that do not exist for other immigrants. However, the interaction of this contextual dimension with individual characteristics can lead to very different outcomes: If for refugees with professional or business skills, governmental assistance is a means to accelerate social integration and economic mobility; for those lacking these resources, it can be a means to perpetuate social dependence and economic marginalization.[29]

Labor markets represent the second dimension in contexts of reception. Clearly, several features affect the economic prospects for immigrants. These features—such as stage in the business cycle, demand for specific kinds of labor, and regional wage differentials—have been discussed at length in the economic literature as potential determinants of earnings. However, there is a sociological aspect of labor markets that is perhaps more significant, namely, the manner in which particular immigrant groups are typified. Employers as a whole may be indifferent toward a particular group, or they may have a positive or negative view of it. Positive or negative typification of a specific minority can take, in turn, different forms. For example, widespread discrimination may hold that certain groups should be confined to low-wage menial labor ("Mexican work" or, in an earlier time, "coolie labor") or it can hold that they are simply too incompetent to be employable at all. In the first instance, discrimination contributes to confinement of the group to the low-wage segment of the labor market; in the second, it contributes to its exclusion and hence unemployment.[30]

Positive typification, as opposed to mere neutrality, has been far less common. Preferential hiring of immigrants as workers tends to occur only when employers are of the same nationality. Hence, when a segment of the local labor market is composed of ethnic firms, immigrants of the same origin often gravitate toward them in search of employment opportunities unavailable elsewhere.[31]

These various labor market situations interact, of course, with individual skills and resources, leading to a plurality of outcomes. The main difference lies in the ability of different types of immigrants to neutralize labor market discrimination. Lack of resources and information makes discrimination most serious for immigrant laborers who are generally trapped in positions held to be "appropriate" for their group. Professionals and business people can escape discrimination either by moving to other parts of the country or by disguising their nationality, a strategy that explains the frequent reluctance of high-status members of stereotyped minorities to identify with their own group.[32]

The ethnic community itself represents the third and most immediate dimension of the context of reception. A first option is that no such community exists, in which case immigrants must confront the host labor market directly. If employers do not discriminate against the newcomers, the situation approaches the ideal one assumed by individualistic human capital models, because presumably only the person's education and other resources will affect his or her earnings. Among present-day immigrants, this situation is most closely approximated by professionals, who frequently accept jobs away from areas of ethnic concentration, and by refugees, resettled by government or voluntary agencies outside the same areas.

Most common, however, is the arrival of immigrants into places where an ethnic community already exists. As seen in chapter 2, a common sociological observation is that such communities cushion the impact of cultural change and protect immigrants against outside prejudice and initial economic difficulties. As important as this observation is the fact that the process of socioeconomic attainment in this context is entirely network driven. Ethnic networks provide sources of information about outside employment, sources of jobs inside the community, and sources of credit and support for entrepreneurial ventures. Because subtracting themselves from the influence of kin and friends is difficult for newcomers in the early stages of adaptation, the characteristics of the ethnic community acquire decisive importance in molding their entry into the labor market and hence their prospects for future mobility.[33]

Ethnic communities vary widely in a number of dimensions, but from the perspective of economic achievement, the central difference is whether they are composed primarily of manual workers or contain a significant professional or business element. All ethnic groups promote their own, but how they do so varies significantly across these situations. For new immigrants in working-class communities, the natural path is to follow the course of earlier arrivals. The help that ethnic networks can provide for securing employment in this situation tends to be constrained by the kind of jobs already held by more established members of the community. In addition, there is often a kind of collective expectation that new arrivals should not be "uppity" and should not try to surpass, at least at the start, the collective status of their elders.

In this fashion, immigrants of above-average ability and motivation find themselves in low-status manual jobs and restricted in their chances for future mobility. Ethnic-network assistance comes at the cost of ethnic pressures for conformity, and the latter often reinforce employers' expectations about the "natural" position of the minority in the labor market. These dynamics help explain the self-perpetuating character of working-class immigrant communities and the frequent tendency among their members to receive lower than average rewards for their past human capital.[34]

The dominant feature of the opposite situation—where a substantial number of community members hold higher-status occupations—is that the support of ethnic networks is not contingent on acceptance of a working-class life-style or outlook. Hence, newcomers, dependent as always on the assistance of kin and friends, may be introduced from the start to the whole range of opportunities available in the host labor market. Within this general pattern, entrepreneurial communities have the additional advantage of being not only sources of information about outside jobs, but sources of employment opportunities themselves. Immigrant firms tend to hire and promote their own; and, as seen previously, they often represent the only segment of the labor market in which newcomers can find employment.

In the past, there was a common belief that jobs in co-ethnic firms were equivalent to those in the lower tier of the outside labor market, insofar as both constrained future mobility opportunities. However, more recent research indicates that this is not the case, because employment within an ethnic enclave is often the best route for promotion into supervisory and managerial positions and for business ownership. These studies have found that education brought from the home country can have a greater economic payoff in ethnic firms than in outside ones and that a key factor promoting business ownership is prior employment in firms owned by persons of the same nationality.[35]

The complexity of modes of incorporation for recent immigrants is more fully appreciated when we combine the three dimensions discussed previously. Figure 3 portrays this diversity. It is a highly simplified portrait because it brings together several of the previously discussed alternatives that are themselves simplifications of real-life situations. Nonetheless, the twelve alternative contexts of incorporation outlined in the figure provide a summary statement of the variety of conditions that newcomers can find on arrival.

The nationalities in each cell are instances of each context of reception as new immigrants from the respective country would have found it at the beginning of the 1990s. To illustrate, recent Argentine immigrants arrive in a situation in which their co-nationals—a relatively small group to begin with—are highly dispersed. Absence of a sizable ethnic community is compensated for in this case by the lack of widespread discrimination because of these immigrants' generally high educations and white features.

Mexicans face a situation in which a concatenation of historical and geographical circumstances has led to the identification of their group as a source of manual wage labor in many

I. U.S. Government Policy:	II. Labor Market Reception:	III. Ethnic Community: None[d]	Working Class	Entrepreneurial/ Professional
Passive acceptance	Neutral or positive[b]	Argentines 92,563 30.9 $35,000 11.3	Italians 580,592 8.6 $29,369 8.0	Greeks 177,398 14.8 $33,500 9.1
	Discriminatory[c]	Nigerians 55,350 64.2 $25,500 13.6	Mexicans 4,298,014 3.5 $21,926 29.7	Jamaicans 334,140 14.9 $30,599 12.1
Active support[a]	Neutral or positive[b]	Romanians 91,106 28.8 $35,000 15.8	Polish 388,328 16.3 $29,948 9.7	Cubans 736,971 15.6 $27,292 14.7
	Discriminatory[c]	Ethiopians 34,805 29.3 $26,000 27.2	Laotians 171,577 5.1 $19,671 40.3	Vietnamese 543,262 15.9 $30,039 25.5

Figure 3.   Contexts of reception of recent immigrant groups in the United States, 1990.

SOURCE: U.S. Bureau of the Census, *The Foreign Born Population in the United States*, CP-3-1 (Washington, D.C.: U.S. Department of Commerce, July 1993), Tables 1, 3, 5; and data drawn from 5% Public Use Microdata Sample (PUMS) of the 1990 U.S. Census, subject to sample variability.

NOTE: The four figures for each nationality are absolute numbers of foreign-born persons from that nationality in 1990, followed by the percentage of adults who completed four years or more of college, the median household income in 1989 dollars, and the poverty rate.

[a] Accorded in recent years only to legal refugee groups.
[b] Accorded primarily to white immigrants.
[c] Experienced primarily by nonwhite immigrants.
[d] Foreign-born groups of fewer than 100,000 not concentrated in a particular location.

regions of the country. Mostly mestizo, new immigrants face stereotypes about what is suitable "Mexican work" and join working-class communities likely to channel them into this type of occupation. Such contexts help explain the consistent labor market disadvantage experienced by Mexicans and their persistent gap in earnings, after controlling for education and work experience.[36]

Another significant contrast in figure 3 is between Jamaican and certain African immigrants, exemplified by the Nigerians. Both are black minorities that face generalized race prejudice in the American labor market. Over the years, however, Jamaicans and other black West Indians have constituted communities with a relatively high proportion of professionals and entrepreneurs. Fifty percent of the U.S. Jamaican population concentrates in New York City; and its rate of self-employment, although still low by U.S. standards, exceeds significantly those of other Caribbean groups such as Dominicans, Haitians, and Puerto Ricans. In 1989, Jamaican household earnings were on a par with the national median.

Nigerians are a much smaller and more recently arrived group that lacks an established ethnic base and must therefore confront U.S. labor market conditions directly. This situation may help explain why, despite very high levels of educational attainment and high proportions in declared professional occupations, Nigerian household incomes are significantly lower than Jamaican and amounted to only 80 percent of the national median in 1989.[37]

Among nationalities formed by recent political inflows and thus eligible for governmental assistance, Ethiopians represent a similar case of a small and recently arrived group. Unlike refugees from Eastern European countries, racial and cultural markers identify Ethiopians as potential targets of labor market discrimination, a disadvantage that cannot be neutralized through participation in a weak ethnic economy. This situation helps explain the high poverty and low median earnings of Ethiopian households in 1989, despite high levels of education and declared professional backgrounds.

This mode of incorporation may be contrasted with that confronting recent Cuban refugees, where an older community has created a fairly stable ethnic economy. In 1989, Cuban household earnings were closer to the national median, despite educational achievements much lower than those of the Ethiopians and other recently arrived groups. The Cuban ethnic economy helps explain why, according to recent evidence, about half the refugees who arrived during the 1980 Mariel exodus were employed in firms owned by co-nationals, and close to 20 percent had become self-employed after only six years of U.S. residence.[38]

Among Southeast Asian refugees, the Vietnamese have started following a similar path, characterized by increasing spatial concentration and an emerging business enclave. Although the Vietnamese are still far below older entrepreneurial groups, their rates of business participation appear to be increasing. This trend contrasts with the situation of other Southeast Asian refugees, best represented by the Laotians, who are far more dispersed and have low rates of business ownership. Existing Laotian communities remain highly dependent on public assistance and on manual wage labor. Hence, despite their comparable lengths of residence in the United States, Vietnamese median incomes in 1989 were far above those of Laotian households. The latter represented about 65 percent of the national figure.

In conclusion, making it in America is a complex process, dependent only partially on the motivation and abilities that immigrants bring with them. How they use these personal resources often depends on international political factors, over which individuals have no control, and on the history of earlier arrivals and the types of communities they have created, about which newcomers also have little say. These complex and involuntary forces confront the foreign born as an objective reality that channels them in different directions.

Afterwards, apologists of successful groups will make necessities out of contingencies and uncover those "unique" traits underlying their achievements; detractors of impoverished mi-

norities will describe those cultural shortcomings or even genetic limitations accounting for their condition. Both are likely
to affirm that, in the end, "if there is a will, there is a way."

Greater knowledge of the contexts immigrants face at present
gives a lie to such assertions because it demonstrates the importance of the modes in which they are incorporated and the
resulting material and moral resources made available by governments, employers, and their own communities. The most
hardworking individuals may thus end up in poor jobs simply
because they perceive no alternatives or none are available; others may rise to the top, riding in the wake of a lucky set of circumstances. Social context renders individualistic models insufficient because it can alter, in decisive ways, the link between
individual skills and their expected rewards.

4

From Immigrants to Ethnics
Identity, Citizenship, and
Political Participation

In 1903, an act promulgated by the U.S. Congress enabled immigration authorities to look for the many radicals allegedly arriving among the masses of European immigrants and deport
them expeditiously. Agents of the Immigration Bureau set out
to canvass ports of entry and processing stations; working with
the Secret Service and local police, they circulated undercover
within immigrant communities in search of the centers of re-
bellion. Few were found. Twenty-three districts out of the thirty
or so covered by the campaign reported no "cases" of radicalism at all; in the remainder, agents managed to uncover a hand-
ful of anarchists who had lived in the country for a long time.[1]
During the 1980s, the U.S. English movement reached nationwide prominence with its campaign for a constitutional
amendment to declare English the official language of the
country. Headed by S. I. Hayakawa, a senator of Japanese immigrant origin, the movement set out to combat what it saw as
the threat of denationalization posed by the new waves of immigrants who speak other languages. Simultaneously, scholars
and nativist organizations sounded the alarm as to the possible
"secession" of the Southwest if massive Mexican immigration
continues unchecked. Because Texas, California, and Arizona
were originally part of Mexico, their reasoning goes, a Mexican

majority in these states would naturally want to return these lands to their original jurisdiction.[2] The passage of Proposition 187 in California in 1994 echoed similar alarms.

Throughout the history of American immigration, a consistent thread has been the fear that the "alien element" would somehow undermine the institutions of the country and lead it down the path of disintegration and decay. Much heated rhetoric and much money has been spent combating these alleged evils; playing on these fears has also proven lucrative for a host of nativist associations and individuals. For the most part, the targets of these efforts, the presumed sappers of democracy, linguistic unity, and territorial integrity, have looked at all these activities with a mixture of resignation and puzzlement. One may surmise the attitudes of poor Italian and Polish immigrants who barely knew the language and struggled daily for survival at the sight of Secret Service agents canvassing their neighborhoods in search of political "extremists."

The response of immigrant communities to nativist fears of yesterday and today have been marked more by passive endurance than active opposition. The notion that California may someday be returned to Mexico is so ludicrous as to preclude any need for a response; the more articulated demands of the U.S. English movement have also gone largely unopposed, however. The view among immigrants who happen to be aware of these demands is that declaring English the official language of the United States is at best a costly redundancy. For illustration, a recent motion before the Metropolitan Commission of Miami to reverse a 1982 ordinance prohibiting the official use of a language other than English was withdrawn at the request of the leading Latin immigrant organizations. Their reasoning was that English was obviously the official language of the nation, and there was no point in alienating the native-American population with such a gesture.[3]

To a large extent, nativist fears and the feverish pitch reached by campaigns based on them are due to the peculiar position of immigrant communities that are "in the society, but not yet of it."[4] Their very foreignness provides fertile ground for all sorts of speculations about their traits and intentions. At the same time, immigrants often lack sufficient knowledge of the new language and culture to realize what is happening and explain themselves effectively. For the most part, the first foreign-born generation lacks "voice."[5] It is on this enforced passivity that the nativist fears of many and the active hostility and lucrative demagoguery of a few have flourished.

Campaigns against the first generation have had a peculiar political consequence, however. Because their targets have been largely illusory, they have never visibly succeeded in their declared goals, be they rooting out political extremism or restoring linguistic integrity. What these campaigns have accomplished, above all, is stirring ethnic militancy among subsequent generations. More attuned to American culture and fluent in English, descendants of the first immigrants have gained "voice" and have used it to reaffirm identities attacked previously with so much impunity. The resilient ethnic identification of many communities and the solidary ethnic politics based on it can be traced directly to this process of "reactive formation."[6] As Nathan Glazer and others have noted, ethnic resilience is a uniquely American product because it has seldom reflected linear continuity with the immigrants' culture, but rather has emerged in reaction to the situation, views, and discrimination they faced on arrival. These experiences turned the circumstance of national origin into the primary basis of group solidarity, overwhelming other competing identifications, such as those based on class.[7]

The immigrant's world has always been a difficult one, torn between old loyalties and new realities. For the most part, the politics of the first generation—to the extent that such politics have existed—have been characterized by an overriding preoccupation with the old country. Early participation in American politics has been limited to the more educated groups, those prevented from going back to their countries of origin, and those exceptional circumstances in which the very survival of the immigrant community has been at stake. Even then, however, old loyalties die hard because individuals socialized in another language and culture have great difficulty giving them up as their primary source of identity.[8]

Throughout the history of immigration, the characteristics of sending countries have also made a significant difference in shaping the politics of the first generation as well as the timing of its shift into American-based concerns. Immigrants in the past or present may have come from stateless nations, divided lands contested by warring factions or occupied by a foreign power; hostile states, dictatorships that oppressed the entire population of their country or singled out the immigrants' own group for special persecution; consolidated but indifferent nation-states, which neither promoted nor acknowledged the emigrants' departure; or states that actually supported and supervised emigration, regarding their nationals' communities abroad as outposts serving their country's interests.

These diverse origins interact with contexts of reception to give rise to different political concerns among the foreign born that mold, in turn, the politics of subsequent generations. Depending on this variable geometry of places of origin and destination, immigrant communities may be passionately committed to political causes back home, either in support of or in opposition to the existing regime; they may see themselves as representatives of their nation-state abroad; or they may turn away from all things past and concentrate on building a new life in America. Examples of these and other possible outcomes are found both at the turn of the twentieth century and at present. We look first at the earlier period in order to provide a backdrop against which to describe contemporary developments.

Immigrant Politics at the Turn of the Century

The Domestic Impact of Immigration

The massive waves of southern and eastern Europeans who crossed the Atlantic in the 1890s and early 1900s and the smaller flows of Asiatic immigrants who traversed the Pacific about the same time altered in multiple ways the fabric of

American society, particularly its political structure. Few could have anticipated at the start that these movements would have such momentous consequences, for they were composed of humble men and women who came to fill the labor needs of an expanding industrial economy. Given the criteria for economic achievement outlined in the previous chapter, turn-of-the-century immigrants were in a uniformly disadvantageous position. With some exceptions, their individual educations and occupational skills were modest, and they confronted a generally unfavorable context on arrival: The U.S. government allowed them in, but did not assume any responsibility for their well-being; employers hired them, but assigned them to the lowest-paid jobs; their own communities helped them, but confined them in the process to the same unskilled, dead-end occupations filled by earlier arrivals.

Despite their concentration at the bottom of the economic and social ladders and their political powerlessness, immigrants were the subject of much agitation. A number of alarming traits and political designs were imputed to them, and, on that basis, nativist organizations mobilized for action. The sins attributed to immigrants were quite different and, at times, contradictory; but the ultimate demand was always the same: containment or suppression of the inflow. On the right, the usual accusation was political radicalism. Immigrant workers transported the "virus" of socialistic ideas that threatened to undermine American democratic institutions:

> In 1919, the Socialist Party of the United States had about 110,000 members, over half of whom belonged to non-English-speaking bodies, the autonomous and practically independent language federations. . . . Ultimately, a split was precipitated and the emergence of the new Communist organizations drew predominantly on these federations.[9]

On the political left, immigrants were accused pretty much of the opposite—inertia, organizational incapacity, and docility—which undermined the efforts of the unions and weakened the political organizations of the working class. The central European peasant, "so steeped in deference, so poor, and so desperate for the American dream that . . . he knelt down and kissed the hand of the boss who sent him to work,"[10] was a favorite of employers, who used him to break the power of the unions. Out West, similar accusations were leveled against Asian immigrants. Chinese immigration, for example, was described as "a more abominable slave traffic than the African slave trade," and the immigrants themselves were portrayed as "half-civilized beings" who spread "filth, depravity and epidemic."[11] The Japanese, who arrived subsequently, fared no better: "Japanese laborers, by reason of race habits, mode of living, disposition, and general characteristics are undesirable . . . they contribute nothing to the growth of the state [California]. They add nothing to its wealth, and they are a blight on the prosperity of it, and great impending danger to its welfare."[12]

The characterization and denunciation of immigrants as either a radical threat or an inferior stock that undermined the welfare of American workers was based on a stereotypical image of all newcomers. Then, as now, all immigrants were portrayed as having similar traits. The reality was quite different. Generalizations about political extremism or political docility each had a basis in fact in the characteristics of *some* groups and were contradicted, in turn, by those of others. Most but not all immigrants arriving at the time were peasants or laborers; they were also skilled industrial workers coming from countries with a well-developed working-class movement. There were, for example, Scandinavian miners and loggers socialized in a strong trade union tradition and artisans and literate merchants from Russia and east central Europe.

Unlike peasant laborers, who could scarcely go lower, these better-educated groups experienced severe downward mobility and confronted American capitalism at its harshest. Their response was governed by their European political experience. Skilled German workers, who grew under the influence of a large and disciplined socialist movement, were notable in this respect. As Fine noted, "It was men trained in such a movement who tried to build up a duplicate in the United States."[13] In the Midwest, Finnish loggers and miners divided between the meek

"Church Finns" and the militant "Red Finns." The latter had also learned working-class politics in their native land, and their experience served them well in union organizing in America. Finnish socialists were the backbone of the Socialist party in many mining and industrial towns, consciously promoting class over ethnic solidarity and proselytizing among the less politically conscious groups, such as Italians and Slavs.[14] Back East, it was the Jewish needle trade workers who formed the core of the union movement. These hardworking immigrants, many refugees from czarist persecution, saw socialism less as a political movement than as a way of life. Their descendants continued this tradition: "In some neighborhoods, one grew up to be a Socialist, a reader of Cahan's *Jewish Daily Forward* in Yiddish or *The Call* in English, and a member of one of the needle trade unions just as naturally as in some other parts of the country one grew up to be a Republican and a reader of the *Saturday Evening Post*."[15]

In the wake of the Russian Revolution of 1917, membership in the Russian-language Federation of the American Socialist party trebled, becoming one of the largest ethnic affiliates. After the split that created the new Workers' (Communist) party, the latter drew most of its membership from workers born in the old czarist empire.[16]

There was, therefore, a basis of fact for the view that immigrants participated in and promoted leftist political organizations. The generalization was inaccurate, however, in the majority of cases. Skilled workers and artisans from an urban-industrial background were the minority among turn-of-the-century arrivals. Even less common were those with extensive political socialization. They were present only among certain nationalities, and even within them they did not always represent a majority. German-born farmers, shopkeepers, and laborers outnumbered militant German workers; the views of "Church Finns" eventually prevailed, and Finnish radicalism faded away; Russian Jewish immigrants became shopkeepers and small entrepreneurs en masse, and their economic progress undermined any support for radical causes.

Most European immigration during this period did not come

from the cities but from rural areas, and it was not formed by skilled artisans, but by peasants. Past political socialization among these masses had exactly the opposite effect as among the literate minority. Not only were party politics foreign to them, but they sometimes could not even tell what nationality they belonged to. Sicilian peasants identified with their village or at best with the surrounding region; in America, they sought the comfort of fellow villagers: "Thus, in the Italian neighborhoods of New York's lower east side in the early 1920s, it was possible to trace, block by block, not only the region of Italy but also the very villages from which the inhabitants had come."[17] Nationality to these immigrants came with their exposure to American society. In Max Ascoli's apt description "they became Americans before they were ever Italians."[18]

Lack of political consciousness among Italian, Slavic, and Scandinavian peasants proved to be a boon to many American employers, who used them as a valuable tool against domestic labor organizations. By dividing workers along national lines and assigning them different pay and working conditions, employers reinforced ethnic identities over class solidarity. Nowhere was this "divide and rule" strategy more effective than in the Pennsylvania coal mines:

> Beginning in 1875 and for at least a quarter-century thereafter, central, southern, and eastern European laborers flowed steadily into the anthracite coal basin of Pennsylvania. . . . This new wave of immigrants doubled the labor supply, reinforcing competition for jobs with competition between cultures and organizational position. The new immigrants received lower pay, exacerbating cultural and occupational tensions, because mechanization was simultaneously depressing the value of skilled career miners.[19]

The antiunion strategy of Pennsylvania collieries and freight railroads proved highly successful and was adopted by other employers. The difficulty in organizing peasant newcomers into labor unions owed much to the absence of relevant political socialization among these immigrants. The problem was compounded, however, by other factors. First, American workers often displaced their hostility from employers engaged in this union-busting strategy toward the peasant immigrants themselves: "Describing new immigrants as probably the offspring of serfs and slaves and . . . as willing to submit to almost any conditions, old labor and its political allies appealed to the free-labor ethos against degradation by the new immigrants."[20]

Second, peasant newcomers were more often than not sojourners whose ultimate goals were in their lands of origin. Although most were to settle eventually in America, this final outcome did not preclude their viewing the journey as temporary and instrumental. Commitment to American political causes, especially those of a radical sort, was not particularly attractive to Hungarian, Italian, or Norwegian peasants whose goal was to save in order to buy land in their home villages. As Rosenblum notes: "Insofar as the late nineteenth and early twentieth century immigration was predominantly economic in orientation, such migrants were, to a large extent, 'target workers' initially seeking the wherewithal to preserve or enhance a position in the society from which they came."[21]

As we saw before, not all immigrants were sojourners, however. Jews leaving the Pale of Settlement and czarist oppression literally "burned their bridges behind them."[22] Other refugees from turbulent European regions never really intended to return. For these groups, politics in the new land was a more serious matter, and they could have been expected to participate more actively. It is thus not surprising that there was a positive, albeit imperfect, correlation between permanent migration and U.S.-based political participation and militancy: Immigrant activists were recruited disproportionately among the settled minorities. This changing geometry of personal skills, past political socialization, and return plans helps explain the basic dissimilarity of behaviors among immigrants during this period. Generalizations about immigrant radicalism or docility at the turn of the century were constantly negated by the actual diversity among the newcomers.

In the end, however, the overall political effect of pre–World

War I immigration was to be conservative. Socialist and Communist movements drew large proportions of their members from the foreign born, but this effect was diluted by the masses of apolitical peasants and laborers arriving during the same period. The question of how these latter groups undermined domestic radicalism is still a subject of debate. For some authors, it was because domestic trade unions were forced to adopt an increasingly conservative position to defend their privileges against the immigrants.[23] For others, it was because settled peasant groups themselves rejected political and labor radicalism in favor of an "instrumental" politics of gradual improvement within the American system.[24] Regardless of the form, the result was the same: A viable labor party never became consolidated, Socialist and Communist ideologies gradually declined, and business unionism under the American Federation of Labor prevailed over the militancy of the Industrial Workers of the World.[25]

Ethnicity, framed by the experiences of the first arrivals rather than class, was to provide the fundamental matrix of American-based politics for subsequent generations. Ironically, the class consciousness of the more literate immigrants faded away while ethnic consciousness, forced on the peasant masses by native discrimination, endured. Because turn-of-the-century immigrants had been defined and treated in America according to their imputed national traits, the politics of later generations pivoted around the same traits seeking their revindication. Hence, ethnic markers, originally used to fragment the working class, were redefined by reactive formation into symbols of pride and rallying points for mass political participation.

Obscure Identities, Split Loyalties

The political equation had another side, however: the countries left behind. Because most late nineteenth- and early twentieth-century immigrants intended to return, they paid more attention, at least initially, to events in the sending countries than in the United States. Political leaders and agitators of all sorts came from abroad to canvass immigrant communities in search of support for their causes. In Nathan Glazer's typology, many immigrants came from nations struggling to become states. The early prototypical example had been the Germans. German immigrants started coming to America in the eighteenth century, long before the consolidation of a German state. United by a common language and culture, they proceeded to re-create a nation in the midst of the American republic, just as their ancestors had done under multiple fragmented principalities in Europe.[26]

By the end of the nineteenth century, other immigrant communities from stateless nations had developed: Poles, Lithuanians, Slovaks, Croatians, Slovenians. The larger these communities became, the stronger their influence on home country politics. Educated immigrants from these lands took the lead in promoting the cause of national political independence. Although the masses of rural immigrants proved uninterested in American class politics, they often could be persuaded to support radical independence movements at home. Nationalist agitation in the United States also had peculiar consequences. According to Glazer, the first newspaper in the Lithuanian language was published in this country, not in Lithuania.[27] The nation of Czechoslovakia was, in a sense, "made in America": "Czechs and Slovaks in this country provided much of the agitation and a large portion of the funds at the time of the World War to disrupt the old Austro-Hungarian empire and to create a Czechoslovak national state."[28] Similarly, the cause of Polish liberation was given a powerful impulse by the organization of the Polish Central Relief Committee in the United States, with Paderewski as honorary president, and by the contributions of hundreds of thousands of dollars by Polish-Americans.[29]

Examples of the significance of immigration for the cause of independent statehood were not limited to Europe, but extended to the New World. The Cuban War of Independence, for instance, was launched from the United States with funds contributed by the émigré communities of New York, Tampa, and Key West. Jose Martí, leader of the Cuban Revolutionary party,

organized the war against Spanish rule from his New York office. After his death in 1895, the Cuban Revolutionary Committee continued a campaign of agitation through the New York
media that contributed, in no small measure, to the entry of the
United States into the war on the rebels' side.[30]

The opposite situation, in Glazer's typology, is that of immigrants leaving states that were not yet nations. These immigrants were eventually to describe themselves as Norwegians,
Greeks, or Albanians, but such self-definitions were not clear at
the start; instead, they worked themselves out in the process of
settlement. According to Greeley: "The Norwegians and Swedes
came to think of themselves as Norwegians and Swedes only
when they banded together to form communities of their fel-
lows, particularly in rural areas."[31]

Southern Italian peasants represented the archetypical example of a group with exclusively local ties that acquired consciousness of their broader identity in America: "Thus the American relatives of Southern Italians (to whom the Ethiopian war
meant nothing more than another affliction visited upon them
by the alien government of the North) became Italian patriots
in America, supporting here the war to which they would have
been indifferent at home."[32]

The contribution of immigration to national consciousness
was not limited to Europeans, but also had its New World
counterpart. South of the border, Mexico achieved statehood
early in the nineteenth century, but the central government's
hold extended precariously into the frontiers of a vast territory.
First Central America and then Texas seceded. The rest of the
North—today the states of California, Arizona, New Mexico,
and Colorado—was lost during the Mexican-American War.
Even in its diminished state, governmental authority continued
to be a remote presence in most indigenous communities and
among rural migrants trekking north.[33] Like Italians and other
European groups in the East, Mexican peasant immigrants
learned to think of themselves as Mexicans by being defined
and treated as such in the American Southwest. The Mexican
Revolution in the second decade of this century increased the

size and diversity of this immigrant flow and heightened its sense of identity. Previously apolitical immigrants contributed men and money to a struggle that only a few years before they had known nothing of or had ignored.[34]

Finally, there were also flows at the turn of the century coming from consolidated nation-states. There was no common pattern within this general category either, nor did the existence of a strong home government facilitate early return or adaptation to the new country. Immigration under these conditions took three forms. It could be "apolitical" and dictated exclusively by economic conditions, "political" in the sense of escape from an oppressive regime, or "politicized" a posteriori by an interventionist state bent on making use of its nationals abroad.

During most of the nineteenth century, British emigration to America was representative of the first type. British labor flows across the Atlantic took place without much interference from the home government, being governed primarily by market conditions at different stages of the economic cycle.[35] British subjects abroad may have remained concerned with events at home, but few were intent on revamping either the English or the American political systems.

Russia was also a consolidated nation-state, but migration from this country took place under very different conditions, exemplifying the second situation. The movement was neither free nor temporary because most of those who escaped the czarist autocracy never intended to return. This was especially the case among the two million Jews who left Russia between 1880 and 1914. In the United States, Russian Jews were simultaneously at the forefront of the American socialist movement and in unanimous opposition to imperial rule at home. Opponents of the autocracy recruited support and funds among this population. Trotsky was in New York at the time of the czar's abdication, and, as seen previously, the Bolshevik triumph led to a rapid rise in Russian affiliations to the American Socialist and Communist parties.[36]

German immigration—previously a stateless flow—became

an example of attempted interventionism as the newly minted German state went on to promote its cause abroad. The growth of the pan-German movement in Berlin coincided in time with the consolidation of the German-American Central Alliance in the United States. By 1914, the alliance and related groups had made German-Americans "by far the best organized of all foreign elements."[37] However, this impressive organization was not created to support global pan-Germanism, but to fight domestic Prohibition. German-Americans saw Prohibition as an Anglo-Puritan threat to their way of life; unfortunately for them, the lines of cleavage on this purely internal matter overlapped with those of the approaching European war. German-American organizations were compelled by the force of events to argue strenuously for neutrality and against British efforts to draw the United States into the conflict.

When war finally came, German-Americans were confronted with one of the most painful choices to be made by any ethnic minority. Having re-created their nation in America, they were now forced to choose unequivocally between the two states. In a country at war, attacks against German-Americans grew in intensity and focused on "swatting the hyphen" from their self-designation. Theodore Roosevelt made the point in no uncertain terms: "The men of German blood who have tried to be both Germans and Americans are no Americans at all, but traitors to America and tools and servants of Germany against America. . . . Hereafter we must see that the melting pot really does not melt. There should be but one language in this country—the English."[38]

The outcome was a surprise by its unanimity and promptness. In April 1918, the German-American Alliance dissolved itself, turning its funds to the American Red Cross; other German-American organizations changed their names and initiated campaigns for the sale of U.S. war bonds; men of German ancestry joined the American armed forces by the thousands. After 1918, visible signs of German *kultur* declined rapidly throughout the country. By their own choice, German-

Americans had "swatted the hyphen" and acceded to Roosevelt's demand for prompt assimilation.

In sum, the politics of immigration was affected as much by events in the sending countries as by those in the United States. Immigrants differed in their past political socialization, commitment to return, and national situations left behind. The combination of these factors affected not only their stance in American domestic politics, but also their orientations and behavior toward the homeland. Depending on the particular mix of factors, some groups struggled for independent statehood for their countries while others did not know that they had left countries behind. Among immigrants from consolidated nation-states, some regarded the homeland political system as a matter of relative indifference; others left to escape its hold; still others had to contend with its expansionist overtures. This diversity negated any easy generalization during the period and simultaneously established a precedent and point of reference for understanding the political behavior of later arrivals.

Immigrant Politics Today

Looking Homeward

In contrast to pre–World War I immigrants, those bound for America today seldom come from stateless lands or lack well-defined national identities. The gradual consolidation of a global interstate system means that most people today not only belong to a nation-state, but are aware of this fact. Consolidated states and strong national identities mean very different things, however, when immigrants see themselves as representatives, in some sense, of their home nations, when they have come fleeing from them, or when their journey has been dictated by purely individual interests and is a matter of official indifference to the sending country. Although, as in the earlier period, these three types are seldom found in pure form, they provide a basic framework for understanding the politics of the first generation.

Early political concerns of the foreign born today seldom have to do with matters American. Instead, they tend to center on issues and problems back home. This is especially the case for sojourners—those whose stay in the United States is defined as instrumental for attaining goals in their own communities and countries. In such cases, there is every reason to regard U.S. politics with relative indifference. The attachment to home country issues persists, however, even among those who have settled here permanently. For political refugees, barred from returning home, it may be the lingering hope of doing so someday, a feeling of seemingly remarkable persistence. For nonpolitical immigrants, the increasing facility for return trips and ease of communication with family and friends at home serve to keep alive the identifications and loyalties into which they were socialized.

Easier transportation and communication go a long way toward explaining contemporary immigrants' strong attachment to the politics of the homeland. Another reason is the very strength acquired by sending states. Even those states for which immigration is a matter of official indifference tend to intervene in national life and the lives of their populations, including immigrants, in far more extensive ways than the disarticulated polities that many turn-of-the-century flows left behind. National governments at present are both more cohesive and generally more visible abroad through elaborate networks of diplomatic representatives and trade offices. These facilities encourage a continuing link between immigrants and their home countries.

The experiences of four different national groups, each documented by a recent study, illustrate the politics of the first generation in each of the three typical situations outlined previously. A first group—Koreans—represents one of the fastest growing immigrant minorities and one that, as seen in chapter 2, has developed sizable concentrations in major cities of both coasts. Most of the Korean-origin population of the United States is foreign born because mass immigration did not start until the mid-1960s. As with other immigrant groups, Koreans have not yet developed a strong presence in local U.S. political affairs, but their organizations have maintained close contact with events back home and at times have played a role in political and economic relations between the two countries.

As described by Kim, the Korean community of New York was until recently a supervised colony, guided by diplomatic representatives of the South Korean government and regarded by the latter as an important outpost in the core of the American economy. The Korean state did not sponsor the emigration of its nationals, but once communities emerged abroad it saw them as an opportunity to promote its economic and political goals. The immigrants responded positively, partly out of nationalism and partly out of economic interests, with the result that their principal organizations became subordinate to home government agencies:

> The South Korean government regards overseas Koreans as its subjects in need of its constant care and protection as well as its "corrective guidance and education." . . . It is no exaggeration to say that the Korean Consulate General is the informal government of New York's Korean community and that the consul general is its "mayor."[39]

Diplomatic representatives have stressed the need for "unity" in the community and supported the existence of complementary rather than competing associations. The Korean Association of Greater New York has been designed by the consulate as the overall umbrella organization, and attempts to establish alternative ones have been discouraged. A small group of business leaders has actively engaged in officially sponsored organizations as a self-conscious strategy for gaining trading and other privileges from the Korean government or even political appointments back home. At least for this group, paths of upward mobility are defined by its activities on American soil as evaluated not by U.S. authorities or public, but by South Korean officials.[40]

This type of "sponsored" immigrant politics has several advantages, such as the financial and moral support given by the home government to community activities, the sense of security among immigrants who feel themselves represented by accredited diplomats, and the presence of higher authority that can mediate or resolve petty community struggles. As Kim points out, however, the situation also has serious drawbacks such as the subordination of immigrant interests to those of a remote government, the potential antagonism created by foreign loyalties among the native-born population, and the persecution of political opponents of the home regime.[41]

The "Koreagate" scandal, which featured a Korean rice dealer attempting to bribe U.S. congressmen on behalf of his government, the antics of Reverend Moon's Unification Church, and the increasing hostility faced by Korean merchants among blacks and other inner-city minorities have convinced many immigrant Koreans of the need to abandon "sponsored" politics under the consulate's guidance and shift toward autonomous community organizations. Produce dealers and other small merchants, who have become increasingly active in community affairs in recent years, succeeded in wresting control of the Korean Association of Greater New York from the traditional clique. The new leadership has reoriented the organization toward local "ethnic" concerns rather than home country politics. Nevertheless, the influence of the Korean government and its interventionist policies continue to be felt both in New York and in other places with large Korean-American concentrations.

Recent Dominican and Colombian immigrants have also created sizable communities in New York, but their circumstances are altogether different. As seen in chapter 3, the background and context of incorporation of these Latin American groups are distinct from the Koreans, resulting in large gaps in average incomes and rates of business ownership. Their politics are also different. Dominicans and Colombians leave formally democratic nations whose governments do not officially promote their departure nor attempt to supervise their settlement abroad. Under circumstances of official indifference, the collective concerns of immigrant communities and the organizations that emerge to address them have not had to contend with systematic outside interference. On the cost side, absence of governmental support has made these organizations more fragile.

According to Sassen-Koob, the Dominican population of New York clusters in Manhattan's Upper West Side, especially in the Washington Heights section, with smaller concentrations in the Lower East Side and the Corona section of Queens. It is primarily a working-class community with origins in the small and middle peasantry of the Cibao region as well as in the urban lower middle class of Santo Domingo and Santiago. Most Dominican organizations are nonpolitical—sports, recreational, and educational groups. Their basic goal appears to be cushioning the impact of adaptation to life in New York through the reproduction of familiar cultural forms.[42]

The Colombian population concentrates in Queens—Jackson Heights, Jamaica, Elmhurst—with a significant number having moved to Long Island. It is also a working-class population, but with a visible professional and entrepreneurial element. Sassen-Koob attributes this diversity to the origins of Colombian immigration in various segments of the urban middle class. Although most newcomers experience downward mobility, a certain sector manages to retain its old class position or climb back into it after a few years. Colombian organizations are also primarily nonpolitical. In this case, however, membership criteria are more restrictive than among Dominicans; existing associations attempt to reinforce the image of a "middle-class" life-style by engaging in certain ritual activities such as balls, tea parties, and country tours.[43]

Although not particularly salient, the political concerns of these two communities are noteworthy. In years past, Colombian immigrants have organized for the right to vote in Colombian national and local elections and succeeded in doing so. By the late 1970s, the principal Dominican organization was the National Association of Dominicans Abroad (ANDE, in the Spanish acronym), whose main goal was securing the same electoral rights for Dominicans and which patterned itself consciously after the successful Colombian groups. During the same period, the Colombian Professional Association began a campaign to protest against the negative image of its country-men in the U.S. media, particularly their association with the drug trade. The organization sought external support in this effort, especially from the New York Spanish-language media and the Colombian embassy in Washington.[44]

As befits immigrant communities with a strong sojourner orientation, the Colombian and Dominican communities of New York thus organized primarily with their homelands in mind. Their political orientations went in the same direction, although their evolution over time was quite different than that among Koreans in the same city. Instead of seeking autonomy from an interventionist state, Colombians and Dominicans ac-tually sought more participation by their governments. Clearly, theirs was a quest for "voice" in the affairs of their homelands and for greater attention and support from so far passive states. In this regard, the self-initiated nationalistic efforts of Colom-bian professionals and their call for governmental help repre-sent a different kind of politics than the attempts by Korean merchants to distance themselves from officially sponsored ac-tivities. In both instances, the goal was to improve the immi-grants' local image. But in one case, the effort relied on bring-ing the home government into the fray; in the other, it depended on gaining distance from it.

Immigrants who come fleeing dictatorial regimes tend to de-velop a different kind of politics. Theirs is not a situation in which political concerns may or may not play a primary role in the life of the community, as with other immigrants. Instead, politics is at the very core of refugee communities and is apt to remain so for many years. Militant opposition to the regime that expelled them and an enduring commitment to oppose it is what sets refugees apart from other immigrants. Even in de-feat, this common political ideology tinges their process of in-corporation into American society and tends to produce novel social and economic outcomes.

Cubans represent one of the largest groups of political escap-ees to arrive in the United States during the last three decades.

Coming in successive waves after the advent of Castro's revolution in 1959, they were guided primarily by the hope of return, at least during the early years. As Boswell and Curtis note: "Many of the Cuban refugees who arrived during the early 1960s believed that their stay in this country would be of short duration. They were convinced that the Castro government would soon lose control and they would be able to return to a free Cuba."[45]

Patterns of settlement and economic incorporation of this group have been described in prior chapters. The point to be emphasized here is the extent to which exile politics permeated these and most other aspects of its collective life. Until the Bay of Pigs invasion, all activity within the émigré community of south Florida revolved around the imminent military conflict and plans for subsequent return. The defeat of the exile brigade in April 1961 represented an immense blow to this community's pride and hopes, but military actions against Cuba and efforts to organize a second invasion persisted until the missile crisis of 1962. At that point, the Kennedy administration agreed to rein in the refugees in exchange for the removal of Soviet missiles from the island. From that moment on, all realistic hopes of overthrowing Castro's regime from the outside vanished because exile organizations could not confront Cuba's forces, trained and armed by the Soviet Union, without U.S. support.[46]

In 1963, the principal exile organization—the Cuban Revolutionary Council—dissolved. Thereafter, one could suppose that Cubans would give up the struggle and turn their attention to the serious matter of long-term adaptation to American society. Adaptation did take place but was colored, to a significant extent, by the ideology of intransigent opposition to Castroism and communism in general. Two decades after the Bay of Pigs, the Cuban-American National Foundation—an organization created by wealthy exile businessmen—embraced as its principal cause the creation of Radio Martí, a powerful station transmitting news and antiregime propaganda to Cuba. The Coalition for a Free Cuba, the foundation's political action committee, has made important financial contributions to sympathetic legislators in Florida, Texas, and other states.[47] The Foundation went so far as to help finance anti-Communist struggles abroad, including the UNITA movement in Angola and the "Contra" army in Nicaragua. Just as in the 1960s Hungarian refugees had joined as volunteers the Cuban exile forces against Castro, in the 1980s Cuban exiles were found fighting in Central America against the Sandinista army. Cuban-American doctors, some U.S. born, represented an important element of support for the Nicaraguan "Contra" effort.[48]

The resilience of a political orientation centered on the dream of return had its origins in the dispossessed Cuban upper and middle classes, compelled to leave their country against their will. Although the passing away of the first generation will surely weaken this orientation, the trauma of departure and subsequent military defeat still tinges Cuban-American politics today. Both the Bay of Pigs fiasco and the missile crisis took place during the Kennedy administration, and Cuban refugees have blamed the Democrats for them ever since. As they acquired the right to vote, Cubans lined solidly behind the Republican party, turning it from an insignificant force in south Florida politics into a major power contender.

Whether subject to the influence and guidance of the home government, seeking actively its collaboration, or intransigently opposed to its rule, the politics of the first generation registers a notable power asymmetry between national states and immigrant communities. Gone are the days when expatriate communities could launch a new nation or lead a liberation war to victory. The consolidation of national states and their increasing power makes such projects unlikely at present. Immigrant communities in the United States are thus constrained to play at best a secondary role in influencing home national destinies. Their political activities in this respect are limited generally to supporting the initiatives of either the sending or receiving states. Koreans, until recently, represented an example of the first course; Cubans and other anti-Communist refugee groups have been examples of the second.

Making It Count: Acquiring Citizenship

There is no guarantee that immigrants, even those settling permanently in America, will ever exhibit an interest in domestic political issues and mobilize to influence them. The history of immigration registers instances of groups that have continued being "in the society, but not of it" throughout the first generation. In those cases where homeward politics begins to give way to more pressing issues in the new environment, needs and interests are not enough, however. Immigrant organizations may be highly effective in protecting their members from the trauma of cultural adaptation or in dialoguing with home governments; but to the extent that they are formed by noncitizens, they have little voice in America.

Citizenship acquisition is the first stage for any foreign minority that wishes to make itself heard. Higher numbers, greater concentration, and higher rates of acquiring citizenship all contribute to this goal. As seen in prior chapters, the first two factors vary significantly across immigrant groups; thus it is not too surprising that the third does also. The "propensity" of a particular minority to change flags is a composite of two related but different trends: the numbers that actually acquire U.S. citizenship and the rapidity with which the process takes place. Hence, the political influence of two immigrant groups that exhibit similar rates of naturalization at the end of the first generation will be very different if one completed the change soon after arrival and the other waited until the years of retirement.

Differential propensities for acquiring citizenship combine with the size of eligible pools from each nationality to produce aggregate naturalization trends. Table 12 presents an overview of these trends between 1976 and 1993. During this period, the regions included in the table accounted for 98 percent of the 3.9 million immigrants who became new American citizens. The relative contribution of each region during the decade shifted significantly, however: naturalized citizens of European extraction declined significantly in relative terms over this time;

Table 12
Naturalizations for Selected Countries and Regions, 1976–1993

Region/Country	1976 N (000s)	1976 %[a]	1979 N (000s)	1979 %	1982 N (000s)	1982 %	1986 N (000s)	1986 %	1993 N (000s)	1993 %	Total N (000s)	Total %
Europe	49	34.3	42	25.6	37	21.3	45	16.0	42	13.3	688	17.5
United Kingdom	9	6.3	8	4.9	8	4.6	9	3.2	10	3.2	153	3.9
Asia	47	32.9	64	39.0	80	46.0	135	48.0	145	46.0	1,780	45.4
India	4	2.8	6	3.7	8	4.6	10	3.6	17	5.4	166	4.2
Korea	7	4.9	13	7.9	13	7.5	18	6.4	10	3.2	228	5.8
Philippines	15	10.5	18	11.0	18	10.3	31	11.0	34	10.8	428	10.9
Vietnam	1	0.7	2	1.2	13	7.5	30	10.7	22	7.0	259	6.6
North America	35	24.4	44	26.8	43	24.7	74	26.3	88	27.9	1,011	25.8
Canada	3	2.1	3	1.8	3	1.7	4	1.4	7	2.2	66	1.7
Cuba	15	10.5	13	7.9	10	5.7	14	5.0	15	4.8	231	5.9
Mexico	6	4.2	8	4.9	11	6.3	28	10.0	24	7.6	279	7.1
Central and South America	10	7.0	15	9.1	15	8.6	27	9.6	37	11.7	382	9.7
Total[b]	143	—	164	—	174	—	281	—	315	—	3,924	—

SOURCES: U.S. Immigration and Naturalization Service, *Statistical Yearbooks* (Washington, D.C.: U.S. Government Printing Office, 1987, 1994), 139–141 and 138–139.

[a] Percentage of total number of naturalizations during the year.
[b] Regional percentages do not add up to 100 because Africa and Oceania have been omitted.

those of Asian origin registered a spectacular increase. Western Hemisphere immigrants also increased their aggregate proportion at the expense of the Europeans, although their gain was nowhere near that of Asians.

Aggregate regional figures conceal, however, significant differences among countries. Major flows contributing to the almost two million new citizens of Asian origin came from India, Korea, China, and the Philippines; these nationalities' share of total naturalizations increased only slightly during the last decade and actually declined during its last years. Vietnamese immigrants—originally a refugee minority—increased their representation fifteenfold, becoming, next to the Philippines, the largest national contingent among naturalized citizens by 1986. Similarly, the consistent rise in the North American figures conceals a declining presence of Canadians and Cubans among new U.S. citizens and an increasing weight of Mexicans, who had quadrupled their numbers by 1993.

These aggregate trends are a function of the pool of eligible immigrants from each region or country and their respective propensity to naturalize. To isolate the latter, one must compare the number of naturalizations for different groups, controlling for their absolute size. Following Warren, table 13 analyzes naturalization rates by comparing the numbers changing nationality for different immigrant groups over a period of ten years.[49] The table includes data for the three largest regional sources of immigration (Europe, Asia, and the Americas) and for the three countries of any size closest to the United States (Canada, Mexico, and Cuba). During the 1970s, Mexico was the single largest national source of immigrants and Cuba the largest source of political refugees.

The overall Mexican naturalization rate during this decade was the lowest, representing less than one-seventh of the average for all countries. The Canadian figure was also very low, oscillating between one-fourth and one-fifth of the total. Cuban refugees naturalized at high rates, consistently exceeding the average for all countries. Roughly 20 percent of European and Central and South American immigrants arriving in 1970

Table 13

The 1970 Immigrant Cohort and Its Naturalization History over the Following Decade for Selected Countries and Regions

Region/Country	Cohort 1970	Naturalizations per Year										Total 1970–1979	% of 1970 Cohort
		1970	1971	1972	1973	1974	1975	1976	1977	1978	1979		
Cuba	16,334	0	10	5	7	58	144	1,678	2,444	1,943	1,323	7,621	47
Mexico	44,469	1	11	17	38	78	96	176	296	404	358	1,475	3
South and Central America[a]	31,316	15	69	121	240	322	235	951	1,394	1,480	1,324	6,161	20
Canada	13,804	2	22	8	34	131	102	140	182	121	114	856	6
Western Europe[b]	92,433	17	127	131	305	1,179	1,154	5,103	4,550	3,211	2,188	17,965	19
Asia[c]	92,816	229	857	680	1,062	4,019	3,616	15,129	9,596	5,833	3,533	44,554	48
All countries	373,326	275	1,118	1,127	1,896	6,298	6,095	27,681	22,301	16,143	11,562	94,532	25

SOURCE: U.S. Immigration and Naturalization Service, *Annual Reports* (Washington, D.C.: U.S. Government Printing Office, 1970–1980), tables 6, 44.

[a] Includes Argentina, Brazil, Chile, Colombia, Ecuador, Guyana, Peru, Uruguay, Venezuela, other South American, Dominican Republic, Costa Rica, El Salvador, Guatemala, Honduras, Nicaragua, and Panama.
[b] Includes Austria, Denmark, France, Germany, Greece, Ireland, Italy, Netherlands, Portugal, Spain, Sweden, Switzerland, and the United Kingdom.
[c] Includes China and Taiwan, Hong Kong, India, Indonesia, Iran, Iraq, Israel, Japan, Jordan, Korea, Lebanon, Philippines, Ryukyu Islands, Syria, Thailand, Turkey, Vietnam, and other Asia.

changed nationalities during the following decade, a rate lower than the average but significantly above those for Canada and Mexico. Asian immigrants, like Cubans, more than doubled the European rate, their aggregate figure being twenty-three percentage points above the global average. Asians were also the most prompt to change citizenship: 57 percent of their naturalizations took place during the first seven years after arrival, as compared to 47 percent for all countries. Asian and European naturalizations peaked in the seventh year; those from Mexico and Central and South America had to wait until the ninth.

Figure 4 presents an alternative view of the process by tracing naturalizations of immigrant cohorts that arrived between 1970 and 1979 until the last year (1993) for which information is available. Included in this analysis are the three countries closest to the United States, representative ones from Europe and Asia, and all major sending regions. Results show clearly why Asia has become the preponderant source of new foreign-born citizens: High levels of immigration combine in this case with high propensities to naturalize. By contrast, the North American region—mainly Canada, Cuba, and Mexico plus the Dominican Republic and Jamaica—sent more immigrants than Asia during the 1970s, but its rate of naturalization was less than a third the Asian figure. Europe and South America continued to exhibit intermediate rates that, when combined with stagnant or declining relative pools of immigrants, yielded lower numbers of naturalizations than for other regions.

The two contiguous countries (Mexico and Canada) again had the lowest propensities to change flags of any country or region; Cubans arriving during the 1970s also seemed much less inclined in that direction than earlier cohorts. Their place was taken by Vietnamese refugees, who exhibited the highest rates of naturalization during the last decade. Also high are other Asian groups, such as Filipinos, Chinese, and Koreans.

The second aspect of propensity to naturalize is the relative delay in completing the process. It is possible in theory that minorities with high overall rates of naturalization are not the most diligent in achieving this goal. In practice, this is not the

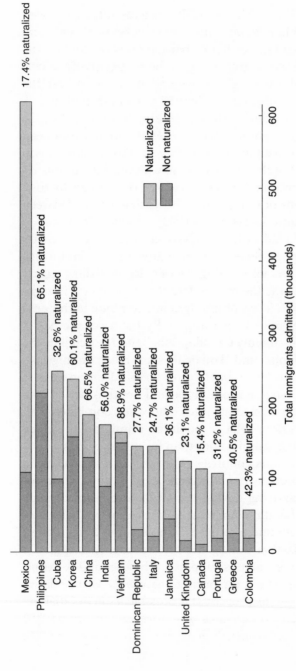

Figure 4. Immigrants admitted, 1970–1979, and proportions naturalized, 1970–1993, by selected countries of birth.

SOURCE: U.S. Immigration and Naturalization Service, *1993 Statistical Yearbook* (Washington, D.C.: U.S. Government Printing Office, 1994), chart R.

NOTE: "China" includes mainland China and Taiwan.

case. Table 14 presents the relevant evidence, aggregated by regions. Results show that over the last twenty years, new citizens of Asian origin have naturalized two to six years earlier than the average for Europeans and South Americans. Immigrants from North American countries are not only the least likely to change citizenship, but the slowest to do so; they have trailed Asians by four to eight years on the average. Only Africans are as diligent as Asians in this respect, but their absolute numbers are still insignificant, although rapidly growing.

European immigrants arriving in the first decades of the century also registered significant variations in their propensities to acquire U.S. citizenship. In 1936, sociologist W. S. Bernard proposed that the gap between "old" (northwestern) and "new" (southeastern) Europeans in acquiring citizenship was due to different levels of literacy and education. Among immigrants arriving at the same time, those with better education could be expected to understand the benefits of naturalization faster and to start the process earlier than others. The observed differences between Italian peasants and north European urban skilled workers could be attributed directly to this factor.[50]

Table 14

*Median Years of U.S. Residence, by Year of
Naturalization and Region of Birth, 1975–1993*

Region	Year of Naturalization			
	1975	1980	1987	1993
Asia	6	7	7	7
Africa	6	7	7	7
Oceania	7	8	9	9
Europe	8	10	9	13
South America	9	9	9	10
North America	9	11	12	15

SOURCE: U.S. Immigration and Naturalization Service, *1993 Statistical Yearbook* (Washington, D.C.: U.S. Government Printing Office, 1994), table J, p. 126.

Bernard's hypothesis has been supported by subsequent studies. As seen in chapter 3, Asian immigrants arriving during the last decades had higher average levels of education and larger proportions of professionals than other nationalities. Table 15 presents additional evidence that Asian professionals in the mid-1970s were already more numerous in both absolute and relative terms than those coming from other regions and that they tended to make disproportionate use of the third preference category—reserved for professionals—for admission into the United States. The single exception was Africa, whose immigrants represented a much smaller contingent. Figures for 1975 are typical of those during the decade that gave

Table 15

*Professional Immigrants and Eastern Hemisphere
Immigrants Admitted Under Third Preference, by Region,
1975*

| Region | N | Professional Immigrants | | Eastern Hemisphere Immigrants Admitted Under Third Preference: Professional Specialty | |
		% of Total	% of Economically Active Immigrants	N	% of Total[a]
Africa	1,521	22.6	47.9	169	3.5
Asia	23,553	17.8	47.6	7,859	8.3
Europe	7,235	9.8	22.5	309	0.5
Oceania	453	13.5	32.3	26	1.2
South America	1,436	6.2	15.2	—[b]	—
North America	4,293	2.9	7.9	—[b]	—
Total	38,491	10.0	25.7	8,363	5.2

SOURCE: U.S. Immigration and Naturalization Service, *1975 Annual Report* (Washington, D.C.: U.S. Government Printing Office, 1976), tables 7a, 8.

[a] Total of immigrants subject to numerical limitations.
[b] Western Hemisphere immigration was not subject to preference system in 1975.

rise to the pool of immigrants eligible for naturalization in the 1980s and 1990s. Hence, it is not surprising that Asian and African immigrants have acquired citizenship at high rates during this period. Only recently has there been a decline in the proportion of professionals among Asian immigrants, due to the increasing use of family reunification preferences, and hence the growing presence of immediate relatives among new arrivals. However, the proportion of professionals increased again after the Immigration Act of 1990 tripled the number of visas available for highly skilled immigrants.

Factors other than education and occupation also play a role in the process. Recent research has identified variables such as the political origin of migration and the geographical proximity of the country of origin as causally significant. Political refugees from Communist-controlled countries naturalize in greater numbers, other things being equal, than other immigrants; those from nearby countries, especially nations sharing land borders with the United States, tend to resist citizenship change more than others. Both results reflect the operation of a more general factor, which may be labeled the "reversibility" of migration: Immigrants for whom it is more difficult to return because of political conditions at home or the high cost of the journey naturalize at higher rates than those for whom return is but a simple bus ride away.[51]

These factors help explain the notorious resistance among Mexican and Canadian immigrants to change flags. Both are primarily economic and easily reversible flows. Cuba is also a nearby country, but the blockage of the return option plays a decisive role in this case. Despite continuous and fierce opposition to the regime on the island, the absence of any realistic opportunity to overthrow it from abroad led Cuban exiles arriving in the 1960s to naturalize in high numbers. The decline in rates of naturalization among later arrivals is probably a function of the more modest educational backgrounds of recent cohorts and their strong tendency to settle within the established Cuban community in south Florida. Relative institutional completeness of this community enables new arrivals to live and work within a familiar cultural environment; although advantageous during the earlier stages of adaptation, this pattern tends to delay naturalization. The Vietnamese, a more recent group of political escapees, have replaced Cubans and others as the most prone to naturalize in both absolute and relative terms. The Vietnamese, who became eligible for citizenship in the early 1980s, are comparable to Cubans in the 1960s in that both were members of early refugee cohorts. As seen previously, earlier refugee arrivals tend to come from higher socioeconomic strata; this factor plus the inability to return seem to have played a decisive role in both cases.

The combined operation of the three variables (educational levels, geographical proximity, and political origin of migration) goes a long way toward explaining differences in naturalization among immigrant groups. A study that examined the joint effects of these variables over ten years found that the three variables combined, plus size of the original cohort, account for over half the group differences in naturalization. According to these results, each additional year of education increases a group's rate of naturalization by about 1.5 percent; coming from Mexico or Canada reduces it by 21 percent; and arriving as a political refugee increases naturalizations by about 13 percent, holding other factors constant.[52]

The Future of Immigrant Politics

Resilient Ethnicity

Time and the passing of the first generation inexorably turn immigrant communities toward American concerns. Contemporary immigration, with all its bewildering variety, is still of recent vintage because most sizable contingents did not start arriving until the late 1960s. Hence, the politics of the first generation, with its strong orientation toward the homeland and varying propensity to naturalize, continues to predominate. In most instances, ethnic communities have not had time to consolidate and develop a distinct political profile in America. However, the exceptions point strongly toward the continuation of trends initiated by earlier European groups. Then, as now, ethnicity has proven a resilient feature; and when immigrant communities finally turn to domestic issues and the vote, they tend to mobilize along national rather than class lines.

Mexicans again furnish the best example. Unlike other Third World immigrants, Mexicans have been arriving in the United States since the nineteenth century and have thus had time to consolidate communities with a sizable American-born component. We have seen how national identity for many nineteenth-century Mexican immigrants emerged out of their North American experience. Despite the first generation's notable resistance to naturalize, their children and grandchildren—U.S. citizens by birth—have become increasingly involved in domestic politics. Thus, looking at the past political experience of this minority is also a way of anticipating the likely course of ethnic groups being created by immigration today, especially those that, like Mexicans, are composed primarily of manual labor migrants.

Although Mexican-American political organizing may be dated back to several turn-of-the-century self-help associations known as the *Mutualistas*, its first real impulse did not occur until World War I and its aftermath. In 1921, returning Mexican-American veterans created in San Antonio the *Orden de Hijos de America*; in 1923, the League of United Latin American Citizens (LULAC) was formed in Corpus Christi. The *Orden*, created to protect the veterans and other members of the minority against discrimination, eventually merged with LULAC, which was to become the oldest and largest Spanish-origin political organization in the country.[53] Thus, at a time when the most urbanized European groups back East continued to be involved in socialism and class politics, Mexican-American political activism in the Southwest already focused on issues of ethnicity and racial-cultural discrimination.

This orientation was to continue and assume more militant overtones after World War II. Thousands of returning Mexican-American veterans, many highly decorated, found that they

were still barred from movie theaters, residential neighborhoods, and even cemeteries in their own hometowns. As a result,
the G.I. Forum was organized in 1948 to defend the interests of
veterans and campaign against racial barriers. By this time, the
process of reactive formation was in full swing: Just as Mexican
immigrants had been made aware of a common identity by being discriminated against together, so their descendants recap-
tured the symbols of that identity and turned them into rallying
points of political solidarity. By 1960, the Mexican-American
Political Association (MAPA) had been formed. It explained its
raison d'être as follows: "MAPA grew out of many and difficult
experiences of thousands of Mexican-Americans throughout
California who have tried so hard to elect representatives to
state and local government. . . . [A]n organization was needed
that would be proudly Mexican-American, openly political, necessarily bipartisan."[54]

Ethnic consciousness and mobilization reached their climax
during the 1960s and early 1970s, driven by an increasingly
vocal U.S.-born generation. Mexican-American politics during
this period were patterned closely after the Black Power movement. As with black groups, older organizations like LULAC
were threatened with displacement by a proliferation of radical youth groups—the United Mexican American Students, the
Mexican American Youth Organization, and the Brown Berets.
Younger intellectuals went beyond pragmatic demands to articulate a vision of collective identity in which race, language,
and culture were paramount. Concepts like Aztlán (the sub-
merged Indo-Mexican nation of North America) and La Raza
(the race—the racial-cultural community of its inhabitants)
were coined and popularized during this period. Like Germans during World War I, Mexican-Americans in the 1960s also
"swatted the hyphen," but they did so in the direction of ethnic
reaffirmation: "Chicano," rather than Mexican-American, became the preferred self-designation. By the end of the decade,
these symbolic developments had reached political expression
in such movements as the Chicano Student Movement of Aztlán (MECHA) and the La Raza Unida party.[55]

The radical period was short-lived, however. La Raza Unida

achieved some notable electoral successes in south Texas, primarily in municipal elections, but by the end of the 1970s, it had effectively disappeared from the political scene. In the 1980s, the older, more moderate LULAC—with branches in forty-one states—and new organizations like the Mexican-American Legal Defense Fund (MALDEF), staffed by professionals and well financed by private foundations, took the lead in Mexican ethnic politics.[56] In retrospect, the militancy of the 1960s can be interpreted as an inevitable reaction, in the context of the time, to the singularly oppressive conditions Mexican migrants and their descendants had endured for decades. Like blacks, Mexican-Americans saw themselves as a simultaneously exploited and despised minority. Because it was difficult to restore ethnic pride under these circumstances, reactive formation among the younger generation necessarily went beyond mild demands to articulate a radical alternative vision of reality.

Chicano militancy accomplished in a few years what decades of past moderate efforts had not. The doors of high political office opened for the first time to Mexican-Americans; citizens of Mexican ancestry finally began registering and voting in high numbers; presidential candidates were increasingly compelled to court the Mexican vote. Because of their concentration in the five southwestern states, Mexican-Americans can play a crucial "swing" role in states that heavily influence electoral college outcomes. As seen in table 16, the Spanish-origin vote in the Southwest represents a much higher proportion than nationwide. The roughly 10 percent of Mexican voters in the region can, when mobilized as a bloc, significantly affect elections in states that jointly control one-fifth of the votes needed to elect a new president. As seen previously, the Mexican-American electorate is potentially much higher because of the large number of nonnaturalized legal immigrants.

During the late 1970s and 1980s, Mexican-Americans were elected to the U.S. House of Representatives, to the governorships of two states, and to mayoralties of major cities such as San Antonio. Mexican-origin state legislators increased fourfold between 1950 and 1983. Ninety percent of the Hispanic caucus in Congress in the early 1980s was Mexican-American.[57]

Table 16
The Spanish-Origin Vote in the Southwest

| | Presidential Vote, 1992 | | | | General Election, 1990 | | |
	Total Vote (000s)	Spanish-Origin Vote (000s)	% Spanish Origin	Electoral College Votes	Total Vote (000s)	Spanish-Origin Vote (000s)	% Spanish Origin
Arizona	1,728	156	9.0	8	1,196	88	7.4
California	11,789	1,135	9.6	54	9,026	843	9.3
Colorado	1,688	136	8.1	8	1,202	64	5.3
New Mexico	675	172	25.5	5	484	126	26.0
Texas	6,817	927	13.6	32	4,972	604	12.1
Total United States	113,866	4,238	3.7	538			

SOURCES: U.S. Bureau of the Census, "Voting and Registration in the Election of November 1990," Current Population Reports, Series P-20, No. 453, October 1991; U.S. Bureau of the Census, "Voting and Registration in the Election of November 1992," Current Population Reports, Series P-20, No. 466, April 1993. World Almanac 1994 (Mahwah, N.J.: Funk and Wagnalls, 1994), 583.

In national elections, the Mexican vote tends to be heavily in favor of the Democratic party. In the 1960 presidential race, for example, districts in El Paso and other Texas cities tallied 100 percent for the Democratic candidate. This was a result of the "Viva Kennedy" campaign orchestrated by major Mexican-American politicians.[58]

In recent years, Republicans have also become aware of this group's growing political clout and have made significant strides, especially during the years of the Reagan presidency. In an effort to solidify this gain, Lauro Cavazos, former Texas Tech University president, was appointed secretary of education in 1988—the first Mexican-American to hold cabinet rank. The important point, however, is that preferences for one or another party among Mexican-American voters do not seem to reflect consistent class differences, but respond instead to the appeal of specific candidates and programs to the minority as a whole. As they were with the Europeans before them, ethnicity and ethnic issues continue to be the fundamental pivot of Mexican-American politics.

Mexican immigrants and their descendants represent an important link between the "old" and "new" immigrations because they partook of both. The flow from south of the border started in the nineteenth century and has never ceased, providing a point of continuity between pre-World War I and contemporary events. Like downtrodden European minorities, Mexicans suffered much poverty and oppression, underwent subsequent reactive processes of ethnic affirmation and radicalization, and gained eventual entry into the mainstream through the electoral system. Their experiences both confirm lessons drawn from European immigrant history and offer a blueprint for the likely political course of recently arrived minorities.

Variations Within a Theme

The Mexican experience does not exhaust all there is to ethnic politics, nor can it be perfectly extrapolated to all contemporary immigrations. Just as in the first decades of the century there were major differences between peasant flows and those formed by urban skilled workers, at present there are significant differences in the background of immigrants and the course of their political incorporation. Thus, within the general themes of gradual shift from homeland to American politics and the enduring role of ethnicity, there is room for significant variation. We have seen already the large divergencies in the first step of entry into domestic politics—naturalization—and its determinants. Differences are likely to persist in subsequent steps as a consequence of variation in both individual characteristics and the interaction between places of origin and of destination.

The typology of contemporary immigration discussed in chapter 1 provides a useful summary of the differences to be expected. Table 17 outlines these differences along four main dimensions. Because each type of immigration comprises a plurality of situations and because the process of political incorporation of today's immigrants is by no means complete, the table should be read as a set of preliminary hypotheses, formulated on the basis of past experience. The rationale for each of them follows.

As seen previously, resistance to naturalization varies inversely with the reversibility of migration and with average socioeducational backgrounds of individual flows. Manual labor migrants tend to be sojourners and come from relatively modest origins. Hence, their rates of naturalization can be expected to be low, especially during the early years. The naturalization patterns of Dominicans and most other Caribbean and Central American groups provide an illustration. Flows with a heavy professional and technical component can be expected to have intermediate rates of naturalization, depending on whether the journey is seen as temporary or permanent. If permanent, professional immigrants can be expected to change nationality promptly because of their high levels of education, knowledge of English, and information about the advantages of U.S. citizenship. The variable presence of sojourners may help explain significant differences between Indian and Egyptian immigrants (professional-type flows with high naturalization rates)

Table 17

Political Orientations of Contemporary Immigrants

	Immigration Type			
Variable	Manual Laborers	Professionals and Technicians	Entrepreneurial Groups	Political Refugees
Propensity to naturalize	low	medium	high	high
Salience of politics	low	medium	medium	high
Locus of early political concerns	external	mixed	mixed	external
Character of ethnicity	reactive	linear	reactive	linear

and those coming from Argentina and other South American countries (also with relatively high proportions of professionals and technicians, but lower rates of naturalization).

Entrepreneurial groups are expected to exhibit a high propensity for naturalization because of their relatively high levels of education, the "rootedness" associated with business ownership, and the added security and advantages derived from citizenship. The behavior of business-oriented immigrant communities from Asia and the Middle East illustrates this trend. Political refugees can also be expected to naturalize at relatively high rates. Continuing preoccupation with events in the home country does not seem to neutralize the effect of a blocked return option. Although the outward ideology of refugee communities may continue to uphold the hope of return, actual reality carries greater weight. The fact that most sanctioned refugee groups today share strong identification with American political values may also facilitate naturalization. Cubans during the 1970s and the Vietnamese during the 1980s and 1990s provide examples.

Manual laborers whose stay is temporary are often more interested in pragmatic economic goals than in politics. As seen in the case of Latin American communities in New York, salient political issues tend to relate to the country of origin. Other nonrefugee flows also share a pragmatic economic orientation, but the salience of politics for them and their attention to U.S. domestic affairs vary. Immigrant professionals and entrepreneurs can be expected to retain a strong interest in home country politics while becoming more attentive to issues in their new environment. In the case of professionals, high levels of education and knowledge of English combine with dispersal across U.S. communities to stimulate growing attention to domestic affairs. For entrepreneurs, issues of a national and local character—trade policies, tariffs, local city ordinances, native population attitudes toward their businesses—can make a difference between success and failure and thus require careful monitoring.[59]

Groups escaping political oppression tend to differ from other immigrants in the high salience of politics in their communities and its overriding external orientation. Although the fading of hopes for return may lead to rapid naturalization, the attention of these communities is often riveted on events back home, and their interest in American politics tends to concentrate on the foreign policy of the U.S. government, particularly toward their respective countries. As the case of Cubans in south Florida illustrates, even subsequent participation in local community politics is colored by the refugee experience.[60]

Finally, the process of reactive formation that played such a crucial role in the political incorporation of European and Mexican immigrants can also be expected to vary significantly at present. The confrontation with concerted attitudes of prejudice on the part of the surrounding population is most likely for manual labor flows settling in highly visible ethnic areas. The Mexican and Central American barrios of East Los Angeles and the Mission District in San Francisco, the Adams Morgan section of Washington, D.C., and the Latin neighborhoods of Manhattan's Lower East Side, Queens, and the Bronx are cases in point. To the extent that a sizable proportion of today's immigrants arriving in these areas settles there, their descendants can be expected to exhibit the same patterns of reactive ethnicity displayed by earlier minorities.

Entrepreneurial groups also tend to be highly visible—whether concentrated in ethnic enclaves or dispersed in "middleman" shops throughout the inner city. Reactions from the surrounding population may include opposition by native whites to the "takeover" by immigrants of certain urban areas or hostility by blacks and other domestic minorities at the "exploitative" behavior of the foreigners. Koreatown in Los Angeles, the growing Chinese and Vietnamese enclaves in Orange County, and Little Havana in Miami are examples. Nativist hostility is not inevitable in such cases, but stereotypes and prejudice often flourish because of salient cultural and linguistic differences between the native population and foreign-born business owners and employees. In this situation, the self-definitions of immigrants and their views of outside society can be strongly colored by the experience of confrontation.

Professionals who pursue careers in the United States are in a different position, insofar as they tend to become dispersed away from areas of ethnic concentration. The result of this mode of incorporation is a relatively low profile vis-à-vis host communities and hence the absence of strong nativist reactions. Indian and Egyptian professionals provide typical examples insofar as their high absolute numbers have not resulted in visible ethnic communities or in a pattern of nativist mobilization directed specifically against them. In these situations, collective identity among immigrants is seldom defined by reactive ethnicity, but continues to be shaped by the cultural experiences transported from the country of origin. Ethnic identity in such instances represents a linear continuation of past experience rather than an emergent reaction to the present.

Lastly, groups that came escaping political oppression also tend to maintain strong collective identities in relative isolation from their new social environment. As noted before, concern with past experiences and political developments at home often render these groups inattentive, at least initially, to reactions in their immediate surroundings. In addition, the ideology of opposition to the home regime—anticommunism in most cases—can be a powerful source of collective solidarity, reinforcing those from a common language and culture. For this reason, refugee groups tend to retain a strong self-identification, defined more by continuity with their own past than by defensive response to events in their present environment. Eastern European and early Cuban and Vietnamese cohorts provide examples.[61]

Emergent Ethnicities

A final point concerns the possibility of future political mobilization on the basis of a larger, supranational identity. We have seen how nationalities were often forged by immigration through the common labeling and stereotyping of groups that shared only a tenuous bond before arriving in America. The consolidation of nation-states during the twentieth century preempted this function so that, by the time that the doors were reopened in 1965 for Eastern Hemisphere countries, most immigrants came with well-defined national identities. But recent years have witnessed the rise of a higher level of collective identification. Colombian immigrants certainly know that they are Colombian and Mexicans that they are Mexican; what they probably do not know when they arrive in the United States is that they belong to a larger ethnic category called Hispanics.

Colombians, Mexicans, Cubans, and other immigrant groups from Latin America are generally aware that they share common linguistic and cultural roots, but this fact seldom suffices to produce a strong overarching solidarity. National experiences are too divergent and national loyalties too deeply embedded to yield to this supranational logic. In Latin America, patriotism is often sharpened by periodic revivals of conflict with a neighboring Latin nation. Thus, Colombians and Venezuelans, Ecuadorians and Peruvians, Chileans and Argentines have traditionally reaffirmed their sense of national pride in actual or symbolic confrontations with each other. Upon arrival in the United States, they learn differently. As Sicilian peasants were informed in New York of their being "Italian," contemporary Latin American immigrants are told—in no uncertain terms—that despite their ancestral differences, they are all "Hispanic."

The experience is not an isolated one. Immigrants from the Far East, especially those with common racial features, are lumped together under the label "Asian" or "Oriental." In this instance, the gap between ethnic labeling and actual reality is even more egregious because groups so designated do not even share a common language. Even so, the labels "Asian" and "Asian-American" figure prominently as categories under which people are counted, students and workers classified, and journalistic articles written.[62]

Ethnicity has always been a socially constructed product,

forged in interaction between individual traits and contextual variables. It is therefore not impossible that these supranational identities will take hold and come eventually to define groups so labeled to others, as well as to themselves. The history of immigration certainly supports this possibility. Students of ethnic mobilization, such as Joane Nagel, have argued strongly that receiving nation-states play a crucial role in the rise of ethnicity through their defining and treating various groups differently.[63] According to them, states can actually "create" ethnic minorities by the simple expedient of acting toward arbitrarily defined aggregates *as if* their internal similarities and external differences with the majority were real.

If this view is accurate, Hispanic-Americans and Asian-Americans are well on their way toward becoming the new ethnic minorities because they are defined as single entities in numerous official publications, lumped together in affirmative action programs, counted together by the census, and addressed jointly in official rhetoric. Academic researchers and the media have contributed significantly to this process of ethnic construction through the same expedient of addressing disparate nationalities "as if" they were part of the same collectivity. To the extent that the process is successful, the ethnic mobilizations to emerge in the Latin barrios and Asian "towns" of major American cities will not be bound by the original national identities, but by the new supranational symbols initially bestowed on them from the outside.

There is impressionistic evidence that these emergent ethnicities are taking hold in certain urban areas, especially where no single nationality predominates. More important, "Hispanic" and "Asian-American" politicians and academics have come to define themselves in these terms rather than as Mexican or Cuban, Korean or Chinese. Yet this is an instance where extrapolating past experience into present reality may not do because strong internal forces countermand these emergent identities. To a certain extent, most Latin American and Asian immigrants will find acceptable a loose common label in the same manner that Germans, British, and Poles do not object to being designated "Europeans." However, the lumping of national self-identifications under a common generic label is likely to find strong resistance.

First, groups so defined are simply too diverse. Under the label "Hispanic," for example, we find individuals whose ancestors lived in the country at least since the time of independence and others who arrived last year; there are substantial numbers of professionals and entrepreneurs, along with farm laborers and unskilled workers; there are "Hispanic" whites, blacks, mulattoes, and mestizos; there are also full-fledged citizens and unauthorized aliens; finally, there are those who came in search of employment and a better economic future and those who arrived escaping political persecution at home.[64]

Second, nation-states are not peasant villages. Their power and increasing reach means they are a continuous presence in the lives of their nationals abroad, whether the latter support or oppose the home regime. For these reasons, official and unofficial efforts in the United States to mobilize groups of separate national origins under a common generic label have tended to break down.[65] "Hispanic" politics in south Florida is very different from that practiced in California; "Asian" attitudes and behavior in San Francisco's Chinatown bear little resemblance to those of similarly designated communities in New York or Washington, D.C.; Mexicans and Puerto Ricans regard events such as the dramatic Mariel exodus as a Cuban problem; similarly, Cubans perceive undocumented migration as a Mexican and Central American issue, quite removed from their concerns.

Until now, attempts to analyze political mobilization under the new ethnic labels have lapsed almost immediately into a discussion of their separate national components. So far, there is no such thing as nationwide "Hispanic" politics or "Asian" mobilization; there are instead Cuban and Mexican, Korean and Vietnamese patterns of political incorporation, as previously described. The new supranational ethnicities may be seen as a reenactment of the historical process by which national identities were created out of village loyalties at the beginning of the century. The outcome at present is, however, far from certain.

Conclusion

In *The Immigration Time Bomb: The Fragmenting of America*, former Colorado governor Richard D. Lamm complains:

> Increasingly, the political power of more than fifteen million Hispanics is being used not to support assimilation but to advance "ethnic pride" in belonging to a different culture. The multiplication of outsiders is not a model for a viable society. . . . If immigrants do not feel that they are fully part of this society, as American as everyone else, then we are failing.[66]

Throughout the history of the United States, immigrants have seldom felt "as American as everyone else" because differences of language and culture separated them from the majority and because they were made painfully aware of that fact. Being "in America, but not of it," even if they wished to, represents an important aspect of the experience of most foreign groups and a major force promoting ethnic identity in subsequent generations. The rise of ethnic pride among the children of recent arrivals is thus not surprising because it is a tale repeated countless times in the history of immigration.

The fostering of "Hispanic pride" is more doubtful because as seen, the existence of this supranational ethnicity is itself problematic. The significant aspect of Lamm's statement is the peril that it outlines and the solution that it proposes. The peril is the "fragmenting of America" by outside cultures, and the solution is rapid assimilation so that immigrants will become "as American as everyone else." As happened at the beginning of the century, immigration is portrayed as somehow un-American; but whereas before the alleged sins were political radicalism or its opposite, political docility, at present they consist of excessive cultural diversity.

Assimilation has seldom taken place in the way recommended by the new nativists. Instead, the reaffirmation of distinct cultural identities—whether actual or invented in the United States—has been the rule among foreign groups and has represented the first effective step in their social and political incorporation. Ethnic solidarity has provided the basis for the pursuit of common goals through the American political system: By mobilizing the collective vote and by electing their own to office, immigrant minorities have learned the rules of the democratic game and absorbed its values in the process.

Assimilation as the rapid transformation of immigrants into residents "as American as everyone else" has never happened. Instead, the definition of the foreign born by their nationality rather than by their class position has meant that the first steps of political apprenticeship consisted of reaffirming symbolically the same national characteristics and organizing along the lines that they demarcated. Italians voted en bloc for Italian candidates in Boston and New York, just as Mexicans do for their own in Los Angeles and San Antonio today.[67] Socialization into American political institutions has taken place through this process. Before Irish, Italian, or Greek politicians entered the mainstream as interpreters of national values and aspirations, their predecessors spent much time in ward politics fighting for their own group's interests.

Ethnic resilience has been the rule among immigrants, old and new, and represents simultaneously a central part of their process of political incorporation. Today, "hispanicity" in the Southwest is a synonym of Mexican-American cultural reaffirmation, a latter-day manifestation of a familiar process. Hence the perils that so much alarm the new patriots are likely to be as imaginary as those that agitated their forebears. The vain search for political radicals in immigrant neighborhoods, described at the beginning of this chapter, finds its present counterpart in the vigorous efforts to eradicate immigrant linguistic diversity through constitutional reform.

Back in the early 1900s, the United States was receiving two to four times the present number of immigrants per year; foreigners represented up to 21 percent of the American labor force and close to half of the urban population; groups like the Germans had succeeded in literally transplanting their nations into America. The country was certainly far more "fragmented" then than now. What held it together then and continues to do so today is not forced cultural homogeneity, but the strength of its political institutions and the durable framework that they offered for the process of ethnic reaffirmation and mobilization to play itself out. Defense of their own particular interests—defined along ethnic lines—was the school in which many immigrants and their descendants learned to identify with the interests of the nation as a whole. With different actors and in new languages, the process continues today.

First Chinese New Year parade held in Monterey Park, California ("the first suburban Chinatown"). Since the 1970s, a large Asian-American enclave has developed in the suburban San Gabriel Valley of Los Angeles, illustrative of a general trend of immigrants settling in suburban, middle-class communities rather than the inner-city locales that have long been associated with immigrant settlements in American urban history. (Photograph by Steve Gold)

Philippine-American Club of Greater Lansing on parade, Lansing, Michigan. Over the past thirty years, only Mexico has sent more immigrants to the United States than the Philippines. (Photograph by Steve Gold)

Indochinese refugees at the Phanat Nikhom refugee camp, Thailand, saying good-bye to family and friends on "the bus to America," leaving for a refugee processing center before coming to the United States. They may never see each other again. (Photograph by Erica Hagen)

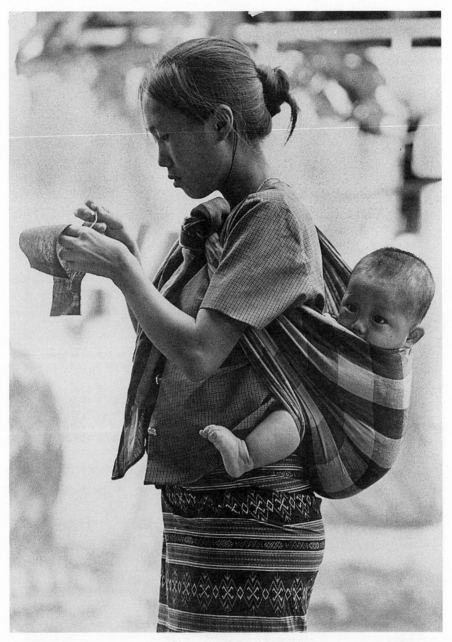

Hmong refugee woman carries her son while doing her needlework. Her husband is a refugee resettlement worker for Catholic Community Services in San Diego. Over one million refugees from Laos, Cambodia, and Vietnam have been resettled in the United States since 1975. (Photograph by Erica Hagen)

Welcoming the newcomers: Soviet Jews in Chabad program, Los Angeles.
(Photograph by Steve Gold)

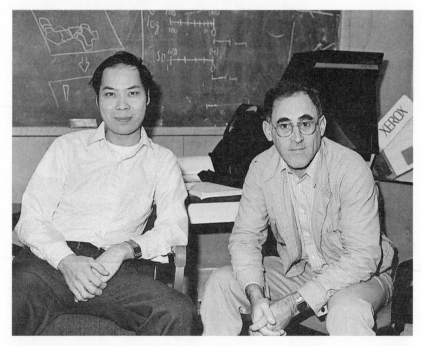

Immigrant computer programmers from Hong Kong and Leningrad at the
University of California, Berkeley. Labeled "brain drain" in the countries of
origin, the immigration of highly trained personnel represents a significant
gain for the United States. (Photograph by Steve Gold)

Trinidadian barber shop, Boston, Massachusetts. (Photograph by Steve Gold)

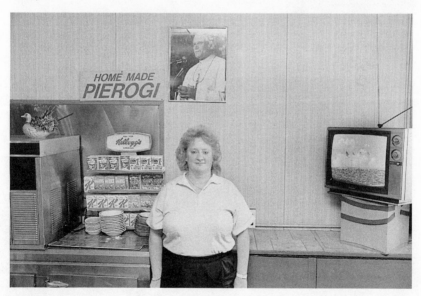

Polish restaurant, Dearborn, Michigan. (Photograph by Steve Gold)

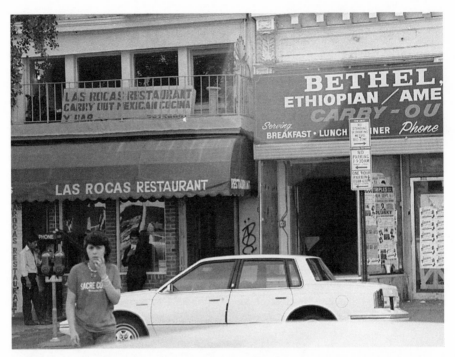

A Mexican restaurant and an Ethiopian restaurant share a wall in Washington, D.C. (Photograph by Luis E. Rumbaut)

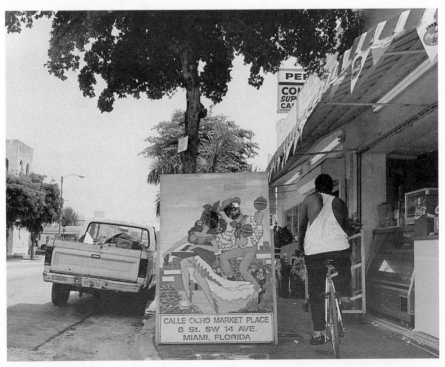

Calle Ocho, Miami, Florida, in the heart of Little Havana. (Photograph by Steve Gold)

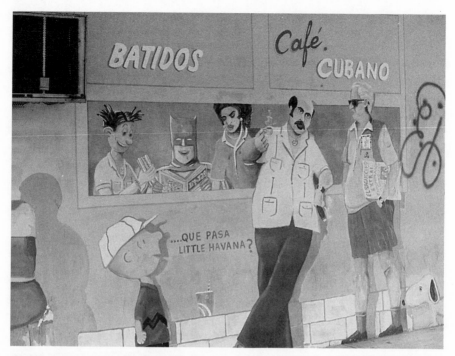

Even Charlie Brown speaks Spanish in Little Havana, Miami, site of the world's largest Cuban community outside Havana itself. (Photograph by Estela R. García)

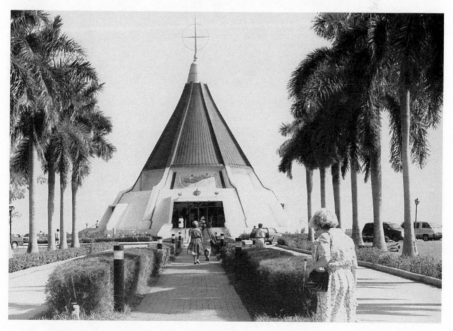

La Ermita de la Caridad: Catholic church built by Cuban immigrants along Biscayne Bay, Miami. The main entrance faces south toward Cuba. (Photograph by Estela R. García)

Vietnamese Catholics celebrate the Feast of the Immaculate Conception, St. Mary's Church, Whittier, California. (Photograph by Steve Gold)

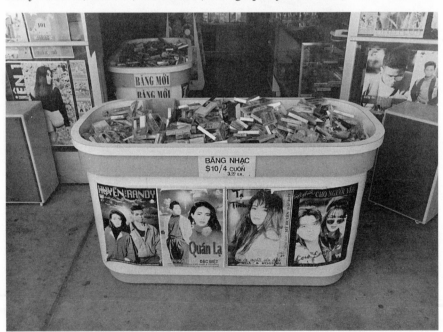

Popular Vietnamese music tapes for sale in Little Saigon, Westminster, Orange County, California. (Photograph by Steve Gold)

During the annual Tet celebration in Little Saigon, an American beer company offers wishes in Vietnamese for "a new year of happiness and success." (Photograph by Steve Gold)

Vietnamese New Year (Tet) celebration, Orange County, California. (Photograph by Steve Gold)

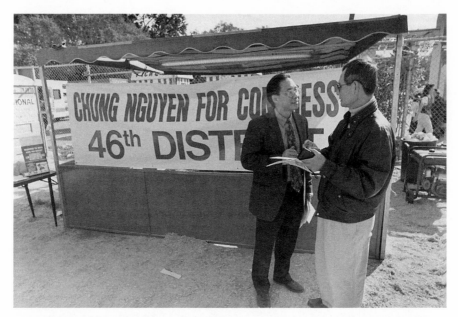

First steps in political incorporation: a Vietnamese immigrant runs for Congress in a heavily Vietnamese district in Orange County, California. (Photograph by Steve Gold)

Vermont Avenue in Koreatown, Los Angeles. Over two thousand Korean immigrant shops such as these were burned in the riots of 1992. (Photograph by Steve Gold)

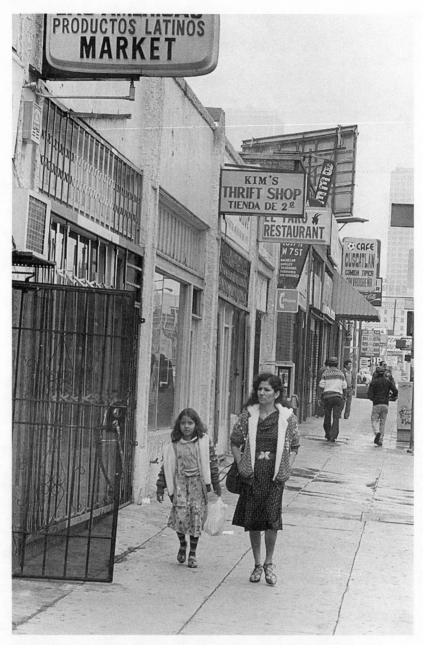

Pico Union area of Los Angeles, home of a major settlement of Central American immigrants, mostly from El Salvador. (Photograph by Steve Gold)

View of Cañón Zapata in Tijuana on the U.S.-Mexican border. Each year during the peak summer months over a thousand undocumented immigrants crossed nightly into the United States from this point. The number of border crossers would fall to a low of about two hundred a day during November and December. The same patterns were observed for many years. (Photograph by Steve Gold)

Mexican migrant farm laborers in northern San Diego County pile on a flatbed truck for a short ride back to camp at the end of a workday. For employers they are a source of abundant and inexpensive labor. For the migrants themselves, the work is a means of survival and a vehicle of economic mobility. (Photographed by Michael Franklin, *The San Diego Union*)

Cramped quarters for migrant workers, these crude cavelike shelters are dug into hillsides and covered with cardboard and chaparral in canyons near farms where migrants seek work. The plastic jugs are used to bring water to the site. A typical shelter sleeps three men for eight months of the year. (Photograph by Michael Franklin, *The San Diego Union*)

Two migrant workers pick tomatoes side by side in a field north of San Diego just as they do in their village in Oaxaca, Mexico. Each year they make the 2,000-mile journey to work in these fields. Growers say the Oaxacans have a gentle way of picking that avoids bruising the fruit. (Photograph by Michael Franklin)

Chabad (Hassidic) day camp for Soviet Jews, West Hollywood, California.
(Photograph by Steve Gold)

Haitian cabbie, Miami Beach. Most Haitian
immigrants in the United States have settled in
two metropolitan areas, New York and Miami.
(Photograph by Steve Gold)

5

A Foreign World

Immigration, Mental Health, and Acculturation

In our old country, whatever we had was made or brought in by our own hands; we never had any doubts that we would not have enough for our mouth. But from now on to the future, that time is over. We are so afraid and worried that there will be one day when we will not have anything for eating or paying the rent, and these days these things are always in our minds. Some nights the sleep hardly comes to me at all. . . . So you see, when you think all of these over, you don't want to live anymore. . . . Talking about this, I want to die right here so I won't see my future. . . . Don't know how to read or write, don't know how to speak the language. My life is only to live day by day until the last day I live, and maybe that is the time when my problems will be solved.

I used to be a real man like any other, but not now any longer. Things I used to do, now I can't do here. I feel like a thing which they say drops in the fire but won't burn and drops in the river but won't flow. So I feel like I have no goal, nothing in the future. . . . We only live day by day, just like the baby birds who are only staying in the nest opening their mouths and waiting for the mother bird to bring the worms. Because we are now like those baby birds who cannot fly yet.

These words could well have been spoken by turn-of-the-century immigrants whose harsh experiences in America were portrayed by William I. Thomas and Florian Znaniecki in *The Polish Peasant in Europe and America* and later by Oscar Handlin in *The Uprooted*.[1] But they are the words of two middle-aged Hmong refugees from Laos—illiterate and of peasant origins—reflecting on their situation in one of the largest cities in the United States. They arrived on the West Coast with their families in 1980, after spending five years in refugee camps in Thailand. The Hmong are a sizable group among the more than one million Southeast Asian refugees resettled in the United States since the end of the Indochina War. To be sure, the economic situation of these refugees is dismal, especially in comparison to the successful experiences of other recent immigrants. Still, their emotional response to circumstances in a foreign world, as illustrated in the opening quotes, underscores the need to take seriously and to understand the *subjective* experience of immigration.

It is commonplace in the literature on migration, mental health, and mental disorder to observe that long-distance journeys entail a set of engulfing life events (losses, changes, conflicts, and demands) that, although varying widely in kind and degree, severely tests the immigrant's emotional resilience. Migration can produce profound psychological distress, even among the best prepared and most motivated and even under the most receptive of circumstances. It is not coincidental that the words *travel* and *travail* share an etymology.[2] But some investigators have remarked on the positive drive and the sense of efficacy and "hardiness" certain groups of immigrants exhibit and on how their victory over adversity promotes increasing self-confidence.[3] Thus, the study of the immigrant experience offers fertile ground to address not merely the "pathogenic" (what makes people ill) but also the "salutogenic" (what keeps people healthy) responses of individuals to conditions of personal crisis.[4] Yet the subjective experience of immigration is an area that, compared to the more objective dimensions of the process examined in prior chapters, has been more difficult to study systematically and comparatively.

Although Thomas and Znaniecki and Handlin would have found the words of our two Hmong informants uncannily familiar, even to these peasant immigrants' almost identical use of agrarian similes to describe their situations, they would have been surprised by the diversity of recent immigrants to the United States. These authors sought, after all, to depict and document not socioeconomic diversity, but the unitary theme of adjustment to crisis that they saw underlying the subjective experience of immigration. Thus, Thomas and Znaniecki focused on the "social disorganization" and the struggle for self-esteem of mostly single, young male laborers from Russian Poland who immigrated to the United States between 1880 and 1910, rather than on immigrants from Austrian or Prussian Poland, who tended to come in entire families.[5] And Handlin, while recognizing that there were differences between the Irish and the Germans and the Poles, nonetheless focused on the common stress of "uprooting" and "arduous transplantation" that constituted the "universality of the migration experience." Thus, his history of immigration became a history of alienation and its consequences:

> The immigrants lived in crisis because they were uprooted. In transplantation, while the old roots were sundered, before the new were established, the immigrants existed in an extreme situation. The shock, and the effects of the shock, persisted for many years. . . . Their most passionate desires were doomed to failure; their lives were those of the feeble little birds which hawks attack, which lose strength from want of food. . . . Sadness was the tone of life. . . . The end of life was an end to hopeless striving, to ceaseless pain, and to the endless succession of disappointment.[6]

The themes of alienation and loneliness permeated the sociological literature on the immigrant experience in America prior to World War I. Although, as with other generalizations, the theme was probably exaggerated, there is no doubt that it reflected an underlying reality. Perhaps more than today, the lot of most turn-of-the-century immigrants was a harsh one, resembling that of our contemporary Hmong refugees more than that of luckier Asian professionals or Caribbean entrepreneurs. Because so much of our understanding of the world of immigrants is molded by ideas and concepts coined during that earlier period, it is important to probe further into it as a prelude to examining subjective aspects of immigration today.

Marginality and Freedom

A step ahead of the stories of unmitigated woe that composed the standard fare of the earlier immigration literature was the concept of marginality. In his essay "Human Migration and the Marginal Man," published in 1928, Robert Park portrayed the immigrant as a personality type, a hybrid on the margin of two worlds. He was a stranger fully belonging to neither, in whose mind colliding cultures met and fused. Although highly stressful, the situation had its positive aspects. Most important among them was the liberation of the person from the shackles of tradition and the expansion of individual initiative: "Energies that were formerly controlled by custom are released. . . . [Immigrants] become in the process not merely emancipated but enlightened. The emancipated individual becomes in a certain sense and to a certain degree a cosmopolitan. . . . The effect of migration is to secularize relations which were formerly sacred."[7]

To be sure, the experience of transition and crisis also confronts the "marginal man" with such characteristics as inner turmoil, instability, restlessness, and malaise. This counterpoint between newly found enlightenment and the stresses associated with it was to permeate analyses of the phenomenology of immigration for years to come. One of Park's disciples, Everett Stonequist, developed in ample detail the theme of a liberating but contradictory social location. Resorting to French, he labeled immigrants both *déclassé* and *déraciné* (uprooted), a term that was to become standard in the literature on the migration experience:

The conflict of cultures working in the immigrant's mind is more intricate and profound than that expressed by the concept of the *déclassé*. The idea of the "uprooted" comes nearer to the heart of the problem. The individual undergoes transformation in the social, mental, and emotional aspects of his personality, each reacting upon the other. Some immigrants speak of these changes as constituting a second birth or childhood.[8]

The same author observed that the immigrant's response to his condition of marginality could vary widely, from amusement to despair, from stimulation to depression. At a minimum, however, it entailed a subtle, perhaps indefinable sense of estrangement and malaise.[9] The empirical literature of the time reflected the same theme, but gave greater credence to the stressful aspects of marginality. On the whole, immigrants were able to cope, and some may have found removal from their tradition-bound birthplaces exhilarating; but many were not making it, as reflected in that most compelling indicator of distress: suicide.

In 1930, the suicide rate among the foreign born in Chicago was 38.8 per 100,000, compared to less than one-third that figure (12.4) for the native born, and the suicide rate for each immigrant group in the United States was found to be two to three times higher than for the same nationality in Europe.[10] Along the same lines, an ecological study of psychopathology in Chicago found that cases of mental disorder showed a regular decrease from the center to the periphery of the city and that rates of schizophrenia and alcoholic psychoses were highest in the neighborhoods of first immigrant settlement with a high proportion of foreign-born residents.[11]

Early Psychopathology:
The Eugenics Approach to Mental Illness

The association between immigration and mental disturbances was consistently supported by early epidemiological studies, based on rates of hospital admission. Sociologists such as Park,

Thomas and Znaniecki, and Stonequist had focused on the whole of the immigrant population or at least on an entire national inflow. For these authors, the higher incidence of mental disturbances among the foreign born was evidence of the trauma of settlement and marginality, but such outcomes were regarded as exceptional.

Psychiatrists and clinical epidemiologists dealing with an inmate population had a different vision of the problem. In many localities, foreigners made up the bulk of the patient population institutionalized in mental asylums, and this situation encouraged quite a different set of explanations. The first epidemiological study of psychopathology and immigration in the United States was done by Edward Jarvis in 1855. He began by noting the rapid increase in the foreign population of Massachusetts: from an estimated 9,620 in 1830, to 34,818 in 1840, to 230,000 by 1854. But the proportion of lunatics among immigrants was notably larger: Although the insane represented 1 in 445 in the native population, they amounted to 1 in 368 among aliens in the state.[12] Jarvis framed the question of causation in terms that were to become standard in subsequent debates among scientists and policymakers alike: "[E]ither our foreign population is more prone to insanity or their habits and trials, their experiences and privations . . . are more unfavorable to their mental health than to that of the natives."[13]

With considerable analytic acumen, Jarvis noted that 93 percent of foreign lunatics in Massachusetts asylums were paupers and that, while only one in sixty-six of the whole native population was in this bottom social category, among the aliens they represented one in twenty-five. Thus, he reasoned, "most of the foreigners are poor . . . and they must, therefore, have a larger proportion of lunatics to their whole number than the Americans."[14] Further, he speculated on the consequences of stressful life events. Prefiguring by decades the sociological analysis of marginality, he observed how "being in a strange land and among strange men and things," immigrants frequently endeavored to accomplish impractical goals, meeting with repeated and harrowing disappointment and defeat.[15]

This emphasis on the importance of class and context was unfortunately set aside subsequently in favor of more simplistic explanations. A growing interest in migration and mental illness reflected underlying policy concerns over the public cost of caring for dependent populations and deeper nativist fears about the impact of increased immigration on American society. As the inflow grew rapidly in the mid-nineteenth century, the foreign born increasingly made up the inmate population of lunatic asylums as well as of poorhouses, penitentiaries, "houses of refuge" for neglected children, and reformatories. In New York, Massachusetts, Ohio, Minnesota, and Wisconsin, anywhere from half to three-quarters of the inmates in lunatic asylums were immigrants, and similar rates were reported in other custodial institutions.[16]

By the early twentieth century, these concerns had fused with those about European immigrant radicalism to become the basis of xenophobic arguments against continuing immigration. Racist theories were given a major impetus by the new vogue of Social Darwinism, Mendelian genetics, and the new "science" of eugenics. Advocates of these views raised alarm over the defective biological "stock" of immigrants, adding to the outcries for restriction stemming from the political right.[17] This was the time in which scientific experts wrote about the "remarkable tendency to suicide" among the Japanese in California, "the strong tendency to delusional trends of a persecutory nature" in West Indian Negroes, the frequency of "hidden sexual complexes" among the Hebrews, and "the remarkable prevalence of mutism" among Poles.[18] Hospital superintendents and other officials, blaming the "tremendous increase in mental diseases and defects" on immigrants, declared that states were expending "millions of dollars annually for the care and maintenance of an alien population which should have been excluded by the federal government."[19]

While such campaigns were raging in the media and in public life, researchers were discovering the significance of age in the explanation of differences in rates of mental illness between foreigners and the native born. Rates of mental disorder vary directly with age, increasing from adolescence to old age. Compared to the native population, there were few children among newly arrived immigrants. Thus, when age-specific rates of mental hospital admission were calculated, the result was to reduce considerably the disproportionately high levels of disorders observed among the foreign born.[20] A second variable of interest uncovered during the period was the relative spatial distribution of both populations. It turned out that the foreign born were disproportionately concentrated in northeastern states, where hospitalization of the mentally ill was much more likely to occur, rather than in southeastern states, where native whites predominated but hospitalization was much less common. Hence, immigrants were more likely to be "counted" in epidemiological studies based exclusively on rates of hospital admission.[21]

These healthy cautions on the interpretation of mental disorder differentials between immigrants and natives evaporated, however, in the heat of political agitation for restriction. The most influential arguments, buttressed by the now prevailing eugenics ideology, brushed aside empirical findings to focus on the gross differences in disturbance rates between native and foreign born. Typical in this regard was the role of Dr. Harry Laughlin, appointed as the "expert eugenics agent" to the House Committee on Immigration and Naturalization.[22] Laughlin's testimony to the committee in 1922 concluded, "In the United States, the foreign-born show an incidence of insanity in the State and Federal hospitals 2.85 times higher than that shown by the whole population, which latter are descended largely from older American stock."[23]

Laughlin did not make any allowances for the roles of socioeconomic status, age differences, or spatial distribution, dismissing such considerations as "special pleading for the alien."[24] The tide was clearly in favor of such explanations, and they were to lead to passage of the most restrictive immigration legislation in the history of the nation. The National Origins Act of 1924 not only effectively barred further entries from most countries, but did so on the basis of explicitly racial considerations. Asians and southeastern Europeans were the groups most heavily penalized by the new law.[25]

The sharp reduction of immigration after passage of the 1924 act was followed by a corresponding decline in the polemics about mental health and the foreign born. Still, predominant scholarly views about the psychology of immigration continued to focus on unique traits imputed to certain nationalities or to the migrant contingent among them. Thus, a detailed analysis of the mental health of Norwegian immigrants in Minnesota from 1889 to 1929 found that it was significantly worse than among both the native population of that state and the nonimmigrant population of Norway. Upon finding that returnees to Norway exhibited "even more insanity" than was found among settled immigrants in Minnesota, the author—a highly respected psychiatric epidemiologist—concluded that there was something pathological about the immigrant personality:

> If the life situation of the immigrants were the main reason for their high ratio of insanity, we might expect to find a lower ratio among those who "save themselves" and go back to their native country. . . . But instead we find that it is probably even higher. This speaks definitely in favor of the theory that the high incidence of mental diseases in the immigrant population is due to a prevalence of certain psychopathic tendencies in the constitution of those who emigrate.[26]

Alternative explanations, such as the experience of objective failure in the adopted country and the trauma of return after such failure, did not enter at all into these conclusions.

Up to World War II, analyses of the subjective world of immigrants thus featured a peculiar bifurcation. On the one hand, a growing research literature suggested that it was not intrinsic characteristics of the immigrants, but rather such objective variables as poverty, age distribution, and spatial concentration that accounted for differential rates in mental disorders. On the other hand, public discourse—including that of most scientific experts—rejected such findings to emphasize, again and again, the inferior psychological makeup of immigrants, especially those of Asian and southeastern European stock. Sociological analyses of the traumas of adaptation and the complex situation of marginality were also swept aside in the enthusiasm to depict the immigrant as an intrinsically pathological figure. That such beliefs were of more than passing consequence is shown by their enactment into law. The National Origins Act of 1924 was to have major consequences for the composition of the American population for decades to come and to pattern the growth of its foreign-born component along explicitly racial lines.

From Nationality to Class and Context: The Changed Etiology of Mental Illness

During and after World War II, vast new international population movements brought renewed interest in the social and psychological consequences of emigration, particularly of *forced* emigration. Massive numbers of "displaced persons" in Europe and elsewhere, and the traumatic conditions of their expatriation, led to the formal recognition of "refugees" as a special category of migrant by the United Nations and, beginning with the Displaced Persons Act of 1948, by the United States.[27] The plight of the refugees contributed in no small measure to a momentous change in the public and academic understanding of the subjective world of immigrants. The period saw a significant shift of theoretical interest away from "selection" factors and toward a new emphasis on the effect of environmental stressors and other objective social conditions.

Apart from the vivid experience of the refugees, World War II also contributed to this conceptual shift through repeated clinical observations of "combat stress" among soldiers who had been previously screened for mental disorders. Impairment scales developed during the war permitted analyses of a more complex array of depression and anxiety reactions that went well beyond earlier gross classifications of psychiatric disorders.[28] Clearly, the fact that such impairments affected "American boys" at the front could not be attributed to their intrinsic psychological inferiority, and the new emphasis on environmental stressors was carried to other settings—including those where the foreign born concentrated.

Beginning in the 1950s, large-scale community surveys based on probability samples of the general population became common, providing a methodological tool superior to earlier studies based on rates of hospital admissions. For the first time, it became possible to obtain psychiatric profiles of various segments of the population unbiased by such factors as the differential availability of hospital care or of knowledge about it. The new methodology was not without its problems, including the difficulty of measuring various types of mental disturbances in "natural" settings.[29] However, it had a definitely greater scope and representativeness than the earlier hospitalization approach. Community surveys moved gradually away from the notion of innate psychological shortcomings to focus on contextual and objective factors, particularly on the role of socioeconomic differences in mental health and mental disorders.

The study by Hollingshead and Redlich, conducted during the 1950s, was among the most influential in establishing a causal link between social class and mental illness. A decade later a survey of the research literature reviewed forty-four major studies that confirmed the role of social class as a major predictor of psychological disturbances. Other related research found that the sheer number of reported "life stress" factors most efficiently accounted for mental health risk, but that when life stresses were held constant, the risk was highest among those of lowest socioeconomic status.[30]

Community surveys also established a series of robust findings concerning psychological distress and associated disturbances that could be summarized in four basic patterns: the higher the socioeconomic status, the lower the distress; women were more distressed than men; unmarried people were more distressed than married people; and the greater the number of undesirable life events, the greater the distress.[31] These results can be subsumed theoretically under the more general concepts of powerlessness and alienation. Inability to reach one's goals in life and powerlessness to control or affect events—more common among lower-class people, women, and the less socially established—result in greater levels of distress and associated mental disorder. Although most research of the period was not concerned directly with immigration, its implications were obvious: The marginal position of immigrants is one of powerlessness and alienation; like other subordinate groups, they would be expected to exhibit higher rates of psychopathogenic symptoms.

This prediction was tested directly in a large New York City study conducted during the late 1950s and dubbed the Midtown Manhattan Project. Sociologist Leo Srole and his associates divided their large sample by immigrant generation—from the foreign born to native Americans of native parentage. They found that immigrants had the expected higher prevalence of distress symptoms, but that the difference disappeared when controlling for age and social class.[32] Most of the foreign born in this sample had arrived after the restrictive 1924 legislation and were thus a highly selected group who had managed to overcome the "formidable screen" of visa requirements prior to entry. Among this group, mental health impairment was infrequent (18.5 percent) and significantly lower than among pre-1920 arrivals. Over a third of the latter (34.3 percent), a group formed primarily by immigrants of European peasant origin, exhibited significant symptoms of mental pathology. The authors concluded:

> What is decisive among immigrants is *not* transplantation to the American metropolis per se, but resettlement in the American metropolis from a *particular kind* of overseas milieu, namely from the low socioeconomic strata in farm, village, or town. . . . To compress the profound historical changes of a revolutionizing century into a few

adult years of an individual life cycle may exact a high price in psychological well-being.[33]

Srole and his associates reached a synthesis of the plausible but until then disjointed themes that had emerged as an alternative to earlier theories of intrinsic racial/cultural differences. Social class and social context were such themes emphasized, respectively, by empirical community surveys and by theoretical elaborations on the earlier concept of marginality. The Midtown Manhattan Project brought both themes together by noting that the trauma of resettlement and marginality was not experienced equally by all immigrants. It was the *social distance* traveled from place of origin to place of destination that accounted for the magnitude of the shock and the ability to cope with it. For immigrants of urban origin, higher education, and middle-class backgrounds, that distance was less; hence, the difficulties of adaptation—of accomplishing their "sociopsychological vault from one place to the other"—became more manageable. Conversely, a greater sense of powerlessness and alienation was the lot of immigrants of lower status, and with it came the familiar psychopathologies associated with the foreign born.

The postwar years thus witnessed a remarkable turnaround both in the objective situation of the foreign born and in the public and academic perceptions of it. The 1924 act reduced immigration to a trickle of highly selected individuals and, modified by later legislation after World War II, to contingents of displaced persons who met with considerable public sympathy. With fears of a foreign invasion left behind, research could proceed in a calmer social environment and communicate its results more effectively. The psychological status of immigrants thus ceased to be a uniquely pathogenic condition and became essentially one more manifestation of a general syndrome affecting other relatively powerless segments of the population. Class of origin and context of reception emerged as the key factors molding the content, challenges, and resilience of the immigrants' world.

Immigrants and Refugees: Contemporary Trends

The contemporary period has seen a rapid diversification in types of immigration and contexts of reception, as seen in prior chapters. This diversity is reflected in the psychological response evident among different categories of immigrants and in their perceptions of American society. Class of origin remains as important as ever in explaining subjective well-being and adaptation, but the diversity of current flows has shifted the locus of the context with which class backgrounds are expected to interact. In Srole's time and earlier, the *context of reception* posed the challenge for newcomers; today the *context of exit* has become equally if not more important. The distinction in chapter 1 between immigrants and refugees becomes crucial at this point because the latter category has emerged as a subject of increasing concern.

Typically, the distinction hinges on the notion of refugees as involuntary and relatively unprepared migrants "pushed out" by coercive political conditions or by an "exposure to disaster," *versus* immigrants as voluntary and better prepared movers "pulled in" by perceived opportunities for economic advancement or family reunification.[34] The distinction is actually more elusive than this definition suggests. So-called voluntary migrations are not always as voluntary and planned as described, and there are wide differences in the degree of urgency, suddenness, and "acute flight" experiences of different refugee groups. In addition, as seen in chapter 1, "refugee" is not a self-assigned label, but one assigned by the host government. Thus, two groups subject to similar conditions of stressful flight may be defined differently on arrival, one granted the status of bona fide "political" refugees and the other labeled clandestine "economic" immigrants. Differential labeling by the U.S. government has marked, for example, the divergent official receptions and subsequent adaptation experiences of Southeast Asian boat people, on the one hand, and Central American escapees, on the other.[35]

Nor is it true that "refugees" did not exist before the contemporary period. What did not exist in earlier times was the appropriate term of reference to identify this situation. Turn-of-the-century "immigrants" such as Russian Jews escaping czarist persecution and pogroms probably experienced conditions of exit as traumatic as many present-day refugees. The advent of the term has finally brought attention to different contexts of expulsion and thus introduced an important new variable in our understanding of immigrant mental health, absent from earlier analyses. Thus, the recent research literature has suggested that several features of stressful life events that accompany immigration are associated with subjective distress: Although both refugees and immigrants must cope with a significant amount of life change, "refugees" appear to experience more threat, more undesirable change, and less control over the events that define their context of exit.

A study of "acculturative stress" among ethnic minorities in Canada found, for example, that highest scores were exhibited by Vietnamese refugees, as compared both with Korean immigrants and domestic minorities. Korean immigrants had a psychological profile that was actually quite close to that of the Canadian native-born population. As in other studies in the United States, higher stress was found among females, the elderly, those unable to speak English, the uneducated, and the unemployed. Social support variables—as in the case of newcomers who had sponsors and close co-ethnic friends—reduced the experience of stress. These objective variables accounted for most, but not all, the differences between refugees and other ethnic minorities.[36]

More poignant evidence supporting the significance of contexts of exit comes from comparisons between Asian immigrants and Indochinese refugees in California. A recent study in Santa Clara County ("Silicon Valley") compared large samples of Chinese immigrants with Vietnamese, Cambodian, and ethnic Chinese refugees from Southeast Asia along various dimensions of mental health need. As with Koreans in Canada, Chinese immigrants in California exhibited an enviable psychological profile, including much lower indicators of distress than the native-born population. All refugee groups scored worse, but there were vast differences in their mental health profiles. First-wave Vietnamese refugees approximated the levels of need of the general population, followed in order of distress by the ethnic Chinese, recently arrived Vietnamese "boat people," and Cambodians.[37]

Some of these differences were clearly attributable to the effect of social class because the rank order of groups along this variable is identical to that of mental health need: Chinese immigrants had by far the highest levels of education, professional training, and income; Cambodians had the lowest. Still, these and other controls do not entirely account for effects attributable to contexts of exit. Cambodians, in particular, had extraordinarily high levels of distress and dysfunction, with fully three-fourths of the sample requiring some form of mental health assistance. Post-traumatic stress disorders, including recurrent nightmares, intrusive "flashbacks" of traumatic experiences, depression, and "numbing," were far more common among this refugee minority than in almost any other group for which reliable data are available. This situation corresponds to the depth and intensity of the respective flight experiences. The same study reported an analysis of questions pertaining to contexts of exit that clearly differentiated the Cambodians from other refugee groups along variables reflecting extreme danger and privation, including the death or disappearance of friends and kin.[38]

Similar symptoms of "post-traumatic stress disorder" have been reported among recent Salvadorans and Guatemalans who came to the United States escaping civil war conditions in their respective countries. Although not recognized as refugees by the U.S. government, many Central Americans have endured experiences prior to departure as traumatic as those reported by other officially sanctioned refugee groups.[39]

Final evidence that escapees from war-torn contexts constitute a distinct class of immigrants from the point of view of psychological well-being and subjective outlook comes from another study of Indochinese refugees in the San Diego metropolitan area. Depressive symptoms among the various Indochinese nationalities were found to be socially patterned, confirming findings from prior research. Significantly higher depression levels were found, for example, among women, respondents over fifty years of age, persons of rural background, the least educated and English proficient, and the unemployed. Lower depression levels were found for those who were married and who had more relatives and friends nearby, underscoring the buffering effects of co-ethnic social support. However, when all variables were combined in a predictive analysis of depression, reported experiences prior to and during escape emerged as the most powerful predictor. The stressful events that defined the contexts of exit of these refugee groups are summarized in table 18. The study concludes that people of the same social class emerged from the experience of flight in very different mental conditions, depending on what they had to witness and endure.[40]

Contexts of exit account, to a large extent, for the considerable differences in depression found among the various groups in the study: highest for Cambodians and Hmong and lowest for ethnic Chinese and first-wave Vietnamese arrivals. Table 19 presents the distribution of depressive symptoms (demoralization) for these refugee samples in 1983 and again in 1984, broken down by gender and education. Aside from national differences, it is worth noting that the level of demoralization, as measured by a widely used screening measure (the General Well-Being Scale) is much higher among the Indochinese as a whole than among the general American population.[41] Although 26 percent of Americans report such symptoms, the rate was three times higher (78 percent) for the Indochinese in 1983. A year later there was noticeable psychological improvement for the refugees overall, especially among men and the better educated, but their rate was still high (66 percent). In

Table 18

Contexts of Exit: Stressful Life Events in the Post-1975 Migration of Indochinese Refugees Resettled in San Diego County

Event	Hmong (N = 109) %	Cambodian (N = 120) %	Chinese (N = 114) %	Vietnamese (N = 157) %	Total (N = 500) %
Reported death of family members	59.6	65.8	32.5	39.5	48.6
Family member in prison in homeland	11.9	5.5	13.6	42.0	20.2
Fled alone, without immediate family	19.3	29.2	11.4	13.4	18.0
Gave bribes to exit	21.3	19.3	71.7	32.7	35.9
Assaulted in escape	25.7	25.2	36.8	30.6	29.6
Feared would be killed during escape	92.7	80.7	73.7	73.2	79.4
Spent over 2 years in refugee camps	72.6	75.9	29.3	22.1	47.7
Cannot communicate with family left behind (unknown whereabouts)	18.4	76.3	16.1	41.0	26.5

SOURCES: Rubén G. Rumbaut, "Mental Health and the Refugee Experience," in Southeast Asian Mental Health, ed. T. C. Owan (Rockville, Md.: National Institute of Mental Health, 1985), table 1; and Rubén G. Rumbaut, "Portraits, Patterns, and Predictors of the Refugee Adaptation Process," in Refugees as Immigrants: Cambodians, Laotians, and Vietnamese in the United States, ed. D. Haines (Totowa, N.J.: Rowman & Littlefield, 1989), table 2.

NOTE: With the exception of the bottom row, which refers to personal situation in 1984, events reported took place after April 1975 and prior to arrival in the United States.

Table 19

Prevalence of Demoralization Among Indochinese Refugees in San Diego County,
by Ethnic Group, Gender, and Level of Education

| | Year | % Demoralization | | | | |
		Hmong (N = 109)	Cambodian (N = 120)	Chinese (N = 114)	Vietnamese (N = 157)	Total (N = 500)
Gender						
Male	1983	84.0	89.7	58.2	70.6	75.0
	1984	63.3	77.6	60.0	38.8	57.5
Female	1983	89.8	85.2	75.9	73.2	80.7
	1984	65.5	91.9	77.6	62.0	73.9
Education						
0–5 years	1983	89.2	84.9	64.3	70.6	81.0
	1984	69.6	89.2	78.0	70.6	77.2
6–11 years	1983	75.0	90.0	69.4	61.2	71.5
	1984	33.3	83.3	72.0	42.9	60.4
12+ years	1983	—	93.8	68.2	79.5	79.3
	1984	—	68.8	45.5	43.8	47.7
Total	1983	87.2	87.4	67.3	71.8	77.9
	1984	64.5	85.0	69.0	49.4	65.7

SOURCES: Rubén G. Rumbaut, "Mental Health and the Refugee Experience," in *Southeast Asian Mental Health*, ed. T. C. Owan (Rockville, Md.: National Institute of Mental Health, 1985), table 6; and Rubén G. Rumbaut, "Portraits, Patterns, and Predictors of the Refugee Adaptation Process," in *Refugees as Immigrants: Cambodians, Laotians, and Vietnamese in the United States*, ed. D. Haines (Totowa, N.J.: Rowman & Littlefield, 1989), table 7.

1983, the most educated refugees actually showed higher levels of demoralization than all but those with no education at all, suggesting the psychological impact of status loss. However, by 1984, the best-educated group had made a remarkable turnaround, with the data showing the same linear relationship between psychological well-being and education found in earlier research on social class and mental illness.[42]

What is the influence of time on the mental outlook of immigrants subject to traumatic departure experiences? The same San Diego study, which followed Indochinese refugees over a twelve-month period, found that effects of such past experiences tend to decline while those associated with their present condition become increasingly important. In other words, contexts of exit gradually lose significance as contexts of reception gain salience. However, the relationship between time and mental health is, more accurately, curvilinear. The first year in the United States is a relatively euphoric period, and the lowest depression scores and highest levels of well-being are usually reported during this time. By contrast, depression and demoralization hit their highest levels during the second year, a period that may be identified as one of "exile shock." After the third year, a process of psychological rebounding seems to take place, as indicated by a significant decrease in depressive symptomatology for refugees who have been in the country for over thirty-six months.[43]

This U-shaped temporal patterning—from elation to depression to recovery—has been observed in a number of other displaced minorities, such as Hungarians, Czechoslovakians, Lithuanians, Cubans, and Ugandan-Asians.[44] For each group, high satisfaction with their successful escape was followed by a psychological downturn marked by the renewed salience of past experiences. Time attenuates the severity of these symptoms, although it does not entirely erase differences among groups subject to varying degrees of predeparture stress. Figure 5 summarizes the theoretical relationship between time and mental health for different categories of the foreign born. For

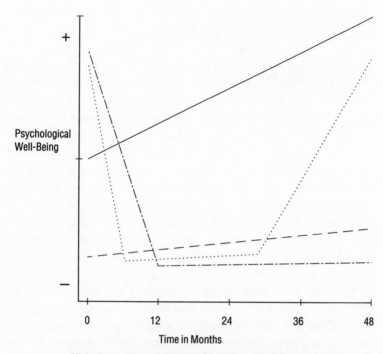

Psychological
Well-Being

0   12   24   36   48

Time in Months

———— High-class origin, nonescapees (e.g., Asian professionals, entrepreneurs)
– – Low-class origin, nonescapees (e.g., Mexican, Caribbean laborers)
····· High-class origin, escapees (e.g., first-wave Cubans and Vietnamese)
-—- Low-class origin, escapees (e.g., Cambodian, Hmong herdsmen, farmers)

Figure 5.   Mental health over time for different immigration
categories.

"regular" immigrants, the relationship is expected to be positive
and linear, with those of higher class backgrounds making a
significantly more rapid psychological adjustment. For escapees from war-torn countries, the relationship is curvilinear, but
higher social class again facilitates adjustment once the period
of recuperation sets in. Chinese and Korean professional immigrants, on the one hand, and Cambodian and Hmong peasant refugees, on the other, illustrate the polar extremes of this
theoretical continuum.

Contexts of Incorporation:
Mental Health and Help Seeking

Unlike escapees, the subjective world of "regular" immigrants tends to be governed from the start by socioeconomic variables and by the context of reception. As seen in prior chapters, Mexicans in the United States are the prototypical example of manual labor immigration because the majority comes from modest educational and social origins. Two large studies of Mexican immigrants in California, conducted by William Vega and his associates, provide evidence of the effect of conditions in places of destination. The first was a survey of a rural sample of Mexican farmworkers in the San Joaquin Valley, who number over one million during the peak of the state's agricultural season. These migrant workers were found to be at much higher risk for depression than the general population, resembling other low-status groups in levels of symptomatology. The highest distress scores were observed for young males and for middle-aged farmworkers of both genders. Their rural context and marginality effectively ruled out access to professional help for mental health problems.[45]

The second study surveyed a sample of 1,825 Mexican immigrant women in San Diego. Depressive symptoms in this urban sample were high, with 41 percent of the women meeting the case criteria for depression, as opposed to the usual 16 to 18 percent found in the general U.S. population. Mexican women were not homogeneous in this respect, however; depression scores declined significantly for married respondents and for those with higher family incomes and increased among the poorly educated and the unemployed. As with refugees, time since arrival led to a slow, gradual decline in symptoms, a pattern that supports the theoretical relationship portrayed in figure 5. Presence of friends and kin and perceived difficulty of reuniting with them were also significant predictors of mental health, indicating once again the importance of co-ethnic networks among immigrants.[46]

The process of incorporation affects not only prospects for psychological well-being, but also the probability that those in need will seek and find professional help. This aspect is brought to light in a recent comparison of Cubans coming to the United States during the 1980 Mariel exodus and Haitians arriving in Florida during the same period. As seen in prior chapters, the U.S. government refused to grant asylum to either group, assigning to them instead the label of "entrant, status pending." Despite this similarity, there are significant differences between these groups in individual characteristics and in contexts of reception. Table 20 presents results of a large survey of these groups conducted in 1987. Despite comparable low levels of education, Mariel entrants were found to earn significantly higher incomes than Haitians after seven years in the United

Table 20
*Sociodemographic and Mental Health Characteristics
of Cuban and Haitian Entrants in Miami, 1987*

Characteristic	Cubans (N = 452) %	Haitians (N = 500) %
Male	59.3	50.2
Married	42.7	60.2
8 or more years of education	52.6	50.0
No income	26.5	39.7
Income above $8,500	43.1	21.7
Major depressive disorder[a]	7.7	4.0
Anxiety disorder[a]	5.9	4.2
Alcohol disorder[a]	5.4	0.6
Psychotic symptoms[b]	8.4	6.0

SOURCE: Alejandro Portes, David Kyle, and William Eaton, "Mental Illness and Help-Seeking Behavior Among Cuban (Mariel) and Haitian Refugees in South Florida." *Journal of Health and Social Behavior* 33 (December 1992): 283–298.

[a] DIS/DSM III scores based on last six months' symptom prevalence.
[b] Screening items based on last six months' symptom prevalence.

States; but this economic advantage did not translate into superior psychological well-being among the Cubans. On the contrary, as the bottom rows of table 20 indicate, the Mariel group exhibited consistently higher levels of psychological disorder than the Haitians.

On the surface, differences in indicators of various mental disorders between the two groups can be seen as a classic instance of the "immigrant versus refugee" distinction. However, Haitians in this sample arrived in the United States after eluding a repressive regime and risking a seven-hundred-mile journey aboard barely seaworthy crafts. Their context of exit seems every bit as traumatic as that confronting many Indochinese refugees. Mariel Cubans came as part of an organized flow in boats chartered in Florida for this purpose and with the consent of the Cuban government. Differences between the two entrant groups can reasonably be attributed less to the trauma of departure than to different levels of selectivity: Haitians are a self-selected group that willingly undertook a perilous journey; Mariel Cubans left because relatives came to take them away or because the Cuban government encouraged their departure.[47]

The positive selectivity of the Haitians did not translate into a more favorable situation in the United States. As shown, their average income level after seven years of U.S. residence is quite low and inferior to that of Mariel Cubans. Table 21 indicates that practically no one in the Haitian sample sought professional help to cope with psychological problems of adaptation to the new environment. Almost 13 percent of Cuban entrants sought such help, a figure twelve times higher than among Haitians and significantly larger than the rate in comparable samples of the native population.[48] Need accounts partially for the difference because depression and symptoms of distress were more common among Mariel Cubans. However, this is an insufficient explanation because such symptoms were also present among Haitians without generating commensurate help seeking.

The difference is best explained by the unequal contexts of reception awaiting the two groups. Haitians came to a place where no one spoke their language and where their own group

Table 21
*Help Seeking for Emotional Problems and Facilitational
Factors, Cuban and Haitian Entrants, 1987*

	Cubans (N = 452) %	Haitians (N = 500) %
Help Sought From		
General medical practitioner	3.1	0.2
Psychiatric clinic	7.5	0.2
Social worker or other human service worker	2.0	0.2
Facilitational Factors		
Knows where to obtain treatment for a mental or emotional problem	70.0	36.0
Has health insurance or other coverage that pays for treatment of mental health problems	46.0	13.0
Has known someone who was treated by a mental health professional	70.0	15.0

SOURCE: William W. Eaton and Roberta Garrison, "The Influence of Class and Ethnic Status on Psychopathology and Help Seeking Among Two Latin American Refugee Groups," progress report (Baltimore, Md.: Johns Hopkins University, School of Public Health, 1988), tables 6, 7.

represents a poor and discriminated-against minority. Mariel Cubans were received into the diversified ethnic community created by their settled co-nationals. The Cuban enclave contains an extensive network of clinics and other medical services linked to the Miami Mental Health Center and other large facilities.[49] Spanish is spoken as a matter of course in these clinics; hence, it is not difficult for new arrivals to obtain both information and assistance. The difference is illustrated in the bottom rows of table 21, which indicate that, in comparison with Haitians, Mariel entrants were twice as knowledgeable about where to seek help for emotional problems, three times more likely to have health insurance or other medical coverage, and almost six times as likely to know others who had received professional mental health assistance in Miami.

Acculturation and Its Consequences

In the past, cultural assimilation or "acculturation" has frequently been assumed to have beneficial consequences for both economic progress and psychological well-being. Just as better knowledge of the language and relevant occupational skills should propel immigrants and their descendants in the labor market, so leaving behind the remnants of old cultures and fully embracing the new one should eliminate much of their distress.[50] Although these assumptions seem plausible, several recent findings cast doubt on them.

A study of Mexican immigrants, native-born Mexican-Americans, and non-Spanish whites in "Silicon Valley" found the usual positive correlation between immigration and depressive symptomatology. However, although immigrants had a significantly higher prevalence of depression, the density of their "Mexican heritage"—as measured by the number of ties to Mexican-born relatives—did not increase these symptoms. On the contrary, the study found that a pervasive sense of cultural heritage was *positively* related to mental health and social well-being among both immigrants and native Mexican-Americans.[51]

A recent analysis of data from the Epidemiological Catchment Area (ECA) study in Los Angeles examined in greater detail the effects of acculturation on mental health in a sample of 1,243 Mexican immigrants and Mexican-Americans. Acculturation was measured by an extensive standardized scale with high levels of reliability.[52] No relationship between acculturation and prevalence of disorder was found for major depression, dysthymia, obsessive-compulsive disorder, or panic disorder. Significant associations were found for four other types of disorder (alcohol and drug abuse or dependence, phobia, and antisocial personality), even after controlling for age and sex. However, the associations ran contrary to conventional expectations. That is, the *higher* the level of acculturation (or "Americanization"), the greater the prevalence of these disorders.[53]

Other results from the same study confirm this surprising finding. Disorders were significantly more prevalent among U.S.-born Mexican-Americans than among immigrants, and the latter had a lower prevalence of major depression and dysthymia than natives as a whole, despite the immigrants' lower incomes and educations. In a separate analysis, the only significant difference found within the Mexican-born subsample was for drug abuse/dependence, with higher rates among the "highly acculturated." In attempting to explain this finding, the study noted the ready availability of drugs in Los Angeles, where their recreational use tends to be condoned among large segments of the native population. Less acculturated immigrants are not only less exposed to these practices, but are under the influence of the stronger families ties, social controls, and traditional values associated with their cultural heritage.[54]

In fact, recent research has shown a striking relationship between acculturation and risky behaviors, which in turn are associated with poorer health as well as mental health outcomes. Data from the 1982–84 Hispanic Health and Nutrition Examination Survey (HHANES), with an exceptionally large regional sample, indicated that marijuana use is five to eight times higher among highly acculturated Mexican-Americans and Puerto Ricans compared to those who are not, net of other sociodemographic factors. Studies based on these data have also documented adverse effects of acculturation among Hispanic groups with respect to cocaine use, alcohol consumption, and, among immigrant women, use of cigarettes and poorer dietary intake. Moreover, drug use and acculturation conflicts have been related to increased suicide attempts among Cuban, Nicaraguan, and other Latin American adolescents in the Miami area. Results from the HHANES have also shown that the rate of low-birth-weight infants born to second-generation Mexican-American women was two to four times higher than that among comparable first-generation immigrant women, despite the fact that the latter had a lower socioeconomic status, a higher percentage of mothers over thirty-five years of age, and less adequate prenatal care.[55] This pattern of superior infant health outcomes found among less acculturated immigrants, despite their socioeconomic disadvantages and high-risk profiles, has been referred to as an "epidemiological paradox" because it goes against conventional expectations, but it has been observed among a wide range of other foreign-born groups from coast to coast.[56]

At Boston City Hospital, a study of 817 low-income black women found significant differences in health behaviors and birth outcomes between natives and immigrants—the latter mostly from Haiti, Jamaica, and other Caribbean and African countries. Compared to the U.S. born, the immigrant women had better pre-pregnancy nutrition; were far less likely to use cigarettes, marijuana, alcohol, cocaine, or opiates during pregnancy; and gave birth to healthier babies.[57] And in the San Diego metropolitan area, a study of all live births and infant deaths for the decade from the late 1970s to the 1980s revealed that the infant mortality rate was lowest for the Vietnamese (5.5 per 1,000 live births) and Cambodians (5.8), followed by the Chinese, Japanese, and Filipinos (7.0), and Mexican-Americans (7.3)—mostly immigrant groups—but notably higher for both native whites (8.0) and African-Americans (16.3). The most positive outcomes were all the more remarkable because the Indochinese refugee groups had significantly higher rates of poverty, unemployment, welfare dependency, fertility, and later use of prenatal care than any other ethnic groups in the San Diego area, and because a high proportion of refugee mothers came from rural backgrounds with little or no prior education or literacy, or easily transferable occupational skills.[58]

The fact that rapid acculturation does not necessarily lead to conventionally anticipated outcomes is illustrated by research on other aspects of the immigrants' subjective world. The comparative study of Cuban and Mexican immigrants described in earlier chapters collected extensive data on the respondents' perceptions of American society, perceptions of discrimination against their own group, and patterns of social relations within and beyond their respective ethnic communities. As shown in table 22, perceptions of discrimination increased significantly

Table 22
*Perceptions of Discrimination Among Cuban and
Mexican Immigrants, 1973–1979*

| | "Is there discrimination against Cubans/ Mexicans in the United States?"[a] | | | | |
	Yes (%)	No (%)	Don't Know (%)	Total (%)	N
Cubans					
1973[b]	4.6	69.0	26.5	100.0	590
1976	26.3	67.8	5.9	100.0	426
1979	26.4	62.5	11.2	100.0	413
Mexicans					
1973[b]	21.7	61.5	16.8	100.0	816
1976	40.0	48.3	11.7	100.0	437
1979	36.3	53.8	9.9	100.0	455

SOURCE: Alejandro Portes and Robert L. Bach, *Latin Journey: Cuban and Mexican Immigrants in the United States* (Berkeley: University of California Press, 1985), table 92.

[a] Question phrased according to respondent's nationality.
[b] Year of arrival for legal residence in the United States.

during the first three years of U.S. residence and remained essentially constant during the next three years. The increase was particularly sharp among Cubans, almost none of whom had reported discrimination at the time of arrival but whose views turned decidedly more negative later on.[59]

The same study developed a scale of perceptions of American society, including perceptions of discrimination, with higher scores indicating a more critical stance toward the new environment. Items forming this scale and indicators of its reliability are presented in table 23. Conventional theory would lead to the expectation that education, knowledge of English, information about U.S. society, and related variables should be negatively associated with scores on this scale. That is, the more acculturated immigrants are, the more positive should be their views of the host society.[60]

Table 23
Perceptions of American Society and Its Correlates, Cuban and Mexican Immigrants

A. Scale Components

	Mexicans r_{it}^a	Cubans r_{it}
There is racial discrimination in economic opportunities in the U.S.	.455	.431
American way of life weakens family ties	.394	.359
Relations with Anglo-Americans are cold	.596	.563
Relations with Anglo-Americans are distant	.572	.587
Relations with Anglo-Americans are hostile	.528	.533
Anglo-Americans discriminate against Mexicans/Cubans	.542	.533
In relation to Mexicans/Cubans, Anglo-Americans feel superior	.485	.495
Scale reliability[b]	.821	.830

B. Correlation with Positive Perceptions of U.S. Society

	Mexicans		Cubans	
	1976	1979	1976	1979
Education on arrival	−.09*	−.10*	−.10*	−.21**
Education in the U.S.	−.13*	−.14*	−.15*	−.16**
Knowledge of English on arrival[c]	−.10*	−.10*	−.15**	−.15**
Knowledge of English at present[c]	−.12*	−.23**	−.25**	−.22**
Information about U.S. society[d]	−.04	−.19**	−.22**	−.13**
Modernity[e]	−.22**	−.37**	−.13*	−.20**
Length of U.S. residence	−.18**	−.19**	—[f]	—[f]

SOURCE: Alejandro Portes and Robert L. Bach, *Latin Journey: Cuban and Mexican Immigrants in the United States* (Berkeley: University of California Press, 1985), tables 94, 95, 96.

[a] Correlation between item and total scale corrected for autocorrelation, 1979.
[b] Unit-weighted maximum likelihood omega coefficients, 1979.
[c] Measured by a 9-item objective test of English comprehension. Scale reliabilities (omega) are .90 or above for both samples.
[d] Measured by a 9-item test of factual knowledge about political and economic matters. Scale reliabilities are .673 (Mexicans) and .773 (Cubans).
[e] Scores in Inkeles and Smith's OM-5 Scale of Psycho-social Modernity.
[f] Length of U.S. residence in the Cuban sample is constant.
* Probability of chance relationship less than .05.
** Probability of chance relationship less than .01.

The bottom panel of table 23 presents the relevant correlations for Cuban and Mexican immigrants after three and six years of U.S. residence. The coefficients are small in size, but they run, without exception, in the direction *opposite* to that expected. That is, the more educated, proficient in English, and informed immigrants are, the more critical their views and the greater their perceptions of discrimination. The same is true for those with more modern orientations and with longer periods of U.S. residence. The fact that the same results hold for two independent samples at two different points in time makes them compelling.

The meaning of these findings is not immediately clear. Do they signify that more acculturated immigrants are more alienated and hostile? Table 24 presents results that contradict this conclusion by showing high levels of satisfaction with present lives and commitment to stay in the United States among both immigrant samples. Moreover, life satisfaction, intentions to remain in the country, and plans to acquire U.S. citizenship all tend to increase over time. Hence, it is not widespread alienation that leads to critical views. A more plausible conclusion is that the latter represent a realistic appraisal of the immigrants' new social environment. In other words, the more educated and informed immigrants become, the more they come to understand American society as it actually is, including its various shortcomings and the lingering reality of discrimination. This awareness may not detract from their decision to stay, but it is certainly at variance with the idealized image often held by starry-eyed new arrivals.

Results of these studies show that acculturation is not a simple solution to the traumas of immigration because it can itself be a traumatic process. Among lower-class immigrants, premature acculturation may lead to a higher incidence of mental illness and to drug dependence as they lose their sense of identity and traditional social controls while being exposed to deviant practices in their new environment. For the better educated, acculturation implies shedding idealized perceptions and confronting the host society's complex and sometimes

Table 24
Satisfaction and Plans, Cuban and Mexican Immigrants,
1976 and 1979

	Mexicans		Cubans	
	1976 (N = 439) %	1979 (N = 454) %	1976 (N = 427) %	1979 (N = 413) %
Dissatisfied with present life in the U.S.	1.1	0.4	3.0	0.9
Satisfied or very satisfied	79.1	78.8	81.3	93.7
Plans to stay permanently in the U.S.	85.2	88.3	88.5	95.9
Plans to become U.S. citizen	67.6	71.0	77.2	85.7

SOURCE: Alejandro Portes and Robert L. Bach, *Latin Journey: Cuban and Mexican Immigrants in the United States* (Berkeley: University of California Press, 1985), tables 86, 87.

harsh realities. The best way of dealing with the challenge of acculturation is apparently to balance its progress with a parallel reaffirmation of primary social ties within the ethnic community.[61] In immigrant families, however, there is often a vast gap in the degree of acculturation between parents and children, from which generational conflicts and role reversals may ensue. This is a more complex issue, which we discuss in detail in chapter 7.

Conclusion: The Major Determinants of Immigrant Psychology

Contexts of exit have been shown to have a decisive effect on the early adaptation process of certain foreign minorities. However, over time, contexts of reception take over, influencing both the mental health and the perceptual outlooks of immigrants. Acculturation per se is not the decisive variable in this situation because, depending on specific circumstances, it can lead to widely different outcomes. The real question is what kind of acculturation do immigrants undergo, and the long-term answer appears to be determined by two main variables: the receptivity found by newcomers in American society and their social class of origin.

As seen earlier in the chapter, the pivotal role of social class in immigrants' psychological adjustment has been recognized at least since World War II. What is different at present is the heterogeneity of contexts of reception with which class must interact, far more diversified than at the time Srole and his associates conducted their study in Manhattan. In chapter 3, we saw that this diversity is determined by a variety of factors, including the policies of the U.S. government, the role of employers, and the character of preexisting ethnic communities. For purposes of simplification, the various contexts of reception are summarized as a continuum in figure 6. Handicapped contexts are those in which governments take a dim view of the newcomers, employers openly discriminate against them, and the ethnic community either does not exist or is too feeble to generate autonomous employment opportunities. At the polar opposite, receptive contexts are those in which government takes an active role in facilitating the adaptation of new arrivals and their own community is sufficiently developed to further their economic prospects.[62]

The conceptual space thus created helps define the objective conditions different immigrant groups confront today, as well as the probable subjective outlook of their individual members. Figure 6 illustrates this range of possibilities on the basis of five ideal-typical instances. Unsanctioned lower-class escapees from war-torn countries and undocumented immigrant laborers tend to approach one extreme in which the depression and distress associated with poverty are compounded by vulnerability and frequent disorientation in a foreign environment. Networks of kin and friends provide the only social shelter under these circumstances, but they are frequently formed by people in almost as precarious a situation as the recipients themselves. Knowledge of the new social environment is very limited, and there is a good chance for deviant acculturation

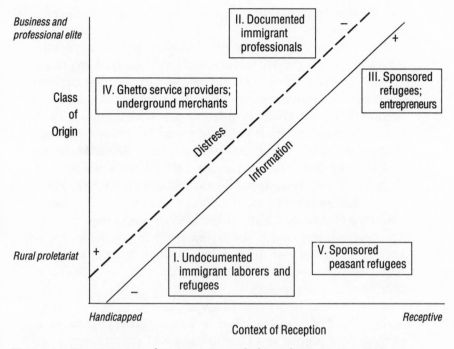

Figure 6.   Determinants of immigrant psychological orientations and types.

because crime and drugs are a constant presence in the dilapi-
dated neighborhoods where immigrants often settle.

At the other extreme, sanctioned upper-class refugees coming in the initial waves of a political exodus tend to undergo a
fairly rapid process of psychological adaptation. Theirs is, by
comparison, a "golden exile" in which the losses and fears experienced before and during departure are compensated for
by a favorable public reception and better chances to rebuild
their economic status in the United States.[63] Elite refugees,
like documented professional immigrants, tend to develop a
highly informed view of American society—including a realistic awareness of its major problems—and to report high levels of satisfaction. Although their conditions of exit are quite
different, the long-term prognosis for upper-class refugees
and immigrants is similar in the relative scarcity of severe

mental symptoms and in their effective adaptation to the new environment.

Less common is the situation of former high-status persons who join an unauthorized refugee or labor flow. Foreign professionals who find themselves in these situations often become ghetto service providers, practicing their careers clandestinely among their own group or other downtrodden minorities. A second common niche is as "middleman" merchants and contractors in underground economic activities. South American and Asian professionals who arrive in the United States illegally or overstay their visas approximate this situation.[64] Because of their small numbers and clandestine status, little is known about the mental health and subjective outlook of these groups. The severe downward mobility that such immigrants experience, added to the insecurity of their position, leads us to expect high levels of stress-related symptoms and a highly critical perception of the host society.

More familiar is the case of lower-class persons who arrive at the tail end of a sanctioned refugee flow. Mariel Cubans, Vietnamese boat people, and Cambodian and Laotian arrivals are among the best-known examples. As the quotes at the start of this chapter suggest, legal arrival does not spare these refugees the traumas associated with their past experience. However, they at least have ready access to governmental aid and assistance. Community networks also provide opportunities for employment and entrepreneurship, especially when prior arrivals have developed a viable ethnic economy.[65] The more favorable prognosis for these groups due to a more receptive context is illustrated by the significant differences in mental help seeking and in access to existing facilities between Mariel Cubans and Haitians, despite the apparently worse psychological condition of the former.

The ideal-typical instances represented in figure 6 do not, of course, exhaust the range of possible situations in which immigrants can find themselves today or their psychological consequences. Nor do they provide a final statement on the groups that most closely approximate each case because many pieces of factual information are still missing. The typology highlights instead the diversity of contemporary immigration and the principal dimensions along which psychological variation has taken place. For all immigrants, America is a foreign world, but the hues in which this world is painted and the emotional reactions that it elicits vary widely under the influence of forces often removed from the initial will or knowledge of the newcomers.

6

Learning the Ropes

Language and Education

The U.S. National Spelling Bee champ in 1988 was a 13-year-old girl in a California public school: Rageshree Ramachandran, who was born in India and correctly spelled *elegiacal* to beat out runner-up Victor Wang, a Chinese-American. The 1985 winner was Indian-born Chicago schoolboy Balu Natarajan, who speaks Tamil at home.[1]

Also in 1988 the two highest honors in the national Westinghouse Science Talent Search went to immigrant students in New York City public schools: Chetan Nayak, from India, and Janet Tseng, from Taiwan. In 1991, Ms. Ramachandran, the spelling bee champ, herself won one of the top ten honors in that national science contest. During the previous decade, almost one-third of the scholarship winners in this high school competition, the oldest and most prestigious in the United States, were Asian-Americans.[2]

A few years ago, an affiliate of the National Coalition of Advocates for Students interviewed several hundred immigrant students in public schools in California about their experiences. What it found was less sanguine than the popular portrayals of success cited above. Here are some excerpts:

A twelfth-grade Lao Mien boy who immigrated at age fourteen tells an interviewer: "The school was so big! There was no one who could speak Mien and explain to me. My uncle had told me if I needed any help to go to the Dean. My teacher asked me something and I didn't understand her. So I just said 'Dean, Dean' because I needed help. That is how I got my American name. She was asking me 'What is your name?' Now everybody calls me Dean. Now it is funny, but it is also sad. My name comes from not knowing what was going on."[3]

A ninth-grade Filipino girl who immigrated with her parents declares: "Our parents don't come [to school functions] because they don't know any English. I don't even tell them when they are supposed to come. They dress so different and I don't want our parents to come because the others will laugh at them and tease us. We are ashamed."[4]

In an elementary school in San Francisco, a teacher is playing "hangman" with her class as a spelling lesson. One "Limited-English-Proficient" (LEP) student, a Cambodian refugee, bursts into tears and becomes hysterical. Later, through an interpreter, the teacher learns that the student had witnessed the hanging of her father in Cambodia.[5]

An eleventh-grade Mexican boy who immigrated at age eleven: "I don't have immigration papers and I feel afraid of getting caught. I work at night so it's hard to study. All I want is for my family to stay together and not have problems with la Migra. My uncle says we may not be able to work anymore and may have to go somewhere else. My teacher asks for my mother to sign a paper, but I'm afraid to have her name in the school file. I'm afraid they will deport her."[6]

Learning to live simultaneously in two social worlds is a requisite of "successful" immigrant adaptation. In a world so different from one's native land, much has to be learned initially to cope—especially, the new language. With few exceptions, newcomers unable to speak English in the Anglo-American world face enormous obstacles. Learning English is a basic step to enable them to participate in the life of the larger community, get an education, find a job, obtain access to health care or social services, and apply for citizenship. Language has often been cited as the principal initial barrier confronting recent immigrants, from the least educated peasants to the most educated professionals.[7] To be sure, the process of language learning—played out, particularly for the children of the new immigrants, in the institutional context of the public schools—is a complex story of mutual adaptation, of the accommodation of two or more ethnolinguistic groups in particular structural contexts. It is also, as the vignettes opening this chapter illustrate, a story of considerable diversity, fraught with irony and controversy.

In this chapter, we focus on the process of "learning the ropes" in the domains of language and education, with particular attention to immigrant youth and their adaptation to the world of the American public school. Language shift and language acquisition parallel in many ways the story of immigrant adaptation to the American culture, polity, and economy told in earlier chapters. Yet the process is not simply a reflection of the immigrant experience in these other realms, for language in America has a meaning that transcends its purely instrumental value as means of communication. Unlike in several European nations, which are tolerant of linguistic diversity, in the United States the acquisition of nonaccented English and the dropping of foreign languages represent the litmus test of Americanization. Other aspects of immigrant culture (religion, cuisine, and community celebrations) often last for several generations, but the home language seldom survives.

Linguistic transition, its forms and its implications, are the subject of this chapter. As with politics and mental health, we must start with the historical record in order to place the analysis of present experience in an appropriate context.

Patterns of English Language Acquisition in the United States

Bilingualism in Comparative Perspective

"What do you call a person who speaks two languages?"
"Bilingual."
"And one who knows only one?"
"American."[8]

Contrary to what may seem to be true from a purely domestic angle, the use of two languages is not exceptional, but normal, in the experience of a good part of the world's population. Over five billion people speak an estimated five thousand languages in a world of some one hundred eighty autonomous states. Thus, there are about thirty times as many languages as there are states; and the dominance of certain languages (such as Chinese, Hindi, Russian, Spanish, and English)—combined with global communications and transportation technologies, international trade, and immigration—contributes to the proliferation of bilingualism.[9] Over the past two centuries, the United States has probably incorporated more bilingual people than any other country in the world. Yet the American experience is remarkable for its near mass extinction of non-English languages: In no other country, among thirty-five nations compared in a detailed study by Lieberson and his colleagues, did the rate of mother-tongue shift toward (English) monolingualism approach the rapidity of that found in the United States. Within the United States, some relatively isolated indigenous groups (such as the Old Spanish, the Navaho and other American Indians, and the Louisiana French) have changed at a much slower rate; but language minority immigrants shifted to English at a rate far in excess of that obtained in all other countries.[10]

Other studies of the languages of European and older Asian immigrant groups in the United States have documented a rapid process of intergenerational "anglicization" that is effectively completed by the third generation. Bilingualism, American style, has been unstable and transitional—at least until recently. The general historical pattern seems clear: Those in the first generation learned as much English as they needed to get by but continued to speak their mother tongue at home. The second generation grew up speaking the mother tongue at home but English away from home—perforce in the public schools and then in the wider society, given the institutional pressures for anglicization and the socioeconomic benefits of native fluency in English. The home language of their children, and hence the mother tongue of the third generation, was mostly English.[11]

The remarkable rapidity and completeness of language transition in America is no mere happenstance, for it reflects the operation of strong social forces. In a country lacking centuries-old traditions and culture and receiving simultaneously millions of foreigners from the most diverse lands, language homogeneity came to be seen as the bedrock of nationhood and collective identity. Immigrants were not only compelled to speak English, but to speak English *only* as the prerequisite of social acceptance and integration. We showed in chapter 4 how the perfectly bilingual German-American community was forced to "swat the hyphen" and abandon German-language schools and newspapers shortly after the start of World War I. Under less dramatic circumstances, other immigrant groups were nudged in the same direction. The nemesis of German-American biculturalism, Theodore Roosevelt, put the general rule in stark terms: "We have room for but one language here, and that is the English language; for we intend to see that the crucible turns our people out as Americans, and not as dwellers in a polyglot boardinghouse; and we have room for but one sole loyalty, and that is loyalty to the American people."[12]

During the nineteenth and early twentieth centuries, pressures against bilingualism had actually two distinct, albeit related strands. First, there was the political variant—represented by Roosevelt and others—that saw the continuing use of foreign languages as somehow un-American. Pressure along these lines led to rapid linguistic loss among immigrant minorities and to the subsequent rise of ethnic reactive formation processes, as seen in chapter 4. Second, there was a scientific and educational literature that attempted to show the intellectual limitations associated with lack of English fluency. Paralleling in many ways the evolution of theories about migration and mental health, these works gave scientific legitimacy to the calls for restriction and linguistic assimilation so common in the political discourse of the time. We turn now to a review of these studies and their conclusions.

Language and Achievement at the Turn of the Century

By the early twentieth century, the scientific debate did not revolve around the close relationship between lack of English and lower intelligence—a settled matter at the time—but around the direction of causality: Did the immigrants' lack of intelligence cause their lack of English or vice versa? At about this time, the development by Alfred Binet of a test of "mental age," soon after translated into English by H. H. Goddard, provided a powerful new tool to the eugenics perspective on immigration. In a 1917 study, Goddard administered the English version of the Binet IQ test to thirty newly arrived Jewish immigrants on Ellis Island and found twenty-five of them to be "feebleminded." Taking the validity of the test for granted, he argued on the basis of their responses to a section of the test measuring word fluency that "such a lack of vocabulary in an adult would probably mean lack of intelligence" and concluded, "[W]e are now getting the poorest of each race."[13]

When World War I broke out, Goddard and his colleagues persuaded the U.S. Army to test some two million draftees, many of whom were foreign born and illiterate in English. Perhaps the most influential analysis of these data was *A Study of American Intelligence*, published in 1923 by Carl Brigham, who concluded, "The representatives of the Alpine and Mediterranean races in our immigration are intellectually inferior to the representatives of the Nordic race." A confirmed hereditarian, Brigham further insisted that "the underlying cause of the nativity differences we have shown is race, and not language."[14] Along the same lines, in his 1926 volume *Intelligence and Immigration*, Clifford Kirkpatrick argued against expecting much progress among immigrants through the reform of school programs, because "High grade germplasm often leads to better results than a high per capita school expenditure. Definite limits are set by heredity, and immigrants of low innate ability cannot by any amount of Americanization be made into intelligent American citizens capable of appropriating and advancing a complex culture."[15]

Educational psychologists who shared similar hereditarian views and whose work was shaped by the larger zeitgeist followed with a string of studies seeking to demonstrate that the cause of low IQ among bilingual immigrant schoolchildren was based on genetic factors (nature) rather than on a "language handicap" (nurture). One line of argument claimed that the inferiority of foreign-born children on tests of mental age persisted even after the children had had time to learn English. Another, typified by the influential work of Florence Goodenough, reviewed numerous studies of immigrant children that showed a negative correlation between group IQ and the extent of foreign language use in the home.

From such correlational evidence, Goodenough argued against a "home environment" theory that would interpret the data to mean that "the use of a foreign language in the home is one of the chief factors in producing mental retardation as measured by intelligence tests" and instead proposed a different causal sequence in favor of innate differences: "A more probable explanation is that those nationality groups whose average intellectual ability is inferior do not readily learn the new language."[16] In other words, for early psychologists of this school, lack of English was not a cause but an effect of inferior intelligence, and the disproportionate presence of feeble-minded aliens was blamed on "selective immigration."

Educational psychologists who stressed not heredity but the environment of the bilinguals came to diametrically opposite interpretations regarding causality, but until the early 1960s, most reached equally negative conclusions about immigrant attainment. From this point of view, low intelligence and poor academic achievement were caused by a learned characteristic: bilingualism itself. Beginning in the early 1920s, in tandem with the flourishing of psychometric tests, the overwhelming majority of these studies consistently reported evidence that bilingual children suffered from a "language handicap." Compared to monolinguals, bilingual children were found to be inferior in intelligence test scores and on a range of verbal and nonverbal linguistic abilities (including vocabulary, grammar, syntax, written composition, and mathematics). Such findings were interpreted as the effects of the "linguistic confusion" or "linguistic interference" supposedly suffered by children who were exposed to two languages at once. That handicap, in turn, was viewed as a negative trait of the bilingual person's mind. Bilingualism in young children particularly was said to be "a hardship and devoid of apparent advantage," bound to produce deficiencies in both languages being learned and to lead to emotional as well as educational maladjustment.[17]

Perhaps most influential in advancing these views was the work of Madorah Smith, whose research on the speech of preschool Chinese, Filipino, Hawaiian, Japanese, Korean, and Portuguese children in Hawaii concluded that the attempt to use two languages was "an important factor in the retardation in speech" found among these youngsters. The bilinguals fared poorly in comparison to a monolingual sample of children from Iowa, based on her method for analyzing proper English usage in speech utterances.[18] This and similar studies reinforced the popular nostrum that bilingualism in children was a serious handicap and English monolingualism for immigrant youngsters, the proper course to follow.

Bilingualism Reassessed: Current Evidence

This negative view dominated academic circles until the early 1960s, oblivious of the fundamental methodological flaw of the research on which it was based. With few exceptions, none of these studies—whether approached from hereditary or environmental perspectives—had introduced controls for social class. They had also typically failed to assess the immigrant children's actual degree of bilingualism, itself a complex issue (in one study, bilingualism had been determined by looking at the child's name).[19] These and other methodological problems fatally flawed the validity of early research findings purporting to document the negative effects of immigrant bilingualism on intelligence and achievement.

In an influential 1962 study in Montreal, Peal and Lambert pointed out that earlier research often compared high-status English-speaking monolinguals with lower-class foreign-born bilinguals, obviously stacking the results a priori.[20] In their study, Peal and Lambert distinguished between two types of bilinguals: true or "balanced" bilinguals, who master both languages at an early age and can communicate competently in both, and "semi-" or "pseudo-" bilinguals, who know one language much better than the other and do not use the second language in communication. They carried out a carefully controlled study of ten-year-old children, classified into groups of French monolinguals and French-English balanced bilinguals, finding that the bilingual group had, on the average, a higher socioeconomic level than the monolinguals. Of more consequence, with socioeconomic status controlled, the bilingual group performed significantly better than the monolinguals on a wide range of verbal and nonverbal IQ tests—contradicting four decades of prior research.

In particular, controlling for social class and demographic variables, the bilinguals in this study performed best on the type of nonverbal tests involving concept formation and cognitive or symbolic "flexibility." Peal and Lambert offered several hypotheses to explain the advantages observed for the bilinguals. They suggested, following Leopold's extensive case study, that people who learn to use two languages have two symbols for every object.[21] Thus, from an early age, they become emancipated from linguistic symbols—from the concreteness, arbitrariness, and "tyranny" of words—developing analytic abilities to focus on essentials and to think in terms of more abstract concepts and relations, independent of the actual word.

In switching from one language to another, the balanced bilingual uses two different perspectives and is exposed to the "enriched environment" of a wider range of experiences stemming from two cultures. By contrast, monolinguals "may be at a disadvantage in that their thought is always subject to language" and "may be more rigid or less flexible than the bilinguals on certain tests."[22] It bears emphasizing, however, that these and subsequent positive evaluations in the literature are built on a considerable body of evidence concerning the performance of fully (or "true") bilingual children. By contrast, little research has been done on limited (or "semi-") bilinguals.

A recent comparative study of students in the San Diego Unified School District (the nation's eighth largest) provides a unique opportunity to look more closely at this issue. The study collected data for the entire 1986–87 and 1989–90 high school cohorts, a combined total of nearly 80,000 seniors, juniors, and sophomores. Over a third of this sample are Hispanics—overwhelmingly Mexican immigrants and Mexican-Americans (20 percent); Filipinos (7 percent); Vietnamese and other Indochinese refugee groups (7 percent); and East Asians—Chinese, Japanese, and Koreans (less than 3 percent). Their growing proportions in the school district are commensurate with the fact that San Diego is a major area of settlement for immigrants from those countries. As table 25 shows, some three-fourths of the Hispanic and Asian students spoke a language other than English at home, usually a good indicator of second-generation status—that is, of children born in the United States of immigrant parents or brought at a young age from abroad. Such students are classified by the school district, based on standardized assessments of their English proficiency, as Limited English Proficient (LEP) or Fluent English Proficient (FEP). The significance of the study is that it correlated the students' English language status (English monolingual, FEP, and LEP) with various indicators of school achievement. The FEP-LEP distinction corresponds closely to Peal and Lambert's distinction between "true" and "semi-" bilinguals; hence, their hypotheses concerning differential achievement, untested in the Montreal study, can be examined directly.[23]

Table 25
Percentage Classified as LEP, FEP, and English-Only Among Two Cohorts of San Diego High School Students, 1986–1987 and 1989–1990, by Selected Ethnic Groups and English Language Status

Ethno-linguistic Group	School Year	N^a	English Language Classification at School		
			LEP[b] %	FEP[c] %	English Only %
East Asian	1987	826	13.7	26.6	59.7
	1990	1,050	10.7	39.0	50.4
Chinese	1987	166	41.0	59.0	—
	1990	248	21.4	78.6	—
Korean	1987	56	41.1	58.9	—
	1990	99	33.0	67.0	—
Japanese	1987	111	19.8	80.2	—
	1990	156	12.8	87.2	—
Indochinese	1987	2,388	68.7	25.4	5.9
	1990	3,102	52.0	42.5	5.5
Vietnamese	1987	1,184	61.9	38.1	—
	1990	1,618	43.9	56.1	—
Hmong	1987	113	73.5	26.5	—
	1990	170	57.1	42.9	—
Lao	1987	560	83.2	16.8	—
	1990	728	66.5	33.5	—
Cambodian	1987	391	91.8	8.2	—
	1990	415	77.8	22.2	—
Filipino	1987	2,064	11.4	50.1	38.5
	1990	3,311	6.6	56.6	36.8
Hispanic	1987	7,007	29.7	37.5	32.8
	1990	8,193	20.1	54.1	25.8
Totals	1987	12,288	33.1	36.6	30.3
	1990	15,656	22.9	51.3	25.8

SOURCE: Rubén G. Rumbaut, "The New Californians: Comparative Research Findings on the Educational Progress of Children of Immigrants," in *California's Immigrant Children: Theory, Research, and Implications for Educational Policy,* ed. Rubén G. Rumbaut and Wayne A. Cornelius, table 2.6 (La Jolla: Center for U.S.-Mexican Studies, University of California, San Diego, 1995).

[a] N [1986–1987] = 12,288 and N [1989–1990] = 15,656 high school seniors, juniors, and sophomores, San Diego Unified School District
[b] LEP: "Limited English Proficient"; primary home language other than English.
[c] FEP: "Fluent English Proficient"; primary home language other than English.

In 1986–87, 30 percent of these students spoke English only at home, with the proportion ranging from almost 60 percent among East Asians to less than 6 percent among the Indochinese. The other 70 percent spoke a language other than English at home: 37 percent were designated as FEP and 33 percent as LEP. Over two-thirds of the Indochinese (and among them, over 90 percent of the Cambodians) were classified as LEP, reflecting the fact that they were the most recently arrived immigrant group. By contrast, less than a third of the Mexican-origin (Hispanic) students were LEP, and less than 15 percent of the East Asians and Filipinos. For the 1989–90 cohort, the proportion of FEPs increased notably, and the proportion of LEPs decreased, for all groups without exception, while the relative rank order of the ethnic groups remained stable.

To examine their actual intellectual accomplishments, table 26 presents data on cumulative grade point averages earned by the students in high school academic courses since the ninth grade. As a point of reference, the overall GPA in the school district was 2.11; the GPA for white Anglo students (2.24) was above that norm, but it was surpassed by those of all of the Asian nationalities listed in table 26. At the top were Chinese (with GPAs exceeding the norm by a full grade point), Korean, Japanese, and Vietnamese students. Clearly FEP students do significantly better than their LEP co-ethnics. More important, in 1986–87 and again in 1989–90, fluent bilinguals surpassed English monolinguals by a significant margin—and this applied to their English-only co-ethnics as well as white majority students. The gap is greatest among nationalities with highest average grades (East and Southeast Asians and Filipinos) and becomes smaller among the low-performing groups.

An analysis of the students' scores on standardized tests of English comprehension and mathematical skills told a somewhat different story. English monolinguals tend to have the highest scores in reading comprehension, with white Anglo students at the top of the distribution. This result essentially confirms the validity of the linguistic classification of students by saying that those who are supposed to know English best actually do so. The situation changes, however, with math scores.

Table 26
Academic Grade Point Averages of Two Cohorts of San Diego High School Students, 1986–1987 and 1989–1990, by Selected Ethnic Groups and English Language Status

| Ethno-linguistic Group | School Year | GPA[a] by English Language Classification | | | Total |
		LEP[b]	FEP[c]	English Only	
East Asian	1987	2.83	3.05	2.38	2.62
	1990	2.86	3.02	2.58	2.78
Chinese	1987	2.94	3.40	—	3.21
	1990	2.95	3.26	—	3.19
Korean	1987	2.76	3.00	—	2.90
	1990	2.90	2.81	—	2.84
Japanese	1987	2.56	2.70	—	2.67
	1990	2.69	2.80	—	2.79
Indochinese	1987	2.30	2.88	2.66	2.47
	1990	2.35	2.94	2.72	2.62
Vietnamese	1987	2.38	2.96	—	2.60
	1990	2.47	3.02	—	2.78
Hmong	1987	2.27	2.66	—	2.37
	1990	2.42	2.84	—	2.60
Lao	1987	2.18	2.63	—	2.26
	1990	2.26	2.72	—	2.41
Cambodian	1987	2.30	2.77	—	2.34
	1990	2.21	2.82	—	2.35
Filipino	1987	2.02	2.53	2.33	2.39
	1990	1.94	2.49	2.38	2.41
Hispanic	1987	1.71	1.85	1.81	1.79
	1990	1.74	1.91	2.01	1.90
Totals	1987	2.00	2.21	2.03	2.09
	1990	2.06	2.27	2.23	2.21

SOURCE: Rubén G. Rumbaut, "The New Californians: Comparative Research Findings on the Educational Progress of Children of Immigrants," in *California's Immigrant Children: Theory, Research, and Implications for Educational Policy,* ed. Rubén G. Rumbaut and Wayne A. Cornelius, table 2.6 (La Jolla: Center for U.S.-Mexican Studies, University of California, San Diego, 1995).

NOTE: N [1986–1987] = 12,288 and N [1989–1990] = 15,656 high school seniors, juniors, and sophomores, San Diego Unified School District.

[a] GPA = Cumulative grade point average since ninth grade, excluding Physical Education; in mean scores on a 4-point scale, where A = 4, B = 3, C = 2, D = 1, F = 0.
[b] LEP: "Limited English Proficient"; primary home language other than English.
[c] FEP: "Fluent English Proficient"; primary home language other than English.

Once again, fluent bilinguals have significantly higher math scores than English monolinguals overall and for every nationality. The exceptions are low-performing groups, for whom the difference is trivial.[24]

In addition, the San Diego study included both "active" (currently enrolled) students as well as "inactive" students who entered their respective high school cohort in the ninth grade but later dropped out of school or left the district. Hence, the data do not suffer from the common bias of selection in favor of those who remain in school; they thus allow an examination of dropout rates as an additional criterion of scholastic achievement. Table 27 presents annual dropout rates for the 1989–90 high school cohort, broken down by ethnic origin and language status. The lowest rate was observed for Chinese language-minority students, who also had the highest GPAs. Dropout rates for the Cambodians actually exceeded the overall rate for Mexican-origin students—who, along with Pacific Islanders, have the highest rate in the school district. The data indicate that limited bilinguals are far more at risk to leave school than those fluent in both languages: The overall LEP rate of 14.4 percent doubled the FEP rate of 7.7 percent. The sizable gap between both categories is repeated, virtually without exception, for every immigrant nationality. More important, fluent bilinguals had significantly lower dropout rates than English monolinguals among all Asian groups (Mexican-origin students were the sole exception in the 1989–90 cohort).

These results lend strong support to Peal and Lambert's hypothesis by showing that there is nothing in bilingualism as such that detracts from scholarly achievement and that, on the contrary, "true" bilingualism is positively associated with the latter. In contrast to decades of psychological research that reported the opposite, these figures indicate that loss of the mother tongue and a complete shift into English is not necessarily associated with greater ability or performance. The meaning of these findings must be carefully weighed, however: The positive association between fluency in two languages and school test scores does not "prove" that one causes the other.

Table 27
Annual Dropout Rates for the 1989–1990 Cohort
of San Diego High School Students, in Rank Order,
by Selected Ethnic Groups and English Language Status

Ethno-linguistic Group	N^b	% Dropped Out[a] by English Language Classification			
		LEP[c]	FEP[d]	English Only	Total
East Asian	1,050	10.7	2.2	5.3	4.7
Chinese	248	5.7	1.0	—	2.0
Korean	88	17.2	1.7	—	6.8
Japanese	156	15.0	3.7	—	5.1
Filipino	3,311	15.4	4.5	5.5	5.6
Indochinese	3,102	11.0	3.5	7.0	7.6
Vietnamese	1,618	10.7	3.4	—	6.6
Hmong	170	5.2	5.5	—	5.3
Cambodian	415	14.9	5.4	—	12.8
Lao	728	9.9	2.5	—	7.4
Hispanic	8,193	17.9	10.9	9.9	12.1
Totals	15,656	14.4	7.7	7.8	9.3

SOURCE: Rubén G. Rumbaut, "The New Californians: Comparative Research Findings on the Educational Progress of Children of Immigrants," in *California's Immigrant Children: Theory, Research, and Implications for Educational Policy,* ed. Rubén G. Rumbaut and Wayne A. Cornelius, table 2.7 (La Jolla: Center for U.S.-Mexican Studies, University of California, San Diego, 1995).

[a] Percentage of students in grades 10–12 who dropped out of school during a given academic year.
[b] N [1989–1990] = 15,656 high school seniors, juniors, and sophomores, San Diego Unified School District
[c] LEP: "Limited English Proficient"; primary home language other than English.
[d] FEP: "Fluent English Proficient"; primary home language other than English.

The two may actually be consequences of a third factor not taken into account, such as type of immigration or social class of origin. Unfortunately, the San Diego School District collects no information on these or other pertinent variables. Social class, in particular, can determine the proclivity of foreign-born families to promote home language retention *and* scholastic achievement among their offspring. We will return to this point in the last section of this chapter.

Language Diversity and Resilience in the United States Today

Recent Immigrants

Is the United States becoming a polyglot country? The previous results suggest that multilingualism may not be such a bad idea, at least in terms of the intellectual abilities and skills associated with it. Yet nativists may object to it on the basis of the need for "national identity," "cultural homogeneity," and the like. It is thus important to examine the evidence concerning both the extent of bilingualism in the country and its resilience over time. The best sources for this purpose continue to be the 1980 and 1990 Censuses, which included several relevant questions not included in previous ones.

The first such question asked whether the respondent spoke a language other than English at home. In 1990, 31.8 million people or 14 percent of the population aged five years or older answered in the affirmative. Because the question did not ask whether this was the "usual" language spoken at home or how frequently it was used relative to English, it probably elicited an overestimate. Still, the data point to the presence of a substantial minority of those who are not English monolinguals. Among all immigrants aged five years or older who came to the United States between 1980 and 1990, 88 percent spoke a language other than English at home. The figure declines to 72 percent among pre-1980 immigrants and to only 8 percent among the native born. The vast majority of the population, over two hundred million, spoke only English.[25]

These results suggest that the United States is far from becoming a multilingual nation. Yet before reaching a final conclusion, we must look at variability within national groups as well as to the evolution of bilingualism over time. Table 28 introduces these aspects by presenting data on home language use for the largest non-English immigrant cohorts, the total

Table 28

Language Spoken at Home and Related Characteristics for Selected Immigrant Groups and the Native-Born, 1990, Ranked by Proportion of Foreign-Born Who Speak English Only

Country of Birth	Persons Aged 5 Years and Older (N)	Language Spoken at Home[a] English Only (%)	Language Spoken at Home[a] Other than English (%)	Immigrated 1980–1990 (%)	Median Age (yrs)	College Graduates[b] (%)	Professionals and Managers[c] (%)
Germany	709,052	41	59	11	53	19	33
Italy	579,442	22	78	6	59	9	20
Poland	386,931	20	80	30	57	16	21
Former Soviet Union	327,635	20	80	39	55	27	31
Japan	281,938	16	84	53	38	35	39
India	445,433	12	88	56	36	65	48
Philippines	906,672	11	89	49	39	43	28
Greece	176,991	11	89	13	49	15	29
Iran	209,554	8	92	50	35	51	42
Korea	562,072	7	93	56	35	34	25
Portugal	209,012	6	94	22	40	5	9
Haiti	221,386	6	94	59	35	12	14
Cuba	734,951	5	95	26	49	16	23
Colombia	282,966	5	95	51	35	15	17
Taiwan	242,600	5	95	65	33	62	47

Dominican Republic	341,775	4	96	53	34	7	11
Nicaragua	165,105	4	96	75	30	15	11
Mexico	4,195,626	4	96	50	30	3	6
Vietnam	538,990	4	96	62	30	16	17
China	526,382	3	97	54	45	31	29
Guatemala	221,930	3	97	68	30	6	7
El Salvador	458,620	3	97	75	29	5	6
Laos	167,997	2	98	76	27	5	7
Cambodia	116,697	2	98	86	29	5	9
Post-1980 Immigrants[a]	8,402,549	12	88	100	27	24	17
Pre-1980 Immigrants[a]	11,103,689	28	72	0	47	19	26
Total Native-Born	210,939,539	92	8	—	33	20	27

SOURCE: U.S. Bureau of the Census, *The Foreign-Born Population in the United States*, CP-3-1 (Washington, D.C.: U.S. Department of Commerce, July 1993), tables 1, 3, 4.

[a] Persons 5 years or older.
[b] Persons 25 years or older.
[c] Employed persons 16 years or older.
[d] Includes immigrants from English-speaking countries.

pre- and post-1980 foreign-born populations, and the native born.[26] Two main conclusions can be derived from these results. First, recently arrived immigrants tend to remain loyal to their native language, regardless of age and education. Although there is some evidence that nationalities with high proportions of college graduates and professionals shift toward English more rapidly, the vast majority of recent arrivals retains its own language at home. Second, time has a strong eroding effect on native language retention: As seen in the upper rows of the table, only one-eighth of recently arrived immigrants use English at home, but more than one-fourth of immigrants with longer U.S. residence do so.

Language transition among recent immigrants has a second aspect, namely, the extent to which they have learned English. In other words, use of the native language at home does not indicate whether users are non-English monolinguals, or limited or fluent bilinguals. The 1990 Census did not test for English knowledge objectively, but included a self-report of ability to speak English very well. Table 29 presents the relevant figures, broken down by year of immigration and age group. Self-reported fluent bilinguals among 1980–90 immigrants represented only about one-third of the total, but that proportion had grown to nearly one-half of the pre-1980 immigrants.

Even more impressive is the rapidity with which English fluency is acquired by immigrant children, underscoring the importance of age at arrival. As shown in table 29, among youth under eighteen years of age who speak another language at home, 43 percent of those who immigrated in 1980–1990 already could speak English "very well," as could fully three-fourths of those who came before 1980. At the other extreme are immigrants in "linguistically isolated" households in which no person aged fourteen or older speaks English only or very well. About two-fifths of post-1980 immigrants lived in such limited bilingual or non-English monolingual households in 1990, although the proportion among pre-1980 immigrants dropped sharply to less than one-fifth.

A fuller picture of today's linguistic diversity is provided in

Table 29
*Language Spoken at Home, Ability to Speak English "Very Well,"
and "Linguistically Isolated" Households
Among Immigrants, by Year of Immigration and Age Group*

Characteristics	Immigrated 1980–1990	Immigrated Pre-1980	Total
Persons Aged 5 Years or Older	8,402,549	11,103,689	19,506,238
Language Spoken at Home[a]			
% speak English only	12.0	27.6	20.9
% speak other than English	88.0	72.4	79.1
% Speak English "Very Well"[b]	31.9	48.7	40.6
Ages 5–17	43.3	76.2	48.5
Ages 18–64	30.0	50.1	40.5
Ages 65 and Over	14.5	37.3	34.0
% "Linguistically Isolated" Households[c]	41.6	18.0	28.2

SOURCE: U.S. Bureau of the Census, *The Foreign-Born Population in the United States,* CP-3-1 (Washington, D.C.: U.S. Department of Commerce, July 1993), table 3.

[a] Persons 5 years or older.
[b] Based on response to census question on English speaking ability; the options were "very well," "well," "not well," or "not at all." Includes persons 5 years or older who speak a language other than English at home; excludes immigrants who speak English only.
[c] Defined by the Census Bureau as a household in which no person aged 14 or older speaks English only or very well.

table 30, which breaks down these data on English speaking ability for the largest non-English-origin nationalities. The highest levels of fluent bilingualism among both post-1980 and pre-1980 immigrants are seen for the Germans, Indians, and Filipinos, the latter two coming from countries where English is either the official language or the language of educated discourse. Between two-thirds and three-fourths of these immigrants are able to speak English "very well." Most others, however, fall well below those levels of self-reported fluency. Immigrants from Southeast Asia and Central America, China, Mexico, and the Dominican Republic, as well as the most recently arrived refugees from the former Soviet

Table 30
Ability to Speak English "Very Well" and "Linguistically Isolated" Households Among Selected Immigrant Groups, by Year of Immigration

Country of Birth	Immigrants[a] Aged 5 Years and Older (N)	Speaks English "Very Well"[b]			Linguistically Isolated Households[c]		
		Immigrated 1980–1990 %	Immigrated Pre-1980 (%)	Total (%)	Immigrated 1980–1990 %	Immigrated Pre-1980 (%)	Total (%)
High English Fluency							
Germany	408,599	73	78	77.3	9	6	6.4
India	394,910	62	79	69.4	17	6	11.7
Philippines	800,314	59	69	63.9	16	9	12.0
Iran	192,423	45	71	57.7	31	12	21.2
Near Average							
Greece	160,179	47	47	47.3	25	17	18.4
Italy	455,489	49	46	46.5	22	17	17.4
Haiti	209,647	34	52	41.6	43	20	33.2
Poland	309,946	33	46	41.6	47	24	31.1
Taiwan	232,856	31	56	39.7	51	22	41.0
Portugal	192,578	31	42	39.2	44	23	27.4
Cuba	698,500	24	41	36.7	49	30	35.0
Former Soviet Union	265,656	22	48	35.8	64	24	39.9
Colombia	268,980	28	44	35.7	47	24	35.6
Japan	237,171	26	43	33.2	53	15	34.3
Korea	520,003	25	44	33.0	54	22	40.1

High Linguistic Isolation

Nicaragua	158,610	26	49	31.8	51	22	43.2
Vietnam	521,207	24	45	31.6	55	28	44.3
Dominican Republic	328,320	23	35	28.5	53	32	43.1
Guatemala	214,550	21	39	26.9	57	28	47.2
Mexico	4,032,703	19	34	26.5	57	30	43.5
Laos	164,150	23	38	26.3	58	36	52.7
Cambodia	113,720	24	37	25.8	57	34	53.4
El Salvador	445,144	23	34	25.5	55	33	49.0
China	506,653	20	31	25.1	57	34	46.4

SOURCE: U.S. Bureau of the Census, *The Foreign-Born Population in the United States*, CP-3-1 (Washington, D.C.: U.S. Department of Commerce, July 1993), table 3.

[a] Persons 5 years or older who speak a language other than English at home; excludes immigrants who speak English only.
[b] Based on response to census question on English speaking ability; the options were "very well," "well," "not well," or "not at all."
[c] Defined by the Census Bureau as a household in which no person aged 14 or older speaks English only or very well.

Union, are far more likely to be found in linguistically isolated households.

Fluent bilingualism thus eludes the majority of recent immigrants, although there is significantly more variation in English ability than in home language use. If immigrants from English-speaking countries are excluded, however, the majority of recent arrivals continue to be monolingual in the mother tongue. This situation may suggest that the foreign born actually resist learning English. This is not the case, however, as indicated by both qualitative evidence and statistical data on the evolution of linguistic preferences over time.

Linguistic Shifts, by Nativity and Age

In 1986, at the time that Proposition 63—the initiative declaring English as the state's official language—was being passed in California, over forty thousand immigrant adults were being turned away from English as a second language (ESL) classes in the Los Angeles Unified School District alone. The supply of services could not meet the demand. Available classes remain to date filled to capacity, and similar strong demand for English instruction has been reported in other areas of immigrant concentration.[27]

More impressive evidence of the low resilience of non-English monolingualism comes from data on the influence of generation on linguistic preferences. Table 31 presents the preferences of children and adults of various ethnic minorities as reported by a unique study. With the exception of Cubans and Koreans, most children were U.S. born; with the exception of Portuguese, Mexicans, and Japanese, most adults (age eighteen and above) were foreign born. Included in this table are Latin American groups, which, as seen previously, are among the most prone to remain non-English monolinguals in the first generation. The data reveal two principal tendencies: First, the larger the proportion of an ethnic group that is U.S. born, the stronger is the shift toward English; second, minority children consistently prefer English to the mother tongue,

Table 31

Generation, Nativity, and Language Use Among Selected Foreign-Origin Groups, 1976

Ethnicity	Age	Born in U.S. (%)	Language Usually Spoken (%)		
			Mother Tongue Only	Mother Tongue Mainly	English Mainly or Only
Hispanic					
Mexican	5–17	89	3	19	78
	18+	69	21	23	56
Cuban	5–17	42	1	26	73
	18+	3	33	41	26
Central and South American	5–17	60	7	19	74
	18+	7	26	29	45
Asian					
Japanese	5–17	90	1	2	97
	18+	68	8	9	83
Chinese	5–17	62	3	16	81
	18+	21	25	28	47
Filipino	5–17	59	0	5	95
	18+	17	6	25	69
Korean	5–17	31	0	26	74
	18+	5	32	20	48
European					
Portuguese	5–17	66	3	26	71
	18+	65	16	8	76

SOURCE: David E. López, *Language Maintenance and Shift in the United States Today*, vol. 1 (Los Alamitos, Calif.: National Center for Bilingual Research, July 1982), tables II-D, II-E. Nativity data from vols. 3 and 4. Based on data from the Survey of Income and Education, 1976.

exceeding—in most cases, by a large margin—the frequency of English use among their elders.

Within this general picture, there are significant variations. Asian immigrants appear consistently more inclined to shed their native tongue than those from Latin America. For example, although the proportion of foreign-born adults is the same among Mexicans and Japanese, the latter exceed the Mexicans' adoption of English by almost 20 percent. Similarly, although Koreans and Cubans have about the same small proportions of native-born adults, the latter tend to remain more loyal to Spanish than Koreans do to their language. These differences are significant but do not detract from the general trend. The latter is illustrated more clearly in table 32, which compares adults from four Spanish-origin minorities, including Puerto Ricans.

Among these groups—presumably the most resistant to abandoning their mother tongue—Spanish monolingualism does not outlast the first generation. The shift toward English is massive, with up to 96 percent of U.S.-born adults adopting it as their main or only language. Mexicans continue to prove the most resilient Spanish speakers, but even among them, the evidence of linguistic shift is unmistakable. A minority of about 20 percent of U.S.-born Mexicans, Puerto Ricans, and Cubans continue to report use of Spanish as their preferred, though not exclusive, language. Among Cubans, the most recently arrived group, the figure provides evidence of some continuing language loyalty in the second generation. Among Mexicans and Puerto Ricans, it is not clear whether this preference also extends to the third. We address this issue in the next section.

Generational Patterns

There are scarcely any systematic three-generation analyses of language maintenance and shift in the research literature. An exception is the work of David López, who conducted two such studies among Spanish-origin minorities in the United States. The first involved a 1973 survey of a representative sample of

Table 32
Monolingualism and Bilingualism Among Hispanic Adults in the United States, by Nativity, 1976

Ethnicity	Persons Aged 18 Years and Older (%)	Language Usually Spoken (%)		
		Mother Tongue Only	Mother Tongue Mainly	English Mainly or Only
Mexican				
Foreign born	32	50	28	22
U.S. born	68	7	21	72
Puerto Rican				
Island born	80	27	41	32
Mainland born	20	0	16	84
Cuban				
Foreign born	97	34	41	25
U.S. born	3	1	19	80
Central and South American				
Foreign born	93	27	31	42
U.S. born	7	0	4	96

SOURCE: David E. López, *Language Maintenance and Shift in the United States Today*, vol. 3 (Los Alamitos, Calif.: National Center for Bilingual Research, July 1982), tables III-2, III-3, V-2, V-3, VI-2, VI-3, VII-2, VII-3. Analysis based on data from the Survey of Income and Education, 1976.

1,129 Mexican-origin couples in Los Angeles. His findings document a pattern of rapid language transition across the three generations that contradicts the assumption of unshakable Spanish-language loyalty among Mexican-Americans. Among first-generation women, for example, he found that 84 percent used Spanish only at home, 14 percent used both languages, and only 2 percent used English solely. By the third generation, there was almost a complete reversal, with only 4 percent speaking Spanish at home, 12 percent using both, and 84 percent shifting to English only.[28]

Figures for men were similar, except that the first- to second-generation shift to English was still more marked. The study also attempted to examine the determinants and consequences of language transition. It found that generation had the strongest causal effect, exceeding by far those of age, rural origin, and other predictors. Spanish maintenance appears to have some positive occupational advantages—controlling for education and other factors—among the immigrant generation, but none for subsequent ones. Among the latter, residual Spanish monolingualism is associated with poor schooling and low socioeconomic status. López concluded that the appearance of high language loyalty among Mexican-Americans is due largely to the effect of continuing high immigration from the country of origin.[29]

A second study by the same author assessed language patterns across three generations, this time for different Spanish-origin groups on the basis of data from the 1979 Current Population Survey. The study confirmed the same negative association between Spanish monolingualism and social class as measured by such variables as education, occupational prestige, and income. For the entire sample, as well as for each national group, adoption of English was positively associated with both higher education and higher socioeconomic status. However, López also uncovered a second trend that differed from both monolingual patterns in which Spanish maintenance was associated with high social class and greater English fluency.[30]

This latter trend was clearer among Spanish-origin groups

other than Mexican-Americans and may help explain why third-generation bilingualism is relatively higher among Hispanics overall than among other foreign-origin groups. In effect, despite strong pressures toward anglicization, this evidence documents the existence of a small but resilient group of high-achieving bilinguals across generations. Thus, López's findings raise again the issue of "elite" versus "folk" bilingualism or "fluent" versus "limited" use of two languages, discussed earlier. Although the intergenerational trend toward English monolingualism is unmistakable and by far the dominant one for all immigrants, this last intriguing set of results compels us to probe deeper into the relationships between social class, language, and academic achievement.

Assimilation and Linguistic Pluralism in America
Adding and Subtracting

Language learning is only one dimension, though a fundamental one, of the process of acculturation. Until recently, the prevailing notion, derived from the assimilationist perspective, was that of a zero-sum process: Acculturation involves shedding the old and assimilating the new and hence a necessary trade-off between the native language and English. To learn English and become American means, from this point of view, that immigrants should not maintain their mother tongues: In the final analysis, this is the litmus test of Americanization. Bilingualism is seen as unstable and transitional, for, as Roosevelt stated, there is no room for two languages and two ethnic identities under the same national roof. In theory, however, English monolingualism and abandonment of the mother tongue represent only one possible linguistic outcome of the process of immigrant incorporation. As portrayed in figure 7, others include continued mother tongue use, limited bilingualism, and fluency in both languages. Still, assimilationists have continued to emphasize use of English as the proper end result of the process.[31]

English-Language Acquisition

	−	+
−	I. Limited bilinguals	II. English monolinguals
+	III. Mother-tongue monolinguals	IV. Fluent bilinguals

Mother-Tongue Retention

Figure 7.   Language retention and acquisition among immigrant groups: a typology.

The call for prompt linguistic assimilation has not been motivated exclusively by concern with the inferior intellectual performance of immigrants. Similar concerns have been voiced, albeit in a different tone, when immigrants actually outperformed natives. An example comes from a Canadian study conducted in the mid-1920s that departed markedly from the familiar reporting of intellectual inferiority among the foreign born. Five hundred Japanese and Chinese children attending public schools in Vancouver were tested in the study. The Japanese median IQ score was 114.2, and the Chinese 107.4, both well above the white norm. The authors found these results "surprising, even startling," and concluded:

> There is every reason for believing that the Japanese are the most intelligent racial group resident in British Columbia, with the Chinese as a more doubtful second. The superiority is undoubtedly due to selection. In the main, it is the Japanese and Chinese possessing the qualities of cleverness, resourcefulness, and courage who emigrate. . . . But the presence of so many clever, industrious, and frugal aliens, capable (as far as mentality is concerned) of competing successfully with the native

whites . . . constitutes a political and economic problem of the greatest importance.[32]

Half a century later a leader of the U.S. English movement in Miami was to express a similar concern by complaining that "the Latins are coming up fast" and that he and other natives had not come to Miami "to live in a Spanish-speaking province."[33] The meaning of such calls is further clarified when the attempt to compel immigrants to shed their language is contrasted with the efforts of many native-born middle-class youth to acquire a foreign tongue in universities and other institutions of higher learning. There is irony in the comparison between the hundreds of hours and thousands of dollars put into acquiring a halting command of a foreign language and the pressure on fluent foreign-born speakers to abandon its use. These contradictory goals—English monolingualism for the immigrant masses but bilingualism or multilingualism for domestic elites—shed light on the actual underpinnings of linguistic nativism.

The pressure for immigrants to learn English can be attributed reasonably to the need to maintain a fundamental element of American identity and culture. The pressure to learn English *only*, especially when contrasted with the efforts of many Americans to do exactly the opposite, must be sought in other factors. The conclusions of Peal and Lambert's study concerning the cognitive advantages accruing to fluent bilinguals are relevant at this point. Knowledge of more than one language represents a resource both in terms of expanding intellectual horizons and of facilitating communication across cultures. This resource and its associated advantages can come to represent a serious threat to monolinguals who must compete in the same labor markets. It is for this reason that calls for subtractive acculturation—not English, but "English only"—find a receptive audience among less educated segments of the domestic population.[34]

Although the sense of threat among those exposed to labor market competition with the foreign born is understandable, we must ask whether virulent campaigns to compel immigrants to abandon their cultural heritage are justified. In chapter 4, we saw how such campaigns leveled against turn-of-the-century immigrants gave rise to processes of reactive formation and ethnic strife later on. Reactive ethnic mobilizations came, however, without the benefit of fluent bilingualism, sacrificed by earlier generations seeking to Americanize as quickly as possible. To the personal suffering inflicted on the first generation by nativist attacks must be added the net loss of intellectual and economic resources for the society at large. Is American culture any richer when its newest participants are told to forget rather than contribute their knowledge?

There is evidence that more recent arrivals have not waited for an enlightened outside answer to this question, but have taken matters into their own hands. The ability to balance the demands of the host society with the preservation of a linguistic and cultural heritage is not, however, within the reach of everyone; it varies significantly with a number of factors.

The Role of Social Class

By the mid-1970s, one-fifth of all U.S. physicians were immigrants. By the mid-1980s, foreign-born students were collecting over half of all doctoral degrees in engineering awarded by U.S. universities, most staying to live in America. One in every three engineers with a doctoral degree working in U.S. industry then was an immigrant. It is estimated that well over 75 percent of engineering professors in U.S. universities today are foreign born, including the majority of assistant professors under thirty-five years of age.[35] These successful immigrant professionals and entrepreneurs are, for the most part, fluent bilinguals. There is little reason to suspect that the pattern of native language use at home—found to be predominant among the first generation—does not apply to them. There is also little reason to suspect that they would want their children to be exclusively monolingual.

We have seen earlier how students classified as fluent bilinguals tend to excel in school, surpassing the performance of both English monolinguals and limited bilinguals. This positive association may be due to the effects of bilingualism on cognitive skills, an argument in line with Peal and Lambert's hypothesis; but it may also be due to the effect of other factors, such as family socioeconomic status, that account for *both* language knowledge and academic performance.

The San Diego School District study reported previously lacked sufficient data to disentangle these causal patterns, but another study of Indochinese refugees in the same city provides the necessary information. The study, described in chapter 5, collected data over time on a probability sample of 340 Indochinese students attending San Diego secondary schools. Complete academic histories for these children were obtained and matched with a comprehensive data set on their parents and households. The characteristics of this sample generally correspond to those reported previously by the larger school district project: 40 percent of respondents were classified as fluent bilinguals (FEP) and 60 percent as limited bilinguals (LEP); the rank order of GPA and standardized test scores among the Indochinese nationalities included in both studies are the same.[36]

Fluent bilingual students were significantly more likely to come from intact families with higher average levels of education, income, and U.S. residence. Along with age and time in the United States, the most significant predictors of fluency in both languages were parental education, occupation, and knowledge of English. Average grade point average in this Indochinese sample was significantly higher than among white Anglo students. A multivariate analysis indicated that fluent bilinguals had a significantly higher GPA, controlling for other factors. Objective family characteristics did not affect GPA directly, a result suggesting that their influence is mediated by other factors, possibly including language knowledge.[37]

A subjective family characteristic did have, however, a direct positive effect on students' performances. This is a summed index measuring the degree to which parents agreed that (1) their ethnic group must stay together to preserve their own culture even as they adapt to the American economy; (2) they should stick together for social support and assistance; (3) they should live in co-ethnic neighborhoods; and (4) they would *not* return to their homelands even if there were a change in government. Hence, the index provides a general measure of cultural reaffirmation among parents who intend to settle permanently in the United States. The parents' scores on this index remained a significant positive predictor of their children's GPA three and even six years later. The overall analysis indicates significant positive associations between parental socioeconomic status and bilingual skills and between the latter and school performance. In addition, it is not parents most willing to assimilate—in the sense of "subtracting" from their cultural background—who seem to motivate their children effectively, but those most inclined to reaffirm their cultural heritage within ethnic networks.

Research findings elsewhere confirm that immigrants from higher class backgrounds are most able to cope with contradictory demands through an "additive" approach that incorporates knowledge of the new language and customs while preserving the old. An example is provided by a 1985 survey of 622 adult Korean immigrants in Chicago. These immigrants, ranging in age from thirty to fifty-nine, had been in the United States for an average of eight years. Their English ability was tested through an objective vocabulary scale drawn from the Wechsler Adult Intelligence Test (WAIS) and through subjective self-reports. English ability and English language use at home decreased with age but increased with time in the United States, as did the proportion of respondents who regularly read American newspapers and magazines—while *also* maintaining fluency and usage of the Korean language, including reading of Korean newspapers. This additive pattern was strongest for college graduates, who maintained more ethnic attachments with Korean friends and organizations. Over time, the more educated the Koreans in this sample, the more they fit the pattern of high-achieving balanced bilingualism noted by López among non-Mexican Hispanics.[38] Similar findings have been reported for Asian Indians in New York, a group of highly educated professional immigrants who travel periodically back to India. These bilingual immigrants differed from the Koreans particularly in the nature of their prior education: Over 80 percent of a sample interviewed in New York had received high school instruction in English in India, and 95 percent had used English in college.[39]

This pattern of additive linguistic adaptation contrasts with the non-English monolingualism found in many immigrant communities and with the wholesale shift into English advocated by assimilationists. Fluent bilingualism is not at the reach of everyone, however, and is most commonly associated with professionals (engineers, physicians, and scientists) and upper-class refugees. These are also the groups most inclined to pass on their skills to their children and hence to give rise to a bilingual second generation.

At the other extreme, immigrant workers and peasant refugees often experience great difficulty in acquiring even limited English proficiency. Theirs are lower-class communities of non-English monolinguals and thus most vulnerable to outside discrimination. Their offspring are usually limited bilinguals, although the character of this handicap varies over time: For children born abroad and brought to the United States, the most common limitation is lack of knowledge of English, a frequent pattern among the Indochinese. For those born here or with longer periods of U.S. residence, the limitation shifts to the home country language: Having learned it only through "folk" usage at home and without extensive formal exposure to the home country's culture, they are not likely to preserve the mother tongue. This is especially the case when immigrant children see its use denigrated by their native-born peers. This kind of limited bilingualism is only a short step away from full English monolingualism, which, as seen earlier, has been the normative pattern for most ethnic minorities.

Types of Immigrants and Their Contexts

The typology of contemporary immigrants that has accompanied us throughout this book—primarily a classification of fundamental differences in social class background and skills—now serves to highlight the principal differences in the process of linguistic adaptation. Before doing so, however, we must again take into account the social context in which immigrants settle. For our purposes, the basic difference is between immigrants who cluster in ethnic communities and those who become dispersed throughout the country.

The fundamental impact of context in the course of linguistic adaptation has been documented consistently by past research. A large study of bilingualism in Canadian cities found, for example, that French and English usage among urban groups was closely related to the proportion of other-tongue speakers in the same city. In general, the more each group found itself in a linguistic minority, the greater the pressure to become bilingual. Because of the national dominance of English, a greater concentration of French speakers was needed to induce bilingualism in native English speakers than vice versa. The pressure was mainly occupational, resulting in more bilingual men than women, given the higher rate of labor force participation among males. Thus, the greater the occupational demand for one language, the greater the pressure for native speakers of the other to become bilingual.[40]

Labor market pressures in the United States also lead in the direction of prompt English acquisition, but their effect is attenuated by the presence of a large and diversified ethnic community. The latter tends to encourage use of the immigrants' native tongue during off-work hours and results in spin-off commercial and service opportunities that *require* fluent knowledge of the non-English home language. That is why use of these languages tends to flourish in entrepreneurial ethnic enclaves. Linguistic requirements in the outside labor market also vary significantly. For most high-status occupations, fluent and even nonaccented English is required. For many manual-level jobs, however, English may be almost unnecessary. In some extreme cases, employers may actually prefer non-English monolinguals, whom they perceive as more docile sources of labor.[41]

Figure 8 summarizes the interplay between type of immigration, context, and expected social and linguistic outcomes. Working-class immigrants and refugees who become dispersed throughout the country tend to have minimal impact in the communities where they settle. Adult immigrants must perforce learn some English, and their children are likely to become English monolinguals. Working-class immigrants who cluster in certain areas give rise to homogeneous ethnic neighborhoods that help preserve mother-tongue monolingualism among adults. Their children are likely to be limited bilinguals because they are insufficiently exposed to English, as is the case with recent arrivals, or to full use of the mother tongue, as is the case with the U.S. born.

Entrepreneurial groups that disperse after arrival tend to give rise to middleman-type businesses, as seen in earlier chapters. They must perforce learn some English in order to carry out transactions with their domestic customers. Their children are prone to become English monolinguals because of outside pressures for assimilation and the absence of ethnic supports for mother-tongue use. A different story is that of entrepreneurial groups that give rise to ethnic enclaves. English is learned, but there is less pressure for adults to do so given the possibility of conducting business in the mother tongue. But the children of enclave entrepreneurs are likely to become fluent bilinguals because of access to quality English language education financed by their parents' resources combined with strong ethnic support for continuing use of the mother tongue. Fluent bilingualism in these contexts is associated with superior economic opportunities.[42]

As seen in chapter 2, immigrant groups with a strong professional component tend to become dispersed upon arrival. The more dispersed they are, the less impact they have on the communities where they settle. Immigrant professionals become fluent, though not necessarily "accentless" bilinguals by force of circumstance and because of their higher education. Although they may try to transmit full bilingualism to their children, the absence of outside ethnic supports makes this a futile

Figure 8. Type of immigration, social context of settlement, and hypothetical community and linguistic outcomes.

enterprise in most instances. But some professional-level immigrants and many upper-class refugees settle where their own group concentrates. Their presence gives to ethnic enclaves or preexisting ethnic neighborhoods a more diversified educational and occupational character. Linguistic transition in these contexts is slower because the community tends to attenuate outside pressures for assimilation.[43] Absence of fluent bilingualism among adults is compensated by its presence among children. The mechanism leading to this outcome is exactly the same as in the case of entrepreneurial communities.

Other individual and collective factors affect language use among immigrants and their descendants.[44] Thus, the outcomes summarized in figure 8 must be read as a set of tendencies, based on past experience. The figure highlights the three core findings of the existing research literature on language adaptation, namely, that home-country monolingualism seldom outlasts the first generation, that English monolingualism is the dominant trend among the second generation, and that preservation of fluent bilingualism is an exceptional outcome, dependent on both the intellectual and economic resources of parents and the presence of outside social structural supports.

Conclusion

> Wide open and unguarded stand our gates,
> And through them presses a wild motley throng . . .
> Accents of menace alien to our air,
> Voices that once the Tower of Babel knew![45]

The author of these lines, Thomas B. Aldrich, was the eminent editor of the *Atlantic Monthly*, penning his poem in the same period that Emma Lazarus contributed hers to the pedestal of the Statue of Liberty in New York harbor. Although the gates are less "unguarded" today than they were at the turn of the century, one can only imagine what Aldrich might have written of the far greater linguistic diversity of the newest immigrants to the United States. Yet he might have saved his muse for a better cause. A rapid transition to English has been the lot of the vast majority of foreign groups in the history of American immigration and continues to be so today.

The shift to English is both an empirical fact and a cultural requirement demanded of foreigners who have sought a new life in America. In its most extreme version, the requirement has included both the acquisition of English and the loss of anything else immigrants might have brought with them. Research on intelligence and the psychology of mental ability until mid-century served to buttress this position by documenting the intellectual inferiority of immigrant children and debating whether it caused lack of English fluency or vice versa. The introduction of controls for social class background after decades of such reports reversed the finding, indicating that fluent or "true" bilingual children actually outperformed monolinguals on a variety of achievement tests. The expansion of intellectual horizons associated with bilingualism must have been suspected earlier by members of the domestic elite, who devoted much effort to acquiring foreign tongues, often the same ones immigrants were being told to forget.

Calls for subtractive assimilation have persisted and have gained renewed vigor in recent years with the advent of U.S. English and other militant nativist movements.[46] The significant new ingredient brought about by contemporary immigration is, however, the presence of a sizable minority of educated newcomers who are both able to understand the advantages of fluent bilingualism and to maintain it. Giving up a foreign language means sacrificing the possibility of looking at things from a different perspective and becoming bound to the symbols and perceptions embedded in a single tongue. Like educated Americans, educated immigrants have sought to avoid these limitations and to transmit this advantage to their children. Their efforts, however, will have only a limited collective effect. First, the vast majority of immigrants do not belong to this privileged stratum, and their adaptation is likely to follow the time-honored pattern toward English monolingualism in the course of one or two generations. Second, bilingual parents who try to educate their children in their mother tongue confront the immense pressure for cultural conformity from peers, friends, teachers, and the media. In the absence of a sizable and economically potent ethnic community to support language maintenance, fluent bilingualism in the second generation is likely to prove an elusive goal.

These conclusions reverse the usual concerns and alarms found in the popular literature, which call attention to the proliferation of foreign languages and to the threat they pose to English dominance. Historical and contemporary evidence indicates that English has never been seriously threatened as the dominant language of the United States and that—with over two hundred million monolingual English speakers—it is certainly not threatened today. The real threat has been to the viability of other languages, which have mostly succumbed in the wake of U.S.-style acculturation. To the extent that language fluency is an asset and that knowledge of a foreign tongue represents a scarce resource, immigrants' efforts to maintain this part of their cultural heritage and pass it on to their children seem worth supporting. Although in the course of time they too may be destined to disappear, the existence of pockets where Chinese, Spanish, German, or Italian continue to flourish enriches American culture and the lives of native and foreign born alike.

7

Growing Up American
The New Second Generation

Since Oscar Handlin noted that to write the history of immigrants in America is to write American history, the phrase has become de rigueur in any introduction to the subject. In reality, however, American history is not so much the history of its immigrants as of their descendants, for it is they who, as citizens and full participants in the culture, have had the heaviest role in the evolution of American society. In the previous chapters, we have examined the diversity of contemporary immigration, its settlement patterns, and its modes of incorporation into the American economy and polity. It is time now to consider how the children of these immigrants are adapting to their role as American citizens.

After the three decades following the Immigration Act of 1965, a large new second generation formed by children of immigrants born in the United States or brought at an early age from abroad has emerged. Most of its members are still in school, but many will enter adulthood during the 1990s. During this decade, the prior record of 28 million native-born citizens of foreign parenthood, reached by descendants of Europeans in the 1940s, will be breached. Immigrants contributed a full 39 percent of the country's population growth between 1980 and

1990. Their offspring will represent as well a significant part of the new generation of young Americans.[1]

At first glance and based on the experience of the children of earlier European groups, we could anticipate that the adaptation process of the new second generation would be relatively straightforward. Children gradually leave foreign languages and identities behind, embrace American culture, and claim and gain their rightful place in the social mainstream. As we will see, this straight-line vision fits present experience only partially.

Sons and daughters of Asian and Latin American immigrants often encounter obstacles in their path that render their successful adaptation and economic advancement problematic. In today's context, many of these children face the paradox that assimilating to their American surroundings may derail their successful adaptation, while remaining firmly ensconced in their parents' immigrant communities may help further it. This paradox stems from the complexities of late twentieth-century American society and the unexpected effects that it has on newcomers. We will inquire into these dynamics after reviewing what is known about the number, location, and attitudes of this emerging population.

The New Second Generation at a Glance

The 1990 Census, like its predecessor in 1980, omitted questions about the nationality of parents, thus preventing a full description of the number and characteristics of today's second generation. Faced with this difficulty, demographers have tried a number of alternative tacks of which the most successful has been the analysis of children living in households headed by immigrant parents. Jensen and Chitose argue, for example, that the relative recency of the new immigration leads to a still youthful second generation most of whose members live with their parents. To the extent that this is the case, an analysis of immigrant-headed households will provide a fairly accurate portrayal of this new population.[2]

Table 33 provides a summary of Jensen and Chitose's findings based on that assumption. From the 1990 Census household sample, these authors selected all households with children under eighteen whose heads or spouses of heads were foreign born. The data allow a distinction between native- and foreign-born children in immigrant households. For comparison, a sample of native-born children of native parentage was also drawn. Table 33 presents these results. It shows that children of immigrants are much more likely to live in metropolitan areas and in the top five states of immigration than native-parentage youth. Not surprisingly, the second generation is also more likely to speak languages other than English at home, with Spanish being by far the most common.

Foreign-born children of immigrants tend to live in poorer households than the native born, whether the latter's parents are natives or immigrants. The same is true of average household incomes but, in this case, the native-born second generation has a slight advantage over children of native parentage, with both categories being economically far ahead of households with foreign-born children. These figures, as well as those on housing tenure, reflect the economic disadvantages of recent immigrant families and the rapid progress achieved, in most cases, by those with longer residence in the country whose children are U.S. born.

The last panel of table 33 shows that immigrant households are much less likely to be white and much more likely to be Asian or Hispanic than those headed by natives. Immigrant households also contain an adult male and are headed by intact married couples more frequently than those of natives. Relative to the latter, the education of immigrant parents is clearly bimodal: There are slightly more college graduates among immigrant than native household heads but, at the other extreme, the foreign born are far more likely to have eight years or less of formal education. That figure is still higher in households where the children are themselves foreign born. This would seem to indicate a declining level of education among the most recent arrivals, except that a more refined analysis reveals higher average education among this group (1985–90 immigrants) than among those arriving ten or twenty years earlier.[3]

These census data pertain to the homes and the parents of the second generation rather than to the children themselves. A recent study of over five thousand children of immigrants in Southern California and South Florida schools affords a direct glimpse of the identity and attitudes of the second generation. The study surveyed eighth- and ninth-grade students in the schools of Miami/Ft. Lauderdale and San Diego who had at least one foreign parent and who themselves were born in the United States or had lived in the country for at least five years. The average age of the sample is fourteen and it is evenly divided between boys and girls and between the native born and the foreign born. By limiting sample selection to the eighth and ninth grades, the survey avoided the bias introduced by selective dropping out of school by students in the higher grades. The sample is considered representative of the universe of second-generation students in these school grades in the two areas surveyed.[4]

Table 34 presents results of this study broken down by the principal immigrant nationalities in each area. In south Florida, these are Cubans, Haitians, Nicaraguans, Colombians, Jamaicans, other West Indians, and other Latin Americans; in southern California, they include Mexicans, Filipinos, Vietnamese, Laotians (Lao and Hmong), Cambodians, other Asians, and other Latin Americans. Table 34 shows considerable variation among children of different national origins in their preference and use of English, relationships with parents, perceptions of discrimination against themselves, and self-esteem. The vast majority of this second-generation sample is fluent in English but, in addition, three-fourths prefer to speak English over any parental language. Exceptions are children of Vietnamese, Lao, and Mexican origin, half of whom or less prefer English. Regardless of their preferences, most second-generation children speak a language other than English at

Table 33
Characteristics of Second Generation Children, 18 Years or Less, Living in Immigrant-Headed Households, 1990

	Second Generation (Foreign-born Parents)			Third Generation and Higher (Native-born Parents)
	Foreign-born Children %	Native-born Children %	Total %	%
Metropolitan Residence, %	96.4	94.0	94.6	79.9
State of Residence, %				
California	39.7	32.3	33.9	8.3
New York	12.5	11.4	11.7	5.7
Texas	9.5	11.6	11.1	7.0
Florida	7.1	6.3	6.5	4.1
Illinois	4.1	5.3	5.1	4.6
Language Spoken at Home, %				
English only	7.7	19.1	16.5	88.6
Spanish	47.3	45.8	46.2	7.2
Other Indo-European language	15.3	16.2	16.0	3.4
Asian–Pacific Island language	26.3	15.5	17.9	0.3
Other	3.4	3.4	3.4	0.5

Poor Households, %[a]	32.3	18.7	21.8	16.5
Household Income ($000s)	33.4	42.8	40.7	40.9
Parents Own Home, %	32.5	58.7	52.8	66.8
Race/Ethnicity, %				
White	30.1	59.6	53.2	83.8
Black	13.1	11.4	11.7	14.5
Asian	55.9	28.2	34.2	0.5
Hispanic[b]	47.4	44.2	44.9	5.5
Household Heads, %				
Male	80.3	83.8	83.0	76.1
Married	83.4	87.9	86.9	78.1
Household Head Education, %				
College graduates	25.4	34.6	33.7	31.7
Eight years or less	35.1	22.9	25.7	3.4

SOURCE: Leif Jensen and Yoshimi Chitose, "Today's Second Generation: Evidence from the 1990 U.S. Census," *International Migration Review* 28 (Winter 1994): 714–735.

[a] 100 percent or less of official poverty line in 1990.
[b] Hispanics can be of any race.

Table 34
Situation and Experiences of Second Generation Students in South Florida and Southern California Schools, 1992

	Latin America and Caribbean								Asia							Total
											Laos					
Characteristics	Mex-ico	Cuba	Nica-ragua	Colom-bia	Other Latin America	Haiti	Ja-maica	Other West Indies	Philip-pines	Viet-nam	Lao	Hmong	Cam-bodia	Other Asia	Total
Prefers English, %	45.2	82.3	74.4	70.5	73.6	80.9	71.0	85.9	88.3	51.5	52.3	64.2	65.6	75.3	71.7
Speaks English with parents, %	19.3	36.8	11.1	19.8	33.1	44.4	74.8	88.7	84.4	9.7	7.7	1.9	12.5	53.1	38.3
Father college graduate, %	7.3	25.4	38.4	24.2	28.0	10.1	23.9	17.9	29.0	15.1	10.3	1.9	5.2	42.0	22.3
Mother college graduate, %	4.2	20.9	28.5	19.4	22.0	11.2	30.3	23.6	38.1	8.6	3.9	0	4.2	25.9	20.0
Both natural parents at home, %	59.3	58.7	62.8	58.6	57.3	44.9	39.4	46.2	79.5	73.1	71.6	77.4	68.8	77.8	63.3
Embarrassed by parents, %	8.1	16.5	16.9	16.3	12.1	25.3	6.5	13.2	17.2	25.9	20.7	35.9	31.3	33.3	16.7
Discrimination against self, %	64.9	38.1	51.2	45.3	48.7	62.7	74.2	61.9	63.5	67.2	72.1	55.8	59.6	59.4	55.1
Self-esteem score (1–4)[a]	3.17	3.40	3.37	3.41	3.33	3.4	3.49	3.44	3.25	3.10	3.1	2.99	3.07	3.32	3.29
N	757	1227	344	277	478	178	155	106	818	371	155	53	96	162	5127

SOURCE: Rubén G. Rumbaut, "The Crucible Within: Ethnic Identity, Self-Esteem, and Segmented Assimilation Among Children of Immigrants," International Migration Review 28 (Winter 1994): 748–794.

[a] Rosenberg's self-esteem scale. Higher scores indicate higher self-esteem.

home. The exceptions are those of Jamaican, other West Indian, and Filipino origin, whose parents are commonly English speakers.

Only about 20 percent of these children have fathers or mothers who are college graduates, but two-thirds live in intact families with both natural parents at home. These figures are in rough correspondence with those drawn from census data, although again there are wide differences among nationalities. The same is the case when we turn to these children's outlooks and experiences. Only 8 percent of Mexican-American students report themselves to feel embarrassed by their parents' foreign ways, but the figure climbs to 36 percent among the Hmong. Less than 40 percent of mostly white Cuban children report ever being discriminated against, but among mostly black Jamaican-Americans, the figure reaches 74 percent. High self-esteem levels are found among youths of West Indian and Cuban origin; Laotian- and Cambodian-Americans have the lowest levels.

There are, of course, variations *within* as well as between nationalities that these average figures conceal. However, the between-group differences are neither random nor trivial. They reflect the characteristics that particular immigrant groups bring along with them as well as their mode of incorporation into American society. As we saw in chapter 3, the combination of these factors significantly affects the economic progress of the first generation. That combination also creates the context where the second generation emerges and grows. We will return to these survey figures later on to illustrate these contexts and the effect that the patterns of acculturation that they foster have on second-generation adaptation.

Leaving the Parental Fold

One of the poignant features of immigrant adaptation to a foreign society is that the roles of parents and children are often reversed. In these situations, children become, in a very real sense, their parents' parents. This happens when their learning of the new language and culture has moved so far ahead as to create a vast gap with the first generation, forcing elders to rely on their youngsters for guidance. Mary Antin's popular autobiography, serialized in the *Atlantic Monthly*, describes how a child of Russian Jewish immigrants saw the process at the turn of the century:

> My parents knew only that they desired us to be like American children. . . . In their bewilderment and uncertainty they needs must trust us children to learn from such models as the tenements afforded. More than this, they must step down from the throne of parental authority and take the law from their children's mouths; for they had no other means of finding out what was good American form. The result . . . makes for friction and sometimes ends in breaking up a family. . . . It is part of the process of Americanization.[5]

Today, the story repeats itself with the children of Asian and Latin American immigrants. The proportion of children who report feeling embarrassed by their parents' ways in table 34 reflects the same attitude. This dissonance is a common feature of the process of acculturation, but it is by no means universal. The same results also indicate that while such rejection of the parental culture reaches high levels among the offspring of several nationalities, it is much lower among other groups.

We can think of these differences as a continuum ranging from situations where parental authority is fully preserved to those where it is thoroughly undermined by the second generation. Acculturation is the first step of the adaptation process where both parents and children learn the ways and the language of their new country. Yet, the rates at which they do so and the extent to which this learning combines with retention of the home culture varies, with decisive consequences for the immigrant family. Parental authority is maintained in those admittedly rare instances where little acculturation takes place in either generation. More commonly, that authority is preserved where sufficient resources exist to guide second-generation acculturation. These resources are of two kinds: first, parental education, allowing the first generation to "keep up" with their children's learning and to monitor its course; second, ethnic bonds, creating incentives for youth to comply with community norms and to combine them with American cultural patterns. Immigrant communities that are sufficiently integrated to reward and sanction their members for observance of their norms can encourage this pattern of selective acculturation, preventing generational role reversal.

Figure 9 summarizes these possible relationships across generations as the process of acculturation proceeds. Generational *consonance* occurs when: (1) both parents and children remain unacculturated; (2) both acculturate at roughly the same rate; (3) the immigrant community encourages selective second-generation acculturation. Generational *dissonance* occurs when second generation acculturation is neither guided nor accompanied by changes in the first generation. This situation leads directly to role reversal in those instances when first-generation parents lack sufficient education or sufficient integration into the ethnic community to cope with the outside environment and hence must depend on their children's guidance. Consonant resistance to acculturation occurs among isolated immigrant groups that are strongly oriented toward return and hence regard their presence in the host society as temporary. These are exceptional cases. More common is consonant acculturation, particularly in families of educated immigrants living among the native born. Selective acculturation is found in immigrant enclaves, being positively associated with the size and resource of these communities.

The literature on the earlier European second generation in America commonly assumed that generational dissonance and even role reversal were normal parts of the process of successful adaptation. In his study of Italian-American youth, Irvin Child, for example, reserved the terms "in-grouper" and "apathetic" for those members of the second generation unable to

Children's Learning of American Culture and Language	Parents' Learning of American Culture and Language	Children's Insertion into Ethnic Community	Parents' Insertion into Ethnic Community	Type	Predicted Consequences
−	−	+	+	Consonant resistance to acculturation	Family isolation within the ethnic community
+	+	−	−	Consonant acculturation	Family search for integration and acceptance into social mainstream
+	−	−	+	Dissonant acculturation (I)	Rupture of family ties and children's abandonment of ethnic community
+	−	−	−	Dissonant acculturation (II)	Loss of parental authority and role reversal
+	+	+	+	Selective acculturation	Preservation of parental language and ethnic community resources

Figure 9. Types of acculturation across generations.

break away from the ethnic fold. "Rebels," on the other hand, were those with sufficient courage to do so and thus join the American mainstream.[6] At present, however, that mainstream has become so fragmented as to offer no certainty that breaking away from the immigrant community is the best way to achieve social acceptance and economic mobility. Indeed, the opposite can be the case, as the following experiences show.

Dissonant and Selective Acculturation: Four Examples

Vietnamese in New Orleans

In their study of the Vietnamese community of New Orleans, Zhou and Bankston note how, despite their poverty, Vietnamese families have managed to maintain close generational ties and forge strong institutions centered around the Catholic Church:

> More than 80 percent of Vietnamese in the community are Catholics and the Mary Queen of Vietnam Church has served not only as a place of worship but also as the focal point of secular community activities. After-school classes for young people take place in the building behind the church. Community meetings to discuss problems and goals are held at the church at irregular intervals. Every Saturday morning, the church grounds are turned into an open air market, where all Vietnamese in the neighborhood can sell their goods.[7]

As a result of the tight integration of this community, second-generation Vietnamese children have adopted a distinct pattern of acculturation that combines school achievement and high educational aspirations with retention of parental norms. Despite the low quality of the inner-city schools that these children attend, most excel academically, a feat that is rewarded by approval from the community at large:

> Both parents and children are constantly observed as under "a Vietnamese microscope." If a child flunks out or drops out of school, or if a boy falls into a gang or a girl

becomes pregnant without getting married, he or she brings shame not only to himself or herself but also to the family. On the contrary, if a child makes good grades or wins awards in school, the community honors both the individual and the family.[8]

Punjabi Sikhs in Northern California

Valleyside (a fictitious name) is a northern California community where the primary economic activity is orchard farming. Farm laborers in this area often come from India; they are mainly rural Sikhs from the Punjab. By the early 1980s, second-generation Punjabi students already accounted for 11 percent of the student body at Valleyside High. An ethnographic study in 1980–82 revealed a very difficult process of acculturation for Punjabi Sikh students. According to its author, Margaret Gibson, Valleyside is "redneck country," and white residents are extremely hostile to immigrants who look different and speak a different language: "Punjabi teenagers are told they stink, told to go back to India, physically abused by majority students who spit at them, refuse to sit by them in class or in buses, throw food at them or worse."[9]

Despite these attacks and some evidence of discrimination by school staff, Punjabi students performed better academically than majority Anglo students. About 90 percent of the immigrant youths completed high school, compared to 70–75 percent of native whites. Punjabi boys surpassed the average grade point average, were more likely to take advanced science and math classes, and expressed aspirations for careers in science and engineering. Girls, on the other hand, tended to enroll in business classes, but they paid less attention to immediate career plans, reflecting parental wishes that they should marry first. This gender difference is indicative of the continuing hold exercised by the immigrant community over its second generation.

According to Gibson, Punjabi parents pressured their children against too much contact with white peers who may "dishonor" the immigrants' families, and defined "becoming Americanized" as forgetting one's roots and adopting the most disparaged traits of the majority, such as leaving home at age eighteen, making decisions without parental consent, dating, and dancing. At the same time, parents urged children to abide by school rules, ignore racist remarks and avoid fights, and learn useful skills, including full proficiency in English.[10]

The New Orleans Vietnamese and California Sikh communities provide examples of the pattern of selective acculturation in figure 9. Immigrant parents have become sufficiently aware of American cultural ways to learn both of the opportunities and perils that they entail. They generally succeed in steering their children toward educational achievement and away from deviance and premature freedom because of the support of a well-integrated ethnic community. Without the moral and material resources that community networks provide, poor first-generation immigrants would be at a loss as to how to maintain authority over their Americanizing youngsters. This is indeed what happens in other cases reported in the recent literature.

West Indians in New York

Among black West Indian immigrants in New York City, Waters describes a variety of acculturation patterns, some of which resemble the experience of second-generation Vietnamese and Punjabis, but others that reflect increasing dissonance across generations. Immigrants that experience this pattern also possess a distinct profile:

> [F]amilies are composed of single working mothers and children. These mothers have not been able to supervise their children as much as they would like, and many do not have any extended family members or close friends available to help with discipline and control. Even families with two spouses often have been apart for long periods because one spouse preceded the family in migration. Often children have been left on the island or sent ahead with relatives to New York and as teenagers reunited with parents who then try to assert their authority. The generational conflict which often ensues tends to create greater pressure for students to want to be "American" to differentiate themselves from parents.[11]

In this instance, "Americanization" is not to the middle-class mainstream but to the inner city, a process that entails adopting its distinct dress, walk, and speech patterns. Use of "Black English" and acceptance of inner-city negative attitudes toward education drive an additional wedge between parental and children's attitudes and aspirations, leading in some cases to family breakups.

Mexicans in Central California

A similar story is told by M. E. Matute-Bianchi in her study of Mexican students in a California high school. Field High (the name is fictitious) is located in a small coastal community of central California whose economy has long been tied to agricultural production and immigrant farm labor. About 57 percent of the student population is of Mexican descent. This population divided itself and was categorized by others in several distinct types. First-generation immigrant children generally used their Mexican education and experiences as points of reference. They remained firmly under the guidance of parents and extended families and were generally regarded by teachers and staff as serious and well-behaved students. Most Mexican-origin seniors graduating at the top of their class belonged to this group.[12] On the other hand, children and grandchildren of settled immigrants often belonged to two other, and quite different, categories.

Chicanos were by far the largest Mexican-descent group at Field High. They were mostly U.S.-born second- and third-generation students whose primary loyalty was to their in-group, seen as locked in conflict with white society. Chicanos referred derisively to successful Mexican students as "schoolboys" and "schoolgirls" or as "wannabes." According to Matute-Bianchi, "To be a Chicano meant in practice to hang out by the science wing . . . *not* eating lunch in the quad where all the 'gringos' and 'schoolboys' hang out . . . cutting classes by faking a call slip so you can be with your friends at the 7–11 . . . sitting in the back of classes and not participating . . . *not* carrying your books to class . . . *not* taking the difficult classes . . . doing the minimum to get by."[13]

Chicanos merge imperceptibly into the last category, the *Cholos*, who were commonly seen as "low riders" and gang members. They were also native-born Mexican-Americans, easily identifiable by their deliberate manner of dress, walk, speech, and other cultural symbols. Chicanos and Cholos were generally regarded by teachers as "irresponsible," "disrespectful," "mistrusting," "sullen," "apathetic," and "less motivated," and their poor school performance was attributed to these traits. According to Matute-Bianchi, Chicanos and Cholos were faced with what they saw as a forced-choice dilemma: either "acting white," that is, doing well in school, or being seen as disloyal to one's group.[14]

At the time of Child's study of Italian-Americans, dissonant acculturation could lead second-generation youths to join the American mainstream, at least that tail end formed by the white industrial working class of the time. Today, as Waters notes, immigrants do not enter a society with a monolithic culture but rather a consciously pluralistic society in which a variety of racial and ethnic subcultures coexist. Hence, the central question is not whether children of immigrants acculturate, but *to what sector* of American society they acculturate to. For, as the cases of black West Indians and Mexican-Americans illustrate, "Americanization" may not entail socialization into middle-class norms and values at all. In these contexts, rejecting first-generation parents in favor of one's native-born peers may not be a ticket to social acceptance and economic progress, but can lead exactly in the opposite direction.

Acculturation, Assimilation, and Contexts of Adaptation

We have seen that *acculturation* is the first step of the adaptation process and is defined by different patterns of learning the language and culture of the host country. The final stage of the same process can be labeled *assimilation*. In the past, this concept has been associated with the notion of a straight-line movement into the social and economic mainstream by children of immigrants, accompanied by the loss of their original language and culture.[15] In the present case, we use the concept to highlight just the opposite, namely the expectation that outcomes of the adaptation process will not be uniform. Assimilation outcomes have become *segmented* as a consequence of the interaction between the social context in which children of immigrants grow up at present and the acculturation patterns just described. Second-generation acculturation is affected by resources that families and communities can bring to bear on it, but it is also influenced with other outside factors. There are today three contextual factors constraining the chances for successful adaptation of children of immigrants: The first is color; the second is geographic location; and the third is changes in the structure of labor markets.

As seen in table 33, close to half of second-generation children are nonwhite. Although this racial feature may appear at first glance to be a characteristic of individuals, in reality it is a trait belonging to the host society. Prejudice is not intrinsic to a particular skin color or racial type, and, indeed, many immigrants never experienced it in their native lands. It is by virtue of moving into a new social environment, marked by different values and prejudices, that physical features become stigmatized and defined as a handicap.

The concentration of immigrant households in metropolitan areas and, in particular, central cities is, to a large extent, a consequence of their initial poverty. This settlement pattern has an unanticipated consequence, which is to bring children of immigrants into close contact with the urban underclass. During the last third of a century or so, American central cities have gradually become the repository of the children and grandchildren of earlier migrants, who failed to move up the socioeconomic ladder. To a large extent, this failure was the direct consequence of racial discrimination coupled with changing requirements of the labor market; but, regardless of its causes, the end result was to foster the development of an adversarial outlook toward middle-class culture.[16]

The bearers of this outlook, who are the offspring of earlier

immigrants and domestic migrants, can exercise a powerful influence on newly arrived youth by reinterpreting for them the
difficult conditions of adaptation. While immigrant parents see
in these conditions the necessary first steps for intergenerational mobility, the inner-city subculture defines them as a permanent feature of the lives of nonwhite minorities in American
society. Thus, an objective factor, namely the physical settlement patterns of immigrant groups, can affect the acculturation process by exposing immigrant youth to a particular
segment of American society. This segment, which is the outgrowth of a past history of discrimination and blocked mobility,
espouses values that are often at odds with those of immigrant
parents, creating the conditions for a problematic mode of dissonant acculturation.

The main arena where the encounter between descendants
of past and present labor migrants takes place is the central-city
schools that both groups attend because of their poverty. The
socialization process that takes place in this setting encourages
newcomers to shift loyalties toward the common adversarial
stance of their native-born peers. To strive for academic
achievement is to "act white," leading directly to the forced-
choice dilemma exemplified by Mexican-American students in
California schools. The end result of this process is summarized by anthropologist Marcelo Suárez-Orozco as "learning
not to learn."[17]

The third contextual factor has to do with changes in the
American labor market that have led to the evaporation of occupational ladders for intergenerational mobility. Immigrant
workers form today the backbone of what remains of labor-
intensive manufacturing in cities as well as in their growing
personal services sector, but these are niches that seldom offer
channels for upward mobility. Rapid de-industrialization
means that the structure of the American labor market looks
less and less like a pyramid, where successive generations can
move up gradually along multiple layers of blue-collar and
white-collar occupations. Instead, it begins to resemble an
"hourglass," where labor demand exists for minimally paid oc-

cupations at the bottom and for those requiring advanced training at the top, but where the middle layers of jobs that provided mobility opportunities for earlier children of immigrants are thinning.[18]

This situation implies that, to avoid confinement to the bottom of the economic hourglass, second-generation youth must race to acquire the educational credentials required for better-paid employment in a few years' time. A college education, previously a dream accomplished after three or four generations in America, must now be acquired in the course of one. Otherwise these children run the risk of being trapped into the same low-paid occupations held by their parents, confirming the dismal portrayals of a permanent underclass.[19]

The combination of these three contextual factors renders the adaptation of today's second generation to American society problematic. Resisting discrimination, countermanding the adversarial stance of the inner city, and traversing the narrowing path toward professional and managerial jobs commonly require strong family support as well as whatever resources the immigrant community can muster. It is here that the typology of acculturation patterns in figure 9 becomes relevant. Acculturation interacts with these outside contextual factors leading to predictable adaptation outcomes. For instance, consonant acculturation where parents and children learn a new language and culture together does not guarantee upward assimilation, but it increases its probability. When outside discrimination is not overwhelming and some family resources exist to support children's educational efforts, this pattern can lead to ready assimilation into the American middle class. Immigrant professional families commonly exemplify this outcome.

Selective acculturation where learning American ways combines with continuing strong bonds with the ethnic community can also be expected to lead to a positive outcome. Selective acculturation is particularly helpful for children of nonwhite immigrants, subject to outside discrimination and exposed to inner-city schools. As illustrated by the New Orleans Vietnamese, the immigrant community protects children from these dangers, while making available a variety of resources to promote educational achievement. Entrepreneurial enclaves provide common examples of this pattern.

Finally, dissonant acculturation may not necessarily lead to downward assimilation, but it increases its probability. This pattern severs ties between children and the immigrant community, depriving youths of privileged sources of material and moral support while leaving them exposed to all the challenges of outside society. In this context, some second-generation youth *may* succeed on the strength of their own talent and determination, but many others will undergo downward mobility. This is especially the case in communities of nonwhite immigrant workers living in close proximity to the inner city.

Figure 10 portrays these relationships more systematically by combining acculturation patterns with the effects of contextual factors. For simplicity, the latter is portrayed in terms of two polar situations: contexts where high outside discrimination combines with a relative dearth of family and community resources *versus* those where the opposite combination obtains. The interaction between these ideal contexts and the four types of acculturation patterns described previously leads to eight polar outcomes. These should not be seen as exhaustive of all possible forms, but rather as covering the range of possibilities encompassed by the concept of segmented assimilation. Figure 10 summarizes relationships between the concepts that have grounded our analysis so far: second-generation adaptation as the general process; acculturation as its initial step; and segmented assimilation as its outcome. The distinct types under the latter again point to the lack of uniformity of the process in contemporary American society.

This exercise highlights two contrasts significant for theoretical as well as practical reasons. First, when the outside context is highly adverse, consonant acculturation may not lead to a desirable outcome. These are situations where immigrants and their offspring give up their home culture, seeking acceptance and mobility in their new country, only to be rebuffed because of their race or their poverty. As seen in chapter 4, this

Type of Acculturation	Social Context		Segmented Assimilation Outcomes
	(I) Discrimination High; Family/ Community Resources Low	(II) Discrimination Low; Family/ Community Resources High	
Consonant Resistance to Acculturation	×		Downward: probable return to home country
		×	Stagnant: perpetuation of distinct ethnic subculture
Consonant Acculturation	×		Downward: blocked entry into American mainstream; reactive ethnicity
		×	Upward: integration into mainstream and gradual abandonment of parental culture
Dissonant Acculturation	×		Downward: socialization into urban underclass roles; adoption of adversarial stance toward the mainstream
		×	Uncertain: contingent on individual traits and resources
Selective Acculturation	×		Upward: slow mobility into white-collar occupations
		×	Upward: rapid mobility into professional and managerial occupations

Figure 10. Types of acculturation, social context, and predicted second-generation outcomes.

type of blocked mobility is likely to turn into reactive ethnicity, creating the basis for a confrontational attitude toward society's mainstream. The process is, of course, similar to that which gave rise to the adversarial inner-city stance in the first place. In contrast, even with a hostile external context, selective acculturation can lead to upward mobility. This is so because a cohesive community may still marshall the resources to avoid role reversal and provide the encouragement required for educational achievement, even if confronted with a difficult external context.

Segmented Assimilation: Five Examples

The Haitian immigrant community of Miami is composed of some 100,000 legal and clandestine immigrants, many of whom sold everything in order to buy passage to America. First-generation Haitians are strongly oriented toward preserving a strong national identity, which they associate both with community solidarity and with social networks promoting individual success. In trying to instill national pride and an achievement orientation in their children, however, they clash with the youngsters' everyday experiences in school. Little Haiti is adjacent to Liberty City, the main ghetto area of Miami, and Haitian adolescents attend predominantly inner-city schools. Native-born minority youth stereotype Haitians as too docile and too subservient to whites and they make fun of French and Creole and of the Haitians' accent. As a result, second-generation Haitian children find themselves torn between conflicting ideas and values: To remain "Haitian" they would have to face social ostracism and continuing attacks in school; to become "American" (black American in this case), they would have to forgo their parents' dreams of making it in America on the basis of ethnic solidarity and preservation of traditional values.[20]

Academically outstanding Haitian-American students have consciously attempted to retain their ethnic identity by cloaking it in black-American cultural forms. Many others, however, have followed the path of least effort and become thoroughly assimilated. "Assimilation" in this instance is not to the mainstream, but to the values and norms of the inner city. In the process, the resources of solidarity and mutual support within the immigrant community are dissipated.

Across town, children of early anti-Castro Cuban exiles face an entirely different set of circumstances. In chapter 3 we saw the favorable mode of incorporation that greeted first-generation Cubans. On that basis, these refugees were able to develop an enclave economy in Miami and to progress economically. At $41,619, Cuban family incomes were the highest of any Latin American–origin group in 1990, coming close to the national average. A central aspect of the development of this ethnic enclave was the growth of a system of bilingual private schools. Children of middle-class refugees attending these schools are effectively insulated both from outside discrimination and from inner-city influence. Staffed mostly by other first-generation immigrants, the schools reinforce the values and outlooks of parents, blocking any possibility of role reversal.[21]

In terms of the typology of acculturation in figure 9, Haitian-American teenagers oscillate between the selective acculturation strongly supported by their parents and the dissonant acculturation pressed on them by their school peers. The Cuban-American youth in bilingual private schools, on the other hand, are firmly ensconced in a selective acculturation pattern since there is no school counterculture that opposes parental beliefs. Private bilingual schools teach English and regular academic subjects but they do so while preserving Spanish and a strong attachment to the immigrants' national history. Combining these patterns with the outside contexts outlined in figure 10, expectations for second-generation adaptation look very different. Children of the early waves of Cuban exiles who attend private schools are almost always white, and the strength of the ethnic economy provides them with a wealth of family and community resources. As black immigrants, Haitian parents face, on the other hand, pervasive discrimination; unemployment and poverty prevents most of these immigrants from leaving the inner city or neutralizing its negative influence. The expected outcomes in this case range from downward assimilation to slow upward mobility based exclusively on family moral resources and support.

The survey of second-generation youth in Florida and California, described in table 34, provides additional data to round up the profile of these two groups in the following section. In addition, however, it is important to consider the experiences of three other immigrant communities that either exemplify alternative paths or provide examples of dissonant and selective acculturation in a different context.

West Indians in south Florida differ from both Cubans and Haitians in that the group is composed, to a large extent, of well-educated English-speaking black immigrants. They have used their material resources to settle away from the inner city, but have lacked the numbers and economic means necessary to develop a distinct ethnic enclave. Like Haitians, they are subject to racial discrimination and to pressures to assimilate to inner-city culture. West Indians frequently resist these outside forces on the strength of their education and superior command of English.[22] In terms of the typology in figure 9, this group represents a clear example of consonant acculturation where both parents and children learn American norms and values jointly. In terms of predicted outcomes (figure 10), everything depends on whether social acceptance and economic mobility are blocked by racism or whether immigrant families are able to bypass this barrier on the strength of their educational and material resources.

Mexican immigrants in California are a much older presence but, as we saw earlier, the menial jobs toward which they have been channeled for decades conspire against the emergence of a socially stable and economically strong community. The fluidity of the movement back and forth across the border and the continuous presence of new arrivals gives to Mexican neighborhoods an unsettled, transient character. Many years of uninterrupted migration have created a sizable Mexican population in southern California, but the relegation of its members to the bottom of the labor market and unabated discrimination have turned some Mexican-American areas into the *core* of inner cities in this region. The adversarial reaction to this permanent situation of subordination has its clearest expression in the emergence of Chicano and Cholo subcultures.

In terms of our typology of acculturation, many Mexican-American youths oscillate between consonant resistance to acculturation, based on the proximity to Mexico and the prospects for family return there, and dissonant acculturation among settled immigrant families. Given outside discrimination and generalized poverty among first-generation immigrants, prospects for their offspring's upward mobility are dim. The combination of dissonant acculturation and an adverse social context puts many Mexican-American youth at risk of downward assimilation.

The condition of the Vietnamese in southern California is similar to that described by Zhou and Bankston in New Orleans. They form a tightly knit community that, in recent years, has become increasingly entrepreneurial. Although the Vietnamese have lacked the resources for building a private school system, they compensate for this with dense social networks and close monitoring of children of parents and other kin. Like Cubans in Miami, the Vietnamese exemplify a pattern of selective acculturation, although, in their case, it combines with lesser material resources and greater evidence of discrimination. Nevertheless, the resources of family and community appear sufficiently strong to anticipate solid upward mobility among the Vietnamese second generation, including entry into professional and managerial tracks.

Achievement and Identity: Survey Evidence

Before discussing the statistical profile of these groups, a cautionary word must be said about internal differences within each. The data refer to *averages* within each community and hence conceal potentially significant variation. In practical terms, this means that not all Haitian- or Mexican-origin youth are at risk of downward assimilation or that all Cuban-Americans or Vietnamese-Americans will be successful. There are many individual exceptions, just as there are other forms of assimilation not covered by our theoretical model. The statistical averages reflect tendencies or modal patterns that suggest differences between immigrant nationalities. These differences are made intelligible by the particular mode of incorporation of each group in its area of settlement and its resulting patterns of acculturation.

Table 35 presents the distribution of Haitian, Cuban, West Indian, Mexican, and Vietnamese second-generation youth on an array of variables that reflect their particular social contexts and acculturation patterns. For Cuban-American youth, the analysis here focuses on the subsample of students attending bilingual private schools in Miami. These results illustrate empirically some of the theoretical combinations presented in figure 10. Respondents in this sample are still too young to examine assimilation outcomes on the basis of completed education, occupation, or incomes. Instead, we focus on those characteristics of adolescents that provide some clue as to the general direction that the process is taking. Ethnic self-identification, educational and occupational aspirations, and academic achievement scores are the variables examined.

The first panel of the table presents characteristics of each immigrant group drawn from the 1990 Census. With the exception of community size, these are national figures and, hence, not strictly representative of the particular features of local communities. Nevertheless, they provide an indication of the overall economic condition of first-generation immigrant groups that furnish, in turn, the context for second-generation adaptation. Wide differences are observable in average family incomes and poverty rates. Mexicans rank at the bottom in these indicators, with Haitians having the next lowest average incomes. A high poverty rate among the Vietnamese indicates that this is not a particularly well-off group, although it does exhibit a high level of entrepreneurship, as indicated by

Table 35
Profile of Five Second Generation Nationalities, 1992

Characteristics	Haitian	Cuban[a]	West Indian[b]	Mexican	Vietnamese	V or ETA[c]
Context						
Community						
Size (000s)[d]	83.2	497.6	105.3	413.8	20.4	—
Average family income[e] ($000s)	32.6	41.5	39.7	26.6	36.9	—
Poverty rate[e]	20.9	11.5	11.1	27.4	23.8	—
Self-employment rate[f]	3.6	7.2	3.8	4.5	6.1	—
Professional specialty occupation (%)	13.8	22.7	21.4	5.8	16.9	—
Family						
Father has some college education (%)[g]	23.5	61.1	34.1	16.3	26.6	.30
Mother has some college education (%)	30.7	60.5	43.4	11.2	16.8	.39
Father's occupational status (1–100)[h]	38.3	52.6	43.4	34.9	41.3	.41
Mother's occupational status (1–100)	40.3	51.1	44.4	34.2	39.8	.41
Family upper-middle class or wealthy (%)[i]	37.9	57.0	49.1	32.2	31.6	.14
Intact family (%)[j]	44.9	73.3	42.6	59.3	73.1	.23
Discrimination						
Has been discriminated against (%)	62.7	29.1	67.4	64.9	67.2	.23
Will be discriminated against even with college education (%)	34.6	12.2	33.3	21.2	24.3	.15

Acculturation						
Fluent in English (%)[k]	95.4	98.8	98.9	86.9	81.3	.22
Fluent in parental language (%)[k]	49.7	94.2	—[l]	86.0	60.3	.45
Most friends have immigrant parents (%)	44.4	93.6	39.4	48.4	53.9	.29
Nationality of friends						
Has friends from Haiti (%)	69.9	0.0	33.0	0.4	0.0	.68
Has friends from Cuba (%)	20.9	97.1	23.3	2.6	0.8	.76
Has friends from West Indies (%)	41.8	0.0	61.3	0.4	0.3	.69
Has friends from Mexico (%)	0.0	0.0	1.1	75.1	13.7	.73
Has friends from Vietnam (%)	0.0	0.0	0.0	3.7	76.5	.80
Spends two or more hours daily on homework (%)	42.5	39.5	46.6	26.0	57.3	.25
Resistant to acculturation (%)[m]	4.6	1.7	3.6	9.0	1.1	.13
Believes U.S. is best country in the world (%)	18.9	54.6	16.1	25.5	31.8	.23
Assimilation						
Ethnic self-identity:[n]						
American (%)	16.3	33.1	15.8	2.6	3.4	
Hyphenated American (%)	37.9	59.3	30.5	29.5	39.9	
Hispanic (%)	2.0	3.5	0.7	28.8	0.0	
Black (%)	12.4	0.0	8.2	0.3	0.0	
Parents' Nationality (%)	26.1	3.5	35.1	18.9	38.8	.32
Aspirations						
Expects to complete college (%)	85.0	97.1	83.9	61.6	76.3	.28
Aspires to a professional/managerial occupation (%)	72.6	72.1	68.9	60.7	69.0	.10
Achievement						
Average math score (1–100)[o]	46.3	78.8	50.1	31.8	60.3	.48
Average reading score (1–100)[o]	30.1	68.1	43.1	26.2	36.9	.40
Grade point average	2.31	2.64	2.46	2.24	3.04	.31
N	178	172	261	757	371	

(Continued on next page)

Table 35   (*continued*)

SOURCES: U.S. Bureau of the Census, *1990 Census of Population, Social and Economic Characteristics*, 1990 CP-2-1 (Washington, D.C.: November 1993); U.S. Bureau of the Census, *The Foreign-Born Population in the United States*, 1990 CP-3-1 (Washington, D.C.: July 1993); Children of Immigrants project. See table 34 above.

[a] Cuban second-generation sample is restricted to children attending private schools in Miami.

[b] Community figures for West Indians are computed as the sum of Jamaicans, Trinidadians, Grenadians, Bahamians, and Barbadians for size and the weighted average of Jamaicans and Trinidadians for socio-economic indicators.

[c] Cramer's *V* for contingency tables; ETA for analysis of variance tables. Both are measures of strength of association.

[d] Estimated 1990 population of foreign-born Haitians, Cubans, and West Indians in Miami/Hialeah metropolitan area and Mexicans and Vietnamese in San Diego metropolitan area, based on census figures.

[e] Families nationwide.

[f] Employed workers 16 years of age and over, nationwide.

[g] One year of college or more.

[h] Treiman's Standardized International Occupation Prestige Scale.

[i] Student's self-placement.

[j] Family headed by biological father and mother.

[k] Speaks, reads, writes, and understands the language very well.

[l] Most West Indian parents are English speakers.

[m] Both respondents and parents "never" or "almost never" prefer American ways.

[n] Column percentages do not add up to 100 because of exclusion of "other" category.

[o] Percentile scores on standardized Stanford Achievement Test.

self-employment rates. Cuban and West Indian immigrants earn the highest average incomes and are most frequently occupied in professional-level jobs.

A similar pattern emerges when we consider family characteristics in the second panel of table 35. Cuban-origin children attending private schools have by far the best-educated parents and those in higher-status occupations. They are followed by West Indians, indicating again the relatively high socioeconomic status of this black immigrant group. Mexican parents rank consistently at the bottom in all indicators of family status. It is also noteworthy that Vietnamese families again exhibit relatively modest educational and occupational levels. Hence, whatever advantage Vietnamese children derive from membership in this community, it is not by virtue of its superior socioeconomic status.

Part of what constitutes the Vietnamese advantage is reflected in the bottom row of the same panel indicating that, along with Cubans, the Vietnamese have by far the greater proportion of intact families. Close to three-fourths of these children grow up in households with father and mother present, a figure that drops to less than half among Haitian and West Indian families. There are no direct indicators of level of discrimination in the data, but we have the students' reports of present and expected discrimination against themselves. As seen already in table 34, Cuban-American youth are in a class apart on this variable. The still lower levels of reported discrimination among Cubans attending private schools highlight the role of these contexts in screening negative outside messages and protecting students' self-esteem.

A consistent two-thirds of the other four groups report having experienced discrimination in the past. These figures drop significantly for all children when asked whether they would still be discriminated against if they achieved a high level of education. In this case, it is the two black immigrant groups that stand out since fully one-third of second generation Haitians and West Indians believe that they would still suffer discrimination under these conditions. The adverse social context created by prejudice against these black immigrants and their children is well reflected in these figures.

Based on the first row of the third panel of table 35, acculturation is proceeding swiftly among all second-generation children, since over four-fifths of all respondents are already fluent in English. The figure reaches 99 percent among West Indian youth, whose parents are English speakers, and among Cuban-Americans. Some evidence for selective acculturation is presented in the second row of this panel, which shows that, along with English, Cuban-Americans are the most prone to preserve their parental language. Mexican-Americans also rank high in fluent bilingualism, followed by the Vietnamese. At the other extreme are Haitian-Americans, half of whom have already lost fluency in French or Creole.

The next rows present data concerning the social relationships of second-generation youth. The two black Caribbean groups are the most outgoing in terms of having friendships with native-parentage American peers. This greater exposure to the outside is supplemented by a greater number of reported friendships with children from other immigrant origins. Cuban-American students in private schools, followed by the Vietnamese, are the most ethnically isolated. Fully 94 percent of the first group reports that most of their friends are other Cuban-Americans; they also have zero friends among the other four immigrant groups. These figures point toward the selective acculturation that these children are undergoing and their relative isolation from both native and other foreign minorities. In the past, this pattern was interpreted as a symptom of "escapism" and a negative influence on academic performance. This is not the case at present, as results presented below indicate.

Less than half of Mexican-American students report that most of their close friends have immigrant parents, but 76 percent report having friends from Mexico. The difference is explainable by the ties between this second-generation group and higher-generation Mexican-Americans. As seen earlier, Mexicans are an older presence in southern California, with third- and even fourth-generation youth still living in barrios. This community also fosters significant resistance to acculturation, as indicated by the proportion of families in which both parents and children reject American ways. That pattern comprises a tiny minority of all groups, except among Mexican-Americans, where it reaches close to 10 percent.[23]

The final rows of this panel provide a glimpse of two other important aspects of acculturation among second-generation adolescents, namely their dedication to academic tasks, as measured by hours of school homework, and their attitudes toward their new country. On the first variable, the Vietnamese are in a class apart. The proportion of Vietnamese-Americans that report spending two or more hours daily on school homework far exceeds all other groups. This contrast reflects the pressure exercised by Vietnamese parents and kin on their children to compensate academically for their relatively modest socioeconomic status. On the question of attitudes, Cuban-Americans, the most ethnically enclosed students, are simultaneously the most enthusiastic about their country, with over half agreeing that the United States is "the best country in the world." Absence of discrimination coupled with the relative economic success of first-generation parents may account for this response. By contrast, children of Haitian and West Indian immigrants, the groups most subject to racial discrimination, display a distinctively less enthusiastic stance.

The last panel of table 35 identifies preliminary assimilation outcomes in this adolescent sample. On the question of ethnic self-identification, it is clear that a "plain American" identity is still the exception rather than the rule among second-generation youth. The modal pattern is hyphenated American identities, followed by nonhyphenated parental (foreign) nationalities. This is the case of Vietnamese children, almost none of whom call themselves American and who oscillate between adding or omitting the hyphen after their parents' country. A second pattern is self-identification with a panethnic label denoting a native-born minority. Twenty-nine percent of Mexican-origin children have given up their parents' nationality in favor of "Hispanic"; 12 percent of Haitian-Americans have done so in favor of "Black."

The most successful immigrant groups appear more resistant to adopt these pan-ethnic labels. Just 8 percent of West Indians call themselves "Black," while "Hispanics" among Cuban-Americans represent a tiny 3 percent. Self-identification among this latter group is noteworthy: Cuban-American youth attending ethnic schools in the heart of the Cuban enclave of Miami are the most likely to call themselves plain Americans and the least likely to use their parents' nonhyphenated national identity. These patterns reflect the progress of the adaptation process, as well as its different outcomes: Children of immigrants experiencing the most difficult economic and social conditions are more prone to see themselves as part of undifferentiated American minorities. Those for whom consonant or selective acculturation is the norm either retain their nationalities in hyphenated form or shift directly into an unhyphenated "American" identity.

Educational and occupational aspirations among all second-generation youth are very high. As shown in the next rows of table 35, majorities of all groups expect to graduate from college and aspire to a professional or executive occupation. A partial exception are Mexican-Americans, whose average aspirations are relatively modest. But even among this group, the majority of children have high hopes for the future. Such hopes are an important assimilation outcome, indicative of what these new Americans are willing to settle for. The figures show awareness that only through an advanced education and high-level occupations can status goals and consumption expectations be satisfied. Yet, as we contrast these lofty goals with the modest resources of some of these immigrant communities, there is reason for concern that the race toward fulfillment of these aspirations can be lost. As seen earlier, only a combination of strong family solidarity and community support offers a high probability of success; not all of these children will enjoy this advantage.

The bottom rows of table 35 indicate wide differences in academic achievement, as measured by standardized math and reading scores. Average math scores are highest among children of Cuban and Vietnamese origin and lowest for Mex-

ican-Americans, with the two black Caribbean groups in between. English reading scores are again highest among Cuban
youth in ethnic private schools. They are followed by West Indians, who show in this fashion their language advantage. Lowest scores are found among children of Haitian and, again,
Mexican immigrants. Insofar as academic achievement represents the most tangible outcome of adaptation among second-
generation children, these large differences provide a telling
sign of the process's segmentation. The pattern is confirmed by
differences in grade point averages. In this case, results favor
Vietnamese-Americans, highlighting again their strong motivation toward academic achievement.

It is possible that these differences in standardized scores
may be due to differences in the socioeconomic status of parents, the length of time children have spent in the United
States,[24] or the different age and sex composition of each group.
If this is the case, the preceding arguments about the role of the
immigrant community in fostering distinct assimilation outcomes would be greatly weakened. To examine that question,
we make use of multiple regression to render groups statistically equivalent in these dimensions, so as to clarify the net effects associated with different immigrant groups. For this
analysis, the rest of the sample, comprising all other nationalities, is used as the term of reference. Individual nationality effects are computed relative to this sample average.[25]

Table 36 presents the results. The bottom rows of this table
show the powerful influence of parental socioeconomic status
on both math and English reading scores, as well as the significant effect of length of U.S. residence on the latter variable.
Controlling for these effects plus those of age, sex, and area of
residence does not obliterate the role of membership in different immigrant communities. Cuban and Vietnamese youth still
display superior math performance after removing the influence of socioeconomic status and other variables. This net advantage is considerable: about 11 percentile points for each
group. Cuban-Americans also retain a similar advantage on
English performance. By contrast, the West Indian superiority

Table 36
*Net Effects of Immigrant Community
on Academic Achievement*

Nationality	Standardized Math Score[a]	Standardized Reading Score[a]
Haitian	−8.84	−11.24
Cuban[b]	11.77	12.48
West Indian	−7.72	n.s.
Mexican	−16.67	−12.78
Vietnamese	10.47	n.s.
Parental SES[c]	9.61	10.88
Length of U.S. Residence	n.s.[f]	4.22
Area of Residence[d]	3.07	n.s.
Age	−4.05	−2.84
Sex[e]	2.71	3.74
R²	.180	.203
N	4229	4229

[a] Regression coefficients indicating percentile changes in standardized scores per unit charge of each predictor. All effects presented are significant at the .01 level or higher.
[b] Cuban-origin students in private schools in Miami.
[c] Socioeconomic status index composed of the sum of standardized measures of father's and mother's education, father's and mother's occupation, and home ownership. Collapsed categories.
[d] Miami/Ft. Lauderdale coded *1*; San Diego *0*.
[e] Girls coded *1*; boys coded *0*.
[f] Statistically nonsignificant effects.

on this variable disappears after introducing the controls, indicating the weaker role of the immigrant community on these youths' academic performance.

At the other extreme, Mexican-American and Haitian-American students are at a considerable disadvantage, even when their families' modest economic circumstances are factored out. Haitian-origin students score about 10 percentile points lower than the average in both achievement measures, net of other factors. The Mexican gap is still higher. These results are in line with what is known about the modes of incorporation of first-generation immigrants from these countries and their resulting patterns of acculturation. Overall, findings show that there is *something* in the character of ethnic communities that is not fully explained by their average status, location, or length of U.S. residence. The particular history of each community, the contexts that it faces, and its ability to steer its young along certain acculturation paths play a significant role in academic achievement, arguably the most important assimilation outcome at this stage of the process.

Conclusion

In her study of black West Indians in New York, Waters quotes the views of a teenage girl, closely identified with her family:

> There was a time back in the 40s and 50s and 60s or whenever that people was actually trying to keep down black people. . . . But, you know, some black people now, it's like they not actually trying to make it better, you know? . . . and they sulk and they cry about it, and they're not really doing that much to help themselves. . . . It's just like hyping the problem if they keep saying everything is racial.[26]

In the last section, we saw how Haitian and West Indian teenagers are very aware of the reality of racial discrimination in America. But "race" can have two meanings for these black youths. For those acculturating to the views of the inner city, it is an explanation for permanent subordination and a justification for an oppositional attitude toward the middle-class mainstream. For those whose families have managed to implement a pattern of selective acculturation, it is a challenge to be overcome on the way to educational and occupational attainment. For this last group, exemplified by Waters's informant, the inner city provides the model of what *not* to become.

This dual meaning of race illustrates how much assimilation has changed since the time that social scientists were writing about the experiences of European-Americans. Joining society's mainstream was seen at the time as both proper and inevitable. Old loyalties were left behind and descendants of foreigners gradually entered American social circles as they learned the "right" values and demeanor. At present, the same process can be observed among some second-generation adolescents, but not among others. Growing up American today means being caught in a vastly more complex social world that carries along both the achievements and the failures of the past. Among the latter, none is more important than the consequences of pervasive racial discrimination and the adversarial reactions that it helped create.

Immigrants who settle in metropolitan areas—the vast majority—confront this reality as a *fait accompli* whose consequences affect them in manifold ways. The irony of the present situation is that certain immigrant groups have come to embody those exemplary values associated with the American mainstream, to which earlier immigrants were supposed to assimilate. It is perhaps for this reason that a pattern of selective acculturation connects so well with society's mainstream and that role reversal, where children's acculturation leaps ahead of their parents', is today more a danger signal than a first step toward successful adaptation.

The contrasting experiences that we have seen in this chapter carry practical weight as well. Together, acculturation, contexts of reception, and the assimilation outcomes that they create will affect the future of millions of new Americans and, along with them, the prospects for the entire society. America in 2050 will be a different place, but its culture and quality of life will be shaped, in no small measure, by what happens to today's children of immigrants. On balance, the resources and motivation of these children and their parents provide grounds for optimism. But, along with it, it is clear that adaptation is not unproblematic, and that some are at risk of reenacting the collective failures and consequent frustrations of America's past.

8

Conclusion

Immigration and Public Policy

There is a sense in which current immigration policy is
Adolf Hitler's posthumous revenge on America. The U.S.
political elite emerged from the war passionately concerned to cleanse itself of all taints of racism or xenophobia. Eventually it enacted the epochal Immigration Act of
1965. And this, quite accidentally triggered a renewed
mass immigration, so huge and so systematically different from anything that had gone before as to trans-
form—and ultimately perhaps even destroy—the one un-
questioned victor of World War II: the American
nation. . . .

So I suggest that the critics of immigration adopt a
name that has a long and honorable role in American history. They should call themselves—"Patriots."

Peter Brimelow, *Alien Nation* (1995, 254)

Periods of high immigration are invariably marked by a tide of
nativist resistance that characterizes the waves of newcomers
as a threat to the integrity of national culture and a source of
decay of the qualities of the native population. Such pronounce-
ments are issued both by crusading journalists and politicians
and by academics who cloak it in the garb of scientific knowledge. The statement that opened this final chapter is but a re-

cent example of a trend dating back to the origins of the republic and whose earlier manifestations at the beginning of this century we have already examined.

These statements are also part of the profoundly ambivalent ways in which immigration is portrayed and understood by the native population: reviled when it is actually taking place and celebrated after a period of time, when the first generation has passed from the scene and its descendants—now American citizens—are able to revindicate its achievements. A good part of American literature is made up of nostalgic retrospectives of the trials and accomplishments of immigrants by its children and grandchildren—Jews and Italians earlier on in the century; Chinese, Cubans, and Mexicans today.[1] Based on the record, it is just as predictable that nativist voices will continue to rise in the coming years against the looming immigration "disaster," as that a revisionist history about current arrivals from Asia and Latin America will be written sometime in the next century.

This cycle of negative and positive stereotyping only skims the surface of the phenomenon of immigration and its determinants. This is so because these successive images emerge in the realm of public opinion, where serious understanding of the dynamics underlying the process, including the role of public opinion itself, is lacking. The well-entrenched public view is that immigration is a consequence of the initiative of immigrants themselves, who come in search of a better life; they are allowed to settle because of the laxness of government controls and a tolerant attitude among the natives. If such an attitude disappears and the government tightens controls, immigration will certainly go away.[2] As in the opening quote, it is the "U.S. political elite" that is seen as responsible for the present situation because of its excessively liberal orientation.

These views are erroneous. Immigrant flows are not initiated solely by the desires and dreams of people in other lands, but by the designs and interests of well-organized groups in the receiving country, primarily employers. Up to a point, public opposition to immigration can play into the hands of these groups by maintaining the newcomers in a vulnerable and dependent position. Similarly, governments are not omnipotent in their regulation of immigration. In particular, governmental attempts at reversing well-established immigrant flows do not generally have the intended effect because of the resistance of dense social networks linking places of origin and destination.[3]

This chapter aims at teasing out these complex dynamics in order to lay the basis for a sound understanding of the origins of contemporary immigration and of viable policies toward it. To do so, we examine both past causal theories about determinants of these flows and recent legislative attempts to deal with them. An initial proposition that both the historical record and present experience can support is that an *inverse* relationship often exists between public perceptions of immigration and its functionality for the economic groups that promote it. The utility of immigrant workers for their prospective employers is usually at its peak during periods in which public opposition to the newcomers' presence is highest. That utility tends to decline as these groups become settled and they and their descendants are better integrated into American social circles and culture.

Theories of Immigration

The Push-Pull Model

The most common theoretical approximation to the origins of immigration is the push-pull model. It is constructed around "factors of expulsion" (economic, social, and political hardships in the sending countries) and "factors of attraction" (comparative economic and political advantages in the receiving countries). The model has a close affinity to the "cost-benefit" approach to immigration advanced by several labor economists and corresponds to the popular view that the movement occurs primarily because of the motivations and actions of the newcomers.[4]

The model assumes that greater disadvantages (factors of expulsion) will naturally lead to greater migration as individuals seek to escape their situation. On the surface, this assumption is quite plausible: People migrate from Mexico and Vietnam to the United States and from Algeria to France rather than vice versa. A moment's reflection will persuade us, however, that the model has little predictive value and that it consists primarily of a *post hoc* recitation of factors that contribute but do not suffice to trigger migration flows. If all there was to the origin of such flows were differentials of advantage, we would expect that they would originate mainly in the most impoverished countries (places like Gabon, Ethiopia, Myanmar, Bolivia, or Paraguay) and, within them, in the most impoverished regions. This prediction seldom coincides with empirical reality.

Instead, international migration, including labor migration, often originates in countries at intermediate levels of development and, within them, in urban and rural sectors possessing some economic resources.[5] In addition, there are marked differences in propensities to migrate among countries and communities at comparable economic levels. The Philippines, a mid-income distant country, is a more likely source of migration to the United States on a per capita basis than a comparable Asian country, such as Pakistan, or a more proximate one, such as Colombia. Studies in Mexico and the Dominican Republic have found significant migration differentials among towns and small cities of comparable socioeconomic development and even located in close proximity to one another.[6]

Undeniably, individual migration is determined by calculations of advantage, but these are embedded in a context that "push-pull" or "cost-benefit" models fail to apprehend. To do so effectively, we must consider two different types of social structures: those linking sending and receiving countries and those linking communities and families in places of origin and destination.

Structural Imbalancing of Peripheral Societies

The present system of international migration registers a close association between the history of prior contact, colonization, and influence of powerful "core" nations in weaker or "peripheral" lands and the onset of migratory movements out of the latter. The history of contact between the United States and the Latin American countries that supplied the major contingents giving rise to today's "Hispanic" communities in the United States provides a suitable example. Each of these countries—Mexico, Puerto Rico, and Cuba—was, each in its time, a target of a North American expansionist pattern that remolded its internal economic and social structures to the point that would-be migrants were already presocialized in American ways even before starting the journey.[7]

The concepts of influence in the core-periphery system and of *structural imbalancing* provide an alternative perspective on the origins of migration that moves us away from exclusively individualistic theories. According to these concepts, the initiation of sizable and durable population flows out of certain peripheral countries is commonly based on a history of prior contact with countries of destination and the consequent growth of a structure of relationships that induces out-migration in various forms. Mexico, the principal source of U.S.-bound labor immigration, is also the prime example of a pattern of external intervention and internal imbalancing.

The Mexican framework of economic and political life constructed under Spanish colonial rule was severely undermined by contact with its more powerful North American neighbor. The Mexican-American War in the 1840s reduced Mexico's territory by almost half and, as Mexican-American scholars are wont to repeat, converted a good part of the country's population into foreigners in its own land.[8] North American expansion did not stop at military conquest, however, because rapid economic growth in what had been the northern provinces of Mexico reclaimed labor from the portion of the country left south of the Rio Grande.

In a pattern typical of the beginning of sizable labor flows elsewhere, Southwest growers and railroad companies started an active recruitment program where paid agents were sent into the interior of Mexico to offer free rail travel and cash advances as incentives for local peasants to come north. The result was to trigger a sizable rural labor outflow that, over time, became self-sustaining. At the time of the early recruitment waves in the nineteenth and early twentieth centuries, the U.S. southwest border was scarcely enforced. As original settlers of the land, Mexicans came with the territory, and the arrival of new contract laborers and the movement back and forth across the Rio Grande met with little official resistance. Mexicans were thus an integral part of the Southwest population before they became immigrants and much before they became "illegal" immigrants.[9]

Hence, contrary to today's portrayal of Mexican immigration as a movement initiated by individual calculations of gain, the process had its historical origins in U.S. geopolitical and economic expansion that first remolded the neighboring nation and then proceeded to organize dependable labor flows out of it. Such movements across the border of the reduced Mexican republic were a well-established routine in the Southwest before they became redefined as "illegal" immigration.

The process of structural imbalancing of peripheral areas of the world economy, followed by sustained immigration, has taken successive forms during the history of capitalism. Deliberate labor recruitment, such as the employer initiatives that gave rise to U.S.-bound Mexican migration, represents an intermediate form of a historical process that has ranged from coerced labor extraction (slavery) beginning in the sixteenth century to the present self-initiated labor flows. Migrant labor recruitment saw its height during the second half of the nineteenth century and the first two decades of the twentieth, when it was responsible for the onset of Italian and Polish as well as Mexican labor migrations to the United States, and for the growth of sizable Italian and Asian populations in other countries of the Western Hemisphere such as Brazil and Argentina.[10]

Self-initiated migrations are a product of the twentieth century, where external imbalancing of peripheral societies does not take the form of organized coercion or deliberate recruitment. Instead, mass diffusion of new consumption expectations and the electronic transmission of information about life standards in the developed world suffice to encourage emigration. The gap between modern consumption standards and the economic realities of backward countries plus increasing information about work opportunities abroad provide enough incentives to generate an almost limitless supply of would-be migrants. The global dominance of Western culture and consumption patterns places the advanced countries in the role of regulators of a seemingly inexhaustible flow of foreign workers who are willing to pay their transportation costs and assume all the risks of the journey. This new mode of imbalancing via electronic diffusion is less costly than earlier modes and affects a broader cross section of the population of potential sending countries. Not surprisingly, the sources of U.S.-bound migration, as well as migration toward other developed countries, have begun to diversify in terms of both national origins and class composition of newcomers during the last two decades.[11]

Despite the universal appeal of Western consumption standards, the specific historical ties between receiving and sending countries—primarily the impact on the latter of colonial and neocolonial episodes—continue to be clearly reflected in the major immigrant flows today. In 1990, the top five countries sending legal immigrants to the United States were Mexico, the Philippines, China/Taiwan, South Korea, and Vietnam; the top two sending unauthorized immigrants were Mexico and El Salvador; and the four principal sources of refugees were Vietnam, Laos, Cambodia, and Cuba.[12] A moment's reflection will bring to light the close historical ties between each of these countries and the United States, forged during successive North American interventions—from the Mexican and Spanish wars in the last century to successive anti-Communist struggles in the post–World War II period.

Overall, the close linkage between past colonial experiences, the economic and cultural penetration of peripheral societies, and the onset of large-scale migration flows indicates the limitations of push-pull models based on individualistic calculations of advantage. Equally underdeveloped countries have had different migration histories, and sizable outflows have originated in more- rather than less-developed regions. The reason is that the beginnings of these movements are rooted in a history of prior economic, political, and cultural contact between sending and receiving nations. Through these processes, social structures are molded that render subsequent calculations of "rewards" and "costs" intelligible. Today, sizable Mexican, Filipino, Korean, and other ethnic communities in the United States represent the direct, living outgrowth of political and economic restructuring of sending societies that set the stage for subsequent labor flows out of them.

Social Networks: The Microstructure of Migration

Not only differences between countries but differences *within* countries in propensities to migration require explanation. Again, a push-pull model proves insufficient at this level since families and communities of similar socioeconomic condition can produce very different migration histories. The main alternative explanation at this level is based on the concept of social networks. Once an external event such as the presence of labor recruiters or the diffusion of information about economic opportunities abroad triggers the departure of a few pioneering migrants, the migration process may become self-sustaining through the construction of increasingly dense social ties across space.

The return of successful migrants and the information that they bring facilitate the journey of others. To the extent that migration abroad fulfills the goals of individuals and families, the process continues to the point that it becomes normative. When this happens, going abroad ceases to be an exceptional affair and becomes the "proper thing to do," first for adult males and then for entire families. At some moment, networks across international borders acquire sufficient strength to induce migration for motives other than those that initiated the flow. People move to join families, care for children and relatives, or avail themselves of social and educational opportunities created by the ethnic community abroad.

The notion that international migration is simultaneously a network-creating and a network-dependent process was established by a string of sociological studies dating back to classics in the field such as Thomas and Znaniecki's *The Polish Peasant in Europe and America*.[13] More recent research has been able to determine the importance of such ties quantitatively. In a study of 822 adult male Mexican immigrants arriving in two Texas ports of entry during 1973–74, Portes and Bach found that over 90 percent of their respondents had obtained legal residence through family and employer connections in the United States. Seventy percent of these men had already traveled and lived in the North, mostly as unauthorized immigrants. They had been able to secure their legal papers mostly through family and work connections established during this period. The remainder also came, with few exceptions, by making use of the family reunification provisions of the U.S. immigration law.[14]

During the 1980s, sociologist Douglas Massey and his associates applied the concept of social networks to account for the differential migration propensities of nineteen Mexican communities. He classified these communities into four stages—from the stage where migration is exceptional to that in which it reaches a mass (normative) level. The differentiating factor, in his view, is the timing of the first pioneering trips abroad. Once some adult males had been recruited as laborers or went abroad on their own, their returns led to the gradual consolidation of cross-national networks along the lines described previously.[15]

The portrait of a self-sustaining migration process and the resilience of well-established flows to changes in economic incentives contrasts markedly with a static push-pull account of the origins of migration. By and large, migration by isolated individuals based on cost-benefit calculations is an exceptional event. For the most part, the decision to migrate is group mediated and its timing and destination determined largely by the social context of networks established over time.

Immigration Controls

The federal government as well as the governments of several states have attempted various measures to stem the tide of unauthorized labor migration and refugee flows in recent years. By and large, such measures have been implemented without taking into account either the historical origins or social underpinnings sustaining these movements. Instead, policies have commonly been based on some version of push-pull theory, seeking to manipulate short-term incentives in the expectation that would-be migrants can be dissuaded from starting the journey. For the most part, these measures have been ineffective. In this section, we consider two examples: the Immigration Reform and Control Act of 1986 and Proposition 187, passed by the State of California in 1994.

Public outcry about the growth of the foreign population and the pressure of influential newspapers and public policy centers led the U.S. Congress in the mid-1980s to consider a series of alternatives to bring unauthorized immigration under control. Following recommendations of the congressionally appointed Select Commission on Immigration and Refugee Policy and after lengthy debate, a series of sweeping measures were passed by both houses. The resulting Immigration Reform and Control Act (IRCA) became law in 1986 and led immediately to a number of important changes in the character and legal treatment of labor immigrants.

As an instrument for immigration control, the new law offered two provisions: 1) an amnesty program to regularize the situation of unauthorized immigrants with some time of residence in the United States; and 2) the civil and criminal sanctioning of employers who engaged in a pattern of repeated hiring of these immigrants. The reasoning behind the law was that the first provision would bring the unauthorized population to the legal surface and discourage it from further lawbreaking, while the second would change the structure of incentives by making it more difficult for new migrants to find U.S. employment.

Supporters of IRCA believed that rewards and sanctions focused on individuals would suffice to bring the flow under control. They did not consider the strength of forces assembled against this goal, which included both the social networks supporting immigration and the organized political resources of its North American sponsors. As noted at the start, mass labor migration does not arise out of the desires of would-be migrants, but out of the needs and interests of powerful groups in the receiving country. As we also saw, Mexican immigration—by far the largest contributor to the unauthorized flow—was initiated by deliberate recruitment and continues to our day to be a preferred labor supply by agricultural and urban employers.[16]

This labor flow is so well-entrenched that its supporters succeeded in turning the public outcry against immigration in their favor. This feat was accomplished via two legal devices. First, a provision was inserted into the amnesty program allowing for the legalization of "special agricultural workers" or SAWs, defined as unauthorized immigrants who had worked in U.S. agriculture for at least ninety days between May 1985 and May 1986. Riddled with fraud, this program nonetheless succeeded in legalizing 1.2 million unauthorized immigrants who, added to the 1.7 million amnestied through the general legalization program, guaranteed to rural and urban employers an ample labor supply for the immediate future.[17]

Second, the same groups succeeded in preventing the employer sanctions provision of the law from including a check for fraudulent documentation. The law provides penalties for engaging in a pattern of "knowingly hiring" illegal aliens. Operationally, this translates into a requirement that employers check prospective employees' documents certifying legal residence. However, firms are not required to verify the authenticity of these documents. Predictably, a counterfeit industry promptly emerged to satisfy the demand for such documentation. Immigrant workers who did not have it were often told by employers to go get their papers (false or otherwise) and then return.[18] More generally, employer sanctions did not stop the inflow of unauthorized workers, but merely rechanneled it into new forms. As predicted by immigration experts at the time, some of it went further underground, becoming better concealed from the authorities, and the rest found employment in the multitude of firms willing to comply with the letter but not the spirit of the law.[19]

On their part, newly amnestied immigrants did not stay put. The program was conceived with individuals in mind without taking into account that most such immigrants are part of extended networks. Soon, the consequences of this oversight became clear. The question promptly arose as to what to do with the immediate relatives of legalized aliens who themselves were ineligible for amnesty. The Immigration and Naturalization Service was forced to deal with this dilemma through ad hoc administrative measures until the Immigration Act of 1990 created a special category of visas for family members of amnestied immigrants.[20]

Legal immigration will increase not only through the amnestied immigrants and their immediate relatives, but also through the capacity of this newly legalized population to reestablish ties with places of origin. Legalized immigrants can now travel back and forth without fear of deportation. After a period of only three years, they become eligible for permanent residence and hence are able to legally petition for other relatives. After another period of three to five years, they can become U.S. citizens and, hence, bring immediate relatives outside quota limits. Through the operation of these networks as well as the effective resistance of labor immigrants and their North American sponsors, a law designed to address the public outcry about immigration ended up *increasing* the flow of both legal and unauthorized immigrants. The experience provides an object lesson in the less-than-straightforward effects of public opinion and the consequences of ignoring the social structures through which migration takes place.

Public opposition to immigration is amorphous and mostly disorganized. By contrast, the structures that sustain the movement are highly focused and well grounded in the history of sending and receiving places. The clash between both forces can result in unanticipated consequences, at variance with the manifest intent of control measures. A second example, still unfolding at the time of this writing, is the approval of a package of anti-immigration measures, via plebiscite, by the State of California. Proposition 187, as this set of measures is known, was passed by a 3-to-2 margin of the California electorate in November 1994.[21]

The purpose of these measures, advertised by its creators as the "save-our-state" (SOS) initiative, is to discourage immigration by barring illegal aliens from access to government services. According to the new law, illegal aliens will become ineligible for a panoply of government programs including public education and all public health services, except for emergency care. Schools are further ordered to report students and their parents if school officials "reasonably suspect" that the student is an illegal alien.[22]

Once again, these provisions seek to control immigration by manipulating the balance of individual incentives and disincentives without regard to broader social forces. For the most part, unauthorized immigrants do not come seeking welfare privileges, but jobs. A study conducted in an immigrant-sending community deep in the interior of Mexico after passage of Proposition 187 revealed that a remarkable 90 percent knew about this measure, but that close to 80 percent indicated that it would have no effect on their plans to work or live in California. Of the remaining 20 percent, most believed erroneously that a new Border Patrol enforcement operation in San Diego was mandated by Proposition 187 and were somewhat concerned about the greater difficulty in crossing. The author of the study concludes:

People from communities like this do not migrate to the United States expecting hand-outs from the government.

The universally held view in this community of migrants was that economic necessity, not laws and policies of the United States, will determine whether a community resident migrates or not.[23]

A flurry of legal challenges, especially to the public education provisions of this measure, have so far prevented its implementation. If put into practice, Proposition 187 will have an important effect—namely, to increase the vulnerability of immigrant workers vis-à-vis prospective employers by removing emergency income sources and social protections. Paradoxically, this greater vulnerability of unauthorized immigrants will make them *more* attractive to California firms as a ready pool of pliant labor. Since the need for jobs and resilient cross-border networks will sustain the flow, the end result is that Proposition 187 will, in all probability, increase the unauthorized migration that it seeks to prevent.

As the preceding examples suggest, the thorny problem of immigration control is not efficiently addressed by legislation that attempts to respond to public fears by punishing immigrants while neglecting the broader determinants on which their decisions are grounded. Such quick fixes, based on a naive view of the process, end up doing more harm than good, as they seriously erode the credibility of government institutions and the law. The next section summarizes what has been learned about the sources of unauthorized migration as a prelude for discussion of an alternative policy approach.

Determinants of Unauthorized Immigration: A Summary

The play of macro- and microstructural forces reviewed previously leads to a series of individual consequences that represent, in turn, the immediate determinants of migration decisions. The process can be portrayed as a sequence of mutually reinforcing events increasing the probability of a given outcome.

A pro-migration cycle is the result of the interplay of forces that ideally proceeds as follows:

1. There is a history of prior external intervention and internal restructuring of the sending society and culture. The process culminates with the reorientation of the economy to play a complementary role vis-à-vis that of the dominant country and the diffusion of consumption patterns from the latter.

2. Once the process of internal restructuring is under way, it becomes easier to activate the potential for labor migration through deliberate recruitment. As a subsistence peasantry becomes incorporated into the money economy, the meaning of higher wages abroad gains significance both as a mechanism to resolve disruptions of the household economy and to satisfy new consumption aspirations. The successful experience of "pioneer" migrants encourages others to follow suit, and supportive social networks begin to emerge, connecting places of origin and of destination.

3. At the individual level, consequences of these macrostructural forces are felt as an increasing disruption of traditional life-styles and a growing gap between new consumption aspirations and the material means to satisfy them. As modern life patterns become normative and the viability of the prior subsistence economy declines, a search for suitable means of economic adaptation begins. Long-distance migration is *one* such solution that competes with others, such as an increasing labor offer by household members, cyclical migration to nearby cities, and even withdrawal to more remote subsistence areas untouched by modernization.

4. At this point, the presence of microstructural forces becomes decisive. The probability of individual and household decisions to migrate are greatly increased when labor recruiters encourage the process through various incentives and when kin and friends do likewise. Although deliberate recruitment is likely to activate the potential for migration in the first place, it is

the consolidation of social networks that gives the process its self-sustaining and cumulative character.

In reality, causal forces at different levels seldom cohere
perfectly in this ideal sequence. Instead, we encounter a variety
of possible combinations between countries and across historical periods. The exercise of political and economic hegemony
may not be accompanied by deliberate labor recruitment, a pattern that leads to the absence or relatively slow onset of labor
flows. U.S. relations with most Third World countries outside of
its immediate periphery may be characterized in this manner.
A second pattern involves the absence of colonial or quasi-co-
lonial ties, compensated subsequently by vigorous labor recruitment. This is exemplified by the systematic recruitment
activities of West Germany in Turkey, Greece, and other Mediterranean countries during the 1960s.[24] Finally, a third variant
features established labor flows created by a prior history of
economic expansion, labor recruitment, and network consolidation that are subsequently declared outside the law and suppressed. The United States and Mexico illustrate this variant, as
well as the instability and uncertainty to which it gives rise.

In all cases, the central point is that immigration does not
arise because, on a given day, some Third World workers decide
to seek their fortunes abroad. Instead, it is a process condi-
tioned by contextual forces ranging from the historical relation
of two states and cultures to the web of social relations in which
individual and family life takes place. Efforts to reverse ongo-
ing migration must take into account the complex series of
steps that gave rise to it in the first place, lest they end up reinforcing the process.

Immigration Types and the Law

In contrast to this conclusion, the common public perception
is that governments are capable of easily reversing historical
trends. As we have seen, the experience of IRCA provides a telling example of how governmental measures in the field of immigration can end up having effects opposite to those intended.

An earlier illustration of the same point was the termination of the contract labor agreement or Bracero Program with Mexico in 1964. This decision was prompted by a similar public outcry about the presence of so many low-wage foreign workers. The measure did not stop the Mexican labor inflow, which went underground and then expanded rapidly.[25]

In addition to the recognition of these limits, policy recommendations in this area should balance carefully the pros and cons of different types of immigration, going beyond the current vagaries of public opinion. A first step consists of breaking down the amorphous concept "immigrant" into the distinct flows coming today into the country and considering the contribution and problems associated with each. The typology of immigration that has accompanied us throughout the book provides a basis for this analysis.

Manual Labor Migration

Figure 11 presents a summary of the major types of immigration, the legal categories under which they come, their legal steps toward citizenship, and major representative nationalities. There is no doubt that the largest category and the prime target for control measures is manual labor migration. As we have seen, the bulk of it comes surreptitiously and has so far defied attempts at stopping or significantly reducing it. A first step in an alternative policy approach is to examine seriously whether this inflow is detrimental to the national interests. Despite the rising wave of anti-immigrant sentiment whipped up by a number of xenophobic tracts, there is evidence that manual labor migration can make some significant economic contributions.

First, the evidence that immigrant workers negatively affect the employment chances and earnings of the native born is mixed at best. Waters provides a detailed ethnographic account of how black West Indian immigrants displaced African-American workers in a mid-size service firm in New York. Similarly, Kircheman and Neckerman and Aponte have shown how employers' preferences in their Chicago sample adversely affected

Type	Mode of Entry	Legal Status	Next Legal Step	Representative Nationalities
Manual Labor Migrants	Mostly surreptitious as (a) legal border crossers (b) visa overstayers. Some legalized under IRCA[a] amnesty program. Some legal entrants under family reunification provisions of immigration law.	Mostly unauthorized. Some permanent legal residents.	*For the unauthorized:* Permanent residence under family reunification provisions or future amnesty program. Return to home country if unsuccessful. *For legal residents:* Citizenship acquisition in 3–5 years.	Mexicans Dominicans Salvadorans Guatemalans
Professionals and Entrepreneurs	Mostly legal under occupational preferences and family reunification provisions. Some visa overstayers.	Mostly legal, permanent.	Citizenship acquisition in 3–5 years. For visa overstayers: Seek permanent residence under occupational preferences or family reunification provisions.	Filipinos Koreans Asian Indians

Refugees/Asylees	Refugee status granted by INS[b] official abroad. Request for asylum upon arrival in the U.S.	Legal, temporary. Illegal if asylum request denied.	Adjustable to legal permanent residence in 1 year. Deportable if asylum request denied.	Refugees: Former Soviet Union Vietnamese Iranians Asylees: Former Soviet Union Former Yugoslavia Syrians

[a] Immigration Reform and Control Act of 1986.
[b] U.S. Immigration and Naturalization Service.

Figure 11. Types of immigration and modes of entry.

the employment chances of African-Americans and Puerto Ricans and favored those of Mexican unauthorized immigrants.[26] On the other hand, these displacement effects seldom show up in aggregate statistics based on census data or larger surveys.[27]

Other studies have found that unauthorized immigrants do not exert any significant impact on the wages of the native born. Table 37 presents results of one such study that estimated wage changes for white, black, and Hispanic natives relative to the number of working-age immigrants living in the same metropolitan area. Results indicate that the number of Hispanic immigrants tends to *increase* the wages of native workers, albeit by a marginal amount. Similarly, a team of researchers at the Urban Institute analyzed data on earnings and unemployment for white and Mexican-origin males in forty-seven standard metropolitan areas of the Southwest. They found that a 10 percent increase in unauthorized immigration from Mexico would

Table 37
Effects of the Presence of Immigrant Workers on Native Workers' Wages, 1980

	Proportional Change in Wages of:		
With Respect to the Number of:	White Natives	Black Natives	Spanish-Origin Natives
Spanish-origin immigrants	.002[a]	.014[b]	.024[b]
Asian immigrants	−.003	−.007	−.025[b]
White immigrants	−.042[b]	−.024	−.005[b]

SOURCE: George J. Borjas, "Immigrants, Minorities, and Labor Market Competition," *Industrial and Labor Relations Review* 40 (April 1987): table 5.

NOTE: Figures are elasticities of factor prices calculated for individuals aged 18–64 who were not in the military, were not self-employed, and had complete information on the variables used in the analysis. See text for an interpretation of results.

[a] Two-stage least squares estimates of cross-price elasticities, controlling for education and work experience.
[b] Significant at the 5 percent level.

increase white male wages by 0.4 percent and those of Mexican-origin males by 0.12 percent while reducing the probability
of white unemployment by 3 to 4 percent.[28] Overall, results of
aggregate statistical studies reveal an insignificant or slightly
positive effect of unauthorized labor migration on the earnings
and employment of the native born.

Second, the presence of foreign workers can help sustain the
pace of economic growth and revive declining sectors such as
manufacturing. According to Muller and Espenshade, immigrants garnered most manufacturing jobs created in Los Angeles during the 1970s and early 1980s and replaced another
55,000 native workers who found jobs elsewhere. The result
was some decline in wages, but the simultaneous stabilization
of that sector's labor force.[29] For Sassen, Waldinger, Zhou, and
other researchers, the presence of foreign workers, including
the unauthorized, has been central to the survival of the garment, footwear, furniture, and other low-tech industries during
the 1980s, as well as to the booming sector of custom-made
goods and services for upscale consumers.[30]

On balance, displacement of native workers in particular
firms, documented by ethnographic research, seems to be
compensated by the economic dynamism created by the presence of low-wage immigrant workers, which opens up new
sources of employment. Above all, these workers provide a
source of highly motivated, hardworking labor whose skills and
energy expand the human resources of the nation. Suppressing
this labor stream altogether may not be wise policy. Instead,
alternative measures should be developed to regulate the inflow
in order to eliminate the undeniable problems associated with
it. These include exploitative labor practices that take advantage of the legal vulnerability of the undocumented, discour-
agement of technological innovation because of the availability
of an abundant low-wage labor supply, and the possibility that
the sheer number of foreign workers may overwhelm the domestic population in certain localities.[31] In addition, for unauthorized immigrant workers, there is the problem of their children's adaptation to American society. As seen in chapter 7,

these children are commonly at risk of downward assimilation because of their disadvantaged situation.

For a number of reasons, it is not likely that border interdiction alone will succeed in controlling the unauthorized inflow. Recent experiments, such as Operation Hold-the-Line in El Paso, succeed in controlling the local traffic, but only shift long-distance migration from the interior of Mexico to less accessible locations along the border.[32] In light of what is known about the origins of this movement, there are only two ways to effectively bring it under control: reduce the interest of U.S. employers in using this source of labor and reorient the social networks of migration toward investment and entrepreneurship in the country of origin.

The laws required to achieve the first objective are already in the books, except that they are poorly and haphazardly enforced. They consist of the set of labor protections—including minimum wage, overtime compensation, workplace safety, old-age and accident insurance, and others—enacted to protect *all* workers whether foreign or native born. Systematic enforcement of these laws would simultaneously lower the motivation to hire unauthorized immigrants because of their vulnerability and increase the supply of domestic workers willing to work at these jobs. Coupled with some tightened program of sanctions based on tamper-proof work permits, enforcement of labor standards may go a long way toward accomplishing the first objective above. Unfortunately, the trend today runs in the opposite direction. As Cornelius notes, competition among states and localities to create a "favorable regulatory climate" for business has led to the weakening of labor standards enforcement to the point that a single California labor inspector is supposed to monitor compliance by tens of thousands of firms in San Diego and Orange counties.[33] Similarly, Fernández-Kelly and García document how the understaffed and undermanned Wage and Hour Division of the U.S. Department of Labor can only monitor the most blatant violators, allowing employers of immigrants in south Florida and southern California to violate protective labor codes with impunity.[34]

But, as shown by numerous studies, it is the transnational networks that families and communities build that provide the backbone for the continuing labor flow. They do so out of economic necessity, within the macroeconomic conditions created for them by the prior penetration of North American interests into their country. Reversing this movement will require, inescapably, transforming the economic conditions of these communities and the coping strategies to which they give rise. For this purpose, programs must be enacted in cooperation with the governments of sending countries, particularly Mexico, to foster small-scale entrepreneurial opportunities in these areas that generate both employment and chances for upward mobility for the local population.

These programs should include loans for land acquisitions by peasant families, agricultural credit and technical support, loans and training programs for grassroots enterprises in the cities, and cooperative development. Some international organizations such as Acción Internacional and the Inter-American Foundation have acquired a wealth of knowledge on the successful implementation of grassroots economic initiatives, although their limited resources have limited the scope of these projects.[35] Fortunately, the existing evidence suggests that people do not migrate out of invidious comparisons with the sending country, but in order to survive and prosper in the country of origin.[36] Translated into practical terms, this means that wage levels in Mexico and other emigration countries need not equal U.S. levels for labor migration to subside. What is needed is that these wages provide a reasonable livelihood and a chance for gradual progress within the local economy. In cooperation with the Mexican government, the United States could reallocate some of the resources now wasted in the hopeless effort to track unauthorized labor migrants into a large-scale program of land acquisition and small-scale entrepreneurial development in the interior of Mexico. Placed in the hands of experienced nongovernmental organizations, rather than government bureaucracies, the program would stand a good chance of succeeding.

Congressional approval of the North American Free Trade Agreement (NAFTA) in 1993 would seem to provide a suitable framework for this cooperative endeavor. Unfortunately, NAFTA has focused so far on large-scale financial and industrial transactions and led directly to a neoliberal set of policies by the Mexican government designed to increase "export efficiency." Among them, the Mexican program of agricultural modernization is designed to consolidate production into large-scale units, which will inevitably shrink labor demand and, hence, reduce opportunities for small farmers. The economic modernization policies linked to NAFTA are thus likely to *increase*, at least in the medium term, the supply of migrants by closing employment opportunities in the interior of Mexico.[37] In the absence of a large-scale program targeted on the development of small-scale agriculture in rural areas and small enterprise in the cities, family and community networks will continue to move people north for the foreseeable future.

Small-scale production stimulated by the binational program proposed here could also be oriented toward exports within the framework of NAFTA. This would open new markets and increase the viability of these enterprises beyond local demand. The experience of small, flexible industries oriented toward exports in other countries offers a viable set of models for such a program.[38] If successful, such initiative would not only retain labor in sending areas but encourage some immigrant workers to return. This second effect would have the added benefit of reducing the problem posed by children growing up in North American cities under conditions of exceptional disadvantage.

For settled immigrant workers in the United States, policies will have to be developed that seek to reinforce parental authority and the cohesiveness of ethnic communities as a means to ward off the danger of downward assimilation. This set of policies should run contrary to the misguided effort of many teachers and schools today to promote "Americanization" at any cost. Such effort often ends up by weakening the hold that parents and communities have on their young, leading to dissonant acculturation. As seen in chapter 7, consequences of this path can be highly negative for the long-term adjustment of the second generation.[39]

Professionals and Entrepreneurs

On the surface, highly skilled foreign professional and business people present much less of a problem than manual laborers. As seen in previous chapters, immigrant scientists, engineers, and physicians reinforce the nation's supply of scarce talent and mix easily with the domestic population by becoming dispersed throughout the country. Foreign entrepreneurs bring capital and business expertise and help fill commercial niches neglected by mainstream firms, such as inner-city retailing and distribution of imported foods and exotic goods. Finally, the majority of these immigrants come legally; hence, the problems associated with the unauthorized do not materialize.

Difficulties with professional and entrepreneurial immigrants are of a different sort. The obvious gain to the United States from these newcomers' skills and resources often comes at the expense of impoverished sending countries. The magnitude of the loss is compounded by the investment of these nations' scarce resources in training scientists, engineers, and physicians who leave after graduation seeking more promising jobs abroad. Similarly, entrepreneurial migrations reduce not only the sending countries' pool of business talent, but also their capital resources.

Professional and entrepreneurial migrations do not always have these negative consequences. In this regard, it is important to distinguish between relatively more advanced countries with a fairly large pool of professional talent and those in the bottom rungs of the development ladder. In the first instance, immigration abroad may even be beneficial as networks of expatriate professionals maintain contact with the home country and provide sources of information and expertise not available otherwise. Similarly, entrepreneurial communities may generate demand for new lines of exports and generate commercial and financial entry points into the North American market. Korean businesses in Los Angeles and East Coast cities offer a clear illustration of this pattern. Indian professionals and academics throughout the United States exemplify the contribution that talented émigrés can make to their home scientific communities.[40]

"Brain-drain" migration becomes a more serious problem when it literally empties the supply of trained personnel so that business and government bureaucracies cannot function efficiently. In Jamaica, Haiti, and other small island nations of the Caribbean, the outflow of professionals is reported to have reached such a level, with obvious deleterious consequences for national development.[41] The same is true of the most impoverished African and Asian nations. In these instances, developed countries—including the United States—should move to balance the free international movement of talent with programs designed to enable these countries to preserve an adequate domestic supply. The requirement that foreign students in North American universities return to their home countries, at least for a few years, is a positive step in this direction. Usually attached to scholarships granted by official and private organizations to Third World students, this requirement should be maintained and strengthened.

Similarly, it is important that the U.S. government support programs of less developed countries designed to repatriate some of their professionals and retain those trained domestically. The rationale for such a policy is more moral than economic. Table 38 presents economic and social indicators for several of the principal countries contributing to professional immigration and compares them with equivalent data for the United States. Clearly, though we benefit from the skills of educated immigrants, their loss is often suffered by countries that can least afford it. For years, the Philippines, China, India, and Korea have been major sources of U.S.-bound professional migration, a role recently joined by Eastern European and African countries. To the extent that an adequate supply of professional and entrepreneurial talent promotes economic development

Table 38

Economic and Social Indicators of Source Countries of U.S.-Bound Professional Emigration

Country	GNP per Capita (1992 U.S. $)	Population, 1992 (000s)	Life Expectancy at Birth	Secondary School Enrollment Rate	Percent Urban Population	Immigrants to U.S. Classified as Professionals and Managers, 1993
China	470	1,162,000	69.1	51	26.8	13,954
Philippines	770	64,259	65.0	74	43.9	11,164
India	310	884,000	61.1	44	26.0	10,210
Poland	1,910	38,365	70.5	83	62.6	6,074
Ireland	12,210	3,547	75.2	100	57.6	3,312
Dominican Republic	1,050	7,231	67.5	74	62.1	2,912
South Korea	6,790	43,663	70.9	90	74.3	2,416
Iran	2,200	59,607	65.5	57	58.3	2,093
Jamaica	1,340	2,396	73.6	62	53.5	1,141
Nigeria	320	102,000	51.8	20	36.8	1,102
United States	23,340	255,000	76.6	90	75.6	—

SOURCES: International Bank for Reconstruction and Development/The World Bank, *World Tables* (Baltimore: Johns Hopkins University Press, 1994); U.S. Immigration and Naturalization Service, *1993 Statistical Yearbook* (Washington, D.C.: U.S. Department of Justice), 1994.

and that the latter provides a basis for social and political stability in the Third World, helping these countries retain high-level human resources is in the long-term interests of the advanced countries, including the United States.

Refugees and Asylees

Since the Refugee Act of 1980, the United States has brought its official policy into line with those of international organizations concerning the definition and treatment of refugee groups. In practice, however, the 1980s continued to see a heavy bias in favor of escapees from Communist-controlled nations and against those from more friendly regimes. The collapse of the Communist camp put a partial end to this bias although, as seen in table 39, new refugee migration to the United States continues to be dominated by the last stages of the Cold War. Remaining Communist countries continue to be major sources

Table 39

Refugee Arrivals in the United States by Selected Nationalities and Presumed Reasons for Departure

Country	Number of Refugees Admitted in the U.S. 1987–1993	Reason for Departure
Soviet Union	262,952	Communist regime and instability following its downfall
Vietnam	173,116	Communist regime
Laos	75,554	Communist regime
Iran	29,236	Anti-U.S. Islamic regime
Cuba	22,158	Communist regime
Romania	20,999	Communist regime and instability following its downfall
Ethiopia	17,994	Same
Afghanistan	14,514	Same
Poland	14,016	Same
Cambodia	9,603	Same

SOURCE: Figures from U.S. Immigration and Naturalization Service, *1993 Statistical Yearbook* (Washington, D.C.: U.S. Department of Justice), 1994.

of refugee migration, a role in which they are joined by the anti-U.S. regime of Iran. The massive increase in refugees from the former Soviet Union coincided with the years of *perestroika* and the end of Communist rule. The decision to open the door wide to Soviet refugees was guided, in part, by the wish to provide a safety valve during this crucial political transition. Hence, geopolitical considerations and related definitions of "friendly" and "hostile" countries continued to dominate refugee admissions during this period.

The best theoretical analysis of the origins of contemporary refugee crises is that of Zolberg and his associates, who define them as the consequence of ethnic and class struggles during the construction of national states or for control of these states.[42] As seen in chapter 4, many European migration flows to North America earlier in the century originated in nations that were not yet states and in states that were not nations. Today, similar situations exist in several areas of Eastern Europe, Asia, and Africa, giving rise to violent conflicts and massive population displacements. The aspiration of suppressed ethnic minorities to their own independent states has triggered protracted wars in places as far apart as Palestine, Northern Ireland, and Bosnia-Herzegovina. Efforts by existing states to consolidate the hold of a dominant ethno-cultural group have triggered massacres and mass escapes in Rwanda, the former Yugoslavia, and Chechnya. Irreconcilable differences between clans of roughly equal power have destroyed national states, as in Somalia.

Situations such as these are likely to continue throughout the Third World and Eastern Europe, as different countries struggle toward definitions of nationhood and stable political systems. Hence, refugee flows cannot be regarded as isolated and short-lived contingencies, but as a stable part of the global scene for years to come. Neither the United States nor any other developed country can be expected to absorb all victims of these dislocations, but their policies in this area should go beyond calculations of narrow political self-interest. Refugees must not be regarded as propaganda tools or beneficiaries of a geopolitical safety valve, but as people in urgent need of help to rebuild their lives and those of their families.

A first line of action consists of efforts to eliminate or at least ameliorate the political conflicts that give rise to refugee out-flows in the first place. When this is not possible, the United States should collaborate with international organizations, in particular the United Nations High Commission for Refugees, in efforts to resettle refugees close to their social and cultural milieu and to promote political settlements that encourage their return. When all else fails and long-term resettlement be-comes necessary, the United States and other developed coun-tries should be willing to absorb a "fair share" of the displaced in rough proportion to their resources and on the basis of hu-manitarian and not exclusively political considerations. Such alternative policy will do away with the paradox of the 1980s when peasant escapees from Cambodia and Laos were greeted by U.S. authorities with open arms, while peasants escaping death squads and army persecution in Guatemala and El Sal-vador were defined as illegal aliens and denied any resettlement assistance.

Conclusion

It's evening in Little Havana, Miami, as the Angulo family pre-pares for its modest dinner. Originally from Managua, Nicara-gua, Mr. Angulo holds a degree in chemistry. He and his wife think of themselves as political exiles, but are not recognized as such by U.S. authorities, who regard them as illegal aliens. Be-cause of their lack of papers, the Angulos hold jobs much below their educational credentials. They are unable to move out of their impoverished neighborhood, where their son Ariel at-tends school. Because of his undocumented status, Ariel cannot even apply for a legal summer job. Violence in the school is rampant and academic standards are low. Ariel complains that other students ridicule Nicaraguans and that his parents do not understand the pressures he is under. More troubling still is the fact that he cannot speak Spanish or English fluently. Caught between two worlds, parents and child look with despair toward the future.[43]

A few blocks to the east, the visitor is transported to rural Haiti upon entering the home of Aristide Maillol. Aristide's mother does not speak English and her eyes drift to the floor when explaining in Haitian Creole that her husband is hospitalized and she had to leave her job as a maid in a motel to attend to his needs. Jobless, she worries as to how she will meet her family's immediate needs. But the Maillol home is something else. Amidst the home-country trinkets that adorn all Haitian residences, there is a large bookcase arranged as a living room shrine. Framed by paper flowers, there is a painted portrait of the Maillol couple in crude and radiant colors. Three shelves of photographs below it show Aristide's brother and three sisters. The boy smiles confidently in the cap and gown of a high school graduate. The girls are displayed individually and in clusters, their eyes beaming, their hair pulled back, attired as for a celebration. Next are the various trophies earned by the Maillol children in academic contests. Aristide's older brother received a scholarship to study at Yale. Aristide, who is fifteen and plans to be a lawyer, is confident that he will follow his brother's path. He says: "We are immigrants and immigrants must work hard to overcome hardship. You can't let anything stop you. I know there is discrimination, racism . . . but you can't let that bother you."[44]

As in other periods of high immigration, thousands of individual stories are being woven today into the rich tapestry of cultures and histories that is America. As in the past, despair and failure mix with hope and success as immigrants and their children strive to find a niche in this complex society. Results are sometimes surprising, as when children of destitute black peasants move up on the strength of their will and family solidarity or when immigrant professionals slide downwards because of an adverse legal ruling. But overall, what remains constant is the energy displayed by this vast mass of newcomers and the contributions that it makes to American economic growth and cultural vitality. For unlike several European countries, rich but sclerotic in their isolation, America has retained the vigor of its social life and its capacity for innovation and change. Immigration has been and will continue to be a key factor in this distinct national profile.

Obviously, this country cannot be the repository of all the ambitious and all the displaced from less lucky lands and, for this reason, regulation and control of immigrant flows remain necessary. The crux of the problem is the size of and the abuses linked to unauthorized immigration. We have seen previously how resolution of this problem will require more complex measures than simple border enforcement, a new set of imaginative policies grounded in the history of these flows. Yet, overall, the fears of the rising chorus of nativists and restrictionists are likely to prove as groundless today as they have in the past. Despite different languages and the perils to children of life in a complex society, the present wave of immigration is more likely to add than to subtract from the wealth and cultural vitality of the nation.

Today's anti-immigrant tracts, exemplified by the opening quote in this chapter, bear an uncanny resemblance to those that poured forth in the 1910s and 1920s. They will be equally discredited. Immigrants and refugees will continue to give rise to viable communities, infusing new blood in local labor markets, filling positions at different levels of the economy, and adding to the diversity of sounds, sights, and tastes of American cities. The history of this "nation of nations" has been, to a large extent, the history of the arrival, struggles, and absorption of its immigrants. While the voices of the small-minded—xenophobes of various stripes—have always been heard in periods of high immigration, in the end they have been silenced by the sheer weight of the achievements of the allegedly inferior races and their descendants. Despite the rising chorus of nativism as we pen these lines, the available evidence points to a repetition of the historical record.

Notes

Chapter 1. Introduction

1. García, *Desert Immigrants*.
2. Lamm and Imhoff, *The Immigration Time Bomb*, 226.
3. Ibid.
4. Briggs, "The Need for a More Restrictive Border Policy"; Teitelbaum, "Right Versus Right."
5. U.S. Bureau of the Census, "The Foreign-Born Population," 1993.
6. Bean, Browning, and Frisbie, "What the 1980 U.S. Census Tells Us"; North and Houstoun, "The Characteristics and Role"; Massey, "Do Undocumented Immigrants"; Portes, "Illegal Immigration." See also U.S. Immigration and Naturalization Service (INS), *Report on the Legalized Alien Population*, 1992.
7. Ibid.
8. Cornelius, "Illegal Migration," 4.
9. Bray, "Economic Development"; Grasmuck, "Immigration"; Pessar, "The Role of Households"; Ugalde, Bean, and Cardenas, "International Migration"; Grasmuck and Pessar, *Between Two Islands*.
10. Cornelius, "Mexican Migration," 7.
11. Bray, "Economic Development," 231.
12. Miller, *The Plight of Haitian Refugees*, chap. 4; Stepick, "Haitian Refugees."
13. See Alba, "Mexico's International Migration," 502–513; Portes and Ross, "Modernization for Emigration."
14. Lebergott, *Manpower in Economic Growth*, 39.
15. INS, *1993 Statistical Yearbook*, 159.
16. Portes and Bach, *Latin Journey*, 92–93.
17. INS, *1987 Statistical Yearbook*, tables 5, 6; and INS, *1993 Statistical Yearbook*, table 8.
18. McCoy, "The Political Economy"; Wood, "Caribbean Cane Cutters in Florida"; de Wind, Seidl, and Shenk, "Caribbean Migration."

19. Chávez, *Shadowed Lives*; Hondagneu-Sotelo, *Gendered Transitions*; Cornelius, "Labor Market Impacts"; Fernández-Kelly and García, "Advanced Technology"; Morales and Mines, "San Diego's Full-Service Restaurants"; NACLA, "Undocumented Immigrant Workers"; Sassen-Koob, "Immigrant and Minority Workers"; Urreu Giraldo, "Life Strategies"; Waldinger, "Immigration and Industrial Change"; Grasmuck, "Immigration"; Sassen-Koob, "Changing Composition."

20. Cornelius, "Labor Market Impacts"; Fernández-Kelly and García, "Advanced Technology"; Sassen-Koob, "Changing Composition."

21. For an analysis of employer-oriented loopholes in the 1986 act, see Portes, "Immigration Reform." See also LeMay, *Anatomy*.

22. Chávez, *Shadowed Lives*; Massey et al., *Return to Aztlán*; Grasmuck and Pessar, *Between Two Islands*; Cornelius, "Mexican Migration"; Dinerman, "Patterns of Adaptation"; Pessar, "The Role of Households"; Massey, "Understanding Mexican Migration."

23. INS, *1993 Statistical Yearbook*, table 21.

24. Portes and Ross, "Modernization for Emigration"; Glaser and Habers, "The Migration and Return of Professionals."

25. See Stevens, Goodman, and Mick, *The Alien Doctors*.

26. U.S. Bureau of the Census, "The Foreign-Born Population" (1993), tables 1, 5; Rumbaut, "Origins and Destinies."

27. Light, "Asian Enterprise in America"; Bonacich, Light, and Wong, "Koreans in Small Business"; Min, *Asian Americans*.

28. Díaz-Briquets, "Cuban-Owned Business"; Portes and Stepick, *City on the Edge*; Botifoll, "How Miami's New Image Was Created."

29. Frazier, *The Negro in the United States*. See also Light, *Ethnic Enterprise in America*.

30. Rischin, *The Promised City*; Howe, *World of Our Fathers*; Bonacich and Modell, *The Economic Basis*; Petersen, *Japanese Americans*.

31. Min, *Middlemen*; Bonacich, Light, and Wong, "Koreans in Small Business"; Kim, *New Urban Immigrants*; Portes and Manning, "The Immigrant Enclave."

32. Díaz-Briquets, "Cuban-Owned Business." See also Grenier and Stepick, *Miami Now*.

33. Zolberg, Suhrke, and Aguayo, "International Factors"; Zolberg, "From Invitation to Interdiction."

34. INS, *1993 Statistical Yearbook*, table 35.

35. Rumbaut, "Vietnamese, Laotian, and Cambodian Americans"; Cichon, Gozdziak, and Grover, "The Economic and Social Adjustment"; Rumbaut, "The Structure of Refuge"; Rumbaut and Weeks, "Fertility and Adaptation"; Bach et al., "The Economic Adjustment"; Portes and Stepick, "Unwelcome Immigrants"; Allen and Turner, *We the People*, 190–196.

36. Zolberg, Suhrke, and Aguayo, "International Factors"; Cichon, Gozdziak, and Grover, "The Economic and Social Adjustment"; Portes and Bach, *Latin Journey*, chap. 3.

Chapter 2. Moving

1. Jerome, *Migration and Business Cycles*, 40.
2. See Handlin, *The Uprooted*; Vecoli, "The Italian Americans"; Alba, *Italian Americans*.
3. Lieberson and Waters, "The Location of Ethnic and Racial Groups," 782.
4. Boswell, "A Split Labor Market Analysis."
5. Kivisto, *Immigrant Socialists*.
6. Wittke, *Refugees of Revolution*; Sowell, *Ethnic America*, chap. 3.
7. Lieberson and Waters, "The Location of Ethnic and Racial Groups," 782, 798–799; U.S. Bureau of the Census, *1990 Ethnic Profiles for States*.
8. Ibid.; Allen and Turner, *We the People*, 84–85.
9. Light, *Ethnic Enterprise in America*, 9.
10. Ibid.; Petersen, *Japanese Americans*.
11. Gardner, Robey, and Smith, "Asian Americans"; Wong and Hirschman, "The New Asian Immigrants"; Nishi, "Japanese Americans."
12. Reichert, "The Migrant Syndrome"; Dinerman, "Patterns of Adaptation"; Massey, "The Settlement Process."
13. On West Indian migration, see Anderson, "Migration and Development"; Dixon, "Emigration and Jamaican Employment"; Levine, *The Caribbean Exodus*. On Dominicans, see Grasmuck and Pessar, *Between Two Islands*; Sassen-Koob, "Formal and Informal Associations." On Haitians, see Stepick and Portes, "Flight into Despair." See also Gardner, Robey, and Smith, "Asian Americans"; Bonacich, "Asian Labor"; Hing, *Making and Remaking Asian America*; Min, *Asian Americans*.
14. Portes and Manning, "The Immigrant Enclave"; Kanjanapan, "The Immigration of Asian Professionals"; Rumbaut, "Origins and Destinies."
15. Korean businesses in Los Angeles are found both in the concentrated "Koreatown" enclave and dispersed throughout the metropolitan area. In New York, however, most Korean enterprise appears to be of the "middleman" kind. See Kim, *New Urban Immigrants*; Sassen-Koob, "The New Labor Demand"; Cobas, "Participation in the Ethnic Economy."
16. Díaz-Briquets and Pérez, "Cuba"; Rumbaut, "The Structure of Refuge"; Allen and Turner, *We the People*, 163–164, 193.

17. U.S. Immigration and Naturalization Service (INS), *1993 Statistical Yearbook*.

18. Preliminary evidence suggests that Salvadorans—many of whom had to stay in the country illegally after being denied political asylum—settled in Washington, D.C., because they encountered less harassment by Immigration Service personnel in the capital than in West Coast cities. Reasons for the presence of large numbers of Vietnamese and other legal refugee groups, such as Iranians, in Washington are less clear at present. On the case of Salvadorans, see Repak, "And They Came."

19. The Cuban enclave is discussed in chapter 3. See also Díaz-Briquets and Pérez, "Cuba"; Wilson and Martin, "Ethnic Enclaves"; Portes and Stepick, *City on the Edge*.

20. Pessar, "The Role of Households"; Grasmuck and Pessar, *Between Two Islands*.

21. Sassen-Koob, "The New Labor Demand"; Wong and Hirschman, "The New Asian Immigrants."

22. Hirschman and Wong, "The Extraordinary Educational Attainment"; Sharma, "The Philippines"; Geschwender, "The Portuguese and Haoles."

23. The Korean enclave economy is discussed in chapter 3. See also Min, "Ethnic Business"; and Min, *Asian Americans*.

24. Rumbaut, "Vietnamese, Laotian, and Cambodian Americans"; Forbes, "Residency Patterns."

25. Cornelius, "Illegal Immigration"; Browning and Rodríguez, "The Migration"; Massey, "The Settlement Process."

26. Grasmuck, "Immigration"; Portes, "Illegal Immigration."

27. Recently arrived refugee groups, such as Ethiopians and Afghans, tend to have high proportions of former professionals—a pattern that reproduces that found for early refugee nationalities, such as Cubans and Vietnamese. Yet a recent study found that almost none of these new professionals had achieved comparable employment in the United States during the first three years after arrival. See Cichon, Gozdziak, and Grover, "The Economic and Social Adjustment." See also Stevens, Goodman, and Mick, *The Alien Doctors*; Portes, "Determinants of the Brain Drain"; Rumbaut, "Passages to America"; Kanjanapan, "The Immigration of Asian Professionals."

28. Sassen-Koob, "The New Labor Demand," 149.

29. Ibid., 156. See also Waldinger, "Immigration and Industrial."

30. Ibid.; Portes and Sassen-Koob, "Making It Underground."

31. Sassen-Koob, "The New Labor Demand," 158.

32. Sowell, *Ethnic America*, 277.

33. Lieberson and Waters, "The Location of Ethnic and Racial Groups," 790.

34. Ibid.

35. Ibid. See also Gardner, Robey, and Smith, "Asian Americans"; Bonacich and Modell, *The Economic Basis*.

36. Lieberson and Waters, "The Location of Ethnic and Racial Groups."

37. Baker and North, *The 1975 Refugees*, 52–89. Forbes, "Residency Patterns"; Rumbaut, "Vietnamese, Laotian, and Cambodian Americans."

38. Sowell, *Ethnic America*, chap. 11; Alba, *Italian Americans*; Steinberg, *The Ethnic Myth*.

39. Light, *Ethnic Enterprise in America*; Bonacich and Modell, *The Economic Basis*; Portes and Manning, "The Immigrant Enclave"; Cobas, "Participation in the Ethnic Economy."

40. Dahl, *Who Governs?*; Sowell, *Ethnic America*, chap. 2; Glazer and Moynihan, *Beyond the Melting Pot*.

41. Lamm and Imhoff, *The Immigration Time Bomb*.

42. Moore and Pachón, *Hispanics in the United States*, chap. 10; Camarillo, *Chicanos in a Changing Society*; Barrera, *Race and Class in the Southwest*.

43. Greeley, *Why Can't They Be Like Us?*, 43.

44. Ibid.

Chapter 3. Making It in America

1. Piore, *Birds of Passage*, 17.

2. Borjas, "Statement," 219. See also Borjas, *Friends or Strangers*.

3. U.S. Bureau of the Census, "The Foreign-Born Population"(1993).

4. Rumbaut, "Origins and Destinies."

5. See Rumbaut, "Vietnamese, Laotian, and Cambodian Americans"; Allen and Turner, *We the People*, 190–196; Kelly, *Irangeles*; Cichon, Gozdziak, and Grover, "The Economic and Social Adjustment."

6. See Massey, "The Settlement Process"; Portes and Bach, *Latin Journey*, chap. 5; Grasmuck and Pessar, *Between Two Islands*.

7. Figures presented in table 4 are not limited to legal immigrants because the census counted undocumented immigrants as well. The latter may be presumed to reinforce the modest educational profile of the principal countries from which they originate. There is little doubt, however, that if the count had been limited to legal immigrants from these countries, results would be basically the same. See Passel and Woodrow, "Geographic Distribution"; Bean, Browning, and Frisbie, "The Socio-Demographic Characteristics."

8. Hirschman and Falcón, "The Educational Attainment."

9. Ibid., 102–104.

10. Rumbaut, "Origins and Destinies."

11. Rumbaut, "Vietnamese, Laotian, and Cambodian Americans." Similar patterns of low labor force participation and high unemployment have been found among recently arrived Afghan refugees. See Cichon, Gozdziak, and Grover, "Non-Southeast Asian Refugees."

12. Portes and Bach, *Latin Journey*; Tienda, "Hispanic Origin Workers," chap. 8; Bean and Tienda, *The Hispanic Population*.

13. Light, "Disadvantaged Minorities," 34.

14. Portes and Stepick, "Unwelcome Immigrants"; Waldinger, "Immigrant Enterprise"; Doeringer, Moss, and Terkla, "Capitalism and Kinship."

15. These findings should be kept in perspective because the average size of these ethnic firms is, by national standards, modest. See Granovetter, "Small Is Bountiful."

16. Light, "Immigrant and Ethnic Enterprise."

17. Bonacich, "A Theory of Middleman Minorities"; Bonacich and Modell, *The Economic Basis*.

18. See Rischin, *The Promised City*; Dinnerstein, "The Last European Jewish Migration."

19. Massey, "The Settlement Process"; Reichert, "The Migrant Syndrome"; Dinerman, "Patterns of Adaptation."

20. Piore, *Birds of Passage*.

21. Light, "Disadvantaged Minorities." The same author has moved recently from this original formulation to outline a theory of minority enterprise based on a combination of class and ethnic resources available to different groups. This new theory comes very close to our own interpretation. See Light, "Immigrant and Ethnic Enterprise."

22. See Kim, *New Urban Immigrants*; Boswell and Curtis, *The Cuban-American Experience*.

23. Chiswick, "The Effect of Americanization," 909.

24. Ibid., 914.

25. Reimers, "A Comparative Analysis."

26. Portes and Bach, *Latin Journey*, chap. 7.

27. See Bustamante, "The Historical Context"; Cornelius, "Mexican Migration to the United States: Causes"; Bach, "Mexican Immigration"; Portes, "Illegal Immigration."

28. On manual labor recruitment, see Grebler, Moore, and Guzman, *The Mexican-American People*; Bach, "Mexican Immigration"; Wood, "Caribbean Cane Cutters." On professional recruitment, see Stevens, Goodman, and Mick, *The Alien Doctors*; Portes, "Determinants of the Brain Drain"; Glaser and Habers, "The Migration and Return"; Rumbaut, "Passages to America."

29. The case of recently arrived Afghan refugees is particularly telling in this respect. See Cichon, Gozdziak, and Grover, "The Economic and Social Adjustment." See also Rumbaut, "The Structure of Refuge."

30. See Bonacich, "Advanced Capitalism"; Barrera, *Race and Class*; Portes and Bach, *Latin Journey*, chap. 7.

31. Light, "Immigrant and Ethnic Enterprise"; Wilson and Martin, "Ethnic Enclaves."

32. See Geschwender, *Racial Stratification in America*; Grebler, Moore, and Guzman, *The Mexican-American People*, part 3.

33. See Anderson, *Networks of Contact*; Samora, *Los Mojados*; Sassen-Koob, "Formal and Informal Associations"; Kim, *New Urban Immigrants*.

34. Anderson, *Networks of Contact*; Rumbaut, "The Structure of Refuge"; Tilly, "Migration in Modern European History"; Vecoli, "The Italian Americans."

35. See Portes and Bach, *Latin Journey*, chap. 6.

36. See Browning and Rodríguez, "The Migration"; Nelson and Tienda, "The Structuring of Hispanic Ethnicity"; Bean and Tienda, *The Hispanic Population*.

37. U.S. Bureau of the Census, "The Foreign-Born Population," table 5.

38. Portes and Clark, "Mariel Refugees," 15.

Chapter 4. From Immigrants to Ethnics

1. Rosenblum, *Immigrant Workers*, 152–153.

2. For examples of this literature, see the monthly *FAIR Immigration Report*, edited by the Federation for American Immigration Reform in Washington, D.C. See also Lamm and Imhoff, *The Immigration Time Bomb*; and Brimelow, *Alien Nation*, 35.

3. The motion was submitted by the only Spanish-origin commissioner, Jorge Valdés, during the summer of 1987. Withdrawal took place after a negative reaction by Anglo-American organizations, which obtained support, in turn, from the umbrella Cuban-American group in the area, called UNIDOS. The latter argued that a new referendum would be a source of unnecessary ethnic strife. Valdés withdrew his motion in the late summer. The story was covered extensively by the *Miami Herald* and *Miami News* during July and August.

4. Lipset and Bendix, *Social Mobility*, 104–105.

5. The concept is used here after Hirschman, *Exit, Voice, and Loyalty*.

6. Hechter, *Internal Colonialism*; Greeley, *Why Can't They Be Like Us?*; Portes and Bach, *Latin Journey*, chap. 1.

7. Glazer, "Ethnic Groups in America."

8. Rosenblum, *Immigrant Workers*, 30–39; Greeley, *Why Can't They Be Like Us?*, 1–3; Portes and Bach, *Latin Journey*, 8.

9. Fine, *Labor and Farmer Parties*, cited in Rosenblum, *Immigrant Workers*, 153.

10. Cited in Mink, *Old Labor and New Immigrants*, 61.

11. Cited in Boswell, "A Split Labor Market Analysis," 358.

12. Cited in Daniels, "The Japanese-American Experience, 1890–1940," 257.

13. Fine, *Labor and Farmer Parties*, cited in Rosenblum, *Immigrant Workers*, 152.

14. Gedicks, "Ethnicity, Class Solidarity, and Labor Radicalism."

15. Shannon, *The Socialist Party in America*, cited in Rosenblum, *Immigrant Workers*, 152.

16. Ibid., 154.

17. Greeley, *Why Can't They Be Like Us?*, 39.

18. Cited in ibid., 27.

19. Mink, *Old Labor and New Immigrants*, 63.

20. Ibid., 64.

21. Rosenblum, *Immigrant Workers*, 34.

22. Warner and Srole, *The Social Systems*, 99.

23. Mink, *Old Labor and New Immigrants*, chap. 2.

24. Rosenblum, *Immigrant Workers*, chap. 6.

25. See Edwards, *Contested Terrain*; Geschwender, *Racial Stratification in America*.

26. Glazer, "Ethnic Groups in America"; Wittke, *Refugees of Revolution*.

27. Glazer, "Ethnic Groups in America."

28. Wittke, *We Who Built America*, 417.

29. Ibid. See also Glazer, "Ethnic Groups in America."

30. Thomas, *Cuba*, 291–309, 339–355.

31. Greeley, *Why Can't They Be Like Us?*, 27.

32. Glazer, "Ethnic Groups in America," 167.

33. For historical accounts of the development and early stages of the Mexican state and its relationship to the origins of migration, see Womack, *Zapata and the Mexican Revolution*; Bustamante, "The Historical Context"; Cumbarland, *Mexico*.

34. For historical accounts of Mexican immigration in the late nineteenth century and at the time of the revolution, see Gamio, *Mexican Immigration*; Santibáñez, *Ensayo acerca*; Barrera, *Race and Class*; Samora, *Los Mojados*; Cardoso, *Mexican Emigration*.

35. The best description of transatlantic British labor flows and their relationship to North American economic development is Thomas, *Migration and Economic Growth*.

36. Rosenblum, *Immigrant Workers*, 154.

37. Child, *The German-Americans*, 7.

38. Cited in ibid., 170.

39. Kim, *New Urban Immigrants*, 228.
40. Ibid., chap. 7.
41. Ibid., chap. 8. See also Min, *Middlemen in Contemporary America*.
42. Sassen-Koob, "Formal and Informal Associations."
43. Ibid.
44. Ibid.
45. Boswell and Curtis, *The Cuban-American Experience*.
46. Ibid., chap. 3. See also Pedraza-Bailey, "Cuba's Exiles"; Portes and Bach, *Latin Journey*, chap. 3; Olson and Olson, *Cuban Americans*.
47. Boswell and Curtis, *The Cuban-American Experience*, chap. 10.
48. No scholarly account exists so far of Cuban-American participation in the Central American conflict. Numerous verbal testimonies have appeared in the Spanish-language media of Miami about these activities. However, interviews with former combatants, talk shows discussing Cuban-American support for the Contra cause, and pamphlets in Spanish circulated in the exile community indicate both the extent of these activities and widespread knowledge about them. Author's fieldwork in south Florida, 1985–86.
49. Warren, "Status Report." See also Jasso and Rosenzweig, *The New Chosen People*, chap. 2.
50. Bernard, "Cultural Determinants."
51. Portes and Mozo, "The Political Adaptation Process."
52. Ibid.
53. Gann and Duignan, *The Hispanics in the United States*, 207.
54. Cited in Moore and Pachón, *Hispanics in the United States*, 179.
55. Ibid., 179–184. For examples of scholarly reinterpretations of the history of the minority, see Acuña, *Occupied America*; Barrera, *Race and Class*.
56. Gann and Duignan, *The Hispanics in the United States*, 217–224.
57. Moore and Pachón, *Hispanics in the United States*, 184–186.
58. Ibid.
59. Kim, *New Urban Immigrants*, chap. 8; Waldinger, "Immigration and Industrial Change"; Portes and Manning, "The Immigrant Enclave: Theory and Empirical Examples"; Min, *Middlemen in Contemporary America*.
60. A Miami politician quipped a few years ago that candidates to the local school board seemed to be running for U.S. Secretary of State, so much were their campaigns tinged by foreign policy issues.
61. The subsequent development of a Cuban ethnic economy in south Florida has altered the situation by confronting sectors of this population with outside reactions in the manner outlined previously for entrepreneurial minorities. See Portes, "The Rise of Ethnicity."

62. Since the term "Asian-American" has become institutionalized in academic discourse, it is not difficult to find multiple illustrations in the scholarly literature. See, for example, Gardner, Robey, and Smith, "Asian Americans"; Nee and Sanders, "The Road to Parity." See also Espiritu, *Asian American Panethnicity*.

63. Nagel, "The Political Construction."

64. Portes and Truelove, "Making Sense of Diversity"; Rumbaut, "The Americans."

65. See, for example, the discussion on Hispanic politics in Gann and Duignan, *The Hispanics in the United States*, which devolves immediately into a review of the divergent experiences of Mexicans, Puerto Ricans, and other national components of this ethnic "group." A similar example concerning the economic performance of Asian-Americans is found in Nee and Sanders, "The Road to Parity."

66. Lamm and Imhoff, *The Immigration Time Bomb*, 123–124.

67. The classic statement about the enduring significance of ethnicity for urban politics is still Glazer and Moynihan, *Beyond the Melting Pot*. See also Greeley, *Why Can't They Be Like Us?* For examples of Mexican-American statements about the significance of ethnicity in politics, see Burma, *Mexican-Americans*, 279–324.

Chapter 5. A Foreign World

1. Thomas and Znaniecki, *The Polish Peasant*; Handlin, *The Uprooted*.

2. Furnham and Bochner, *Culture Shock*, 63. See also Rumbaut, "Life Events."

3. Kuo and Tsai, "Social Networking"; Rumbaut and Rumbaut, "Refugees in the United States"; Richardson, "A Theory and a Method."

4. Antonovsky, *Health, Stress, and Coping*; Rumbaut and Weeks, "Unraveling a Public Health Enigma."

5. Thomas and Znaniecki, *The Polish Peasant*.

6. Handlin, *The Uprooted*, 4, 6, 97. See also Handlin, *Boston's Immigrants*. Handlin's work shaped the later anthropological formulation of the concept of "culture shock." See, for example, Oberg, "Cultural Shock"; Garza-Guerrero, "Culture Shock"; Furnham and Bochner, *Culture Shock*. For contemporary historical scholarship on these themes, see Miller, *Emigrants and Exiles*; Bodnar, *The Transplanted*.

7. Park, "Human Migration," 887–888. On this theme of emancipation, see also Shutz, "The Stranger"; Rumbaut and Rumbaut, "The Family in Exile."

8. Stonequist, *The Marginal Man*, 84, 86, 92.

9. Ibid., 159.

10. Ibid., 203.

11. Faris and Dunham, *Mental Disorders*.

12. Jarvis, *Insanity and Idiocy*, 61–62.

13. Ibid., 59.

14. Ibid., 61.

15. Ibid., 62.

16. Rothman, *The Discovery of the Asylum*; Ranney, "On Insane Foreigners"; Robertson, "Prevalence of Insanity"; Salmon, "The Relation of Immigration."

17. Higham, *Strangers in the Land*; Kraut, *The Huddled Masses*. See also Kraut, *Silent Travelers*.

18. Sanua, "Immigration, Migration, and Mental Illness."

19. Ibid. Virtually identical statements about the fiscal costs of the newest immigration have been made in the 1990s. See, for example, Brimelow, *Alien Nation*. For assessments of recent cost-benefit fiscal analyses, see Fix and Passel, *Immigration and Immigrants*; Clark et al., *Fiscal Impacts of Undocumented Aliens*.

20. Malzberg, "Mental Disease and 'The Melting Pot'"; Malzberg, "Mental Disease in New York State"; Malzberg, *Social and Biological Aspects*; Malzberg and Lee, *Migration and Mental Disease*.

21. Malzberg and Lee, *Migration and Mental Disease*. On this topic, see also the groundbreaking paper by Jarvis, "Influence of Distance."

22. Higham, *Strangers in the Land*, 314.

23. Quoted in Malzberg and Lee, *Migration and Mental Disease*, 7–8.

24. Ibid., 8–9.

25. Portes and Bach, *Latin Journey*, 48.

26. Ødegaard, "Emigration and Insanity," 175–176; Ødegaard, "The Distribution."

27. Murphy, *Flight and Resettlement*; Keller, *Uprooting and Social Change*; Zwingmann and Pfister-Ammende, *Uprooting and After*; Rose, "Some Thoughts"; Haines, *Refugees in the United States*; Williams and Westermeyer, *Refugee Mental Health*.

28. Weissman, Myers, and Ross, *Community Surveys*; Dohrenwend, *Mental Illness*; Schwab and Schwab, *Sociocultural Roots*.

29. Kohn, "Social Class and Schizophrenia."

30. Hollingshead and Redlich, *Social Class and Mental Illness*; Dohrenwend and Dohrenwend, *Social Status and Psychological Disorder*; Dohrenwend and Dohrenwend, *Stressful Life Events*; Kohn, "Social Class and Schizophrenia"; Langner and Michael, *Life Stress and Mental Health*. See also Mirowsky and Ross, *Social Causes of Psychological Distress*.

31. Vega and Rumbaut, "Ethnic Minorities and Mental Health"; Mirowsky and Ross, "Social Patterns of Distress"; Seeman, "On the Meaning of Alienation"; Morowsky and Ross, "Paranoia"; Thoits,

"Undesirable Life Events"; Thoits, "Conceptual, Methodological, and Theoretical Problems"; Kessler and Cleary, "Social Class and Psychological Distress."

32. Srole, Langner, and Mitchell, *Mental Health in the Metropolis*.

33. Ibid., 354.

34. Rumbaut, "The Agony of Exile"; Gaertner, "A Comparison of Refugee"; David, "Involuntary International Migration"; Kunz, "The Refugee in Flight"; Kunz, "Exile and Resettlement"; Stein, "The Experience of Being a Refugee"; Pedraza-Bailey, "Cubans and Mexicans"; Tabori, *The Anatomy of Exile*. For an early critique of this distinction, see Portes and Bach, *Latin Journey*, 72–76.

35. Portes and Bach, *Latin Journey*, 72–76; Haines, *Refugees in the United States*. See also Zolberg, Suhrke, and Aguayo, "International Factors"; and Zolberg, Suhrke, and Aguayo, *Escape From Violence*.

36. Berry et al., "Comparative Studies of Acculturative Stress." See also Berry, "The Acculturation Process."

37. Meinhardt et al., "Southeast Asian Refugees."

38. Ibid. The social-psychological literature on post-1975 refugees from Indochina is by far the most extensive yet produced on any immigrant group in the United States. See, for example, Mollica and Lavelle, "Southeast Asian Refugees"; Alley, "Life-Threatening Indicators"; Kinzie and Manson, "Five Years' Experience"; Carlin, "The Catastrophically Uprooted Child"; Chan and Loveridge, "Refugees 'in Transit'"; Lin, Tazuma, and Masuda, "Adaptational Problems"; Masuda, Lin, and Tazuma, "Adaptational Problems"; Nicassio, "Psychosocial Correlates"; Simon, "Refugee Families' Adjustment"; Starr and Roberts, "Attitudes Toward New Americans"; Rahe et al., "Psychiatric Consultation"; Liu, Lamanna, and Murata, *Transition to Nowhere*; Kinzie and Sack, "Severely Traumatized Cambodian Children."

39. Molesky, "The Exiled"; Vargas, "Recently Arrived"; Espino, "Trauma and Adaptation"; Zamichow, "No Way to Escape the Fear."

40. Rumbaut, "Mental Health"; Rumbaut, "Portraits, Patterns, and Predictors"; and Rumbaut, "Migration, Adaptation, and Mental Health."

41. Dupuy, "Utility of the National Center." See also Link and Dohrenwend, "Formulation of Hypotheses."

42. Rumbaut, "Portraits, Patterns, and Predictors."

43. Ibid.

44. Tyhurst, "Displacement and Migration"; Tyhurst, "Psychosocial First Aid"; Mezey, "Psychiatric Illness"; Cohon, "Psychological Adaptation"; Baskauskas, "The Lithuanian Refugee"; Marris, *Loss and Change*; Rumbaut and Rumbaut, "The Family in Exile"; Richardson, "A Theory and a Method." Similar observations of recently arrived immi-

grant patients in the New York Lunatic Asylum at Blackwell's Island were described as long ago as 1850 by Ranney, "On Insane Foreigners," 54–55.

45. Vega, Warheit, and Palacio, "Psychiatric Symptomatology."

46. Vega et al., "Depressive Symptoms"; Vega, Kolody, and Valle, "Migration and Mental Health." On Mexican immigrants, see also Vega, Warheit, and Meinhardt, "Mental Health Issues"; Mirowsky and Ross, "Mexican Culture"; Martínez, "Mexican-Americans"; Rogler, Malgady, and Rodríguez, *Hispanics and Mental Health*.

47. Portes and Stepick, "Unwelcome Immigrants."

48. Eaton and Garrison, "The Influence of Class." For related analyses of differential access to and utilization of health and mental health care services among other immigrant groups, see Rumbaut et al., "The Politics of Migrant Health Care"; Hough, "Utilization of Health."

49. Camayd-Freixas, *Crisis in Miami*. See also Szapocznik, Cohen, and Hernández, *Coping with Adolescent Refugees*; Bernal and Gutiérrez, "Cubans."

50. Child, *Italian or American?*; Warner and Srole, *The Social Systems*; Sowell, *Ethnic America*; Alba, *Italian Americans*.

51. Vega et al., "The Prevalence of Depressive Symptoms"; Warheit et al., "Mexican-American Immigration."

52. Burnam et al., "Acculturation and Lifetime Prevalence."

53. Ibid. See also Kaplan and Marks, "Adverse Effects of Acculturation"; Moscicki et al., "Depressive Symptoms"; Vega and Rumbaut, "Ethnic Minorities and Mental Health."

54. Ibid. For other pertinent data from the ECA study, see Karno and Hough, "Lifetime Prevalence." See also Febrega, "Social Psychiatric Aspects"; Favazza, "Cultural Change and Mental Health."

55. Amaro et al., "Acculturation and Marijuana and Cocaine Use"; Gilbert, "Alcohol Consumption Patterns"; Haynes et al., "Patterns of Cigarette Smoking"; Guendelman and Abrams, "Dietary Intake"; Marks, García and Solis, "Health Risk Behaviors"; Vega and Amaro, "Latino Outlook"; Guendelman et al., "Generational Differences in Perinatal Health."

56. Markides and Coreil, "The Health of Hispanics"; Collins and Shay, "Prevalence of Low Birth Weight"; Rumbaut and Weeks, "Unraveling a Public Health Enigma."

57. Cabral et al., "Foreign-Born and U.S.-Born Black Women."

58. Rumbaut and Weeks, "Infant Health Among Indochinese Refugees"; Weeks and Rumbaut, "Infant Mortality."

59. Portes and Bach, *Latin Journey*, chap. 8.

60. Sowell, *Ethnic America*; Warner and Srole, *The Social Systems*. For a more detailed presentation of this argument, see Portes, Parker, and Cobas, "Assimilation or Consciousness?"

61. Portes and Bach, *Latin Journey*, 333. See also Portes, "The Rise of Ethnicity"; Rumbaut, "The Agony of Exile."

62. The two events need not occur together. That is, a favorable government reception is not always accompanied by the presence of a strong ethnic community or vice versa. They are combined here for purposes of illustration.

63. See Portes, "Dilemmas of a Golden Exile."

64. Sassen-Koob, "New York City's Informal Economy"; Waldinger, "Ethnic Business in the United States"; Min, *Middlemen in Contemporary America*.

65. See Rumbaut, "The Structure of Refuge"; Portes and Stepick, "Unwelcome Immigrants"; Gold, *Refugee Communities*; Kibria, *Family Tightrope*.

Chapter 6. Learning the Ropes

1. *Los Angeles Times*, "Elegiacal"; *Time*, "Immigrants," 29.

2. *New York Times*, "2 in New York"; *Time*, "The New Whiz Kids," 46; *Los Angeles Times*, "San Gabriel Student Garners 'Nobel' "; Butterfield, "Why They Excel."

3. Quoted in Olsen, *Crossing the Schoolhouse Border*, 89.

4. Ibid., 82.

5. Ibid., 66.

6. Ibid., 75. On the case of an illegal immigrant student from Mexico who graduated as valedictorian of his class, see Ibarra, "Looking at Proposition 187."

7. See, for example, Rumbaut, "Passages to America"; Strand and Jones, *Indochinese Refugees in America*; Haines, *Refugees as Immigrants*. See also the research reports of Raul Moncarz on the professional adaptation of Cuban accountants, architects, engineers, lawyers, nurses, optometrists, pharmacists, physicians, pilots, and teachers. His papers are collected in Cortés, *Cuban Exiles in the United States*.

8. Quoted in Görlach, "Comment."

9. Wardhaugh, *Languages in Competition*, 1–22; Mackey, *Bilingualism as a World Problem*, 11; Landry, "Comment."

10. Lieberson, Dalto, and Johnston, "The Course"; Lieberson and Hansen, "National Development." See also Lieberson, *Language Diversity and Language Contact*.

11. Fishman, *Language Loyalty in the United States*; Fishman, "Language Maintenance"; Veltman, *Language Shift in the United States*; López, *Language Maintenance*; Veltman, "Modelling the Language Shift." See also Portes and Schauffler, "Language and the Second Generation."

12. Quoted in Brumberg, *Going to America*, 7. See also Schloss-man, "Is There an American Tradition."

13. Quoted in Hakuta, *Mirror of Language*, 17. Hakuta's book re-mains the best single overview available on the topic of bilingualism in the United States. See also Laponce, *Languages and Their Territories*.

14. Brigham, *A Study of American Intelligence*, 194–197.

15. Kirkpatrick, *Intelligence and Immigration*, 2.

16. Goodenough, "Racial Differences." See also Hakuta, *Mirror of Language*, 28–33.

17. Díaz, "Thought and Two Languages." For an early case study on the question of language and identity, see Child, *Italian or American?*

18. Smith, "Some Light on the Problem."

19. For detailed reviews, see Díaz, "Thought and Two Languages"; Hakuta, *Mirror of Language*; Peal and Lambert, "The Relation of Bi-lingualism."

20. Peal and Lambert, "The Relation of Bilingualism."

21. Leopold, *Speech Development*.

22. Peal and Lambert, "The Relation of Bilingualism," 5–7, 14–15. See also Reynolds, "Language and Learning."

23. Rumbaut and Ima, *The Adaptation*; and Rumbaut, "Immigrant Students." Comparative data from this study on native (English-only) white and black students, as well as Pacific Islanders, American Indi-ans, and other much smaller immigrant groups (Europeans, South Asians, Middle Easterners, Africans), are not included here for ease of presentation. See also Rumbaut, "The New Californians."

24. Ibid. Chapter 7 presents an analysis of determinants of stan-dardized math and reading scores for a large sample of children of immigrants in secondary schools in San Diego and South Florida.

25. U.S. Bureau of the Census, "The Foreign-Born Population" (1993).

26. Excluded from the first group are Great Britain, Canada, and Jamaica, where English is the dominant language. Included are India and the Philippines, where English use is common among the edu-cated classes, but other languages are also spoken.

27. Woo, "Immigrants."

28. López, *The Maintenance of Spanish*.

29. Ibid.

30. López, *The Maintenance of Spanish*.

31. See Marshall, "The Question"; Thernstrom, "Language." For a leading assimilationist statement, see Rodríguez, *Hunger of Memory*.

32. Sandiford and Kerr, "Intelligence."

33. Quoted in Schmalz, "Hispanic Influx." See also Resnick, "Be-yond the Ethnic Community."

34. For an example of the argument for forced linguistic assimila-

tion, see Henry, "Against a Confusion of Tongues." See also the journalistic account of the origins of the U.S. English movement by Crawford, "The Hidden Motives."

35. *Time*, "Wanted"; *Los Angeles Times*, "Threat to Security." See also Rumbaut, "Passages to America."

36. For an overview of the parent study, see Rumbaut, "Portraits, Patterns, and Predictors." See also Rumbaut and Ima, *The Adaptation*; and Rumbaut, "Immigrant Students."

37. Rumbaut and Ima, "Determinants of Educational Attainment." For a follow-up of this study, see Rumbaut, "The New Californians."

38. Kim and Hurh, "Two Dimensions."

39. Sridhar, "Language Maintenance."

40. Lieberson, *Language and Ethnic Relations*.

41. Sassen-Koob, "Exporting Capital"; Bustamante, "Espaldas Mojadas"; Cornelius, "The United States Demand."

42. Doeringer, Moss, and Terkla, "Capitalism and Kinship"; Min, "Ethnic Business"; Gold, "Refugees and Small Business"; Portes, "The Social Origins"; Resnick, "Beyond the Ethnic Community."

43. Portes, Clark, and López, "Six Years Later."

44. See, for example, Laponce, *Languages and Their Territories*; Ben-Rafael, *Language, Identity, and Social Division*; Silva-Corvalán, *Language Contact and Change*; Pinker, *The Language Instinct*. For a discussion of the effect of age on accentless second language acquisition, see Lenneberg, *Biological Foundations of Language*. For a statement on the politics of ethnic language use over time in the context of competitive intergroup relations, see Taylor, "Ethnicity and Language." On language and bicultural identities, see Hoffman, *Lost in Translation*; Pérez Firmat, *Life on the Hyphen*.

45. From Aldrich's poem, "Unguarded Gates," quoted in *Time*, "Immigrants," 31.

46. Crawford, *Hold Your Tongue*; Crawford, "The Hidden Motives"; Loo, "The 'Biliterate' Ballot Controversy." For a concise argument against the U.S. English movement, see Capen, "Languages Open Opportunity's Door." See also Marshall, "The Question," and the entire special issue of the *International Journal of the Sociology of Language* 60 (1986); Crawford, *Language Loyalties*; and Baron, *The English-Only Question*.

Chapter 7. Growing Up American

1. Passel and Edmonston, "Immigration and Race"; Fix and Passel, *Immigration and Immigrants*; Rumbaut, "Origins and Destinies."

2. Jensen and Chitose, "Today's Second Generation."

3. Thirty-five percent of 1985–90 immigrant household heads had

less than 8 years of education while 25 percent were college graduates. These figures compare with 43 percent and 18 percent, respectively, among those arriving between 1965 and 1974. These results are in line with those presented in chapter 3 indicating the lack of evidence for the hypothesis of declining "quality" of education among the most recent immigrant cohorts.

4. For a more detailed explanation of the methodology of this study, see Portes and Schauffler, "Language and the Second Generation"; and Rumbaut, "The Crucible Within."

5. Antin, *The Promised Land*, 271–272.

6. Child, *Italian or American?*

7. Zhou and Bankston, "Social Capital and the Adaptation," 832.

8. Ibid., 831.

9. Gibson, *Accommodation Without Assimilation*, 268.

10. Gibson, *Accommodation Without Assimilation*. For a follow-up to this study, see Gibson, "Additive Acculturation." See also Rumbaut, "Immigrant Students in California," 22–23; and Rumbaut, "The New Californians."

11. Waters, "Ethnic and Racial Identities," 804.

12. Matute-Bianchi, "Ethnic Identities."

13. Ibid., 253.

14. The study is summarized in Rumbaut, "Immigrant Students," 25. For a follow-up to this study, see Matute-Bianchi, "Situational Ethnicity." See also Rumbaut, "The New Californians."

15. The classic treatment of the topic in modern sociology is Gordon's *Assimilation in American Life*. More recent restatements and elaboration of Gordon's analysis are found in Alba, *Italian-Americans*, and Barkan, "Race, Religion, and Nationality." For critical views of the assimilation approach, as originally stated, see Glazer and Moynihan, *Beyond the Melting Pot*; Greeley, *Why Can't They Be Like Us?*; and Portes and Bach, *Latin Journey*.

16. See Ogbu, "Variability in Minority School Performance"; Wacquant and Wilson, "The Cost of Racial and Class Exclusion"; Waters, "Ethnic and Racial Identities"; Gans, "Second Generation Decline."

17. Suárez-Orozco, "Towards a Psychosocial Understanding." See also Fordham and Ogbu, "Black Students"; Matute-Bianchi, "Ethnic Identities"; Vigil, *Barrio Gangs*.

18. Sassen, "New York City's Informal Economy"; Sassen and Smith, "Post-Industrial Growth and Economic Reorganization"; Harrison and Bluestone, *The Great U-Turn*; Waldinger, "Immigration and Industrial Change."

19. The relatively slow mobility toward a college education of succeeding immigrant generations is a standard reference in accounts of the assimilation process of earlier European immigrants. On the

Italian-Americans, see Alba, *Italian-Americans*; on East European Jews, Dinnerstein, "The East European Jewish Migration"; on other European-origin ethnic groups, Greeley, *Why Can't They Be Like Us?*; and Lieberson, *A Piece of the Pie*.

20. Stepick, "The Refugees Nobody Wants"; Stepick, "Miami's Two Informal Sectors"; Portes and Stepick, *City on the Edge*, chap. 8.

21. Pérez, "Cuban Miami"; Fernández-Kelly and Schauffler, "Divided Fates"; Portes and Stepick, *City on the Edge*, chap. 6.

22. Waters, "West Indian Immigrants"; Portes and Zhou, "The New Second Generation."

23. The proximity to the border of San Diego's Mexican neighborhoods, the heavy back-and-forth movement across this border, and the cultural influence of the country of origin may account for this higher-than-average resistance to acculturation among Mexican youth.

24. The study defined "second generation" as native-born children with at least one immigrant parent or as children born abroad who were brought to the United States at an early age. To be included in the sample, children had to have lived in the U.S. for at least five years. Hence, there is variation in length of U.S. residence—from "all my life" to "six years or less." This variation may have significant effects on the academic performance of different nationalities.

25. This residual category ($N = 3,109$) comprises children of over seventy national origins. Individual national samples are mostly small, but the size and diversity of the total provides an adequate standard of reference to evaluate the net performance of the five target groups.

26. Waters, "Ethnic and Racial Identities," 805.

Chapter 8. Conclusion

1. As examples, see Amy Tan, *The Joy Luck Club*, on Chinese-Americans; Cristina García, *Dreaming in Cuban*, on Cuban-Americans; Richard Rodríguez, *Days of Obligation*, on Mexican-Americans. See also Alexandra Portes, "The Longest Migration," on contemporary Mexican-American literature.

2. See, for example, Lamm and Imhoff, *The Immigration Time Bomb*, and the above-cited book by Brimelow. For a more balanced illustration of this belief in the capabilities of government, see Staff Report of the Select Commission on Immigration and Refugee Policy, *U.S. Immigration Policy and the National Interest*, esp. xxxi–lxi.

3. This argument will be developed at greater length in later sections. For introductory statements on the role of social networks in international migration, see Tilly, "Transplanted Networks"; and Massey and García España, "The Social Process of International Migration."

4. For a classic example of this approach, see Brimley Thomas, *Migration and Economic Growth*. For a more recent example, see George J. Borjas, *Friends or Strangers*.

5. Mexican and Colombian migration to the United States and Turkish and Greek migration to Western Europe are examples. A more recent illustration is provided by the large undocumented inflow of Irish to East Coast cities. See Portes, "Illegal Immigration"; Bustamante and Martínez, "Undocumented Immigration"; Castles, Booth, and Wallace, *Here for Good*; Tumulty, "When Irish Eyes Are Hiding."

6. See Reichert, "The Migrant Syndrome"; Massey et al., "Continuities in Transnational Migration"; Grasmuck and Pessar, *Between Two Islands*.

7. For a more extensive presentation of this argument, see Portes, "From South of the Border." See also Bach, "Mexican Immigration"; Rumbaut, "The Americans"; and Barrera, *Race and Class in the Southwest*.

8. Camarillo, *Chicanos in a Changing Society*; Bustamante, "The Historical Context"; Barrera, *Race and Class in the Southwest*.

9. Bach, "Mexican Immigration"; Massey, "Understanding Mexican Migration"; Massey et al., *Return to Aztlán*; Cockcroft, *Outlaws in the Promised Land*.

10. Piore, *Birds of Passage*; de Souza Martins, *Á Immigraçào e a Crise do Brasil Agrario*; Portes and Walton, *Labor, Class, and the International System*, chap. 2.

11. See Portes and Zhou, "Divergent Destinies." On labor migration to Europe, see Castles, "The Guest-Worker in Western Europe"; Justus Veenman, "Ethnic Minorities in the Netherlands"; Bade, "From Emigration to Immigration." See also Rumbaut, "Origins and Destinies."

12. Immigration and Naturalization Service, *1990 Statistical Yearbook*.

13. Originally published in 1920, republished in 1984.

14. Portes and Bach, *Latin Journey*, 92–93, 125–127.

15. Massey et al., "Continuities in Transnational Migration."

16. Smith, "New York in Mixteca"; Roberts, "Socially Expected Durations"; Kircheman and Neckerman, "We Love to Hire Them But...."

17. See Bach and Brill, *Impact of IRCA*; Fix and Passel, "The Door Remains Open."

18. Bach and Brill, *Impact of IRCA*, 57–64.

19. Cornelius, "Illegal Migration to the United States"; Cornelius and Chavez, *Mexican Immigrants and Southern California*; Portes, "Of Borders and States."

20. Fix and Passel, "The Door Remains Open." Immigration and Naturalization Service, *1990 Statistical Yearbook*.

21. Schuck, "The Message of 187."

22. Cornelius, "Appearances and Realities."

23. Cornelius, "Appearances and Realities," 17.

24. Bade, "From Emigration to Immigration."

25. Samora, *Los Mojados*; Bustamante, "The Historical Context"; Portes and Bach, *Latin Journey*, chap. 2.

26. Kircheman and Neckerman, "We Love to Hire Them But . . . "; Waters, "West Indian Immigrants"; Aponte, "Urban Unemployment and the Mismatch Theory." On displacement effects in Chicago, see also Tienda and Stier, "The Wages of Race."

27. Borjas, *Friends or Strangers*, chap. 5; Simon, *The Economic Consequences of Immigration*, chap. 10.

28. Taylor et al., "Mexican Immigrants and the Wages."

29. Muller and Espenshade, *The Fourth Wave*. See also Espenshade and Goodis, "Are Mexican Immigrant."

30. Fernández-Kelly and García, "Informalization at the Core"; Waldinger, "Immigration and Industrial Change"; Sassen, "New York City's Informal Economy"; Zhou, *Chinatown*.

31. Bach, "Immigration"; U.S. Department of Labor, *Report*; Portes and Böröcz, "Contemporary Immigration."

32. See Espenshade, "Using INS Border Apprehension Data."

33. Cornelius, "Appearances and Realities."

34. Fernández-Kelly and García, "Informalization at the Core."

35. Periodic reports of these activities are presented in the Inter-American Foundation magazine, *Grassroots Development*. See also Hirschman, *Getting Ahead Collectively*.

36. This fact helps explain why wage differentials are such poor predictors of international migration either at the individual or collective level. See Tilly, "Transplanted Networks"; Massey, "Social Structure, Household Strategies"; and Portes, "Determinants of the Brain Drain."

37. Cornelius, "Appearances and Realities." Sabin and Hughes, "Economic Integration and Labor Flows."

38. See Kyle, *The Transnational Peasant*; Pérez-Sainz, *El Dilema del Nahual*; Sabel, "Changing Modes of Economic Efficiency"; Capecchi, "The Informal Economy."

39. Rumbaut, "The Crucible Within." See also Rumbaut and Cornelius, *California's Immigrant Children*.

40. See Glaser and Habers, "The Migration and Return"; Portes and Ross, "Modernization for Emigration"; Light and Bonacich, *Korean Entrepreneurs*; Madhavan, "Migration of Skilled People"; Madhavan, "Indian Emigrants"; Rumbaut, "Passages to America."

41. Anderson, "Manpower Losses"; Leaven, *The Caribbean Exodus*; Pastor, *Migration and Development*.

42. Zolberg, Suhrke, and Aguayo, "International Factors." See also Zolberg, "The Next Waves."

43. This vignette is drawn from narratives summarizing in-depth parental interviews conducted in Miami and San Diego as part of the project Children of Immigrants: The Adaptation of the Second Generation. This project is described in chapter 7. This particular narrative is reported in Fernández-Kelly and Schauffler, "Divided Fates," 671–672.

44. Fernández-Kelly and Schauffler, "Divided Fates," 671.

References

Acuña, Rodolfo. *Occupied America: A History of Chicanos*. New York: Harper and Row, 1981.

Alba, Francisco. "Mexico's International Migration as a Manifestation of Its Development Pattern." *International Migration Review* 12 (Winter 1978): 502–551.

Alba, Richard D. *Italian Americans: Into the Twilight of Ethnicity*. Englewood Cliffs, N.J.: Prentice-Hall, 1985.

Allen, James P., and Eugene J. Turner. *We the People: An Atlas of America's Ethnic Diversity*. New York: Macmillan, 1986.

Alley, James Curtis. "Life-Threatening Indicators Among the Indochinese Refugees." *Suicide and Life-Threatening Behavior* 12 (Spring 1982): 46–51.

Amaro, Hortensia, R. Whitaker, J. Coffman, and T. Heeren. "Acculturation and Marijuana and Cocaine Use: Findings from HHANES 1982–84." *American Journal of Public Health*, supplement, 80 (1990): 54–60.

Anderson, Grace M. *Networks of Contact: The Portuguese and Toronto*. Ontario: Wilfrid Laurier University Press, 1974.

Anderson, Patricia. "Manpower Losses and Employment Adequacy Among Skilled Workers in Jamaica, 1976–1985." In *When Borders Don't Divide: Labor Migration and Refugee Movements in the Americas*, ed. Patricia Pessar, 96–128. New York: Center for Migration Studies, 1988.

———. "Migration and Development in Jamaica." In *Migration and Development in the Caribbean*, ed. Robert Pastor, 117–139. Boulder, Colo.: Westview Press, 1988.

Antin, Mary. *The Promised Land*. New York: Houghton-Mifflin, 1912.

Antonovsky, Aaron. *Health, Stress and Coping*. San Francisco: Jossey-Bass, 1979.

Aponte, Robert. "Urban Unemployment and the Mismatch Theory."

Paper presented at the Conference on Urban Poverty, University of Chicago, October 1991.

Bach, Robert L. "Immigration: Issues of Ethnicity, Class, and Public Policy in the United States." *Annals of the American Academy of Political and Social Science* 485 (May 1986): 139–152.

———. "Mexican Immigration and the American State." *International Migration Review* 12 (Winter 1978): 536–558.

Bach, Robert L., and Howard Brill. *Impact of IRCA on the U.S. Labor Market and Economy.* Report to the U.S. Department of Labor, Institute for Research on International Labor. Binghamton: State University of New York, 1991.

Bach, Robert L., Linda W. Gordon, David W. Haines, and David R. Howell. "The Economic Adjustment of Southeast Asian Refugees in the United States." In *World Refugee Survey, 1983*, 51–55. Geneva: United Nations High Commission for Refugees, 1984.

Baker, Reginald P., and David S. North. *The 1975 Refugees: Their First Five Years in America.* Washington, D.C.: New TransCentury Foundation, 1984.

Barkan, Elliott R. "Race, Religion, and Nationality in American Society: A Model of Ethnicity—from Contact to Assimilation." *Journal of American Ethnic History* (Winter 1995): 38–75.

Baron, D. *The English-Only Question.* New Haven, Conn.: Yale University Press, 1990.

Barrera, Mario. *Race and Class in the Southwest: A Theory of Racial Inequality.* Notre Dame, Ind.: Notre Dame University Press, 1980.

Baskauskas, Luicija. "The Lithuanian Refugee Experience and Grief." *International Migration Review* 15 (1981): 276–291.

Bean, Frank D., Harley L. Browning, and W. Parker Frisbie. "The Socio-demographic Characteristics of Mexican Immigrant Status Groups: Implications for Studying Undocumented Mexicans." *International Migration Review* 18 (Fall 1985): 672–691.

———. "What the 1980 U.S. Census Tells Us About the Characteristics of Illegal and Legal Mexican Immigrants." Population Research Center, University of Texas at Austin, 1985. Mimeographed.

Bean, Frank D., B. Lindsay Lowell, and Lowell J. Taylor. "Undocumented Migration to the United States: Perceptions and Evidence." *Population and Development Review* 13 (December 1987): 671–690.

Bean, Frank D., and Marta Tienda. *The Hispanic Population of the United States.* New York: Russell Sage Foundation, 1987.

Ben-Rafael, Eliezer. *Language, Identity and Social Division: The Case of Israel.* New York: Oxford University Press, 1994.

Bernal, Guillermo, and Manuel Gutiérrez. "Cubans." In *Cross-Cultural Mental Health*, ed. Lillian Comas-Díaz and Ezra E. H. Griffith, 233–261. New York: Wiley, 1988.

Bernard, W. S. "Cultural Determinants of Naturalization." *American Sociological Review* 1 (December 1936): 943–953.

Berry, John W. "The Acculturation Process and Refugee Behavior." In *Refugee Mental Health in Resettlement Countries*, ed. Carolyn L. Williams and Joseph Westermeyer, 25–37. New York: Hemisphere, 1986.

Berry, John W., Uichol Kim, Thomas Minde, and Doris Mok. "Comparative Studies of Acculturative Stress." *International Migration Review* 21 (Fall 1987): 491–511.

Bodnar, John. *The Transplanted: A History of Immigrants in Urban America*. Bloomington: Indiana University Press, 1985.

Bonacich, Edna. "Advanced Capitalism and Black/White Relations: A Split Labor Market Interpretation." *American Sociological Review* 41 (February 1976): 34–51.

———. "Asian Labor in the Development of California and Hawaii." In *Labor Immigration Under Capitalism*, ed. Lucie Cheng and Edna Bonacich, 130–185. Berkeley: University of California Press, 1984.

———. "A Theory of Middleman Minorities." *American Sociological Review* 38 (October 1973): 583–594.

Bonacich, Edna, Ivan Light, and Charles Wong. "Koreans in Small Business." *Society* 14 (September–October 1977): 54–59.

Bonacich, Edna, and John Modell. *The Economic Basis of Ethnic Solidarity: Small Business in the Japanese-American Community*. Berkeley: University of California Press, 1980.

Bonilla, Frank A., and Ricardo Campos. "A Wealth of Poor: Puerto Ricans in the New Economic Order." *Daedalus* 110 (Spring 1981): 133–176.

Borjas, George J. *Friends or Strangers: The Impact of Immigrants on the U.S. Economy*. New York: Basic Books, 1990.

———. "Self-Selection and the Earnings of Immigrants." *American Economic Review* 77 (1987): 531–553.

———. "Statement." Hearings before the Subcommittee on Economic Resources, Competitiveness, and Security Economics, U.S. House of Representatives. 99th Cong. Washington, D.C.: U.S. Government Printing Office, 1987.

Boswell, Terry E. "A Split Labor Market Analysis of Discrimination Against Chinese Immigrants, 1850–1882." *American Sociological Review* 51 (June 1986): 352–371.

Boswell, Thomas D., and James R. Curtis. *The Cuban-American Experience*. Totowa, N.J.: Rowman & Allanheld, 1984.

Botifoll, Luis J. "How Miami's New Image Was Created." Occasional Paper 1985-I. Institute of Interamerican Studies, University of Miami, 1985.

Bouvier, Leon F., and Robert W. Gardner. "Immigration to the U.S.: The Unfinished Story." *Population Bulletin* 41 (1986).

Bray, David. "Economic Development: The Middle Class and International Migration in the Dominican Republic." *International Migration Review* 18 (Summer 1984): 217–236.

Briggs, Vernon M. "The Need for a More Restrictive Border Policy." *Social Science Quarterly* 56 (1975): 477–484.

Brigham, Carl C. *A Study of American Intelligence*. Princeton, N.J.: Princeton University Press, 1923.

Browning, Harley L., and Nestor Rodríguez. "The Migration of Mexican Indocumentados as a Settlement Process: Implications for Work." In *Hispanics in the U.S. Economy*, ed. George J. Borjas and Marta Tienda, 277–297. Orlando, Fla.: Academic Press, 1985.

Brumberg, Stephen F. *Going to America, Going to School: The Jewish Immigrant Public School Encounter in Turn-of-the-Century New York City*. New York: Praeger, 1986.

Burma, John D. *Mexican-Americans in the United States: A Reader*. New York: Schenkman, 1970.

Burnam, M. Audrey, Richard L. Hough, Marvin Karno, Javier I. Escobar, and Cynthia A. Telles. "Acculturation and Lifetime Prevalence of Psychiatric Disorders Among Mexican Americans in Los Angeles." *Journal of Health and Social Behavior* 28 (March 1987): 89–102.

Bustamante, Jorge A. "Espaldas Mojadas: Materia Prima para la Exportación del Capital Norteamericano." *Cuadernos del CES*, 9. El Colegio de México, 1975.

———. "The Historical Context of Undocumented Mexican Immigration to the United States." *Aztlán* 3 (Winter 1973): 257–281.

Bustamante, Jorge A., and Gerónimo Martínez. "Undocumented Immigration from Mexico: Beyond Borders but Within Systems." *Journal of International Affairs* 33 (Fall/Winter 1979): 265–284.

Butterfield, Fox. "Why They Excel." *Parade Magazine*, January 21, 1990, 4–6.

Cabral, H., L. E. Fried, S. Levenson, H. Amaro, and B. Zuckerman. "Foreign-Born and U.S. Born Black Women: Differences in Health Behaviors and Birth Outcomes." *American Journal of Public Health* 80, 1 (1990): 70–72.

Camarillo, Albert. *Chicanos in a Changing Society*. Cambridge, Mass.: Harvard University Press, 1979.

Camayd-Freixas, Yohel. *Crisis in Miami: Community Context and Institutional Response in the Adaptation of Mariel Cubans and Undocumented Haitian Entrants in South Florida*. Commissioned report. Boston: Urban Research and Development, 1988.

Capecchi, Vittorio. "The Informal Economy and the Development of Flexible Specialization in Emilia-Romagna." In *The Informal Economy: Studies in Advanced and Less Developed Countries*, ed. A. Portes, M. Castells, and L. A. Benton, 189–215. Baltimore: Johns Hopkins University Press, 1989.

Capen, Richard. "Languages Open Opportunity's Door." *Miami Herald*, October 30, 1988, 15.

Caplan, Nathan, Marcella H. Choy, and John K. Whitmore. *Children of the Boat People: A Study of Educational Success*. Ann Arbor: University of Michigan Press, 1991.

Cardoso, Lawrence A. *Mexican Emigration to the United States, 1897–1931*. Tucson: University of Arizona Press, 1980.

Carlin, Jean E. "The Catastrophically Uprooted Child: Southeast Asian Refugee Children." In *Basic Handbook of Child Psychiatry*, vol. 1, ed. Justin D. Call, Joseph D. Noshpitz, Richard L. Cohen, and Irving N. Berlin, 290–300. New York: Basic Books, 1979.

Castles, Stephen. "The Guest-Worker in Western Europe: An Obituary." *International Migration Review* 20 (Winter 1986): 761–778.

Castles, Stephen, Heather Booth, and Tina Wallace. *Here for Good: Western Europe's New Ethnic Minorities*. London: Pluto Press, 1984.

Chan, Kwok B., and David Loveridge. "Refugees 'in Transit': Vietnamese in a Refugee Camp in Hong Kong." *International Migration Review* 21 (Fall 1987): 745–759.

Chávez, Leo R. "Settlers and Sojourners: The Case of Mexicans in the United States." *Human Organization* 47 (Summer 1988): 95–108.

———. *Shadowed Lives: Undocumented Immigrants in American Society*. San Diego: Harcourt Brace Jovanovich, 1992.

Chávez, Leo R., and Estevan T. Flores. "Undocumented Mexicans and Central Americans and the Immigration Reform and Control Act of 1986: A Reflection Based on Empirical Data." In *In Defense of the Alien*, vol. 10, 137–156. New York: Center for Migration Studies, 1988.

Child, Clifton J. *The German-Americans in Politics, 1914–1917*. Madison: University of Wisconsin Press, 1939.

Child, Irving L. *Italian or American? The Second Generation in Conflict*. New Haven, Conn.: Yale University Press, 1943.

Chiswick, Barry R. "The Effect of Americanization on the Earnings of Foreign-Born Men." *Journal of Political Economy* 86 (October 1978): 897–921.

Cichon, Donald J., Elzbieta M. Gozdziak, and Jane G. Grover. "The Economic and Social Adjustment of Non-Southeast Asian Refugees." Report to the Office of Refugee Resettlement. Department of Health and Human Services, Washington, D.C., 1986. Mimeographed.

Clark, Rebecca L., Jeffrey S. Passel, Wendy N. Zimmerman, and Michael E. Fix. *Fiscal Impacts of Undocumented Aliens: Selective Estimates for Seven States*. Washington, D.C.: The Urban Institute, 1994.

Cobas, José. "Participation in the Ethnic Economy, Ethnic Solidarity, and Ambivalence Toward the Host Society: The Case of Cuban Emigrés in Puerto Rico." Paper presented at the meetings of the American Sociological Association, San Antonio, 1984.

Cockcroft, James D. *Outlaws in the Promised Land: Mexican Immigrant Workers and America's Future*. New York: Grove Press, 1986.

Cohon, J. Donald, Jr. "Psychological Adaptation and Dysfunction Among Refugees." *International Migration Review* 15 (Spring–Summer 1981): 255–275.

Collins, J. W., Jr., and D. K. Shay. "Prevalence of Low Birth Weight Among Hispanic Infants with United States-Born and Foreign-Born Mothers: The Effect of Urban Poverty." *American Journal of Epidemiology* 139, 2 (1994): 184–192.

Cornelius, Wayne A. "Appearances and Realities: Controlling Illegal Immigration in the United States." In *Japanese and U.S. Immigration: Refugee and Citizenship Policies*, ed. M. Weiner and T. Hashami (forthcoming).

———. "Illegal Migration to the United States: Recent Research Findings, Policy Implications, and Research Priorities." Discussion paper C/77-11. Center for International Studies, MIT, 1977. Mimeographed.

———. "Labor Market Impacts of Mexican Immigration: Two Generations of Research." Paper presented at the seminar on the urban informal sector in center and periphery, Johns Hopkins University, Baltimore, June 1984.

———. "Mexican Migration to the United States: Causes, Consequences, and U.S. Responses." Working paper. Center for International Studies, MIT, 1977.

———. "Mexican Migration to the United States: The View from Rural Sending Communities." Discussion paper C/76-12. Center for International Studies, MIT, 1976. Mimeographed.

———. "The United States Demand for Mexican Labor." Paper presented at the workshop on migration issues of the Bilateral Commission on the Future of U.S.–Mexican Relations, San Diego, August 1987.

Cornelius, Wayne A., Leo R. Chávez, and Jorge G. Castro. *Mexican Immigrants and Southern California: A Summary of Current Knowledge*. Research Report Series 36. Center for U.S.–Mexican Studies, University of California, San Diego, 1982.

Cortés, Carlos E., ed. *Cuban Exiles in the United States*. New York: Arno Press, 1980.

Crawford, James. "The Hidden Motives Stain Official English." *Miami*

Herald, November 10, 1988, A13.

—. *Hold Your Tongue; Bilingualism and the Politics of "English Only."* New York: Addison-Wesley, 1992.

—. *Language Loyalties: A Source Book on the Official English Controversy.* Chicago: University of Chicago Press, 1992.

Cumbarland, Charles. *Mexico: The Struggle for Modernity.* New York: Oxford University Press, 1968.

Dahl, Robert A. *Who Governs? Democracy and Power in an American City.* New Haven, Conn.: Yale University Press, 1961.

Daniels, Roger. "The Japanese-American Experience, 1890–1940." In *Uncertain Americans: Readings in Ethnic History*, ed. Leonard Dinnerstein and Frederic C. Jaher, 250–276. New York: Oxford University Press, 1977.

David, Henry P. "Involuntary International Migration: Adaptation of Refugees." In *Behavior in New Environments*, ed. Eugene B. Brody, 73–95. Beverly Hills, Calif.: Sage, 1970.

de Souza Martins, Jose. *Á Immigraçào e a Crise do Brasil Agrario.* Sao Paulo: Livraría Pioneira, 1973.

de Wind, Josh, Tom Seidl, and Janet Shenk. "Caribbean Migration: Contract Labor in U.S. Agriculture." *NACLA Report on the Americas* 11 (November–December 1977): 4–37.

Díaz, Rafael M. "Thought and Two Languages: The Impact of Bilingualism on Cognitive Development." *Review of Research in Education* 10 (1983): 23–54.

Díaz-Briquets, Sergio. "Cuban-Owned Business in the United States." *Cuban Studies* 14 (Summer 1985): 57–64.

Díaz-Briquets, Sergio, and Lisandro Pérez. "Cuba: The Demography of Revolution." *Population Bulletin* 36 (April 1981): 2–41.

Dinerman, Ina R. "Patterns of Adaptation Among Households of U.S.-Bound Migrants from Michoacán, Mexico." *International Migration Review* 12 (Winter 1978): 485–501.

Dinnerstein, Leonard. "The East European Jewish Migration." In *Uncertain Americans: Readings in Ethnic History*, ed. Leonard Dinnerstein and Frederic C. Jaher, 216–231. New York: Oxford University Press, 1977.

Dixon, Heriberto. "Emigration and Jamaican Employment." *Migration Today* 8 (1980): 24–27.

Doeringer, Peter B., Philip Moss, and David G. Terkla. "Capitalism and Kinship: Do Institutions Matter in the Labor Market?" *Industrial and Labor Relations Review* 40 (October 1986): 48–59.

Dohrenwend, Barbara S., and Bruce P. Dohrenwend, eds. *Stressful Life Events: Their Nature and Effects.* New York: Wiley, 1974.

Dohrenwend, Bruce P. *Mental Illness in the United States: Epidemiological Estimates.* New York: Praeger, 1980.

Dohrenwend, Bruce P., and Barbara S. Dohrenwend. *Social Status and Psychological Disorder: A Causal Inquiry*. New York: Wiley, 1969.

Dupuy, Harold J. "Utility of the National Center for Health Statistics General Well-Being Schedule in the Assessment of Self-Representations of Subjective Well-Being and Distress." National Conference on Education in Alcohol, Drug Abuse, and Mental Health Programs. Washington, D.C.: DHEW, 1974.

Eaton, William W., and Roberta Garrison. "The Influence of Class and Ethnic Status on Psychopathology and Helpseeking Among Two Latin American Refugee Groups." Progress report. School of Public Health, Johns Hopkins University, 1988. Mimeographed.

Edwards, Richard C. *Contested Terrain: The Transformation of the Workplace in the Twentieth Century*. New York: Harper Torchbooks, 1979.

"'Elegiacal': It Spells Success for Bee Champ." *Los Angeles Times*, June 3, 1988, I-1.

Entzinger, Hans B. "Race, Class and the Shaping of a Policy for Immigrants: The Case of the Netherlands." *International Migration Review* 25 (March 1987): 5–20.

Espenshade, Thomas J. "Using INS Border Apprehension Data to Measure the Flow of Undocumented Migrants Crossing the U.S.–Mexico Frontier." *International Migration Review* 29 (Summer 1995): 545–565.

Espenshade, Thomas J., and Tracy Ann Goodis. "Are Mexican Immigrant and U.S. Native Workers Substitutes or Complements in Production?" Discussion paper PRIP-UI-3. Washington, D.C.: The Urban Institute, 1988.

Espino, Conchita M. "Trauma and Adaptation: The Case of Central American Children." In *Refugee Children: Theory, Research, and Services*, ed. F. L. Ahearn, Jr., and J. L. Athey, 106–124. Baltimore: Johns Hopkins University Press, 1991.

Espiritu, Yen Le. *Asian American Panethnicity: Bridging Institutions and Identities*. Philadelphia: Temple University Press, 1992.

Fagen, Patricia W. "Central Americans and U.S. Refugee Asylum Policies." Paper presented at the Conference on Immigration and Refugee Policies sponsored by the Inter-American Dialogue and the University of California, San Diego, 1986.

Faris, Robert E. L., and H. Warren Dunham. *Mental Disorders in Urban Areas*. Chicago: University of Chicago Press, 1939.

Favazza, Armando R. "Culture Change and Mental Health." *Journal of Operational Psychiatry* 11 (1980): 101–119.

Febrega, Horacio, Jr. "Social Psychiatric Aspects of Acculturation and Migration: A General Statement." *Comprehensive Psychiatry* 10 (July 1969): 314–329.

Fernández-Kelly, María Patricia, and Ana García. "Advanced Technology, Regional Development, and Women's Employment in Southern California." Discussion paper. La Jolla: Center for U.S.–Mexico Studies, University of California, San Diego, 1985.

———. "Informalization at the Core: Hispanic Women, Home Work, and the Advanced Capitalist State." In *The Informal Economy: Studies in Advanced and Less Developed Countries*, ed. Alejandro Portes, Manuel Castells, and Lauren Benton, 247–264. Baltimore: Johns Hopkins University Press, 1989.

Fernández-Kelly, María Patricia, and Richard Schauffler. "Divided Fates: Immigrant Children in a Restructured U.S. Economy." *International Migration Review* 28 (Winter 1994): 662–689.

Fine, Nathan. *Labor and Farmer Parties in the United States, 1828–1928*. New York: Rand School of Social Science, 1928.

Fishman, Joshua A., ed. *Language Loyalty in the United States*. The Hague: Mouton, 1966.

———. "Language Maintenance." In *Harvard Encyclopedia of American Ethnic Groups*, ed. Stephan Thernstrom, 629–638. Cambridge, Mass.: Harvard University Press, 1981.

Fitzpatrick, Joseph. *Puerto Rican Americans: The Meaning of Migration to the Mainland*. 2nd ed. Englewood Cliffs, N.J.: Prentice-Hall, 1987.

Fix, Michael E., and Jeffrey S. Passel. "The Door Remains Open: Recent Immigration to the United States and a Preliminary Analysis of the Immigration Act of 1990." Report, the Urban Institute and the Rand Corporation, 1991.

———. *Immigration and Immigrants: Setting the Record Straight*. Washington, D.C.: The Urban Institute, 1994.

Forbes, Susan S. "Residency Patterns and Secondary Migration of Refugees." *Migration News* 34 (January–March 1985): 3–18.

Fordham, Signithia, and John U. Ogbu. "Black Students' School Success: Coping With the Burden of 'Acting White'." *Urban Review* 18, 3 (1987): 176–206.

Frazier, E. Franklin. *The Negro in the United States*. New York: Macmillan, 1949.

Furnham, Adrian, and Stephen Bochner. *Culture Shock: Psychological Reactions to Unfamiliar Environments*. New York: Methuen, 1986.

Gaertner, Miriam L. "A Comparison of Refugee and Non-Refugee Immigrants to New York City." In *Flight and Resettlement*, ed. H. B. Murphy, 99–112. Lucerne: UNESCO, 1955.

Gamio, Manuel. *Mexican Immigration to the United States*. Chicago: University of Chicago Press, 1930.

Gann, L. H., and Peter J. Duignan. *The Hispanics in the United States: A History*. Boulder, Colo.: Westview Press, 1986.

Gans, Herbert J. "Deconstructing the Underclass." *APA Journal* 56 (Summer 1990): 1–7.

———. "Second-Generation Decline: Scenarios for the Economic and Ethnic Futures of the Post-1965 American Immigrants." *Ethnic and Racial Studies* 15 (April 1992): 173–192.

García, Cristina. *Dreaming in Cuban*. New York: Ballantine Books, 1992.

García, Mario. *Desert Immigrants: The Mexicans of El Paso, 1880–1920*. New Haven, Conn.: Yale University Press, 1981.

Gardner, Robert W., Bryant Robey, and Peter C. Smith. "Asian Americans: Growth, Change, and Diversity." *Population Bulletin* 40 (October 1985).

Garza-Guerrero, A. C. "Culture Shock: Its Mourning and the Vicissitudes of Identity." *Journal of the American Psychoanalytic Association* 22 (1974): 408–429.

Gedicks, Al. "Ethnicity, Class Solidarity, and Labor Radicalism Among Finnish Immigrants in Michigan Copper Country." *Politics and Society* 7 (1977): 127–156.

Geschwender, James A. "The Portuguese and Haoles of Hawaii: Implications for the Origin of Ethnicity." *American Sociological Review* 53 (August 1988): 515–527.

———. *Racial Stratification in America*. Dubuque, Iowa: William C. Brown, 1978.

Gibson, Margaret A. *Accommodation Without Assimilation: Sikh Immigrants in an American High School*. Ithaca, N.Y.: Cornell University Press, 1989.

———. "Additive Acculturation as a Strategy for School Improvement." In *California's Immigrant Children: Theory, Research, and Implications for Educational Policy*, ed. Rubén G. Rumbaut and Wayne A. Cornelius, 77–105. La Jolla: Center for U.S.–Mexican Studies, University of California, San Diego, 1995.

Gilbert, M. "Alcohol Consumption Patterns in Immigrant and Later Generation Mexican American Women." *Hispanic Journal of Behavioral Sciences* 9 (1989): 299–313.

Glaser, William A., and Christopher Habers. "The Migration and Return of Professionals." *International Migration Review* 8 (Summer 1974): 227–244.

Glazer, Nathan. "Ethnic Groups in America." In *Freedom and Control in Modern Society*, ed. Monroe Berger, Theodore Abel, and Charles Page, 158–173. New York: Van Nostrand, 1954.

Glazer, Nathan, and Daniel P. Moynihan. *Beyond the Melting Pot: The Negroes, Puerto Ricans, Jews, Italians and Irish of New York City*. Cambridge, Mass.: MIT Press, 1970.

Gold, Steven J. *Refugee Communities: A Comparative Field Study*. Newbury Park, Calif.: Sage, 1992.

———. "Refugees and Small Business: The Case of Soviet Jews and Vietnamese." *Ethnic and Racial Studies* 11 (November 1988): 411–438.

Goodenough, Florence. "Racial Differences in the Intelligence of Children." *Journal of Experimental Psychology* 9 (October 1926): 392–393.

Gordon, Milton M. *Assimilation in American Life: The Role of Race, Religion, and National Origins*. New York: Oxford University Press, 1964.

Görlach, Mannfred. "Comment." *International Journal of the Sociology of Language* 60 (1986): 97.

Granovetter, Mark. "Economic Action and Social Structure: The Problem of Embeddedness." *American Journal of Sociology* 91 (1985): 481–510.

———. "Small Is Bountiful: Labor Markets and Establishment Size." *American Sociological Review* 49 (June 1984): 323–334.

Grasmuck, Sherri. "Immigration, Ethnic Stratification, and Native Working-Class Discipline: Comparison of Documented and Undocumented Dominicans." *International Migration Review* 18 (Fall 1984): 692–713.

Grasmuck, Sherri, and Patricia Pessar. *Between Two Islands: Dominican International Migration*. Berkeley: University of California Press, 1991.

Grebler, Leo, Joan W. Moore, and Ralph C. Guzman. *The Mexican-American People: The Nation's Second Largest Minority*. New York: Free Press, 1970.

Greeley, Andrew M. *Why Can't They Be Like Us? America's White Ethnic Groups*. New York: E. P. Dutton, 1971.

Guendelman, Silvia, and B. Abrams. "Dietary Intake Among Mexican American Women: Generational Differences and a Comparison with White Non-Hispanic Women." *American Journal of Public Health* 85, 1 (1995): 20–25.

Guendelman, Silvia, J. Gould, M. Hudes, and B. Eskanazi. "Generational Differences in Perinatal Health among the Mexican American Population: Findings from HHANES 1982–84." *American Journal of Public Health*, supplement, 80 (1990): 61–65.

Haines, David W., ed. *Refugees as Immigrants: Cambodians, Laotians and Vietnamese in America*. Totowa, N.J.: Rowman & Littlefield, 1989.

———. *Refugees in the United States: A Reference Handbook*. Westport, Conn.: Greenwood Press, 1985.

Hakuta, Kenji. *Mirror of Language: The Debate on Bilingualism.* New York: Basic Books, 1986.

Hamilton, Denise. "San Gabriel Student Garners 'Nobel' for High School Science." *Los Angeles Times*, March 5, 1991, A-1.

Handlin, Oscar. *Boston's Immigrants: A Study of Acculturation.* Cambridge, Mass.: Harvard University Press, 1941.

———. *The Uprooted.* 2nd enlarged ed. Boston: Little, Brown, 1973.

———. *The Uprooted: The Epic Story of the Great Migrations That Made the American People.* Boston: Little, Brown, 1951.

Harrison, Bennett, and Barry Bluestone. *The Great U-Turn.* New York: Basic Books, 1988.

Haynes, S. G., C. Harvey, H. Montes, H. Nicken, and B. H. Cohen. "Patterns of Cigarette Smoking Among Hispanics in the United States: Results from the HHANES 1982–84." *American Journal of Public Health*, supplement, 80 (1990): 47–53.

Hechter, Michael. *Internal Colonialism: The Celtic Fringe in British National Development, 1536–1966.* Berkeley: University of California Press, 1977.

Hein, Jeremy. *From Vietnam, Laos, and Cambodia: A Refugee Experience in the United States.* New York: Twayne Publishers, 1995.

Henry, William. "Against a Confusion of Tongues." *Time*, June 13, 1983, 30–31.

Higham, John. *Strangers in the Land: Patterns of American Nativism, 1896–1925.* New Brunswick, N.J.: Rutgers University Press, 1955.

Hing, Bill Ong. *Making and Remaking Asian America Through Immigration Policy, 1850–1990.* Stanford, Calif.: Stanford University Press, 1993.

Hirschman, Albert D. *Getting Ahead Collectively: Grassroots Experiences in Latin America.* New York: Pergamon Press, 1984.

Hirschman, Albert O. *Exit, Voice, and Loyalty: Responses to Decline in Firms, Organizations, and States.* Cambridge, Mass.: Harvard University Press, 1970.

Hirschman, Charles, and Luis Falcón. "The Educational Attainment of Religio-Ethnic Groups in the United States." *Research in Sociology of Education and Socialization* 5 (1985): 83–120.

Hirschman, Charles, and Morrison G. Wong. "The Extraordinary Educational Attainment of Asian Americans: A Search for Historical Evidence and Explanations." *Social Forces* 65 (September 1986): 1–27.

Hoffman, Eva. *Lost in Translation: A Life in a New Language.* New York: Penguin Books, 1990.

Hollingshead, August B., and F. C. Redlich. *Social Class and Mental Illness: A Community Study.* New York: Wiley, 1958.

Hondagneu-Sotelo, Pierrette. *Gendered Transitions: Mexican Experiences of Immigration.* Berkeley: University of California Press, 1994.

Hough, Richard L. "Utilization of Health and Mental Health Services by Los Angeles Mexican Americans and Non-Hispanic Whites." *Archives of General Psychiatry* 44 (August 1987): 702–709.

Howe, Irving. *World of Our Fathers.* New York: Harcourt Brace and Jovanovich, 1976.

Ibarra, Rafael. "Looking at Proposition 187 Through the Eyes of an Illegal Valedictorian." *Los Angeles Times,* November 6, 1994, M-6.

"Immigrants: The Changing Face of America." *Time,* July 8, 1985, 31.

Jarvis, Edward. "Influence of Distance from Nearness to an Insane Hospital on Its Use by the People." *American Journal of Insanity* 22 (January 1866): 361–406.

———. *Insanity and Idiocy in Massachusetts: Report of the Commission on Lunacy, 1855,* intro. Gerald N. Grob. 1855. Reprint, Cambridge, Mass.: Harvard University Press, 1971.

Jasso, Guillermina, and Mark R. Rosenzweig. *The New Chosen People: Immigrants in the United States.* New York: Russell Sage Foundation, 1990.

Jencks, Christopher. *Rethinking Social Policy: Race, Poverty, and the Underclass.* Cambridge, Mass.: Harvard University Press, 1992.

Jensen, Leif. "Children of the New Immigration: A Comparative Analysis of Today's Second Generation." Working paper #1990-32. Institute for Policy Research and Evaluation, Pennsylvania State University, 1990.

Jensen, Leif, and Yoshimi Chitose. "Today's Second Generation: Evidence from the 1990 U.S. Census." *International Migration Review* 28 (1994): 714–773.

Jerome, Harry. *Migration and Business Cycles.* New York: National Bureau of Economic Research, 1926.

Kanjanapan, Wilawan. "The Immigration of Asian Professionals to the United States, 1988–1990." *International Migration Review* 29, 1 (1995): 7–32.

Kao, Grace, and Marta Tienda. "Optimism and Achievement: The Educational Performance of Immigrant Youth." *Social Science Quarterly* 76, 1 (1995): 1–19.

Kaplan, M., and G. Marks. "Adverse Effects of Acculturation: Psychological Distress Among Mexican American Young Adults." *Social Science and Medicine* 31, 12 (1990): 1313–1319.

Karno, Marvin, and Richard L. Hough. "Lifetime Prevalence of Specific Psychiatric Disorders Among Mexican Americans and Non-Hispanic Whites in Los Angeles." *Archives of General Psychiatry* 44 (August 1987): 695–701.

Keller, S. L. *Uprooting and Social Change: The Role of Refugees in Development*. Delhi: Manohar Book Service, 1975.

Kessler, R. C., and P. D. Cleary. "Social Class and Psychological Distress." *American Sociological Review* 45 (June 1980): 463–478.

Kibria, Nazli. *Family Tightrope: The Changing Lives of Vietnamese Americans*. Princeton: Princeton University Press, 1993.

Kim, Illsoo. *New Urban Immigrants: The Korean Community in New York*. Princeton, N.J.: Princeton University Press, 1981.

Kim, Kwang Chung, and Won Moo Hurh. "Two Dimensions of Korean Immigrants' Sociocultural Adaptation: Americanization and Ethnic Attachment." Paper presented at the annual meeting of the American Sociological Association, Atlanta, August 1988.

Kinzie, J. David, and Spero Manson. "Five Years' Experience with Indochinese Refugee Psychiatric Patients." *Journal of Operational Psychiatry* 14 (1983): 105–111.

Kinzie, J. David, and William Sack. "Severely Traumatized Cambodian Children: Research Findings and Clinical Implications." In *Refugee Children: Theory, Research, and Services*, ed. F. L. Ahearn, Jr., and J. L. Athey, 92–105. Baltimore: Johns Hopkins University Press, 1991.

Kircheman, Joleen, and Kathryn M. Neckerman. "We Love to Hire Them But . . . : The Meaning of Race to Employers." In *The Urban Underclass*, ed. C. Jencks and P. E. Peterson. Washington, D.C.: Brookings Institution, 1991.

Kirkpatrick, Clifford. *Intelligence and Immigration*. Baltimore: Williams and Wilkins, 1926.

Kivisto, Peter. *Immigrant Socialists in the United States: The Case of Finns and the Left*. Rutherford, N.J.: Farleigh Dickinson University Press, 1984.

Kohn, Melvin L. "Social Class and Schizophrenia: A Critical Review and Reformulation." *Schizophrenia Bulletin* 7 (Winter 1973): 60–79.

Kraut, Alan M. *The Huddled Masses: The Immigrant in American Society, 1880–1921*. Arlington Heights, Ill.: Harlan Davidson, 1982.

———. *Silent Travelers: Germs, Genes, and the 'Immigrant Menace.'* New York: Basic Books, 1994.

Kunz, Egon F. "Exile and Resettlement: Refugee Theory." *International Migration Review* 15 (Spring–Summer 1981): 42–51.

———. "The Refugee in Flight: Kinetic Models and Forms of Displacement." *International Migration Review* 7 (Summer 1973): 125–146.

Kuo, Wen H., and Yung-Mei Tsai. "Social Networking, Hardiness and Immigrants' Mental Health." *Journal of Health and Social Behavior* 27 (June 1986): 133–149.

Kyle, David. "The Transnational Peasant: The Social Structures of Economic Migration from the Ecuadoran Andes." Ph.D. diss., Johns Hopkins University, 1995.

Lamm, Richard D., and Gary Imhoff. *The Immigration Time Bomb: The Fragmenting of America*. New York: Dutton, 1985.

Landale, Nancy S., and R. S. Oropesa. "Immigrant Children and the Children of Immigrants: Inter- and Intra-Ethnic Group Differences in the United States." Population Research Group (PRG) Research Paper 95-2. East Lansing: Institute for Public Policy and Social Research, Michigan State University, 1995.

Landry, Walter. "Comment." *International Journal of the Sociology of Language* 60 (1986): 129–138.

Langner, Thomas S., and Stanley T. Michael. *Life Stress and Mental Health: The Midtown Manhattan Study*, vol. 2. London: Collier-Macmillan, 1963.

Laponce, J. A. *Languages and Their Territories*. Translated by Anthony Martin-Sperry. Toronto: University of Toronto Press, 1987.

Lebergott, Stanley. *Manpower in Economic Growth: The American Record Since 1800*. New York: McGraw-Hill, 1964.

LeMay, Michael C. *Anatomy of a Public Policy: The Reform of Contemporary American Immigration Law*. Westport, Conn.: Praeger, 1994.

Lenneberg, Eric H. *Biological Foundations of Language*. New York: Wiley, 1967.

Leopold, Werner F. *Speech Development of a Bilingual Child*, vols. 1–4. Evanston, Ill.: Northwestern University Press, 1939, 1947, 1949.

Levine, Barry. *The Caribbean Exodus*. New York: Praeger, 1987.

Lieberson, Stanley. *Language and Ethnic Relations in Canada*. New York: Wiley, 1970.

———. *Language Diversity and Language Contact*. Stanford, Calif: Stanford University Press, 1981.

———. *A Piece of the Pie: Blacks and White Immigrants Since 1880*. Berkeley: University of California Press, 1980.

Lieberson, Stanley, Guy Dalto, and Mary Ellen Johnston. "The Course of Mother Tongue Diversity in Nations." *American Journal of Sociology* 81 (July 1975): 34–61.

Lieberson, Stanley, and Lynn K. Hansen. "National Development, Mother Tongue Diversity, and the Comparative Study of Nations." *American Sociological Review* 39 (August 1974): 523–541.

Lieberson, Stanley, and Mary C. Waters. "The Location of Ethnic and Racial Groups in the United States." *Sociological Forum* 2 (Fall 1987): 780–810.

Light, Ivan. "Asian Enterprise in America: Chinese, Japanese, and Koreans in Small Business." In *Self-Help in Urban America*, ed. Scott Cummings, 33–57. New York: Kennikat Press, 1980.

———. "Disadvantaged Minorities in Self-Employment." *International Journal of Comparative Sociology* 20 (March–June 1979): 31–45.

———. *Ethnic Enterprise in America: Business and Welfare Among Chi-*

nese, Japanese, and Blacks. Berkeley: University of California Press, 1972.

———. "Immigrant and Ethnic Enterprise in North America." *Ethnic and Racial Studies* 7 (April 1984): 195–216.

Light, Ivan, and Edna Bonacich. *Immigrant Entrepreneurs: Koreans in Los Angeles, 1965–1982*. Berkeley: University of California Press, 1988.

Lin, Keh-Ming, Laurie Tazuma, and Minoru Masuda. "Adaptational Problems of Vietnamese Refugees: I. Health and Mental Health Status." *Archives of General Psychiatry* 36 (August 1979): 955–961.

Link, Bruce, and Bruce P. Dohrenwend. "Formulation of Hypotheses About the True Prevalence of Demoralization." In *Mental Illness in the United States: Epidemiological Estimates*, ed. Bruce P. Dohrenwend, 114–132. New York: Praeger, 1980.

Lipset, Seymour M., and Reinhard Bendix. *Social Mobility in Industrial Society*. Berkeley: University of California Press, 1959.

Liu, William T., Maryanne Lamanna, and Alicia Murata. *Transition to Nowhere: Vietnamese Refugees in America*. Nashville, Tenn.: Charter House, 1979.

Loo, Chalsa M. "The 'Biliterate' Ballot Controversy: Language Acquisition and Cultural Shift Among Immigrants." *International Migration Review* 19 (Fall 1985): 493–515.

López, David E. "Chicano Language Loyalty in an Urban Setting." *Sociology and Social Research* 62 (1978): 267–278.

———. *Language Maintenance and Shift in the United States Today: The Basic Patterns and Their Social Implications*, vols. 1–4. Los Alamitos, Calif.: National Center for Bilingual Research, 1982.

———. *The Maintenance of Spanish Over Three Generations in the United States*. Los Alamitos, Calif.: National Center for Bilingual Research, 1982.

Mackey, William F. *Bilingualism as a World Problem*. Montreal: Harvest House, 1967.

Madhavan, M. C. "Indian Emigrants: Numbers, Characteristics, and Economic Impact." *Population and Development Review* 11 (September 1985): 457–481.

———. "Migration of Skilled People from Developing to Developed Countries: Characteristics, Consequences, and Policies." Paper presented at the United Nations Development Program Conference on Transfer of Knowledge Through Expatriate Nations, New Delhi, India, February 1988.

Maldonado, Edwin. "Contract Labor and the Origin of Puerto Rican Communities in the United States." *International Migration Review* 13 (Spring 1979): 103–121.

Malzberg, Benjamin. "Mental Disease and 'the Melting Pot'." *Journal of Nervous and Mental Disease* 72 (October 1930): 379–395.

———. "Mental Disease in New York State According to Nativity and Parentage." *Mental Hygiene* 19 (October 1935): 635–660.

———. *Social and Biological Aspects of Mental Disease.* Utica, N.Y.: State Hospitals Press, 1940.

Malzberg, Benjamin, and Everett S. Lee. *Migration and Mental Disease: A Study of First Admissions to Hospitals for Mental Disease, New York, 1939–1941.* New York: Social Science Research Council, 1956.

Margolis, Maxine L. *Little Brazil: An Ethnography of Brazilian Immigrants in New York City.* Princeton, N.J.: Princeton University Press, 1994.

Markides, K. S., and J. Coreil. "The Health of Hispanics in the Southwestern United States: An Epidemiological Paradox." *Public Health Reports* 101 (1986): 253–265.

Marks, G., M. García, and J. Solis. "Health Risk Behaviors in Hispanics in the United States: Findings from HHANES 1982–84." *American Journal of Public Health*, supplement, 80 (1990): 20–26.

Marris, Peter. *Loss and Change.* Garden City, N.Y.: Doubleday, 1975.

Marshall, David F. "The Question of an Official Language: Language Rights and the English Language Amendment." *International Journal of the Sociology of Language* 60 (1986): 7–75.

Martínez, Cervando, Jr. "Mexican-Americans." In *Cross-Cultural Mental Health*, ed. Lillian Comas-Díaz and Ezra E. H. Griffith, 262–302. New York: Wiley, 1988.

Massey, Douglas S. "Do Undocumented Immigrants Earn Lower Wages than Legal Immigrants? New Evidence from Mexico." *International Migration Review* 21 (Summer 1987): 236–274.

———. "Latinos, Poverty, and the Underclass: A New Agenda for Research." *Hispanic Journal of Behavioral Sciences* 15 (November 1993): 449–475.

———. "The Settlement Process Among Mexican Immigrants to the United States." *American Sociological Review* 51 (October 1986): 670–684.

———. "Social Structure, Household Strategies, and the Cumulative Causation of Migration." *Population Index* 56 (1990): 3–26.

———. "Understanding Mexican Migration to the United States." *American Journal of Sociology* 92 (May 1987): 1372–1403.

Massey, Douglas S., Rafael Alarcón, Jorge Durand, and Humberto González. *Return to Atzlán: The Social Process of International Migration from Western Mexico.* Berkeley: University of California Press, 1987.

Massey, Douglas S., and Felipe García España. "The Social Process of International Migration." *Science* 237 (1987): 733–738.

Massey, Douglas S., and L. Goldring. "Continuities in Transnational Migration: An Analysis of Nineteen Mexican Communities." *American Journal of Sociology* 99 (May 1994): 1492–1533.

Masuda, Minoru, Keh-Ming Lin, and Laurie Tazuma. "Adaptational Problems of Vietnamese Refugees: II. Life Changes and Perceptions of Life Events." *Archives of General Psychiatry* 37 (April 1980): 447–450.

Matute-Bianchi, María Eugenia. "Ethnic Identities and Patterns of School Success and Failure Among Mexican-Descent and Japanese-American Students in a California High School." *American Journal of Education* 95 (November 1986): 233–255.

———. "Situational Ethnicity and Patterns of School Performance Among Immigrant and Nonimmigrant Mexican-Descent Students." In *Minority Status and Schooling: A Comparative Study of Immigrant and Involuntary Minorities*, ed. Margaret A. Gibson and John U. Ogbu, 205–247. New York: Garland, 1991.

McCoy, Terry L. "The Political Economy of Caribbean Workers in the Florida Sugar Industry." Paper presented at the fifth annual meeting of the Caribbean Studies Association, Willemstad, Curacao, May 1980. Mimeographed.

Meinhardt, Kenneth, Soleng Tom, Philip Tse, and Connie Young Yu. "Southeast Asian Refugees in the 'Silicon Valley': The Asian Health Assessment Project." *Amerasia* 12 (1985–1986): 43–65.

Mezey, A. G. "Psychiatric Illness in Hungarian Refugees." *Journal of Mental Science* 106 (April 1960): 628–637.

Miller, Jake C. *The Plight of Haitian Refugees*. New York: Praeger, 1984.

Miller, Kerby A. *Emigrants and Exiles: Ireland and the Irish Exodus to North America*. New York: Oxford University Press, 1985.

Min, Pyong Gap. "Ethnic Business and Economic Mobility: Korean Immigrants in Los Angeles." Paper presented at the meetings of the American Sociological Association, Atlanta, August 1988.

———. *Middlemen in Contemporary America: Koreans in New York and Los Angeles, 1970–1994*. Berkeley: University of California Press, 1996.

———, ed. *Asian Americans: Contemporary Trends and Issues*. Thousand Oaks, Calif.: Sage, 1995.

Mink, Gwendolyn. *Old Labor and New Immigrants in American Political Development*. Ithaca, N.Y.: Cornell University Press, 1986.

Mirowsky, John, and Catherine E. Ross. "Mexican Culture and Its Emotional Contradictions." *Journal of Health and Social Behavior* 25 (March 1984): 2–13.

———. "Paranoia and the Structure of Powerlessness." *American Sociological Review* 48 (April 1983): 228–239.

———. *Social Causes of Psychological Distress*. New York: Aldine de Gruyter, 1989.

———. "Social Patterns of Distress." *Annual Review of Sociology* 12 (1986): 23–45.

Molesky, Jean. "The Exiled: Pathology of Central American Refugees." *Migration World* 14 (1986): 19–23.

Mollica, Richard F., and James P. Lavelle. "Southeast Asian Refugees." In *Clinical Guidelines in Cross-Cultural Mental Health*, ed. Lillian Comas-Díaz and Ezra E. H. Griffith, 262–302. New York: Wiley, 1988.

Moore, Joan, and Harry Pachón. *Hispanics in the United States*. Englewood Cliffs, N.J.: Prentice-Hall, 1985.

Morales, Rick, and Richard Mines. "San Diego's Full-Service Restaurants: A View from the Back of the House." Report. La Jolla: Center for U.S.–Mexico Studies, University of California, San Diego, 1985.

Moscicki, E. K., B. Z. Locke, D. S. Rae, et al. "Depressive Symptoms Among Mexican Americans: The Hispanic Health and Nutrition Examination Survey." *American Journal of Epidemiology*, 130 (1989): 348–360.

Moynihan, Daniel P. *Maximum Feasible Misunderstanding*. New York: Random House, 1969.

Muller, Thomas, and Thomas J. Espenshade. *The Fourth Wave: California's Newest Immigrants*. Washington, D.C.: Urban Institute, 1985.

Murphy, H. B. M., ed. *Flight and Resettlement*. Geneva: UNESCO, 1955.

NACLA. "Undocumented Immigrant Workers in New York City." *Latin American and Empire Report* 12 (November–December 1979), special issue.

Nagel, Joane. "The Political Construction of Ethnicity." In *Competitive Ethnic Relations*, ed. Joane Nagel and Susan Olzak, 93–112. Orlando, Fla.: Academic Press, 1986.

Nee, Victor, and Jimy Sanders. "The Road to Parity: Determinants of the Socio-Economic Achievement of Asian Americans." *Ethnic and Racial Studies* 8 (January 1985): 75–93.

Nelson, Candace, and Marta Tienda. "The Structuring of Hispanic Ethnicity: Historical and Contemporary Perspectives." *Ethnic and Racial Studies* 8 (January 1985): 49–74.

"The New Whiz Kids." *Time*, August 31, 1987, 42, 44, 46.

Nicassio, Perry M. "Psychosocial Correlates of Alienation: Study of a Sample of Indochinese Refugees." *Journal of Cross-Cultural Psychology* 14 (September 1983): 337–351.

Nishi, Setsuko Matsunaga. "Japanese Americans." In *Asian Americans: Contemporary Trends and Issues*, ed. Pyong Gap Min, 95–133. Thousand Oaks, Calif.: Sage, 1995.

North, David S., and Marion F. Houstoun. "The Characteristics and Role of Illegal Aliens in the U.S. Labor Market." Washington, D.C.: Linton, 1976. Mimeographed.

Oberg, K. "Cultural Shock: Adjustment to New Cultural Environments." *Practical Anthropology* 7 (1960): 177–182.

Ødegaard, Ørnulv. "The Distribution of Mental Diseases in Norway." *Acta Psychiatrica et Neurologica* 20 (1945): 247–284.

———. "Emigration and Insanity: A Study of Mental Disease Among the Norwegian-Born Population of Minnesota." *Acta Psychiatrica et Neurologica*, supplement, 4 (1932): 1–206.

Ogbu, John U. "Variability in Minority School Performance: A Problem in Search of an Explanation." *Anthropology of Education Quarterly* 18 (December 1987): 312–334.

Olsen, Laurie. "Crossing the Schoolhouse Border: Immigrant Children in California." *Phi Delta Kappan* 70 (November 1988): 211.

———. *Crossing the Schoolhouse Border: Immigrant Students and the California Public Schools.* San Francisco: California Tomorrow, 1988.

Olson, James S., and Judith E. Olson. *Cuban Americans: From Trauma to Triumph.* New York: Twayne Publishers, 1995.

Ortiz, Vilma. "Changes in the Characteristics of Puerto Rican Migrants from 1955 to 1980." *International Migration Review* 20 (Fall 1986): 612–628.

Park, Robert E. "Human Migration and the Marginal Man." *American Journal of Sociology* 33 (May 1928): 881–893.

Passel, Jeffrey S., and Barry Edmonston. "Immigration and Race: Recent Trends in Immigration to the United States." Paper PRIP-UI-22. Washington, D.C.: The Urban Institute, 1992.

Passel, Jeffrey S., and Karen A. Woodrow. "Geographic Distribution of Undocumented Immigrants: Estimates of Undocumented Aliens Counted in the 1980 Census by State." *International Migration Review* 18 (Fall 1984): 642–671.

Pastor, Robert. *Migration and Development in the Caribbean.* Boulder, Colo.: Westview Press, 1985.

Peal, Elizabeth, and Wallace E. Lambert. "The Relation of Bilingualism to Intelligence." *Psychological Monographs: General and Applied* 76 (1962): 1–23.

Pedraza-Bailey, Silvia. "Cubans and Mexicans in the United States: The Functions of Political and Economic Migration." *Cuban Studies* 11 (July 1979): 79–97.

———. "Cuba's Exiles: Portrait of a Refugee Migration." *International Migration Review* 19 (Spring 1985): 4–34.

Pérez, Lisandro. "Cuban Miami." In *Miami Now!* ed. Guillermo J.

Grenier and Alex Stepick, 83–108. Gainesville, Fla.: University Press of Florida, 1992.

Pérez Firmat, Gustavo. *Life on the Hyphen: The Cuban-American Way.* Austin: University of Texas Press, 1994.

Pérez-Sainz, Juan Pablo. *El dilema del Nahual.* San José: FLACSO Editores, 1994.

Pessar, Patricia R. "The Role of Households in International Migration and the Case of the U.S.–Bound Migration from the Dominican Republic." *International Migration Review* 16 (Summer 1982): 342–364.

Petersen, William. *Japanese Americans: Oppression and Success.* New York: Random House, 1971.

Pinker, Steven. *The Language Instinct.* New York: William Morrow, 1994.

Piore, Michael. *Birds of Passage.* Cambridge, Mass.: Cambridge University Press, 1979.

Portes, Alejandro. "Children of Immigrants: Segmented Assimilation and Its Determinants." In *The Economic Sociology of Immigration: Essays on Networks, Ethnicity, and Entrepreneurship,* ed. Alejandro Portes, 248–279. New York: Russell Sage Foundation, 1995.

———. "Determinants of the Brain Drain." *International Migration Review* 10 (Winter 1976): 489–508.

———. "Dilemmas of a Golden Exile: Integration of Cuban Refugee Families in Milwaukee." *American Sociological Review* 34 (August 1969): 505–518.

———. "From South of the Border: Hispanic Minorities in the United States." In *Immigration Reconsidered: History, Sociology, and Politics,* ed. V. Yans-McLaughlin, 160–184. New York: Oxford University Press, 1990.

———. "Illegal Immigration and the International System: Lessons from Recent Legal Mexican Immigrants to the United States." *Social Problems* 26 (April 1979): 425–438.

———. "Immigration Reform: The Theory and the Realities." *Baltimore Sun,* January 2, 1987, 15A.

———. "The Longest Migration." *The New Republic,* April 26, 1993.

———. "Migration and Underdevelopment." *Politics and Society* 8 (1978): 1–48.

———. "The Rise of Ethnicity." *American Sociological Review* 49 (June 1984): 383–397.

———. "The Social Origins of the Cuban Enclave Economy of Miami." *Sociological Perspectives* 30 (October 1987): 340–372.

———. "When More Can Be Less: Labor Standards, Development, and the Informal Economy." In *Labor Standards and Development in the*

Global Economy, ed. S. Herzenberg and J. Perez-Lopez, 219–237. Washington, D.C.: Bureau of International Labor Affairs, U.S. Department of Labor, 1990.

Portes, Alejandro, and Robert L. Bach. *Latin Journey: Cuban and Mexican Immigrants in the United States*. Berkeley: University of California Press, 1985.

Portes, Alejandro, and József Böröcz. "Contemporary Immigration: Theoretical Perspectives on Its Determinants and Modes of Incorporation." *International Migration Review* 23 (Fall 1989): 606–630.

Portes, Alejandro, and Juan M. Clark. "Mariel Refugees: Six Years Later." *Migration World* 15 (Fall 1987): 14–18.

Portes, Alejandro, Juan M. Clark, and Manuel M. López. "Six Years Later: The Process of Incorporation of Cuban Exiles in the United States." *Cuban Studies* 11/12 (January 1982): 1–24.

Portes, Alejandro, and Robert D. Manning. "The Immigrant Enclave: Theory and Empirical Examples." In *Competitive Ethnic Relations*, ed. Joane Nagel and Susan Olzak, 47–68. Orlando, Fla.: Academic Press, 1986.

Portes, Alejandro, and Rafael Mozo. "The Political Adaptation Process of Cubans and Other Ethnic Minorities in the United States." *International Migration Review* 19 (Spring 1985): 35–63.

Portes, Alejandro, Robert N. Parker, and José A. Cobas. "Assimilation or Consciousness?" *Social Forces* 59 (September 1980): 200–224.

Portes, Alejandro, and Adreain R. Ross. "Modernization for Emigration: The Medical Brain Drain from Argentina." *Journal of Interamerican Studies and World Affairs* 13 (November 1976): 395–422.

Portes, Alejandro, and Saskia Sassen-Koob. "Making It Underground: Comparative Materials on the Informal Sector in Western Market Economies." *American Journal of Sociology* 93 (1987): 30–61.

Portes, Alejandro, and Richard Schauffler. "Language and the Second Generation: Bilingualism Yesterday and Today." *International Migration Review* 28, 4 (1994): 640–661.

Portes, Alejandro, and Alex Stepick. *City on the Edge: The Transformation of Miami*. Berkeley: University of California Press, 1993.

———. "Unwelcome Immigrants: The Labor Market Experiences of 1980 (Mariel) Cuban and Haitian Refugees in South Florida." *American Sociological Review* 50 (August 1985): 493–514.

Portes, Alejandro, and Cynthia Truelove. "Making Sense of Diversity: Recent Research on Hispanic Minorities in the United States." *Annual Review of Sociology* 13 (1987): 359–385.

Portes, Alejandro, and John Walton. *Labor, Class, and the International System*. New York: Academic Press, 1981.

Portes, Alejandro, and Min Zhou. "Divergent Destinies: Immigration,

Poverty, and Entrepreneurship in the United States." In *Poverty, Inequality, and the Future of Social Policy*, ed. K. McFate, R. Lawson, and W. J. Wilson, 489–520. New York: Russell Sage Foundation, 1995.

Rahe, Richard H., John G. Looney, Harold W. Ward, Tran M. Tung, and William T. Liu. "Psychiatric Consultation in a Vietnamese Refugee Camp." *American Journal of Psychiatry* 135 (February 1978): 185–190.

Ranney, M. H. "On Insane Foreigners." *American Journal of Insanity* 7 (July 1850): 53–63.

Reichert, Joshua S. "The Migrant Syndrome: Seasonal U.S. Wage Labor and Rural Development in Central Mexico." *Human Organization* 40 (Spring 1981): 59–66.

Reimers, Cordelia W. "A Comparative Analysis of the Wages of Hispanics, Blacks, and Non-Hispanic Whites." In *Hispanics in the U.S. Economy*, ed. George J. Borjas and Marta Tienda, 27–75. Orlando, Fla.: Academic Press, 1985.

Reimers, David M. *Still the Golden Door: The Third World Comes to America*. New York: Columbia University Press, 1985.

Repak, Terry A. "And They Come on Behalf of Their Children: Central American Families in Washington, D.C." Report prepared for the Conference on Immigration, U.S. Department of Labor, September, 1988.

Resnick, Melvin C. "Beyond the Ethnic Community: Spanish Language Roles and Maintenance in Miami." *International Journal of the Sociology of Language* 69 (1988): 89–104.

Reynolds, Maura. "Language and Learning: Lessons from Canada." *San Diego Union-Tribune*, May 30, 1993, A-1.

Richardson, Alan. "A Theory and a Method for the Psychological Study of Assimilation." *International Migration Review* 2 (Fall 1967): 3–29.

Rischin, Moses. *The Promised City: New York Jews, 1870–1914*. Cambridge, Mass.: Harvard University Press, 1962.

Rist, Ray. "Guestworkers in Germany: Public Policies as the Legitimation of Marginality." *Ethnic and Racial Studies* 2 (October 1979): 401–415.

Roberts, Bryan R. "Employment Structure, Life Cycle, and Life Chances: Formal and Informal Sectors in Guadalajara." In *The Informal Economy: Studies in Advanced and Less Developed Countries*, ed. Alejandro Portes, Manuel Castells, and Lauren Benton, 41–59. Baltimore: Johns Hopkins University Press, 1989,

———. "Socially Expected Durations and the Economic Adjustment of Immigrants." In *The Economic Sociology of Immigration*, ed. Alejandro Portes, 42–86. New York: Russell Sage Foundation, 1995.

Robertson, John W. "Prevalence of Insanity in California." *American Journal of Insanity* 60 (July 1903): 81–82.

Rodríguez, Clara. *The Ethnic Queue in the U.S.: The Case of Puerto Ricans*. San Francisco: R and E Research Associates, 1976.

Rodríguez, Nestor P. "Undocumented Central Americans in Houston: Diverse Populations." *International Migration Review* 21 (Spring 1987): 4–26.

Rodríguez, Richard. *Days of Obligation: An Argument with My Mexican Father*. New York: Viking, 1992.

———. *Hunger of Memory*. Boston: David R. Godline, 1982.

Rogler, Lloyd H., Robert G. Malgady, and Orlando Rodríguez. *Hispanics and Mental Health: A Framework for Research*. Malabar, Fla.: Krieger, 1989.

Rose, Peter I. "Some Thoughts About Refugees and the Descendants of Theseus." *International Migration Review* 15 (Spring–Summer 1981): 8–15.

Rosenblum, Gerald. *Immigrant Workers: Their Impact on American Radicalism*. New York: Basic Books, 1973.

Rothman, David J. *The Discovery of the Asylum*. Boston: Little, Brown, 1971.

Rubenstein, Hyzine. "Remittances and Rural Underdevelopment in the English-Speaking Caribbean." *Human Organization* 42 (Winter 1983): 295–306.

Rumbaut, Rubén D. "Life Events, Change, Migration, and Depression." In *Phenomenology and Treatment of Depression*, ed. William E. Fann, Ismet Karacan, Alex D. Pokorny, and Robert L. Williams, 115–126. New York: Plenum, 1977.

Rumbaut, Rubén D., and Rubén G. Rumbaut. "The Family in Exile: Cuban Expatriates in the United States." *American Journal of Psychiatry* 133 (April 1976): 395–399.

———. "Refugees in the United States: A Mental Health Research Challenge." Paper presented to the Karl Menninger School of Psychiatry, Topeka, Kansas, June 1986.

Rumbaut, Rubén G. "The Agony of Exile: A Study of Indochinese Refugee Adults and Children." In *Refugee Children: Theory, Research, and Services*, ed. F. L. Ahearn, Jr., and J. L. Athey, 53–91. Baltimore: Johns Hopkins University Press, 1991.

———. "The Americans: Latin American and Caribbean Peoples in the United States." In *Americas: New Interpretive Essays*, ed. Alfred Stepan, 275–307. New York: Oxford University Press, 1992.

———. "The Crucible Within: Ethnic Identity, Self-Esteem, and Segmented Assimilation Among Children of Immigrants." *International Migration Review* 28 (Winter 1994): 748–794.

———. *Immigrant Students in California Public Schools: A Summary of Current Knowledge*. Center for Research on Effective Schooling for Disadvantaged Children, Report No. 11. Baltimore: Johns Hopkins University, 1990.

———. "Mental Health and the Refugee Experience: A Comparative Study of Southeast Asian Refugees." In *Southeast Asian Mental Health*, ed. Tom C. Owan, 433–486. Rockville, Md.: National Institute of Mental Health, 1985.

———. "Migration, Adaptation, and Mental Health: The Experience of Southeast Asian Refugees in the United States." In *Refugee Policy: Canada and the United States*, ed. Howard Adelman, 383–427. Toronto: York Lanes Press, 1991.

———. "The New Californians: Comparative Research Findings on the Educational Progress of Immigrant Children." In *California's Immigrant Children: Theory, Research, and Implications for Educational Policy*, ed. R. G. Rumbaut and W. A. Cornelius, 17–70. La Jolla: Center for U.S.–Mexican Studies, University of California, San Diego, 1995.

———. "Origins and Destinies: Immigration to the United States Since World War II." *Sociological Forum* 9 (1994): 583–621.

———. "Passages to America: Perspectives on the New Immigration." In *America at Century's End*, ed. Alan Wolfe, 208–244. Berkeley: University of California Press, 1991.

———. "Portraits, Patterns, and Predictors of the Refugee Adaptation Process." In *Refugees as Immigrants: Cambodians, Laotians and Vietnamese in America*, ed. David W. Haines, 138–182. Totowa, N.J.: Rowman & Littlefield, 1989.

———. "The Structure of Refuge: Southeast Asian Refugees in the United States." *International Review of Comparative Public Policy* 1 (Winter 1989): 97–129.

———. "Vietnamese, Laotian, and Cambodian Americans." In *Asian Americans: Contemporary Trends and Issues*, ed. Pyong Gap Min, 232–270. Thousand Oaks, Calif.: Sage, 1995.

Rumbaut, Rubén G., Leo R. Chávez, Robert J. Moser, Sheila Pickwell, and Samuel Wishik. "The Politics of Migrant Health Care: A Comparative Study of Mexican Immigrants and Indochinese Refugees." *Research in the Sociology of Health Care* 7 (1988): 143–202.

Rumbaut, Rubén G., and Wayne A. Cornelius, ed. *California's Immigrant Children: Theory, Research, and Implications for Educational Policy*. La Jolla: Center for U.S.–Mexican Studies, University of California, San Diego, 1995.

Rumbaut, Rubén G., and Kenji Ima. *The Adaptation of Southeast Asian Refugee Youth: A Comparative Study*. Washington, D.C.: U.S. Office of Refugee Resettlement, 1988.

———. "Determinants of Educational Attainment Among Indochinese

Refugees and Other Immigrant Students." Paper presented at the annual meeting of the American Sociological Association, Atlanta, August 1988.

Rumbaut, Rubén G., and John R. Weeks. "Fertility and Adaptation: Indochinese Refugees in the United States." *International Migration Review* 20 (Summer 1986): 428–466.

———. "Infant Health Among Indochinese Refugees: Patterns of Infant Mortality, Birthweight and Prenatal Care in Comparative Perspective." *Research in the Sociology of Health Care* 8 (1989): 37–196.

———. "Unraveling a Public Health Enigma: Why Do Immigrants Experience Superior Perinatal Health Outcomes?" *Research in the Sociology of Health Care* 13 (1996): 335–388.

Sabel, Charles F. "Changing Modes of Economic Efficiency and Their Implications for Industrialization in the Third World." In *Development, Democracy, and Trespassing: Essays in Honor of Albert O. Hirschman*, ed. M. S. McPherson, A. Foxley, and G. O'Donnell, 27–55. Notre Dame, Ind.: Notre Dame University Press, 1986.

Salmon, T. W. "The Relation of Immigration to the Prevalence of Insanity." *American Journal of Insanity* 64 (July 1907): 53–71.

Samora, Julián. *Los Mojados: The Wetback Story*. Notre Dame, Ind.: Notre Dame University Press, 1971.

Sánchez-Korrol, Victoria. *From Colonia to Community*. Westport, Conn.: Greenwood Press, 1983.

Sandiford, Peter, and Ruby Kerr. "Intelligence of Chinese and Japanese Children." *Journal of Educational Psychology* 17 (September 1926): 366–367.

Santibáñez, Enrique. *Ensayo acerca de la inmigración Mexicana en los Estados Unidos*. San Antonio, Tex.: Clegg, 1930.

Santoli, Al. *New Americans: An Oral History*. New York: Viking, 1988.

Sanua, Victor D. "Immigration, Migration, and Mental Illness." In *Behavior in New Environments: Adaptation of Migrant Populations*, ed. Eugene B. Brody, 291–352. Beverly Hills, Calif.: Sage, 1970.

Sassen, Saskia. "Changing Composition and Labor Market Location of Hispanic Immigrants in New York City, 1960–1980." In *Hispanics in the U.S. Economy*, ed. George J. Borjas and Marta Tienda, 299–322. New York: Academic Press, 1985.

———. "Exporting Capital and Importing Labor: The Role of Caribbean Migration to New York." Occasional Paper no. 28. Center for Latin American and Caribbean Studies, New York University, 1981.

———. "Formal and Informal Associations: Dominicans and Colombians in New York." *International Migration Review* 13 (Summer 1979): 314–332.

———. "Immigrant and Minority Workers in the Organization of the Labor Process." *Journal of Ethnic Studies* (Spring 1981): 1–34.

————. *The Mobility of Labor and Capital: A Study in International Investment and Labor Flow*. New York: Cambridge University Press, 1988.

————. "The New Labor Demand in Global Cities." In *Cities in Transformation*, ed. Michael P. Smith, 139–171. Beverly Hills, Calif.: Sage Publications, 1984.

————. "New York City's Informal Economy." In *The Informal Economy: Studies in Advanced and Less Developed Countries*, ed. A. Portes, M. Castells, and L. Benton, 60–77. Baltimore: Johns Hopkins University Press, 1989.

Sassen, Saskia, and Robert C. Smith. "Post-industrial Growth and Economic Reorganization: Their Impact on Immigrant Employment." In *U.S.–Mexico Relations, Labor Market Interdependence*, ed. J. Bustamante, C. W. Reynolds, and R. A. Hinojosa, 372–393. Stanford, Calif.: Stanford University Press, 1992.

Schlossman, Steven L. "Is There an American Tradition of Bilingual Education? German in the Public Elementary Schools, 1840–1919." *American Journal of Education* 91 (February 1983): 139–186.

Schmalz, Jeffrey. "Hispanic Influx Spurs Step to Bolster English." *New York Times*, October 26, 1988, I-1.

Schuck, Peter. "The Message of 187." *The American Prospect* 21 (Spring 1995): 85–92.

Schwab, John J., and Mary E. Schwab. *Sociocultural Roots of Mental Illness: An Epidemiologic Survey*. New York: Plenum, 1978.

Seeman, Melvin. "On the Meaning of Alienation." *American Sociological Review* 24 (December 1959): 783–791.

Shannon, David A. *The Socialist Party in America*. Chicago: Quadrangle Books, 1967.

Sharma, Miriam. "The Philippines: A Case of Migration to Hawaii, 1906–1946." In *Labor Immigration Under Capitalism*, ed. Lucie Cheng and Edna Bonacich, 337–358. Berkeley: University of California Press, 1984.

Shutz, Alfred. "The Stranger: An Essay in Social Psychology." *American Journal of Sociology* 49 (May 1944): 499–507.

Silva-Corvalón, Carmen. *Language Contact and Change: Spanish in Los Angeles*. New York: Oxford University Press, 1994.

Simon, Julian. *The Economic Consequences of Immigration*. Cambridge, Mass.: Basil Blackwell, 1989.

Simon, Rita J. "Refugee Families' Adjustment and Aspirations: A Comparison of Soviet Jewish and Vietnamese Immigrants." *Ethnic and Racial Studies* 6 (October 1983): 492–504.

Smith, Madorah E. "Some Light on the Problem of Bilingualism as Found from a Study of the Progress in Mastery of English Among

Preschool Children of Non-American Ancestry in Hawaii." *Genetic Psychology Monographs* 21 (May 1939): 119–284.

Smith, Robert C. "Los ausentes siempre presentes: The Imagining, Making, and Politics of a Transnational Community Between New York City and Ticuaní, Puebla." Manuscript. Institute for Latin American and Iberian Studies, Columbia University, October 1992.

———. "New York in Mixtexa: Mixteca in New York." *NACLA Report on the Americas* 26, 1 (1992).

Sowell, Thomas. *Ethnic America: A History*. New York: Basic Books, 1981.

Sridhar, Kamal K. "Language Maintenance and Language Shift Among Asian-Indians: Kannadigas in the New York Area." *International Journal of the Sociology of Language* 69 (1988): 73–87.

Srole, Leo, Thomas S. Langner, and Stanley Mitchell. *Mental Health in the Metropolis: The Midtown Manhattan Study*, vol. 1. Rev. ed. New York: New York University Press, 1962.

Starr, Paul D., and Alden E. Roberts. "Attitudes Toward New Americans: Perceptions of Indo-Chinese in Nine Cities." *Research in Race and Ethnic Relations* 3 (1982): 165–186.

Stein, Barry N. "The Experience of Being a Refugee: Insights from the Research Literature." In *Refugee Mental Health in Resettlement Countries*, ed. Carolyn L. Williams and Joseph Westermeyer, 5–23. New York: Hemisphere, 1986.

Steinberg, Stephen. *The Ethnic Myth*. New York: Atheneum, 1981.

Stepick, Alex. "Haitian Refugees in the U.S." Minority Rights Group Report no. 52. London: MRG, 1982.

Stepick, Alex, and Alejandro Portes. "Flight into Despair: A Profile of Recent Haitian Refugees in South Florida." *International Migration Review* 20 (Summer 1986): 329–350.

Stevens, Rosemary, Louis W. Goodman, and Stephen Mick. *The Alien Doctors: Foreign Medical Graduates in American Hospitals*. New York: Wiley, 1978.

Stonequist, Everett V. *The Marginal Man: A Study in Personality and Culture Conflict*. 1937. Reprint, New York: Russell & Russell, 1961.

Strand, Paul J., and Woodrow Jones, Jr. *Indochinese Refugees in America: Problems of Adaptation and Assimilation*. Durham, N.C.: Duke University Press, 1985.

Suárez-Orozco, Marcelo M. *Central American Refugees and U.S. High Schools: A Psychosocial Study of Motivation and Achievement*. Stanford: Stanford University Press, 1989.

———. "Towards a Psychosocial Understanding of Hispanic Adaptation to American Schooling." In *Success or Failure? Learning and the Languages of Minority Students*, ed. H. T. Trueba, 156–168. New York: Newbury House Publishers, 1987.

Suárez-Orozco, Marcelo M., and Carola Suárez-Orozco. "The Cultural Patterning of Achievement Motivation: A Comparative Study of Mexican, Mexican Immigrant, and Non-Latino White American Youths in Schools." In *California's Immigrant Children: Theory, Research, and Implications for Educational Policy*, ed. Rubén G. Rumbaut and Wayne A. Cornelius, 161–190. La Jolla: Center for U.S.–Mexican Studies, University of California, San Diego, 1995.

Szapocznik, José, Raquel Cohen, and Roberto E. Hernández, eds. *Coping with Adolescent Refugees: The Mariel Boatlift*. New York: Praeger, 1985.

Tabori, Paul. *The Anatomy of Exile: A Semantic and Historical Study*. London: George Harrap, 1972.

Tan, Amy. 1989. *The Joy Luck Club*. New York: Putnam.

Taylor, Donald M. "Ethnicity and Language: A Social Psychological Perspective." In *Language: Social Psychological Perspectives*, ed. Howard Giles, W. Peter Robinson, and Philip M. Smith, 133–139. New York: Pergamon Press, 1980.

Taylor, Lowell J., Frank D. Bean, James B. Rebitzer, Susan Gonzalez Baker, and B. Lindsay Lowell. "Mexican Immigrants and the Wages and Unemployment Experience of Native Workers." Discussion paper PRIP-UI-1. Washington, D.C.: Urban Institute, 1988.

Teitelbaum, Michael S. "Right Versus Right: Immigration and Refugee Policy in the United States." *Foreign Affairs* 59 (1980): 21–59.

Thernstrom, Abigail M. "Language: Issues and Legislation." In *Harvard Encyclopedia of American Ethnic Groups*, ed. Stephan Thernstrom, 619–629. Cambridge, Mass.: Harvard University Press, 1981.

Thoits, P. A. "Conceptual, Methodological, and Theoretical Problems in Studying Social Support as a Buffer Against Life Stress." *Journal of Health and Social Behavior* 23 (June 1982): 145–159.

———. "Undesirable Life Events and Psychological Distress: A Problem of Operational Confounding." *American Sociological Review* 46 (February 1981): 97–109.

Thomas, Brinley. *Migration and Economic Growth: A Study of Great Britain and the Atlantic Economy*. Cambridge: Cambridge University Press, 1973.

Thomas, Hugh. *Cuba: The Pursuit of Freedom*. New York: Harper and Row, 1971.

Thomas, William I., and Florian Znaniecki. *The Polish Peasant in Europe and America*, ed. and abr. Eli Zaretsky. 1918–1920. Reprint, Chicago: University of Illinois Press, 1984.

"Threat to Security Cited in Rise of Foreign Engineers." *Los Angeles Times*, January 20, 1988, I-1.

Tienda, Marta. "Hispanic Origin Workers in the U.S. Labor Market: Comparative Analyses of Employment and Earnings." Final report to the U.S. Department of Labor. Madison: University of Wisconsin Department of Rural Sociology, 1981. Mimeographed.

Tienda, Marta, and Haya Stier. "The Wages of Race: Color and Employment Opportunity in Chicago's Inner City." In *Origins and Destinies: Immigration, Race, and Ethnicity in America*, ed. S. Pedraza and Rubén G. Rumbaut. Belmont, Calif.: Wadsworth, 1996.

Tilly, Charles. "Migration in Modern European History." In *Human Migration, Patterns and Policies*, ed. William S. McNeill and Ruth Adams, 48–72. Bloomington: Indiana University Press, 1978.

———. "Transplanted Networks." In *Immigration Reconsidered: History, Sociology, and Politics*, ed. V. Yans-McLaughlin, 79–95. New York: Oxford University Press, 1990.

Tobar, Hector. "Salvadoran Loyalties Clash in L.A." *Los Angeles Times*, February 12, 1989.

Tumulty, Karen. "When Irish Eyes Are Hiding." *Los Angeles Times*, January 29, 1989.

"2 in New York Are Top Science Winners." *New York Times*, March 1, 1988, I-1.

Tyhurst, Libuse. "Displacement and Migration: A Study in Social Psychiatry." *American Journal of Psychiatry* 101 (February 1951): 561–568.

———. "Psychosocial First Aid for Refugees: An Essay in Social Psychiatry." *Mental Health and Society* 4 (1977): 319–343.

Ugalde, Antonio, Frank D. Bean, and Gilbert Cardenas. "International Migration from the Dominican Republic: Findings from a National Survey." *International Migration Review* 13 (Summer 1979): 235–254.

Urrea Giraldo, Fernando. "Life Strategies and the Labor Market: Colombians in New York in the 1970s." Report. New York: New York Research Program in Inter-American Affairs, 1982.

U.S. Bureau of the Census. *The Foreign-Born Population in the United States*, 1990 Census of Population, CP-3-1. Washington, D.C.: U.S. Department of Commerce, 1993.

———. *1980 Census: Detailed Population Characteristics*. Release PC80-1-D1-A. Washington, D.C.: U.S. Department of Commerce, 1984.

———. *1990 Ethnic Profiles for States*. Release CPH-L-136. Washington, D.C.: U.S. Department of Commerce, 1993.

———. *Socioeconomic Characteristics of the U.S. Foreign-Born Population Detailed in Census Bureau Tabulations*. Washington, D.C.: U.S. Department of Commerce, 1984.

U.S. Department of Justice. *Immigration Reform and Control Act: Report on the Legalized Alien Population*. Washington, D.C.: U.S. Government Printing Office, 1992.

U.S. Department of Labor. *Report of the Department of Labor Legal Immigration Task Force*. Washington, D.C.: U.S. Government Printing Office, 1988.

U.S. Immigration and Naturalization Service (INS). *1987 Statistical Yearbook*. Washington, D.C.: U.S. Government Printing Office, 1988.

———. *1990 Statistical Yearbook*. Washington, D.C.: U.S. Government Printing Office, 1991.

———. *1993 Statistical Yearbook*. Washington, D.C.: U.S. Government Printing Office, 1994.

U.S. Immigration [Dillingham] Commission. *Reports of the Immigration Commission*. Vol. 29. *The Children of Immigrants in Schools*. Washington, D.C.: U.S. Government Printing Office, 1911.

Vargas, Gloria E. "Recently Arrived Central American Immigration: Mental Health Needs." *Research Bulletin*. UCLA Spanish Speaking Mental Health Research Center, Autumn 1984, 1–3.

Vecoli, Rudolph. "The Italian Americans." In *Uncertain Americans: Readings in Ethnic History*, ed. Leonard Dinnerstein and Frederic C. Jaher, 201–215. New York: Oxford University Press, 1977.

Veenman, Justus. "Ethnic Minorities in the Netherlands." In *Poverty, Inequality, and the Future of Social Policy*, ed. K. McFate, B. Lawson, and W. J. Wilson, 607–628. New York: Russell Sage Foundation, 1995.

Vega, William A., and Hortensia Amaro. "Latino Outlook: Good Health, Uncertain Prognosis." *Annual Review of Public Health* 15 (1994): 39–67.

Vega, William A., Bohdan Kolody, and Juan Ramón Valle. "Migration and Mental Health: An Empirical Test of Depression Risk Factors Among Immigrant Mexican Women." *International Migration Review* 21 (Fall 1987): 512–530.

Vega, William A., Bohdan Kolody, Juan Ramón Valle, and Richard Hough. "Depressive Symptoms and Their Correlates Among Immigrant Mexican Women in the United States." *Social Science and Medicine* 22 (1986): 645–652.

Vega, William A., and Rubén G. Rumbaut. "Ethnic Minorities and Mental Health." *Annual Review of Sociology* 17 (1991): 351–383.

Vega, William A., George J. Warheit, Joanne Buhl-Auth, and Kenneth Meinhardt. "Mental Health Issues in the Hispanic Community: The Prevalence of Psychological Distress." In *Stress and Hispanic Mental Health*, ed. William A. Vega and Manuel R. Miranda, 30–47. Rockville, Md.: National Institute of Mental Health, 1985.

———. "The Prevalence of Depressive Symptoms Among Mexican Americans and Anglos." *American Journal of Epidemiology* 120 (October 1984): 592–607.

Vega, William A., George J. Warheit, and Robert Palacio. "Psychiatric Symptomatology Among Mexican American Farmworkers." *Social Science and Medicine* 20 (1985): 39–45.

Veltman, Calvin. *Language Shift in the United States*. Berlin: Mouton, 1983.

———. "Modelling the Language Shift Process of Hispanic Immigrants." *International Migration Review* 22 (Winter 1988): 545–562.

Vigil, James Diego. *Barrio Gangs: Street Life and Identity in Southern California*. Austin: University of Texas Press, 1988.

Wacquant, Loïc J., and William J. Wilson. "The Cost of Racial and Class Exclusion in the Inner City." *Annals of the American Academy of Political and Social Science* 501 (1989): 8–26.

Waldinger, Roger. "Ethnic Business in the United States." Department of Sociology, City University of New York, 1988. Mimeographed.

———. "Immigrant Enterprise: A New Test of Competing Theories." Paper presented at the Symposium on Hispanic enterprise, Arizona State University, April 1987.

———. "Immigration and Industrial Change in the New York City Apparel Industry." In *Hispanics in the U.S. Economy*, ed. George J. Borjas and Marta Tienda, 323–349. New York: Academic Press, 1985.

———. "The Making of an Immigrant Niche." Manuscript. Department of Sociology, University of California, Los Angeles, 1992.

Walker, S. Lynne. "The Invisible Work Force: San Diego's Migrant Farm Laborers from Oaxaca." *San Diego Union*, December 18–22, 1988, A-1.

"Wanted: Fresh, Homegrown Talent." *Time*, January 11, 1988, 65.

Wardhaugh, Ronald. *Languages in Competition: Dominance, Diversity, and Decline*. New York: Basil Blackwell, 1987.

Warheit, George J., William A. Vega, Joanne Auth, and Kenneth Meinhardt. "Mexican-American Immigration and Mental Health: A Comparative Analysis of Psychosocial Distress and Dysfunction." In *Stress and Hispanic Mental Health*, ed. William A. Vega and Manuel R. Miranda, 76–109. Rockville, Md: National Institute of Mental Health, 1985.

Warner, W. Lloyd, and Leo Srole. *The Social Systems of American Ethnic Groups*. New Haven: Yale University Press, 1945.

Warren, R. "Status Report on Naturalization Rates." Working Paper #CO 1326, 6/C. Washington, D.C.: U.S. Bureau of the Census, 1979.

Waters, Mary. "Ethnic and Racial Identities of Second Generation Black Immigrants in New York City." *International Migration Review* 28 (Winter 1994): 795–820.

———. "West Indian Immigrants, African Americans, and Whites in the Workplace: Different Perspectives on American Race Relations."

Paper presented at the meetings of the American Sociological Association, Los Angeles, August 1994.

Weeks, John R., and Rubén G. Rumbaut. "Infant Mortality Among Ethnic Immigrant Groups." *Social Science and Medicine* 33, 3 (1991): 327–334.

Weissman, Myrna M., Jerome K. Myers, and Catherine E. Ross, eds. *Community Surveys of Psychiatric Disorders*. New Brunswick, N.J.: Rutgers University Press, 1986.

Williams, Carolyn L., and Joseph Westermeyer, eds. *Refugee Mental Health in Resettlement Countries*. New York: Hemisphere, 1986.

Wilson, Kenneth, and W. Allen Martin. "Ethnic Enclaves: A Comparison of the Cuban and Black Economies in Miami." *American Journal of Sociology* 88 (1982): 135–160.

Wilson, William J. *The Truly Disadvantaged: The Inner-City, the Underclass, and Public Policy*. Chicago: University of Chicago Press, 1987.

Wittke, Carl. *Refugees of Revolution: The German Forty-Eighters in America*. Philadelphia: University of Pennsylvania Press, 1952.

———. *We Who Built America*. Englewood Cliffs, N.J.: Prentice Hall, 1939.

Womack, John. *Zapata and the Mexican Revolution*. New York: Vintage Books, 1968.

Wong, Morrison G., and Charles Hirschman. "The New Asian Immigrants." In *Culture, Ethnicity, and Identity*, ed. William C. McReady, 381–403. New York: Academic Press, 1983.

Woo, Elaine. "Immigrants: A Rush to the Classroom." *Los Angeles Times*, September 24, 1986, I-1.

Wood, Charles H. "Caribbean Cane Cutters in Florida: A Study of the Relative Cost of Domestic and Foreign Labor." Paper presented at the meetings of the American Sociological Association, San Antonio, Texas, August 1984. Mimeographed.

Zabin, Carol, and Sallie Hughes. "Economic Integration and Labor Flows: Stage Migration in Farm Labor Markets in Mexico and the United States." *International Migration Review* 29 (Summer 1995): 395–422.

Zamichow, Nora. "No Way to Escape the Fear: Stress Disorder Grips Women Immigrants." *Los Angeles Times*, February 10, 1992, B1–4.

Zhou, Min. *New York's Chinatown: The Socioeconomic Potential of an Urban Enclave*. Philadelphia: Temple University Press, 1992.

Zhou, Min, and Carl L. Bankston. "Social Capital and the Adaptation of the Second Generation: The Case of Vietnamese Youth in New Orleans." *International Migration Review* 28 (Winter 1994): 821–845.

Zolberg, Aristide R. "From Invitation to Interdiction: U.S. Foreign Policy and Immigration Since 1945." In *Threatened Peoples, Threat-*

ened Borders: World Migration and U.S. Policy, ed. M. S. Teitelbaum and M. Weiner, 117–159. New York: W. W. Norton, 1995.

———. "The Next Waves: Migration Theory for a Changing World." *International Migration Review* 23 (Fall 1989): 403–430.

Zolberg, Aristide R., Astri Suhrke, and Sergio Aguayo. *Escape from Violence: Conflict and the Refugee Crisis in the Developing World*. New York: Oxford University Press, 1989.

———. "International Factors in the Formation of Refugee Movements." *International Migration Review* 20 (Summer 1986): 151–169.

Zwingmann, C. A., and Maria Pfister-Ammende, eds. *Uprooting and After*. New York: Springer-Verlag, 1973.

Index

Academic achievement. *See* Educational attainment

Acción Internacional, 291

Acculturation: and linguistic transition, 219; and location patterns, 50–51, 53; and mental health, 180–88, 183t, 184–85t; and pluralism, 247; pressure for, 138–39; professional immigrants, 20; second-generation immigrants, 187, 247–48, 267–68; typology of, 241, 242f, 250–53, 252f; and World War I, 106–7, 196. *See also* Assimilation theories; Citizenship, acquisition of; Linguistic transition; Second-generation immigrants

Afghan immigrants, 24, 63, 304n27, 306n11, 306n29

African Americans. *See* Black Americans, U.S.-born; *and specific groups*

African immigrants, 182, 294; citizenship acquisition, 122–23; economic adaptation, 66, 69, 81; educational attainment, 60, 62, 63–64. *See also specific immigrant groups*

Albanian immigrants, 104

Aldrich, Thomas B., 229

"Alien invasion" notion. *See* Nativism

Alien Land Law (1913), 31

American Federation of Labor, 102

Amnesty program, 278–79, 280

ANDE. *See* National Association of Dominicans Abroad (ANDE)

Anti-Communist sentiments, of immigrants, 24, 62

Antin, Mary, 240

Aponte, Robert, 285, 288

Arab immigrants, 75, 132

Argentine immigrants, 88, 132, 135

Ascoli, Max, 100

Asian-Americans, 135, 136, 310n62. *See also* Asian immigrants

Asian immigrants: acculturation, 233; and brain drain, 294; citizenship acquisition, 119, 122; educational attainment, 60, 62, 63–64, 66, 122; income, 79, 80, 81; linguistic transition, 201, 203, 216; location patterns, 35; mental health, 169–70, 171, 172t, 173t, 174–75, 190; occupational attainment, 66, 69, 75; and politics, 98, 132; second-generation, 240. *See also specific immigrant groups*

Assimilation theories, 7–8, 50–51, 53, 138–39. *See also* Acculturation
Asylum, 23. *See also* Refugees
Aztlán, 126

Bach, Robert L., 277
Baltimore, Md., 22, 29, 41
Bankston, Carl L., 243, 256
Bay of Pigs invasion, 76, 113, 114
Bernard, W. S., 121, 122
Bilingualism. *See* Linguistic transition
Binet, Alfred, 197
Black Americans, U.S.-born, 126, 182, 253, 288; and immigrant entrepreneurs, 110, 133; self-employment, 75, 77
Black Power movement, 126
Bonacich, Edna, 76
Boston, Mass., 29
Boswell, Thomas D., 113
Bracero Program (temporary labor), 15–16, 285
"Brain drain." *See* Professional immigrants
Brigham, Carl, 197–98
British immigrants, 64, 69, 105
Brown Berets, 126
Business ownership. *See* Entrepreneurial immigrants; Self-employment

California, 34; and location patterns, 33, 37, 41, 43, 44, 45, 48; nativism in, 14, 94, 98, 214, 281–82; second-generation immigrants in, 235, 244–45, 246–47, 255–56
Cambodian immigrants, 24, 182, 239, 275, 298; economic adaptation, 63, 67, 69, 80; linguistic transition, 203, 205; mental health, 169–70, 171, 172t, 173t, 190

Canadian immigrants, 60, 63, 69; citizenship acquisition, 117, 119, 123, 124
Caribbean immigrants, 11, 12, 69, 182, 294; location patterns, 32, 35. *See also specific immigrant groups*
Carter, Jimmy, 23
Cavazos, Lauro, 129
Central American conflict, 114, 309n48
Central American immigrants, 169, 170, 211; economic adaptation, 63, 69, 80. *See also* Latin American immigrants; *and specific immigrant groups*
Chicago, Ill., 32, 35, 37, 40, 44
Chicano Student Movement of Aztlán (MECHA), 126
Child, Irvin, 241, 243, 247
Children. *See* Second-generation immigrants
Chilean immigrants, 135
Chinese immigrants, 85, 182, 275; citizenship acquisition, 117, 119; economic adaptation, 22, 71, 73, 75, 77, 80, 294; linguistic transition, 201, 203, 211, 220; location patterns, 29, 33, 35, 37, 40; mental health, 169–70, 171, 172t, 173t; and politics, 98, 133
Chiswick, Barry R., 80, 81
Chitose, Yoshimi, 233, 234
Citizenship, acquisition of, 115–24, 116t, 118t; delay in, 119, 121, 121t; and educational attainment, 121–23, 122t, 124; and geographical proximity, 119, 120t, 123
Coalition for a Free Cuba, 113–14
Cold War, end of, 23–24, 296–97
Colombian immigrants, 60, 272, 319n5; and politics, 110–12, 135

Colombian Professional Association, 112

Colonization, 272–73, 275–76

Combat stress, 164–65

Community surveys, 165

Concentration. *See* Location patterns

Consonant acculturation, 241, 242 f, 250, 252 f, 255

Consonant acculturation resistance, 241, 242 f, 252 f, 256

Contemporary immigration: domestic implications of, 26–27; public images of, 6–7, 17, 19; typology of, 14–26, 130–34, 131 t, 284–85, 286–87 f. *See also specific topics*

Context of exit. *See* Exit context, from country of origin; Refugees; *and specific topics*

Context of reception. *See* Reception contexts

Contract labor, 15–16, 285

Core-periphery system, 272–76

Cornelius, Wayne A., 290

Croatian immigrants, 30, 103

Cuban-American National Foundation, 113

Cuban immigrants, 4–5, 307 n3; acculturation, 182–83, 183 t, 184–85 t; citizenship acquisition, 117, 119, 123; educational attainment, 63; as entrepreneurs, 20–21, 22–23; income, 80, 81–82; linguistic transition, 216, 262; location patterns, 33, 34, 35, 37, 40, 45, 52; Mariel boatlift, 24, 43, 45, 91, 177–79, 190; mental health, 174, 177–79, 177 t, 179 t, 181, 190; occupational attainment, 69; and politics, 103–4, 112–14, 132, 133, 134, 309 nn48,60,61; refugees, 22–23, 24, 34; second-

generation, 239, 254–55, 256–67, 258–60 t; self-employment, 75, 76, 77, 306 n15; and structural imbalancing, 275

Cuban Revolutionary Committee, 104

Cuban Revolutionary Council, 113

Culture shock, 310 n6

Curtis, James R., 113

Czech immigrants, 31, 103, 174

Dade County, Fla. *See* South Florida

Demand. *See* Labor markets

Diffusion. *See* Location patterns

Disadvantage theory of entrepreneurship, 77, 306 n21

Discrimination: and economic adaptation, 77, 85, 88, 90–91, 306 n21; and location patterns, 31–32; and mental health, 182–83, 183 t, 186, 187–88 t; and politics, 125–26; second-generation immigrants, 239, 244, 248, 251, 254, 255, 256, 261–62, 263, 267

Displaced Persons Act (1948), 164

Dissonant acculturation, 241, 242 f, 245–47, 251, 252 f, 256

Dominican immigrants, 12, 110–11, 119, 211, 272; economic adaptation, 63, 69, 80; illegal, 11, 44, 63; location patterns, 32, 35, 37, 40, 45

Drug trade, 112

Drug use, 181, 186, 189

Eastern European immigrants, 23, 29–30; economic adaptation, 31, 76, 90; educational attainment, 64, 66; location patterns, 29–30, 31; and politics, 98, 99, 103, 134

Economic adaptation, 57–92; and discrimination, 77, 85, 88, 90–91, 306 n21; and educational attainment, 58–66, 59 t, 61 t, 65 t; and ethnic enclaves, 85–88, 89 f, 91; and government immigration policy, 84–85, 89 f, 306 n29; and income, 77–82, 78–79 t; and labor markets, 85–86, 89 f; modes of, 82–84; and occupational attainment, 66–77; public images of, 7, 18, 57–58; theories of, 75–77, 91–92, 306 n21

Economic modernization policies, 292

Ecuadorian immigrants, 132, 135

Educational attainment, 58–66, 59 t, 61 t, 65 t; and citizenship acquisition, 121–23, 122 t, 124; and dependents, 60, 62; and government immigration policy, 62–64, 65 t; illegal immigrants, 63, 305 n7; and income, 80–81; individual factors, 64, 66; and occupational attainment, 67, 71; and politics, 132; second-generation immigrants, 234–35, 250, 261, 264–67, 266 t, 316–17 n3, 317–18 nn19,24,25

Educational psychology, 198–99

Egyptian immigrants, 130, 134

Elderly people, 80

El Paso, Tex., 37

El Salvador. *See* Salvadoran immigrants

Employers. *See* Labor markets

English acquisition. *See* Linguistic transition

English Only movement. *See* U.S. English movement

Entrepreneurial immigrants, 20–23; and economic adaptation, 83; and government immigration policy, 22, 293–96, 295 t; linguistic transition, 222, 227; and location patterns, 30–32, 33, 35, 45, 48, 303 n15; and nativism, 133–34; and politics, 99, 110, 132, 133–34; second-generation, 250–51. *See also* Self-employment; *and specific topics*

Espenshade, Thomas J., 289

Ethiopian immigrants, 24, 63, 90, 304 n27

Ethnic enclaves, 20–22; and citizenship acquisition, 123–24; and economic adaptation, 71, 85–88, 89 f, 91; and linguistic transition, 226, 227; and location patterns, 32–33, 40, 48; and mental health, 179, 188–89; and politics, 133, 309 n61; and second-generation immigrants, 250–51, 254. *See also* *specific immigrant groups*

Ethnicity: emergent, 95, 100, 134–38; linear, 131 t, 134; reactive, 95, 102, 129, 131 t, 133, 134; resilient, 124–29; socially constructed, 95, 100, 102, 104, 135, 136. *See also* Identity

Eugenics, 159–64

European immigrants, 97–98, 117, 119; economic adaptation, 67, 75, 76, 79; educational attainment, 60, 62, 63, 317–19 n19. *See also* Eastern European immigrants; *and specific immigrant groups*

EWIs, 15

Exit context, from country of origin, 168–75, 178, 187. *See also* Refugees; *and specific topics*

Falcón, Luis, 64, 66

Family reunification provisions, 15, 22, 62, 71, 123, 280
Fernández-Kelly, María Patricia, 290
Filipino immigrants, 60, 182, 272, 275; citizenship acquisition, 117, 119; linguistic transition, 201, 203, 211; location patterns, 32–33, 35, 37, 41, 45, 51; professional, 19–20, 294; self-employment, 73, 77
Fine, Nathan, 98
Finnish immigrants, 30, 98–99
Florida. *See* South Florida
Foreign-poverty theory of immigration, 9–12
Frazier, Franklin, 21
Fresno, Calif., 43

García, Ana, 290
Gary, Ind., 32
Generational relationships, 239–43, 242 f, 245–46; linguistic transition, 214, 215 t, 216, 218–19. *See also* Acculturation; Second-generation immigrants
Gentleman's Agreement (1907), 32
German-American Central Alliance, 106
German immigrants, 30–31, 51, 157, 211; and politics, 98, 99, 103, 105–7
Gibson, Margaret, 244–45
G.I. Forum, 126
Glazer, Nathan, 95, 103, 104
Global cultural diffusion, 12–14, 274–75
Goddard, H. H., 197
Goodenough, Florence, 198
Government immigration policy, 278–82, 300; and economic adaptation, 84–85, 89 f, 306 n29;

and educational attainment, 62–64, 65 t; and entrepreneurial immigrants, 22, 293–96, 295 t; and eugenics, 162–63, 164; family reunification provisions, 15, 22, 62, 71, 123, 280; Immigration Act of 1965, 8, 64, 232, 269; Immigration Act of 1990, 15, 18, 280; Immigration Reform and Control Act (IRCA; 1986), 14, 15, 16, 17, 278–80, 284; and immigration typology, 284–85, 286–87 f; and Japanese immigrants, 31–32; and labor migrants, 14, 15–16, 17, 279, 285, 288–93, 288 t; nativist views of, 269–70; and occupational attainment, 71; occupational preference system, 18, 22, 62, 71, 122, 123; and origin theories, 8–9, 269–71; political restrictions (1903), 93; postwar, 167; and professional/entrepreneurial immigrants, 18, 22, 71, 122, 123, 293–96, 295 t; recruitment, 9, 13, 29–30, 40, 84–85, 273–74; and refugees, 23–24, 62–63, 85, 168–69, 170, 296–98, 306 n29; and second-generation immigrants, 292–93
Greek immigrants, 80, 104; self-employment, 71, 73, 77, 80
Greeley, Andrew M., 55, 104
Guatemalan immigrants, 69, 170, 298
Guyanese immigrants, 35

Haitian immigrants, 12, 32, 73, 182, 294, 299; linguistic transition, 262; mental health, 177–79, 177 t, 179 t, 190; second-generation, 253–55, 256–67, 258–60 t

Handlin, Oscar, 156, 157, 232, 310n6
Hawaii, 37, 41
Hayakawa, S. I., 93
Hirschman, Charles, 64, 66
Hispanic-Americans, 135, 136–37, 138. *See also specific groups*
Hmong immigrants, 43, 239; mental health, 155–56, 171, 172t, 173t
Hollingshead, August B., 165
Honolulu, Hi., 37
Houston, Tex., 35
H-2 workers, 16
"Human Migration and the Marginal Man" (Park), 158
Hungarian immigrants, 30, 174

Identity: collective, 95, 100, 134, 135; ethnic, 95, 100, 102–7, 131t, 134, 256–57, 258t, 263–64; hyphenated American, 104, 106–7, 258t, 263–6; national, 95, 107, 135, 137, 138, 258t, 263–64; non-hyphenated American, 104, 106–7, 258t, 264–64; pan-ethnic, 137, 258t, 263–6; supranational, 136, 137. *See also* Ethnicity
Illegal immigrants, 1–3, 10–11, 14–15, 23; educational attainment, 63, 305n7; location patterns, 44; origin theories, 282–84; second-generation, 289–90, 298–99; and structural imbalancing, 274. *See also* Government immigration policy; Immigration Reform and Control Act (IRCA; 1986)
Immigration Act of 1903, 93
Immigration Act of 1965, 8, 64, 232, 269
Immigration Act of 1990, 15, 18, 280
Immigration origin theories, 8–14, 269–78; foreign-poverty theory, 9–12; global cultural diffusion, 12–14, 274–75; and government immigration policy, 8–9, 269–71; illegal immigrants, 282–84; and labor markets, 13, 270–71; and nativism, 269–70; push-pull model, 271–72, 275–76, 278, 319n5; refugees, 296–98; structural imbalancing, 272–76; transnational networks, 276–78
Immigration policy. *See* Government immigration policy
Immigration Reform and Control Act (IRCA; 1986), 14, 15, 16, 17, 278–80, 284
The Immigration Time Bomb: The Fragmenting of America (Lamm), 138
Income, 77–82, 78–79t
Indiana, 31
Indian immigrants, 60, 66, 67, 117; linguistic transition, 211, 224–25; location patterns, 33, 40; and politics, 130, 134; professional, 5–6, 19–20, 33, 294; second-generation, 244–45; self-employment, 75, 306n15
Indochina War, 156
Indochinese immigrants. *See* Southeast Asian immigrants; *and specific immigrant groups*
Industrial Workers of the World, 102
Intelligence and Immigration (Kirkpatrick), 198
Intelligence testing, 197–99, 220–21
Inter-American Foundation, 291
Iranian immigrants, 24, 60, 63, 73, 80, 304n18
Iraqi immigrants, 24

IRCA. *See* Immigration Reform and Control Act (IRCA; 1986)
Irish immigrants, 30, 51, 54, 69, 157, 319n5
Italian immigrants, 29, 30, 73, 80, 274; educational attainment, 60, 64, 66; and politics, 54, 99, 100, 104, 135; second-generation, 241, 243, 247

Jamaican immigrants, 16, 90, 119, 182, 294; location patterns, 32, 35; second-generation, 239
Japanese immigrants, 98, 161, 182; as entrepreneurs, 21–22, 31–32; linguistic transition, 201, 203, 216, 220; location patterns, 32–33, 51; self-employment, 71, 73, 77
Jarvis, Edward, 160
Jensen, Leif, 233, 234
Jerome, Harry, 28
Jersey City, New Jersey, 22
Jewish immigrants, 21, 52, 161, 169, 197, 240; educational attainment, 63, 64; and politics, 99, 101, 105; self-employment, 75, 76

Kennedy, John F., 113, 114, 129
Kim, Illsoo, 109
Kircheman, Joleen, 285, 288
Kirkpatrick, Clifford, 198
Koreagate scandal, 110
Korean Association of Greater New York, 109
Korean immigrants, 60, 80, 275; citizenship acquisition, 117, 119; as entrepreneurs, 20, 21, 22, 33, 294, 303n15; linguistic transition, 201, 203, 216, 224; location patterns, 33, 41, 303n15; mental health, 169, 175; and politics, 108–9, 114, 133; self-employment, 73, 75, 77

Labor force participation, 66–67, 68t, 69, 306n11. *See also* Occupational attainment
Labor markets, 16–17; and economic adaptation, 85–86, 89f; and educational attainment, 63; and government immigration policy, 278, 279–80, 281–82, 290; and linguistic transition, 226; and origin theories, 13, 270–71; and second-generation immigrants, 249–50. *See also* Occupational attainment
Labor migrants, 14–18; displacement effects, 285, 288–89; and economic adaptation, 85, 86; and government immigration policy, 14, 15–16, 17, 279, 285, 288–93, 288t; linguistic transition, 225, 227; and location patterns, 29–30, 33, 40–41, 45, 48; and politics, 130, 132; two-way flow of, 17–18
Lambert, Wallace E., 200, 201, 205, 221, 223
Lamm, Richard D., 138
Language. *See* Linguistic transition
Laotian immigrants, 24, 43, 63, 239, 275, 298; economic adaptation, 67, 80, 91; mental health, 155–56, 171, 172t, 173t, 190
La Raza Unida Party, 126–27
Latin American immigrants, 216, 233, 240, 273; citizenship acquisition, 117, 119; economic adaptation, 66, 69, 75, 79; educational attainment, 60, 62, 63; mental health, 181, 190; and politics, 132, 135. *See also* Central American immigrants; *and specific immigrant groups*

Laughlin, Harry, 162
Laws. *See* Government immigration policy
League of United Latin American Citizens (LULAC), 125, 126, 127
Lebanese immigrants, 77
Legalization dependents. *See* Family reunification provisions
Leopold, Werner F., 200
Lieberson, Stanley, 195
Light, Ivan, 75
Linguistic transition, 192–231; current evidence about, 199–207, 202t, 204t; extent of bilingualism, 195–96; linguistic diversity, 207–14, 208–9t, 211t, 212–13t, 315n26; and nativism, 207, 214, 219–22, 230, 231; second-generation immigrants, 214, 215t, 216, 218–19, 234, 235, 236t, 238t, 239, 262; shifts, 214–16, 215t, 217t; and socioeconomic status, 206–7, 222–25; turn-of-century attitudes toward, 106, 196–99; typology of, 219, 220f, 225–29, 228f. *See also* Acculturation
Lithuanian immigrants, 103, 174
Location patterns, 28–56; advantages/disadvantages, 53–56; and assimilation theories, 50–51, 53; destination areas, 34–35, 36f, 37; and entrepreneurial immigrants, 30–32, 33, 35, 45, 48, 303n15; and ethnic enclaves, 32–33, 40, 48; future trends, 49–53; and geographical proximity, 29; group destinations, 37, 38f, 39t, 40–41, 42t, 304n18; of illegal immigrants, 44; and recruitment, 29–30, 40; and second-

generation immigrants, 248–49; urban concentration, 43–45, 46–47t, 48–49
López, David, 216, 218–19, 224
Los Angeles, Calif., 8, 24, 133, 180–81; entrepreneurial immigrants, 20, 21, 22; and location patterns, 33, 35, 37, 41, 43, 44, 45, 48
LULAC. *See* League of United Latin American Citizens (LULAC)

MALDEF. *See* Mexican-American Legal Defense Fund (MALDEF)
Manual labor migrants. *See* Labor migrants
MAPA. *See* Mexican-American Political Association (MAPA)
Marginality, 158–59
Mariel boatlift (1980), 24, 43, 45, 91, 177–79, 190
Martí, José, 103–4
Massey, Douglas, 277
Matute-Bianchi, M. E., 246–47
MECHA. *See* Chicano Student Movement of Aztlán (MECHA)
Median household incomes, 10
Mental health, 155–91; and acculturation, 180–88, 183t, 184–85t; culture shock, 310n6; and discrimination, 182–83, 183t, 186, 187–88t; eugenics, 159–64; and exit context, 168–75, 178, 187; marginality, 158–59; postwar studies, 164–67; and reception context, 167, 168, 176–79, 177t, 179t, 188; and socioeconomic status, 165–67, 176, 178, 188; temporal patterning, 174–75, 175f; typology of, 188–91, 189f
Mexican-American Legal Defense Fund (MALDEF), 127

Mexican-American Political Association (MAPA), 126
Mexican-American War, 104, 273
Mexican American Youth Organization, 126
Mexican immigrants: acculturation, 180–81, 182–83, 183t, 184–85t; citizenship acquisition, 117, 119, 123, 124; and discrimination, 77, 85, 90; and displacement effects, 288–89; economic adaptation, 69, 76, 77, 80, 81–82, 88, 90; educational attainment, 60, 63, 66; and government immigration policy, 9, 290; illegal, 1–3, 10–11, 12, 15, 44, 63; linguistic transition, 201, 203, 205, 211, 216, 218, 262; location patterns, 32, 35, 37, 40–41, 45, 51; mental health, 176, 180; and nativism, 93–94; physical health, 182; and politics, 104–5, 125–29, 128t, 135; and push-pull model, 272, 319n5; second-generation, 239, 246–47, 255–67, 258–60t, 318n23; and structural imbalancing, 273–74, 275; and transnational networks, 32, 277, 291
Mexican Revolution, 104–5
Miami, Fla. *See* South Florida
Michigan, 30
Middleman minorities, 22, 33, 227, 303n15
Midtown Manhattan Project, 166
Migration and Business Cycles (Jerome), 28
Milwaukee, Wisc., 32
Minnesota, 30, 31
Missouri, 31
Moon, Sun Myung, 110
Muller, Thomas, 289
Mutualistas, 125

NAFTA, 292
Nagel, Joane, 136
National Association of Dominicans Abroad (ANDE), 111
National Origins Act (1924), 162–63, 164, 167
Nativism, 14, 17, 300; and cultural diversity, 55–56, 138–39; and fiscal costs, 161, 311n19; and linguistic transition, 207, 214, 219–22, 230, 231; and mental health, 161; and origin theories, 269–70; and politics, 93–95, 97–98, 133–34, 138–39; U.S. English movement, 93, 94, 214, 221–22, 307n3
Naturalization. *See* Citizenship, acquisition of
Neckerman, Kathryn M., 285
New Orleans, La., 243–44, 250–51
New York City, 8, 21, 22; labor market, 48–49; and location patterns, 29, 32, 33, 35, 40, 44, 45, 48–49; politics, 109–12, 132, 133
Nicaraguan immigrants, 181, 298–99
Nigerian immigrants, 90
North American Free Trade Agreement (NAFTA), 292
Norwegian immigrants, 51, 52, 104, 163

Occupational attainment, 66–77, 70t; and educational attainment, 67, 71; labor force participation, 66–67, 68t, 69, 306n11; second-generation immigrants, 249–50; self-employment, 71–77, 72t, 74t, 306n15. *See also* Occupational preference system
Occupational preference system, 18, 22, 62, 71, 122, 123

Ohio, 30, 31
Operation Hold-the-Line, 290
Orange County, Calif., 24, 34, 41, 43, 133
Orden de Hijos de America, 125

Pakistani immigrants, 272
Park, Robert, 158, 159–60
Peal, Elizabeth, 200, 201, 205, 221, 223
Peruvian immigrants, 60, 132, 135
Philadelphia, Pa., 29, 41
Philippines. *See* Filipino immigrants
Pioneer migrants, 29–32
Pluralism, 247
Polish Central Relief Committee, 103
Polish immigrants, 24, 69, 103, 274, 277; location patterns, 35, 52; mental health, 157, 161
The Polish Peasant in Europe and America (Thomas & Znaniecki), 156, 277
Political refugees. *See* Refugees
Politics, 93–140; citizenship acquisition, 115–24; and emergent ethnicities, 104–5, 134–38; and immigrant typology, 130–34, 131 t; and location patterns, 54; and nativism, 93–95, 97–98, 133–34, 138–39; and refugees, 112–14, 132, 133, 134; and resilient ethnicity, 124–29, 128 t; and sojourner orientation, 101, 108–12, 130, 132; turn-of-century, 96–107
Portes, Alejandro, 277
Portuguese immigrants, 51, 60, 80
Post-traumatic stress disorders, 170
Preference systems. *See* Government immigration policy

Prejudice. *See* Discrimination
Professional immigrants, 5–6, 10, 18–20, 58; citizenship acquisition, 122–23, 122 t; and economic adaptation, 82–83, 86; and government immigration policy, 18, 71, 122, 123, 293–96, 295 t; linguistic transition, 222, 227, 229; location patterns, 33, 45, 48, 304 n27; and politics, 130, 132, 134; second-generation, 250. *See also* Occupational attainment; *and specific topics*
Prohibition, 106
Proposition 63 (California), 214
Proposition 187 (California), 14, 94, 281–82
Protestant (work) ethic, 75
Puerto Rican immigrants, 216, 288
Puerto Rico, 33, 37
Punjabi immigrants, 244–45
Push-pull model of immigration origins, 271–72, 275–76, 278, 319 n5

Queuing theory, 50

Radio Martí, 113
Railroad labor, 30
Reactive formation, 95, 126, 133, 138, 222, 253
Reagan, Ronald, 23
Recentness of arrival, 80, 81, 83, 210
Reception contexts: and economic adaptation, 84–92; and mental health, 167, 168, 176–79, 177 t, 179 t, 188. *See also specific topics*
Recruitment, 9, 13, 84–85; and location patterns, 29–30, 40; and structural imbalancing, 273–74

Redlich, F. C., 165
Refugee Act (1980), 23, 24, 296
Refugees, 23–25, 26; citizenship
  acquisition, 123, 124; economic
  adaptation, 83, 86; and government immigration policy, 23–
  24, 62–63, 85, 168–69, 170,
  296–98, 306n29; linguistic
  transition, 225, 227; location
  patterns, 33–34, 35, 37, 41,
  304n18; mental health, 164,
  168–75; occupational attainment, 69, 71; origin theories,
  296–98; and politics, 112–14,
  132, 133, 134
Reimers, Cordelia W., 81
Religion, 75–76, 243
Romanian immigrants, 24
Roosevelt, Theodore, 106, 107,
  196, 219
Rosenblum, Gerald, 101
Russian immigrants, 52, 71, 73,
  169, 240; turn-of-century politics, 98, 99, 101, 105. *See also*
  Soviet immigrants
Russian Revolution, 99, 105

Salvadoran immigrants, 69, 170,
  275, 298; location patterns, 35,
  304n18
San Diego, Calif., 37, 43, 45, 182,
  235; school district study, 201,
  202t, 203, 204t, 205
San Francisco, Calif., 21–22, 29,
  33, 35, 37, 133
San Jose, Calif., 43
San Juan, P.R., 37
Santa Ana, Calif., 37
Santa Clara County, Calif., 169–
  70, 180
Sassen-Koob, Saskia, 49, 111,
  289
Scandinavian immigrants, 31,
  51, 52, 98–99, 100

Second-generation immigrants,
  187, 232–68; acculturation typology, 241, 242f, 250–53,
  252f; case studies, 243–47,
  253–56; contextual factors,
  247–50; demographic analysis,
  233–39, 236–37t, 238t; educational attainment, 234–35,
  250, 261, 264–67, 266t, 316–
  17n3, 317–18nn19,24,25;
  generational relationships,
  239–43, 242f; and government
  immigration policy, 292–93; illegal, 289–90, 298–99; linguistic transition, 214, 215t, 216,
  218–19, 234, 235, 236t, 238t,
  239, 262; number of, 232–33;
  segmented assimilation, 248,
  253–56; social relationships,
  262–63; socioeconomic status,
  234, 237t, 257, 261, 265–66;
  statistical profiles, 256–67,
  258–60t
Segmented assimilation, 248,
  253–56
Selective acculturation, 241,
  242f, 243–45, 250–51, 252f,
  254, 256, 262, 267
Self-employment, 71–77, 72t,
  306n15; and economic mobility, 71, 73, 74t; and ethnic enclaves, 88; and income, 80; theories of, 75–77, 306n21. *See also*
  Entrepreneurial immigrants;
  Professional immigrants
Separatism, 54, 55
Serbian immigrants, 30
Sikh immigrants, 244–45
Silicon Valley, Calif. *See* Santa
  Clara County, Calif.
Slavery, 274
Slovakian immigrants, 30, 103
Slovenian immigrants, 30, 103
Smith, Madorah, 199

Social Darwinism, 161
Socialism, 97, 98, 99, 102, 105
Social networks. *See* Ethnic enclaves; Transnational networks
Socioeconomic status: and linguistic transition, 200, 206–7,
222–25; and mental health,
165–67, 176, 178, 188; and
origin theories, 9–12; second-
generation immigrants, 234,
257, 261, 265–66. *See also*
Educational attainment; Occupational attainment
Sojourners, 76, 241; and politics,
101, 108–12, 130, 132
Southeast Asian immigrants, 23,
63, 168–69, 211; economic adaptation, 67, 69, 80, 91; location patterns, 43, 52–53; mental health, 155–56, 169–70,
171, 172t, 173t, 174–75
South Florida, 8, 20–21, 22, 24;
location patterns, 33, 34, 35,
37, 40, 43, 44, 45, 48; politics, 113, 133, 309n60; second-
generation immigrants in, 235,
253–54, 255
Soviet collapse, 23–24, 296
Soviet immigrants, 24, 52, 63, 69,
80, 211
Srole, Leo, 166–67, 168
Stereotypes. *See* Discrimination
Stonequist, Everett, 158, 160
Structural imbalancing, 272–76
A Study of American Intelligence
(Brigham), 197–98
Suárez-Orozco, Marcelo, 249
Suicide, 159
Swedish immigrants, 51

Taiwanese immigrants, 58, 60, 67.
See also Chinese immigrants
Tampa, Fla., 37

Temporary immigrants. *See*
Sojourners
Thomas, William I., 156, 157,
160, 277
Transnational networks, 276–
78, 291; and location patterns,
32–33
Trotsky, Leon, 105
Turn-of-century immigrant politics, 96–107, 140; and domestic politics, 97, 98–102; leftist
movements, 97, 98–99; and nativism, 97–98; and peasant immigrants, 99–102; and sending
countries, 102–7
Turn-of-century immigrants: linguistic transition, 196–99;
mental health, 157–58; public
images of, 6–7. *See also* Turn-
of-century immigrant politics

Ugandan-Asian immigrants, 174
Underground labor flows. *See* Il-
legal immigrants
Undocumented immigrants. *See*
Illegal immigrants
Unemployment, 66–67, 85
Unification Church, 110
Unions, 98–99, 100–101, 102.
See also Socialism
United Kingdom. *See* British
immigrants
United Mexican American Stu-
dents, 126
U.S. English movement, 93, 94,
214, 221–22, 307n3
The Uprooted (Handlin), 156

Valdés, Jorge, 307n3
Vega, William, 176
Venezuelan immigrants, 135
Vietnamese immigrants, 3–4, 24,
34, 63, 182; citizenship acqui-

sition, 117, 119, 124; economic adaptation, 67, 91; linguistic transition, 201, 203, 262; location patterns, 34, 35, 37, 41, 43, 304n18; mental health, 169–70, 171, 172t, 173t, 190; and politics, 132, 133, 134; second-generation, 243–44, 250–51, 255–67, 258–60t, 263; and structural imbalancing, 275
Visa abusers, 15

Wage levels, 11, 16
Waldinger, Roger, 289
Warren, Robert, 117
Washington, D.C., 22, 133; location patterns, 35, 37, 41, 48, 304n18
Waters, Mary, 245, 267, 285
Weber, Max, 75
West Indian immigrants, 16, 90, 161, 262; second-generation, 239, 245–46, 255, 256–67, 258–60t
White Americans, U.S.-born, 182, 203
Wisconsin, 30, 31
Women immigrants, 81, 226; mental health, 165, 166, 169
World War I, 103, 106–7, 125, 196
World War II, 125–26, 164–65, 269

Xenophobia. *See* Nativism

Youth organizations, 126

Zhou, Min, 243, 256, 289
Znaniecki, Florian, 156, 157, 160, 277
Zolberg, Aristide R., 297

Text: 10/13 Aster
Display: Aster
Index: Do Mi Stauber
Composition: G & S Typesetters, Inc.
Printing and binding: Royal Book Co.